CURRENT DEBATES IN INTERNATIONAL ACCOUNTING

Current Debates in International Accounting

Christopher W. Nobes

Royal Holloway, University of London, UK

Edward Elgar
Cheltenham, UK • Northampton, MA, USA

© Christopher W. Nobes 2010

Published by
Edward Elgar Publishing Limited
The Lypiatts
15 Lansdown Road
Cheltenham
Glos GL50 2JA
UK

Edward Elgar Publishing, Inc.
William Pratt House
9 Dewey Court
Northampton
Massachusetts 01060
USA

A catalogue record for this book
is available from the British Library

MIX
Paper from
responsible sources
FSC
www.fsc.org
FSC® C018575

ISBN 978 1 84844 838 4

Printed and bound by MPG Books Group, UK

Contents

Acknowledgments

The author wishes to thank the following whom have kindly given permission for the use of copyright material.

Academy of Accounting Historians, for permission to reproduce: Nobes, C., 'Were Islamic records precursors to accounting books based on the Italian method? A comment', *Accounting Historians Journal*, **28** (2), 2001, 207–14.

American Accounting Association, for permission to reproduce: Nobes, C., 'Rules-based standards and the lack of principles in accounting', *Accounting Horizons*, **19** (1), 2005, 25–34.

Canadian Academic Accounting Association, for permission to reproduce: Nobes, C.W. and Zeff, S.A., 'Auditors' affirmations of compliance with IFRS around the world: an exploratory study', *Accounting Perspectives*, **7** (4), 2008, 279–92.

Elsevier, for permission to reproduce: Nobes, C., 'Observations on measuring the differences between domestic accounting standards and IAS', *Journal of Accounting and Public Policy*, **28** (2), 2009, 148–53; Nobes, C., 'On the myth of Anglo- Saxon financial accounting: a comment', *International Journal of Accounting*, **38** (1), 2003, 95–104; Nobes, C., 'On accounting classification and the international harmonisation debate', *Accounting, Organizations and Society*, **29** (2), 2004, 189–200.

John Wiley and Sons, for permission to reproduce: Nobes, C. and Roberts, A., 'Towards a unifying model of systems of law, corporate financing, accounting and corporate governance', *Australian Accounting Review*, **10** (1), 2000, 26–34; Nobes, C., 'An analysis of the international development of the equity method', *Abacus*, **38** (1), 2002, 16–45; Nobes, C.W., 'Accounting classification in the IFRS era', *Australian Accounting Review*, **18** (3), 2008, 191–8; Nobes, C., '57 varieties of serious defect in IFRS?', *Australian Accounting Review*, **18** (4), 2008, 283–6.

Taylor & Francis, for permission to reproduce: Nobes, C. and Schwencke, H.R., 'Modelling the links between tax and financial reporting: a longitudinal examination of Norway over 30 years up to IFRS adoption', *European Accounting Review*, **15** (1), 2006, 63–87; Nobes, C.W., 'Revenue recognition and EU endorsement of IFRS', *Accounting in Europe*, **3**, 2006, 81–9.

Wolters Kluwer, for permission to reproduce: Nobes, C., 'The survival of international differences under IFRS: towards a research agenda', *Accounting and Business Research*, **36** (3), 2006, 233–45; Kvaal, E. and Nobes, C., 'International differences in IFRS policy choice: a research note', *Accounting and Business Research*, **40** (2),

2010, 173–87; Aisbitt, S. and Nobes, C., 'The true and fair view requirement in recent national implementations', *Accounting and Business Research*, **31** (2), 2001, 83–90; Nobes, C., 'Is true and fair of over-riding importance?: a comment on Alexander's benchmark', *Accounting and Business Research*, **30** (4), 2000, 307–12; Nobes, C., 'The importance of being fair: an analysis of IFRS regulation and practice – a comment', *Accounting and Business Research*, **39** (4), 415–27.

Preface

This book brings together my writings on international accounting that were published in the first decade of the new millennium. It starts where I left off in *International Accounting and Comparative Financial Reporting*, which was also published by Edward Elgar, in 1999.

I hope that this compendium will be useful to researchers, teachers and students of international accounting. The 'Introduction' to this volume examines themes that run through this literature, and puts the papers into the context of the writings of others.

Five of the papers in this volume were co-authored. Chapter 14's co-author was my much-missed colleague and former doctoral student, Sally Aisbitt (see an obituary in *Accounting and Business Research*, **36** (4), 2006). Chapter 1's co-author, Alan Roberts, had contributed much to the writings contained in the previous volume while he was a colleague at the University of Reading. More recently, I have worked with colleagues at the Norwegian School of Management (BI) where I have a part-time post: Hans Robert Schwenke (Chapter 2) and Erlend Kvaal (Chapter 12). For many years, Steve Zeff has provided help and inspiration, and I am pleased to include a paper co-authored with him (Chapter 13).

In the background, continuing to provide valuable advice on most of my output, remains Bob Parker. The most recent papers have also benefited from the advice of my new colleagues at Royal Holloway: Jane Davison, Brendan McSweeney, Christopher Napier and Christian Stadler.

Christopher Nobes
Royal Holloway
31 May 2010

Introduction

The selection

The papers here are all authored or co-authored by the editor of this volume. They all concern international aspects of financial accounting. They were all published in academic journals from 2000 to 2010. Earlier papers on the same topics were collected in *International Accounting and Comparative Financial Reporting* (Edward Elgar, 1999; hereafter referred to as IACFR).

The papers come from eleven different journals: American (four papers), Australian (four papers), British (six papers), Canadian (one paper) and pan-European (two papers). Five of the papers were co-authored with colleagues (two British, two Norwegian and one American). So, there is internationality in more than the topics of the papers.

Comment papers

The word 'debates' in the title of the volume reminds us that any interesting issues are likely to involve different views, which will be refined over time. One way in which this refining occurs is through published 'comments' and 'replies' to them.

In this volume, seven of the papers are 'comments'. In the previous volume (IACFR, referred to above), eight of the twenty papers were 'comments'. In my view, 'comments' can be very valuable. The published exchange between authors can, in a very few pages, advance a debate and add useful clarifications. Occasionally, a brief comment can point out a fatal flaw in a long and previously well-regarded paper.

In my view, a journal editor should impose tough criteria before accepting draft 'comments'. They should of course be subject to blind review, preferably not by the reviewers of the original paper (who might be embarrassed if flaws are pointed out), and obviously not by the author of the original paper. In my experience, both of the above review techniques have happened. However, subject to tough review, editors should in principle be happy to publish comments, for the reasons raised in the previous paragraph.

Of course, editors should also allow the original authors to 'reply', subject to review. In this volume, I do not include the original papers or the replies that relate to my 'comments' (because they are not authored by me) but I refer to them below in the discussion of the content of the volume.

I pay tribute here to all the authors of the papers upon which I commented. Without exception, they engaged in the comment/reply process in a helpful, pleasant and fruitful way.

International development

Part I of this volume contains four papers on international aspects of the development of financial reporting practices over time. In Chapter 1, Nobes and Roberts extend the theorising of Nobes (1998; reproduced as Chapter 9 in IACFR) on the forces that have driven international differences in financial reporting. Chapter 1 adds corporate governance systems to the mix of law, tax and corporate financing. It concludes that the influence of a legal system can be overridden by the needs of users of financial reporting. Corporate governance systems are also seen to flow mainly from types of financing not from types of legal system.

Chapter 2 extends the work of Lamb, Nobes and Roberts (1998, reproduced as Chapter 8 in IACFR). Lamb et al. examined the tax/accounting relationships existing in 1996 in France, Germany, the UK and the US. In Chapter 2, Nobes and Schwencke start by setting up a general model for the mutual influences of tax and financial reporting. They then apply the techniques of Lamb et al. (somewhat refined) to the case of Norway over 30 years. Thus, a theory and a time dimension are added to the literature. One conclusion is that there are competing pressures for connection and disconnection of tax and accounting, but that (at least for consolidated statements) disconnection is likely to be maintained and extended.

Chapter 3 is a 'comment' on the dangers of using data for a purpose not intended by its preparers. This is also one aspect of Chapter 7 of this volume and of Nobes (1981) which was reproduced as Chapter 4 of IACFR. In the case of Chapter 3 of this volume, the data was prepared by me and used by Ding et al. (2007). Those authors use the *GAAP 2001* survey (Nobes, 2001) as data for the measurement of national differences from international standards (then IAS). This was part of their research on the effects of variables such as the legal system and the financing system. Chapter 3 notes that many differences in rules are of little importance for practice. It also questions Ding et al.'s distinction between the absence of an IAS rule and divergence from IAS. In the reply by Ding et al. (2009) several of the suggestions in Chapter 3 are taken up.

Another international issue is the origins of double-entry book-keeping. In a paper of an earlier period (Nobes, 1987), I had commented on a paper by Lall Nigam (1986) which had proposed an Indian origin for double entry. Chapter 4 of this volume is a comment on Zaid (2000) which appears to suggest that Islamic recording practices influenced the development of double entry. My main argument in both comments is that, once we are clear about the definition of double entry (including a full set of entries in the same currency, with periodic balancing), the case for a northern Italian origin in the late thirteenth century remains strong. Elsewhere, there is no set of historical records that shows double entry gradually evolving, no surviving books of account in double entry, and no contemporaneous descriptions of double entry. Zaid (2001) replies to some of the detailed points but agrees that there is no evidence for an Islamic influence on the origins of double entry.

Chapter 5 analyses the evolution of the equity method through the twentieth century and across several countries. I conclude that the method began as a form of proto-consolidation. It gradually spread internationally, having different uses in different countries. The 20 per cent threshold for the identification of associated companies was invented without a theory, and it also gradually spread round the world. It is suggested that the method is not appropriate for most of the uses it has had.

Classification

Part II of this volume contains additions to one of the main themes of my work: classification of financial reporting systems. Earlier papers were included as Chapters

3, 7 and 10 of IACFR. The two-system model (Anglo-Saxon versus continental European) whose development I had contributed to came under criticism from several quarters. In IACFR, Chapter 6 contained a comment on the doubts of Cairns (1997). In this volume, Chapters 6 and 7 are comments on the doubts of Alexander and Archer (2000) and of d'Arcy (2001). In Chapter 6, I suggest that Alexander and Archer concentrate too much on the regulatory system as they seek to show that UK and US accounting are different. If, instead, they had concentrated on financial reporting *practices* (and contrasted UK and US practices to Chinese, French, German or Japanese practices), an Anglo-Saxon system would have been easier to discern. Alexander and Archer (2003) reply, *inter alia*, that Nobes understates the importance of the transatlantic difference in the fairness 'override' (see the discussion about Part IV below).

D'Arcy (2001) used a database of accounting differences to classify the account-ing rules of 14 countries and international standards. She found no Anglo-Saxon grouping, and noted that Australia was an outlier. In Chapter 7, I show that these findings are explained by unreliable data. D'Arcy (2004) replies by explaining various aspects of her work but not by addressing most of the doubts about the accuracy of the data.

Chapter 8 asks whether the arrival of IFRS has made accounting classification a matter for historical interest only. The conclusion is that classification can still be helpful in explaining how countries react to the availability of IFRS. It is also relevant in that much of financial reporting (for example unconsolidated statements) continues to use national rules.

International Financial Reporting Standards

Part III moves to studies specifically about IFRS. Chapter 9 was one of a series of papers of the mid-2000s on principles and rules in accounting (for example Nelson, 2003; Schipper, 2003). Chapter 9 suggests that the need for rules in standards is often caused by having no principle or a bad principle. Examples are given (from IFRS and US accounting) of pension accounting, financial assets, lease accounting, government grants, scope of the group, and use of the equity method. At the time of writing, all of these issues still remain to be resolved by the standard-setters. However, some progress has been made since 2005 in standards or discussion papers, on reducing complexity and removing options and exceptions.

Chapter 10 is a 'comment' on Haswell and Langfield-Smith (2008a). This is partly a detailed debate about the quality of individual standards within IFRS. Haswell and Langfield-Smith had identified 57 'serious defects' but I suggest that some of the items are not defects and some are not serious. Haswell and Langfield-Smith (2008b) reply, *inter alia*, that opinions can reasonably differ on some of the issues.

Chapter 11 examines a topic that was new to the literature: are there national versions of IFRS practice? Chapter 11 sets out the theory by asking whether the reasons for national difference (see Chapters 1–3) might still be relevant under IFRS, and whether there is scope within the rules of IFRS for practices to differ in this way. The conclusion is affirmative in both cases.

The obvious next step is to discover whether such national flavours of IFRS practice actually exist. Chapter 12 examines that issue by looking at the 2005/6 annual reports of companies in the stock market indices of five countries. This provides very strong evidence of country-based choices of options within IFRS.

The last chapter in this part (Chapter 13) examines international differences in audit reports on IFRS. In particular, many audit reports do not refer to compliance with IFRS (as issued by the IASB) even where compliance exists.

On truth and fairness

The four last chapters in this volume (Part IV) concern the 'true and fair view' (TFV) requirement. Many papers have been published on this. Most are set in a single national context. Some of these have been collected together by Nobes and Parker (1994) and by Parker, Wolnizer and Nobes (1996). However, starting in the 1990s, some papers have taken a deliberately international approach. Zeff (1990) examines the Dutch version of the concept, in the context of UK and US wordings. Alexander (for example 1993), Nobes (for example 1993), Ordelheide (for example 1993) and Van Hulle (for example 1992) debate the issue in a comparative European way.

Nobes (1993; reproduced as Chapter 15 in IACFR) looked at the origins of the TFV requirement and at its implementation in the twelve EU member states of the time. The signifiers, the signified and the significance were examined country by country. This work is taken further by Aisbitt and Nobes (Chapter 14 in this volume), who examine the same issues for the three countries that joined the EU in 1995 (Austria, Finland and Sweden) and for Norway as a member of the European Economic Area. Chapter 14 reports that three of the four new laws depart from the TFV signifiers of the related language versions of the Fourth Directive. Startlingly, none of the four laws contains a straightforward TFV 'override', as foreseen in the Directive.

On the subject of the override, Chapter 15 contains a 'comment' on a paper by Alexander (1999) which had set up a useful model of accounting requirements by splitting them into Type A (general, overriding), Type B (framework) and Type C (detailed). Alexander writes approvingly of the TFV override and of its insertion into IAS 1. Chapter 15 raises arguments against this. It is suggested that an override is best used by standard setters and regulators rather than by preparers or auditors. In an international context (compared, for example, to a UK context), there is greater variability in the interpretation of the expression and in the enforcement of its proper use. Alexander (2001) replies by accepting some of these points into his model, and adding examples of the use of the override by preparers.

Chapter 16 is a further 'comment'. It relates the conclusions by Wüstemann and Kierzek (2005, hereafter WK) that the European Commission had endorsed a number of international standards that did not comply with 'the' European TFV. Chapter 16 suggests that there is no single European TFV, and it questions each of WK's allegedly defective endorsements. Wüstemann and Kierzek (2006) reply. They no longer conclude that any of the endorsements were clearly erroneous, but they suggest a different one (IFRS 3).

Chapter 17 contains a wide-ranging commentary on TFV and fair presentation (FP) in the context of financial statements as prepared by UK companies under International Financial Reporting Standards (IFRS). Most of the commentary is also relevant for other EU countries. Chapter 17 analyses the rather complex relationship between national law, the EU Regulation and IFRS. For example, directors are required by IAS

1 to ensure an FP but auditors are required by law to give an opinion on TFV. There is also discussion of the difference between an override in law and one in standards. There is then an examination of the use of the override in practice, with the conclusion that it does not perform a useful function. This reinforces the expectation of Chapter 15.

References

Alexander, D. (1993) 'A European true and fair view?', *European Accounting Review*, **2** (1), 59–80.

Alexander, D. (1999) 'A benchmark for the adequacy of published financial statements', *Accounting and Business Research*, **29**, Summer, 239–53.

Alexander, D. (2001) 'The over-riding importance of internationalism: a reply to Nobes', *Accounting and Business Research*, **31** (2), 145–9.

Alexander, D. and Archer, S. (2000) 'On the myth of Anglo-Saxon financial accounting', *International Journal of Accounting*, **35** (4), 539–57.

Alexander, D. and Archer, S. (2003) 'On the myth of "Anglo-Saxon" financial accounting: a response to Nobes', *International Journal of Accounting*, **38** (4), 503–4.

Cairns, D. (1997) 'The future shape of harmonization: a reply', *European Accounting Review*, **6** (2), 305–48.

d'Arcy, A. (2001) 'Accounting classification and the international harmonisation debate – an empirical investigation', *Accounting, Organizations and Society*, **26**, 327–49.

d'Arcy, A. (2004) 'Accounting classification and the international debate: a reply to a comment', *Accounting, Organizations and Society*, **29** (2), 201–6.

Ding, Y., Hope, O.-K., Jeanjean, T. and Stolowy, H. (2007) 'Differences between domestic accounting standards and IAS: measurement, determinants and implications', *Journal of Accounting and Public Policy*, **26**, 1–38.

Ding, Y., Jeanjean, T. and Stolowy, H. (2009) 'Observations on measuring the differences between domestic accounting standards and IAS: a reply', *Journal of Accounting and Public Policy*, **28** (2), 154–61.

Haswell, S. and Langfield-Smith, I. (2008a) 'Fifty-seven serious defects in "Australian" IFRS', *Australian Accounting Review*, **18** (1), 46–62.

Haswell, S. and Langfield-Smith, I. (2008b) 'Serious IFRS defects a trifling matter? Reply to two commentaries on "57 serious defects in 'Australian' IFRS"', *Australian Accounting Review*, **18** (4), 294–6.

Lall Nigam, B.M. (1986) 'Bahi-Khata: the pre-Pacioli Indian double-entry system of bookkeeping', *Abacus*, **22** (2), 148–61

Lamb, M., Nobes, C.W. and Roberts, A.D. (1998) 'International variations in the connections between tax and financial reporting', *Accounting and Business Research*, Summer, 173–88.

Nelson, M.W. (2003) 'Behavioural evidence on the effects of principles- and rules-based standards', *Accounting Horizons*, **17** (1), 91–104.

Nobes, C.W. (1981) 'An empirical analysis of international accounting principles: a comment', *Journal of Accounting Research*, Spring, 268–70.

Nobes, C.W. (1987) 'The pre-Pacioli Indian double-entry system of bookkeeping: a comment', *Abacus*, **23** (2), 182–4.

Nobes, C.W. (1993) 'The true and fair view requirement: impact on and of the fourth Directive', *Accounting and Business Research*, **24** (93), 35–48.

Nobes, C.W. (1998) 'Towards a general model of the reasons for international differences in financial reporting', *Abacus*, **34** (2), 162–87.

Nobes, C.W. (2001) *GAAP 2001: A Survey of National Accounting Rules* (ed.), Ernst & Young.

Nobes, C.W. and Parker, R.H. (1994) *An International View of True and Fair Accounting*, Routledge, London.

Ordelheide, D. (1993) 'True and fair view: a European and a German perspective', *European Accounting Review*, **2** (1), 81–90.

Parker, R.H., Wolnizer, P. and Nobes, C.W. (1996) *Readings in True and Fair*, Garland Publishing, New York.

Schipper, K. (2003) 'Principles-based accounting standards', *Accounting Horizons*, **17** (1), 61–72.

Van Hulle, K. (1992) 'Harmonization of accounting standards: a view from the European Community', *European Accounting Review*, **1** (1), 161–72.

Wüstemann, J. and Kierzek, S. (2005) 'Revenue recognition under IFRS revisited: conceptual models, current proposals and practical consequences', *Accounting in Europe*, **2** (1), 69–106.

Wüstemann, J. and Kierzek, S. (2006) 'True and fair revisited – a reply to Alexander and Nobes', *Accounting in Europe*, **3**, 91–116.

Zaid, O.A. (2000) 'Were Islamic records precursors to accounting books based on the Italian method?', *Accounting Historians Journal*, **27** (1), 73–90.

Zaid, O.A. (2001) 'Were Islamic records precursors to accounting books based on the Italian method? A response', *Accounting Historians Journal*, **28** (2), 215–18.

Zeff, S.A. (1990) 'The English language equivalent of "Geeft een Getrouw Beeld"', *De Accountant*, No. 2, October, 83.

PART I

INTERNATIONAL DEVELOPMENT

[1]

CHRISTOPHER NOBES AND ALAN ROBERTS

TOWARDS A UNIFYING MODEL OF SYSTEMS OF LAW, CORPORATE FINANCING, ACCOUNTING AND CORPORATE GOVERNANCE

This paper examines the relationships between four systems: legal, corporate financing, financial reporting and corporate governance. Nobes (1998) investigated the linkages between the first three of these. The objectives of this paper are to give further explanation and examples of why legal systems need not be seen as causal factors for accounting systems, and then to suggest linkages with the fourth system, corporate governance. It is proposed that, for any of these systems, developments over time and comparisons across countries are best understood by looking at the four systems together. Preliminary suggestions are made towards a unifying theory for the four systems in the shape of a model containing testable propositions.

Discussions in the areas of concern to this paper are sometimes confusing because of a lack of clarity in the terminology used. For the purposes of this paper, certain terms need to be defined.

The expression "legal system" is used to mean the broad nature of law within a particular jurisdiction. The frequently used distinction between Roman codified law and English common law (eg, David and Brierley, 1985; van Caenegem, 1988) is an example of the level of abstraction intended here.

"Systems of corporate financing" are ways in which classes of company are financed within a jurisdiction. For example, in some countries, there is a class of public companies which are largely funded by equity issues to millions of investors. Several systems of financing may exist simultaneously in a country, but one may dominate economic activity.

The term "system of financial reporting" refers to a set of financial reporting practices held in common by the financial reports of a set of companies. The term (sometimes abbreviated here and elsewhere to "accounting system") covers both measurement and disclosure practices, but is not intended to cover the regulatory system for financial reporting or such issues as audit. Nobes (1998) draws on previous descriptions and classifications to propose two main

Several authors have observed a relationship between a country's type of legal system and its style of financial reporting. Generally, the causality is presumed to be from legal system to accounting system. However, one model of accounting differences suggests that the type of accounting is an influence on the regulatory system rather than vice versa. This helps to explain why the Netherlands has Roman law but approximately Anglo-Saxon accounting. It also allows for the extensive use by European companies of US or international rules. This paper expands on these themes, and extends the model to include corporate governance.

TABLE 1: EXAMPLES OF FEATURES OF THE TWO ACCOUNTING CLASSES

Feature	Class A	Class B
Provisions for depreciation and pensions	Accounting practice differs from tax rules	Accounting practice follows tax rules
Long-term contracts	Percentage of completion method	Completed contract method
Unsettled currency gains	Taken to income	Deferred or not recognised
Legal reserves	Not found	Required
Profit and loss format	Expenses recorded by function (eg, cost of sales)	Expenses recorded by nature (eg, total wages)
Cashflow statements	Required	Not required, found only sporadically
Earnings per share disclosure	Required by listed companies	Not required, found only sporadically

classes of accounting. Table 1 illustrates some features of these. Different types of company in a country can use different systems of financial reporting (Roberts, 1995). Further, a single company might use more than one system at the same time in order to address different users or uses of information.

A "corporate governance system" is taken to comprise the elements whereby companies are controlled and managed, in particular the accountability aspects of governance involving monitoring, evaluation and control of agents to ensure that they behave in the interests of stakeholders (Keasey and Wright, 1993, p. 291). This includes such issues as board structure, how dividend policy is set, whom the auditors report to and who sets management remuneration. It does not include the profile of owners and lenders, which is seen as an aspect of financing. Different classes of companies within a jurisdiction may have different systems of corporate governance.

REASONS FOR INTERNATIONAL DIFFERENCES IN ACCOUNTING

Elsewhere, Nobes (1998) notes that previous writers have suggested a number of reasons for international differences in financial reporting. It is proposed there that most of these factors are either too vague to be useful or are covered by other factors or are results rather than causes. However, two factors stand out as explanations for financing reporting differences across the world: colonial influence and corporate financing.

Most countries exhibit accounting systems imposed by or copied from other influential countries. Thus, colonial or cultural influence overwhelms all other factors, sometimes leading to apparently inappropriate financial reporting. For example, an African country which was once a British colony may have no stock exchange but a British-style system of financial

reporting which seems most suitable for a country with many listed companies, private shareholders, qualified auditors, etc.

In countries which do not fit this description of cultural influence, financial reporting is particularly affected by corporate financing systems. Zysman (1983) classifies financing systems into three types: capital market based; credit-based system (governmental); and credit-based system (financial institutions). Nobes (1998) proposes a development of this classification, as in Table 2. There are equity market financing systems and credit-based systems. For each of these it matters whether the shareholders and creditors are "outsiders" or "insiders". "Outsiders" are not members of the board of directors and do not have a privileged relationship with the company (eg, such as enjoyed by a company's banker who is also a shareholder). "Insiders", on the other hand, are institutions such as governments' families and banks and other financial institutions which do have a close long-term relationship with their investees. This notion of insiders and outsiders is well known in the finance literature (eg, Franks and Mayer, 1992; Kenway, 1994).

The argument advanced in Nobes (1998) is that the equity/credit split explains different measurement practices. Financial reports in strong equity market countries will be largely directed to outside users. Conceptual frameworks in the US and the UK underline this orientation. In strong credit-based countries, however, there is a greater concern for conservative profit measurement and asset valuation, a concern which reflects an orientation towards creditor protection and a prudent calculation of distributable profit.

TABLE 2: FINANCING SYSTEMS

	Strong credit	Strong equity
Insiders dominant	I	III
Outsiders dominant	II	IV

The insider/outsider split explains different disclosure practices. Insiders will often have a private provision of timely and frequent accounting information which reflects their long-term relationship with a company. Outsiders, by contrast, will exert pressure for disclosures of information in the published financial reports since they cannot necessarily benefit from private information sources.

Class A accounting (see Table 1) is caused by an amalgam of equity and outsider features (ie, a Category IV financing system in Table 2). In countries with a Category IV system, the accounting rule-makers tend to be preoccupied with this system, so that Class A accounting is spread even to small private companies which are not financed in a Category IV way.

In countries which have traditionally relied on financing systems I to III, Class A accounting will not be the general system in use. However, as a whole country or particular companies move towards system IV, then Class A accounting will follow. Nobes (1998) gives examples, and some are explained below.

LEGAL SYSTEMS

Previous writers (eg, Nobes and Parker, 1988, ch.1) have noted the correlation between common law countries and Class A accounting, and between codified law countries and Class B accounting. Causality has been assumed to be from law to accounting (eg, Doupnik and Salter, 1995).

One radical feature of the model in Nobes (1998) is that legal systems are not seen as a major and direct explanatory variable for financial reporting systems. Rather, the nature of the regulatory system for financial reporting will follow from the type of financial reporting system, although this in turn will be linked indirectly to the legal system. The argument here is that there are too many major exceptions to the legal causality model.

First, the Netherlands is a Roman/codified law country but with a Class A system of financial reporting,[1] which seems connected with its large equity market (Nobes, 1998, Appendix). The Netherlands would thus have to be seen as an exception to legal causality. Following the logic of Nobes (1998), we would expect to find a private-sector standard-setter and permissive[2] legal regulation, despite Roman law and a civil code. This seems a reasonable description of the Netherlands (Zeff *et al*, 1992; Buijink and Eken, 1999).

An alternative explanation for Dutch Class A reporting despite Roman law is that the Netherlands is a small country with extensive influence from overseas, particularly from Britain in the setting up of its accountancy body in 1895 and in the Anglo-Dutch multinationals (Royal Dutch Shell and Unilever) which exert enormous influence (Zeff *et al*, 1992). This explanation would not run counter to the arguments here; indeed, it emphasises the role of culture as a plausible cause of accounting difference. The point advanced in Nobes (1998) is that culture can often overwhelm other factors in influencing accounting, and countries can usefully be divided into those which are culturally dominant (CD) and those which are culturally influenced (CI). In CD countries, the class of the dominant accounting system in use will generally depend on the strength of the equity market. In CI countries, accounting systems will be imported. Such importation may or may not fit with the nature of the CI country equity market (in the Dutch case it would appear to fit) and may run counter to the nature of the legal system. Dutch accounting may be better explained as an example of cultural influence rather than as a refutation of "law causes accounting".

Second, Italy is a Roman law country but from the late 1970s to 1994[3] had a quite separate regulatory regime for the consolidated financial statements of listed companies. Consolidated financial statements were not required by the civil code, but they were by the regime established and supervised by the stock exchange regulator, CONSOB,[4] established in 1974. The setting up of CONSOB and its interest in consolidated statements can be seen in the light of the establishment in France of the Commission des Opérations de Bourse in 1967, which is ultimately traceable to the American SEC (Scheid and Walton, 1992, p. 71). For consolidated reporting in Italy, special accounting standards *(principi contabili)* were established. These exhibited several Class A features and were written by a private-sector committee including auditors working in the Italian offices of international accountancy firms. The resulting statements, unlike most others in Italy at the time, were also required to be audited by external independent experts *(società di revisione)*.

A third and more recent problem for legal causality concerns the changes that have occurred in France and Germany, both having codified commercial law.

INSIDERS WILL OFTEN HAVE A PRIVATE PROVISION OF TIMELY AND FREQUENT ACCOUNTING INFORMATION WHICH REFLECTS THEIR LONG-TERM RELATIONSHIP WITH A COMPANY.

From the early 1990s, increasing numbers of French and German groups have used US rules or international accounting standards when preparing their consolidated financial statements. This reflects a recognition among those groups of the need to have some international dimension to their financial statements if international capital markets are to be accessed. It is clear that in both France and Germany the constraints imposed by domestic law on individual company accounting do not need to apply to consolidated accounts. This feature in turn reflects the fact that, with certain exceptions, the group is not a taxable entity in these countries.

The French position at the end of 1996 is shown in Table 3 and the German position from 1993 to 1997 is shown in Table 4. In 1998, laws were passed exempting the consolidated statements of certain listed companies from domestic laws if internationally recognised standards are followed instead, under certain conditions.[5] This led to an increased use of Class A accounting, as Table 5 shows for Germany. Both countries have also set up standard-setting bodies.[6]

In summary, all these examples illustrate that Class A accounting is sometimes allowed (or even required) to replace Class B accounting in Roman law countries. Furthermore, a suitable regulatory system for such accounting develops despite the prevailing nature of the country's legal system.

A linkage in a quite different area is proposed by La Porta *et al* (1997) who suggest that the nature of the legal system may affect the development of financing systems in a country. For example, common law systems may predispose a country towards the creation of equity-outsider financing. According to the previous section, this would then lead to generalised use of Class A accounting and private-sector standard-setting.

TABLE 3: FRENCH COMPANIES PUBLISHING 1996 IAS/US DATA

US GAAP			IAS	
'Compatible' national set of accounts		Supplementary set of accounts	'Compatible' national set of accounts	
Fully	With exceptions	(20-F or full annual report)	Fully	With exceptions
• Bull	• Air Liquide	• AB Productions	• Bongrain	• Aérospatiale
• Chargeurs	• Carrefour	• Alcatel Alsthom	• Canal Plus	• Béghin-Say
• Dassault Systèmes	• Danone	• Axa-UAP	• DMC	• Cap Gémini
• Elf	• PSA	• Bouygues Offshore	• Essilor	• Lafarge Coppée
• Legrand	• Technip	• Business Objects	• Moulinex	• LVMH
• Rhône-Poulenc		• Coflexip	• Saint Louis	• Renault
• SEB		• Dassault Systèmes	• SEB	•Saint-Gobain
		• Elf	• Technip	
		• Flamel Technologies	• Thomson	
		• Genset	• Usinor-Sacilor	
		• Ilog	•Valéo	
		• LVMH		
		• Péchiney		
		• Usinor-Sacilor		
		• SCOR		
		• Total		

Source: S. Zambon and W. Dick (1997)

TABLE 4: EXAMPLES OF USE OF IAS AND US RULES FOR CONSOLIDATED STATEMENTS BY GERMAN COMPANIES BEFORE 1998

US GAAP		IAS	
Supplementary set	20-F Reconciliation	Compatible national set of accounts	Supplementary set
Daimler-Benz (1996-1997)	Daimler-Benz (1993-1995)	Bayer (1993-1997)	Deutsche Bank (1995-97)
	Deutsche Telekom (eg. 1997)	Schering (1993-1997)	
		Hoechst (1995-1997)	
		Adidas (1995-1997)	

Table 5: GERMAN USE OF IAS FOR 1998	
US GAAP	**IAS**
Daimler-Chrysler	Adidas-Salomon
Degussa*	Allianz*
Deutsche Telekom**	Bayer
Hoechst**	B. Hypo. Bank*
SAP**	Commerzbank*
Veba**	Deutsche Bank
[BASF]	Dresdner Bank*
[Siemens]	Henkel
	Hoechst
	Lufthansa*
	Schering
	[MAN]
	[Metro]
	[Preussag]
	[RWE]

* = new for 1998.
** = reconciliation
[ ] = announced plans
Source: Adapted from IASC Insight, March 1999

Pagano (1993) suggests that these arguments connecting legal systems to financing systems are "not completely persuasive" (p. 1102). Instead, he proposes the following. In a country with few listed companies, there are capital market imperfections and few opportunities for risk-sharing. Such a country's stockmarket may get trapped at a low level of activity, because a company's choice to go public involves a trade-off between the advantages of diversification and the costs of flotation and loss of control. This suggestion may help to explain why Italian and German equity markets do not keep pace with their economies, but it does not explain how the international difference in the financing systems arose in the first place. For this latter issue, the above legal system argument (for example, by La Porta *et al*) seems the best available so far, although other elements of culture might play a role but remain to be identified.

CORPORATE GOVERNANCE

Just as a country can have more than one type of company, accounting system and regulatory system for accounting, so it can have more than one type of corporate governance system. A clear example of this is the requirement in Germany and the Netherlands for certain companies[7] to have two-tier board structures, with the top board (the supervisory board) required to take account of the interests of the workforce as well as the owners.

Such an element of corporate governance seems not to be caused by the legal system, because most German and Dutch companies are not required to have two-tier boards and most other codified law countries have no such requirements for any compa-

nies. Nor can it easily be tied to the accounting system or to the category of financing system, as there seems to be nothing relevant in common between the Netherlands and Germany which is not also to be found in France,[8] Italy or Spain. Similarly, in the UK, the growth of audit committees and the increased importance of non-executive directors[9] seems not to be linked to a change in category of legal system, accounting system or financing system.

However, a more detailed look at financing may be relevant; in particular at ownership concentration. If ownership is concentrated in the hands of a few owner-managers, there seems to be no need for elaborate corporate governance procedures. If ownership is widely spread, the separation of ownership from management introduces problems which might be addressed by such procedures. One difficulty for this proposal is that German ownership of listed companies is more concentrated than British ownership (eg, Franks and Mayer, 1997) but it is the former country which has supervisory boards designed to control the management, set their salaries and receive auditors' reports. Further, concentration of ownership has greatly increased in the UK over the past three decades (Stapledon, 1996), and this has coincided with a recent increase in the strength of corporate governance procedures designed to control management, such as the rise of non-executive directors and of audit and remuneration committees and the Cadbury (1992) code and subsequent extensions of it.

The explanation may contain three elements. First, there are cultural and political factors. The Germans and the Dutch[10] are more interested in workers' rights than the British or the Americans. Works councils in these countries have extensive rights of information and consultation. The legal requirement for supervisory boards is part of co-determination *(Mitbestimmung)* legislation which is designed to give rights to workers rather than to non-manager shareholders. Further, both the German and the Dutch legislation applies to companies with more than a certain size of workforce[11] whether they are public or private. It became compulsory in Germany in 1951 for the coal, iron and steel industries and in 1976 for other industries. In the Netherlands, it became compulsory in 1971 (Zeff *et al*, 1992, p. 11; Dijskma and Hoogendoorn, 1993, p. 21) in the context of a prevailing wish to control management and give rights to workers. Similarly, the British interest in corporate governance occurred in the 1990s, coinciding with a major swing of political and social mood after the unbridled capitalism of the 1980s.

A second factor is that, in addition to the internal corporate governance mechanisms, there can be external mechanisms such as the market for corporate control. In certain countries, comparatively weak internal mechanisms may be explained by the existence of comparatively strong external mechanisms (Moerland, 1995, p. 22; Short *et al*, 1999, p. 345).

A third explanatory factor returns to the issue of concentration of ownership[12] and rests on an elaboration of the insider/outsider categorisation of shareholders identified in Table 2. Two types of insiders can be identified: (i) owner-managers, and (ii) large institutional, corporate or governmental stakeholders who may be represented by non-executive directors. Figure 1 illustrates this, with concentration decreasing to the right. Private companies are generally dominated by owner-managers, and even some listed companies may be actively controlled by groups of descendants of a founder. Many other continental European or Japanese listed companies are controlled by small numbers of "core" shareholders with substantial share stakes (eg, Cable, 1985; Franks and Mayer, 1997; Renneboog, 1997). In France, for example, the phenomenon of *autocontrôle* exists in many listed companies because large proportions of their shares are owned by their subsidiaries (Maclean, 1999, p. 91). The core shareholders will have formal ways (eg, as non-executive or supervisory board directors) or informal ways of exercising influence and extracting financial information.

Outsiders could be split into a further two groups of shareholders: (iii) institutions with small stakes, and (iv) private individuals. Many UK listed companies have a number of institutional shareholders with small stakes (eg, 5%, see Stapledon, 1996). In 1992, such shareholders were the largest group,[13] owning 22% of the shares of UK companies (Goergen and Renneboog, 2000). Large US listed companies also have a shareholder profile containing many institutional stakes. This is associated with a large number of non-executive directors; indeed, on average more than in the UK (Short *et al*, 1999, p. 340). The non-executive directors do not, in general, directly represent the institutions, but the institutions encourage their existence. Turning to private individuals as shareholders, the US is the country with the most obvious dominance of such shareholders in some companies (Kester, 1992, p. 33).

The proposed model is that elaborate corporate governance systems are most likely to be found in the middle two boxes of Figure 1. This is because, at one extreme, corporate governance is not a problem for owner-managers. At the other extreme, although it is a problem for individual shareholders, they are not powerful enough to impose control on management (except by external mechanisms such as takeovers) and they will free-ride on the monitoring costs of others (Hart, 1995, p. 681). In between, the large institutional stakeholders are powerful enough to appoint non-executive directors (institutionalised as supervisory boards in some countries), and the small institutional stakeholders may be jointly powerful enough to impose their will concerning audit committees, the existence of non-executive directors, the separation of the roles of chairman and chief executive, etc. Unlike most individual shareholders, some "outsider" institutions have expertise and sufficiently large holdings to be taken seriously by management. Short *et al* (1999, p. 343) review the evidence on this issue, and note the type of effects that active institutional shareholders might have; for example, they note a correlation with increased research and development.

The prediction is, then, that corporate governance systems will be weakest in countries and for companies at the two extremes of ownership concentration. A country can exhibit more than one system for different categories of company and ownership. For example, in the US, companies in positions (i), (iii) and (iv) of Figure 1 exist; and, in Germany, those in positions (i) and (ii). As concentration increases in a country for large companies which start from the right of Figure 1, so corporate governance issues get a raised profile. This seems to be the UK position in the 1990s.

SUMMARY AND CONCLUSIONS

This paper makes some preliminary suggestions for a unifying model involving systems of law, financing, financial reporting and corporate governance. The model is one which emphasises linkages between these four systems. Although the model frames these linkages in terms of causal processes, it would be a mistake not to recognise the potential for feedbacks and looping. For many countries, some or all of these

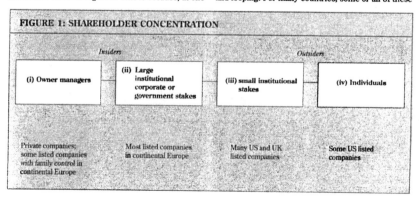

FIGURE 1: SHAREHOLDER CONCENTRATION

Insiders		*Outsiders*	
(i) Owner managers	(ii) Large institutional corporate or government stakes	(iii) small institutional stakes	(iv) Individuals
Private companies; some listed companies with family control in continental Europe	Most listed companies in continental Europe	Many US and UK listed companies	Some US listed companies

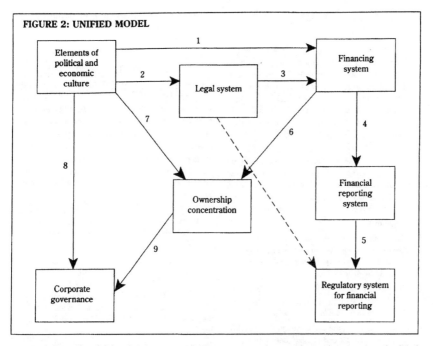

FIGURE 2: UNIFIED MODEL

systems are causally related to their import as a result of colonial or cultural influence. In other countries the linkages are more complex. Figure 2 provides a plausible set of causal links as discussed above and shown in the figure as numbered arrows as follows:

1. Pagano (1993) provides good reasons for small and large equity markets to remain in their respective positions. How they get to their positions in the first place is not well established. Various economic and political reasons may be involved, as well as law (see 3).

2. The legal system can be seen as being determined by culture or as part of culture. Clear explanations of the direction and mechanism of influence seem lacking.

3. La Porta *et al* (1997) provide arguments and evidence for a connection between legal system and financing system.

4. Nobes (1998) suggests that, except for culturally dominated countries, the main influence on class of accounting is type of financing system.

5. It is proposed that the regulatory system for accounting is a result of the class of accounting, not its cause.

6. The degree of ownership concentration will depend partly on the system of corporate financing. Unconcentrated ownership can only exist in equity/outsider systems.

7. Ownership concentration may also be influenced by other economic factors yet to be specified.

8. To the extent that ownership concentration (see 9) does not explain different regimes of corporate gov-

ernance, they may be partly a question of political mood. External, as well as internal, mechanisms should be considered.

9. The concentration of ownership may be an explanation of the corporate governance procedures adopted.

The following propositions form part of this model:

P_1: Common law countries tend to have strong equity markets.

P_2: For culturally dominated countries, the financial reporting system will be imported.

P_3: For other countries, Class A accounting (see Table 1) will be found when there is equity-outsider financing.

P_4: A non-codified regulatory system for financial reporting will be adopted to regulate Class A accounting even in codified law countries.

P_5: Ownership concentration can only be very low in equity/outsider financing systems. Corporate governance systems will be weak for countries or companies with very high or very low ownership concentration.

The authors believe that these propositions, and therefore the model, could be tested. They encourage empirical researchers to attempt this.

Christopher Nobes and Alan Roberts work in the University of Reading. They are grateful for advice from Marc Goergen (University of Manchester), Kevin Keasey (University of Leeds), Mike Wright (University of Nottingham) and a referee of this journal.

NOTES

1 See, for example, Zeff *et al* (1992) or Parker (1998).

2 Dutch accounting regulation in the civil code is largely based on the Fourth and Seventh EU Directives, but the Netherlands has preserved most of the large number of options in the directives. Consequently, it seems legal to obey international accounting standards and even US rules (as, for example, in the annual reports of Royal Dutch/Shell, 1998, pp. 42 and 47).

3 Presidential Degree No. 126 of March 1975 introduced this scheme, under the control of the *Commissione Nazionale per le Società e la Borsa*, which was established in 1974. From 1994, consolidated accounts are regulated by the law of April 1991 which implemented the EU Seventh Directive.

4 See Note 3.

5 The conditions include that EU Directives are obeyed. In France, the internationally recognised standards must be translated into French and approved by the CRC.

6 The *Comité de la Réglementation Comptable* (CRC) began work in 1998, as did the *Deutsches Rechnungslegung Standards Committee*.

7 In Germany, both public (AG) and private (GmbH) companies above a certain size (see Note 11). In the Netherlands, for *structuurvennootshappen*, which are companies above a certain size (eg, 100 employees or more in the Netherlands), whether of public (NV) or private (BV) form.

8 A two-tier structure is allowed in France for the *société anonyme*, but is rare (Scheid and Walton, 1992, p. 35).

9 For example, Stapledon (1996) shows that the proportion of non-executive directors on the boards of listed UK industrial companies increased from 30% in 1979 to 44% in 1993.

10 Eg, Zeff *et al* (1992, p. 350).

11 In Germany, more than 1,000 employees in the coal, iron and steel industries, and more than 2,000 in other industries (Ordelheide and Pfaff, 1994, p. 47). In the Netherlands, 100 or more employees in the country and some other criteria (Dijksma and Hoogendoorn, 1993, p. 21).

12 We are grateful to Marc Goergen for suggesting that market concentration seems a relevant issue.

13 Directors owned 9.9%, companies 6.1%, families and individuals 2.5%. Blocks of 3% or more were counted.

REFERENCES

Buijink, W., and R. Eken, 1999, in S.J. McLeay, *Accounting Regulation in Europe* (Macmillan, London).

Cable, J., 1985, "Capital market information and industrial performance: the role of West German banks", *Economic Journal*, 95, 377, March.

Cadbury, A., 1992, *Report of the Committee on the Financial Aspects of Corporate Governance* (Gee & Co., London).

Caenegem, R.C. van, 1988, *The Birth of the English Common Law* (Cambridge University Press).

David, R., and J.E.C. Brierley, 1985, *Major Legal Systems in the World Today* (Stevens, London).

Dijksma, J., and M.N. Hoogendoorn, 1993, *European Financial Reporting: The Netherlands* (Routledge, London).

Doupnik, T., and S. Salter, 1995, "External environment, culture, and accounting practice: a preliminary test of a general model of international accounting development", *International Journal of Accounting*, 30, 3, 189–207.

Franks, J., and C. Mayer, 1992, "Corporate control: a synthesis of the international evidence", working paper of London Business School and University of Warwick.

Franks, J., and C. Mayer, 1995, "Ownership and control" in H. Siebert, ed., *Trends in Business Organization: Do Participation and Cooperation Increase Competitiveness?* (Mohr, Tübingen), reprinted in A. Soppe, J. Spronk, E. Vermeulen and A. Vorst, eds., *Financiering en Belegging* (Erasmus University, Rotterdam).

Goergen, M., and L. Renneboog, 2000, "Strong managers and passive institutional investors in the UK", in M. Becht and C.P. Mayer, *Ownership and Control: A European Perspective* (Oxford University Press).

Hart, O., 1995, "Corporate governance: some theory and implications", *Economic Journal*, 105 (May), 678–89.

Keasey, K., and M. Wright, 1993, "Issues in corporate accountability and governance: an editorial", *Accounting and Business Research*, 23, 91A, 291–303.

Kenway, P., 1994, "The concentration of ownership and its implications for corporate governance in the Czech Republic", University of Reading, Discussion Papers in Economics, Series A, No. 288.

Kester, W.C., 1992, "Industrial groups as systems of contractual governance", *Oxford Review of Economic Policy*, 8, 3, 24–44.

La Porta, R., F. Lopez-de-Silanes, A. Shleifer and R.W. Vishny, 1997, "Legal Determinants of External Finance", *Journal of Finance*, July.

Maclean, M., 1999, "Corporate governance in France and the UK: long-term perspectives on contemporary institutional arrangements", *Business History*, 41, 1, 88–116.

Moerland, P.W., 1995, "Alternative disciplinary mechanisms in different corporate systems", *Journal of Economic Behavior and Organization*, 26, 17–34.

Nobes, C.W., 1998, "Towards a general model of the reasons for international differences in financial reporting", *Abacus*, 34, 2.

Nobes, C.W., and R.H. Parker, 1988, *Issues in Multinational Accounting* (Philip Allan, Oxford).

Ordelheide, D., and D. Pfaff, 1994, *European Financial Reporting: Germany* (Routledge, London).

Pagano, M., 1993, "The flotation of companies on the stock market: a coordination failure model", *European Economic Review*, 37, 1101–25.

Parker, R.H., 1998, "Financial reporting in the Netherlands", ch. 8 in C.W. Nobes and R.H. Parker, *Comparative International Accounting* (Prentice Hall, Hemel Hempstead).

Renneboog, L., 1997, "Shareholding Concentration and Pyramidal Ownership Structures in Belgium", in M. Balling, E. Hennessy and R. O'Brien, eds., Corporate Governance, *Financial Markets and Global Convergence* (Kluwer Academic Publishers, Amsterdam).

Roberts, A.D., 1995, "The very idea of classification in international accounting", *Accounting, Organizations and Society*, 20, 639–64.

Short, H., K. Keasey, M. Wright and A. Hall, 1999, "Corporate governance: from accountability to enterprise", *Accounting and Business Research*, 30, 4, 337–52.

Stapledon, G., 1996, *Institutional Shareholders and Corporate Governance* (Clarendon Press, Oxford).

Zambon, S., and W. Dick, 1998, "Alternative Standards (IAS/US GAAP) and Continental European Accounts: Evidences of a Competitive Process", University of Reading Discussion Papers in Accounting, Finance and Banking, No. 58.

Zeff, S.A., F. van der Wel and K. Camfferman, 1992, *Company Financial Reporting: A Historical and Comparative Study of the Dutch Regulatory Process* (North-Holland, Amsterdam).

Zysman, J., 1983, *Government, Markets and Growth: Financial Systems and the Politics of Industrial Change* (Cornell University Press, Ithaca and Martin Robertson, Oxford).

[2]

European Accounting Review
Vol. 15, No. 1, 63–87, 2006

Modelling the Links between Tax and Financial Reporting: A Longitudinal Examination of Norway over 30 Years up to IFRS Adoption

CHRISTOPHER NOBES* AND HANS ROBERT SCHWENCKE**

*University of Reading Business School, Reading, UK and **BI, Norwegian School of Management, Oslo, Norway

ABSTRACT The operational links between tax and financial reporting vary on a continuum from country to country and from period to period. We propose a model for how the links vary over time in developed Western countries. This takes account of competing purposes for accounting, and the mutual reactions of taxation and financial reporting authorities. We illustrate the model using the case of Norway over a 30-year period up to the adoption of IFRS. This has the incidental benefit of analysing the operational links for Norway, which has not been done systematically before, at three dates. We also put Norway into the context of four other countries by adopting and somewhat enhancing existing methodology. We show that Norway has moved from a 'continental' position to one that exceeds the disconnection of tax from financial reporting found in the USA or the UK. We raise several research questions related to the generalisability of our model.

1. Introduction

A key feature of international differences in accounting is the connection between tax and financial reporting. This connection is not 'all or nothing' but varies on a continuum from one period to another and from one country to another. As explained below, some research examines the operational links at a particular

Correspondence Address: Christopher Nobes, PricewaterhouseCoopers Professor of Accounting, University of Reading Business School, PO Box 218, Whiteknights, Reading, Berkshire, RG6 6AA, UK. E-mail: c.wright@reading.ac.uk

0963-8180 Print/1468-4497 Online/06/010063–25 © 2006 European Accounting Association
DOI: 10.1080/09638180500510418
Published by Routledge Journals, Taylor & Francis on behalf of the EAA.

date for a particular country or for a few countries comparatively. Also, there is some limited research concerning the change in the links over time in a particular country, but no general model for this.

In this paper, we propose a model for the development of links between tax and financial reporting over time. We then use, as a case study over 30 years, Norway for which the linkage has not previously been documented in detail at any date. We also put Norway into the context of other countries.

In Section 2, we review the literature relevant to this issue, and then set out our proposed contribution in more detail and outline the rest of the paper.

2. Relevant Literature

Writers generally include the connection between tax and financial reporting in lists of features related to international accounting differences (e.g. Doupnik and Salter, 1995; Choi *et al.*, 2002, ch. 2; Radebaugh and Gray, 2002, ch. 2). These writers contrast *countries* with respect to their connections, although Roberts (1995) points out that it would be better to contrast financial reporting *systems*, because a country can contain more than one system. For example, the tax connection may be strong for the financial reporting of individual German companies (Haller, 1992) but weak for the consolidated reporting of German groups using International Financial Reporting Standards (IFRS). It might also be useful to distinguish between private companies and listed companies, with the expectation that the financial reporting of the former would be more influenced by tax.

There have been several studies of the degree of tax/reporting connection. Hoogendoorn (1996) summarises the position for 13 European countries (not including Norway), although his classification conflates the separate issues of the tax/reporting connection and the treatment of deferred tax, making it difficult to interpret the classification. In the same issue of the *European Accounting Review*, there are studies on the 13 countries, though they do not all look at the same topics, and the level of detail varies.

Lamb *et al.* (1998) examine France, Germany, the UK and the USA in more detail than the above studies and systematically. For each country, they look at 15 accounting topics and classify each into one of five cases of connection or disconnection. Lamb *et al.* conclude that it is possible to confirm the assertions in the literature that UK and US financial reporting is noticeably less tax-influenced than German reporting. The French position is intermediate, with French consolidated reporting able to be substantially disconnected from tax.

Table 1 shows the five cases of Lamb *et al.* but, unlike them, we have clearly separated their two examples of 'Accounting Leads', that is, Cases III and III[†]. Case III describes the common position in any jurisdiction of tax practice following a specified financial reporting requirement in the absence of a tax rule because of the widespread principle of tax laws that normal accounting rules are generally to be followed. Case III[†] (Accounting Leads but with reverse effect from tax to

Table 1. Cases of linkage between tax and financial reporting

Disconnection (Case I)	The different tax and financial reporting rules (or different options) are followed for their different purposes.[a]
Identity (Case II)	Identity between specific (or singular) tax and financial reporting rules.
Accounting Leads (Case III)	A financial reporting rule is followed for financial reporting purposes, and also for tax purposes. This is possible because of the absence of a sufficiently specific (or singular) tax rule.
Accounting Leads (but with reverse effect) (Case III†)	Financial reporting rules contain options or allow interpretations, some of which lead to lower or to later profit than others do. This is a motivation for choosing these options so that they will then also be used for tax purposes, in the absence of a specific or singular tax rule.
Tax Leads (Case IV)	A tax rule or option is followed for tax purposes, and also for financial reporting purposes. This is possible because of the absence of a sufficiently specific (or singular) financial reporting rule.
Tax Dominates (Case V)	A tax rule or option is followed for tax and financial reporting purposes instead of a conflicting financial reporting principle.

[a]Such disconnection will be recognised when distinct, independent and detailed tax and financial reporting operational rules exist. Even if measurement outcomes are essentially the same, the particular arena may still be characterised as Case I; the independence and completeness of the sets of rules 'disconnects' tax and accounting in an operational sense.
Source: Adapted from Lamb *et al.* (1998).

financial reporting) occurs where taxpayers have financial reporting choices that would affect tax assessments.

A further issue is the direction of influence between tax and financial reporting. The writers referred to at the start of this section treat international tax differences as a cause of international financial reporting differences, but Nobes (1998) suggests that the influence is primarily the other way round. For example, the relative lack of tax connection in the USA results from the fact that the main purpose of US accounting is not to calculate taxable income but to give useful information to investors. This does not deny that, at a more detailed level, such issues as whether last-in, first-out (LIFO) is acceptable for tax purposes cause international financial reporting differences.

In addition to the operational linkage between tax and financial reporting at a particular date, there is the developing relationship between the tax system[1] and the financial reporting system over time. An implication of Lamb *et al.*'s findings that countries exist on a continuum of degrees of operational linkage is that any particular country's linkage may change on a continuum over time.

For the UK, for example, Freedman (1993, p. 468) identifies a 'see-saw relation-ship', Lamb (1996, p. 933) finds 'effective interdependence of practice', as it develops over time, and Noguchi (2005) looks at how the relationship developed for the particular topic of inventory valuation.

However, the literature does not contain proposals for or applications of a general model of the development of tax/reporting linkages. In this paper, we propose such a model, and use Norway as a case study. Norway is especially interesting because it exhibits several different stages of relationship, including a period in which some tax effects had to be separately disclosed in financial state-ments. As noted above, the specialist literature on tax/reporting links does not cover Norway. The specialist coverage of *accounting* in Norway treats tax briefly but suggests in outline that the tax influence was once strong but has gradually been reduced (e.g. Johnsen, 1993, p. 624; Kinserdal, 1994a, p. 197, 1994b, p. 163). Kinserdal (1995, pp. 2060–2061) and Johnsen and Eilifsen (2001, pp. 1305–1306) also mention the tax/reporting linkage but do not study any topic in detail. Alexander and Schwencke (2003, p. 551) discuss the tax/reporting link, but only for depreciation and only for the 1970s and 1980s. Alexander and Schwencke (p. 562) also mention the general proposition of reduced linkage, but only in relation to 1998 onwards. Of course, at any particular date, practitioners and legislators (especially *tax* practitioners and legislators) would have understood the operational connections between tax and financial reporting in Norway. One of the subsidiary contributions of our paper is to record these connections at several dates in a way that can be compared over time and internationally. We examine Norway through to 2005, from when two financial reporting systems exist because individual companies can choose between Norwegian rules and IFRS.

In summary: (i) tax and financial reporting have important operational links but this varies over time, internationally and even between financial reporting systems within a country; (ii) the literature includes several descriptions of lin-kages at a particular date but the only systematic study is by Lamb *et al.* (1998), who find a continuum of linkage for four countries; (iii) none of this lit-erature on tax linkages includes Norway, and the accounting literature on Norway is thin on the tax linkages, but Norway is especially interesting because of the perceived major change in the linkage over time; (iv) no model of the develop-ment of tax and financial reporting linkage over time is proposed in the literature; and (v) there are no detailed studies of the development of the relationship over time in any particular country.

In the light of this, in Section 3 we propose a model of the longitudinal devel-opment of the tax and financial reporting relationship. Then, Section 4 begins to focus on Norway by identifying three key dates when the relationship changed. In Section 5, Norway is assessed in detail at these dates, using the methodology of Lamb *et al.* In Section 6, we put Norway into the context of the four countries of Lamb *et al.*, somewhat refining their methodology by introducing two indices of tax/reporting linkage. In Section 7, we interpret Norway's changing linkages in terms of our model. In Section 8, several research issues are raised with respect to the model.

3.   Stages in the Development of Tax/Reporting Links

From our observation of changes in Norway (as charted in more detail in Section 5 below and in Appendix A) and of changes in some other developed Western countries (as discussed in the literature cited in Section 2), we now propose a model to describe and explain the historical course of the development of the relationship between tax and financial reporting. In the first instance, we suggest that the model might apply for these developed Western countries, which have a financial reporting history going back at least to the early 20th century. Our model would only be relevant where the countries also have a history of taxation of corporate income. Later, in Section 8, we address the generalisability of this model.

The starting point is the position before the imposition of a tax on corporate income. Accounting already exists for private commercial purposes. If external financial reporting is required, it is for the protection of creditors. There are no mandatory detailed accounting principles.

The next stage is that a tax on corporate income is introduced. The tax system does not invent all of its own accounting rules but uses assessments linked to ordinary commercial accounting practice. This describes the position in many developed Western countries in the early 20th century (e.g. Haddou (1991) or Lemarchand (1995) for France; or Lamb (1996) for the UK). However, the taxation authorities gradually specify tax rules (or, at least, maximum levels of deductibility of expenses) in increasing detail, especially for topics where financial reporting rules are absent, allow choices or require judgement.

In the absence of a major competing purpose for accounting in a country, tax rules and corporate motivations to reduce taxable income will be the main influence on financial reporting. In terms of Table 1, this involves examples of Tax Leads: Case IV and Accounting Leads (but with reverse effect): Case III[†]. Given the absence of a competing purpose, it is unlikely that there will be many financial reporting rules that are unacceptable to the tax authorities. If there are any, a special tax rule will be created (Disconnection: Case I). For any topics on which there are clear financial reporting rules that are acceptable to the tax authorities, any informal reliance of tax on normal accounting rules (Accounting Leads: Cases III or III[†]) can be formalised in tax law, leading to examples of Identity: Case II. Where examples of Tax Leads: Case IV produce practices acceptable for financial reporting, specification of financial reporting rules can also produce Identity: Case II. Examples of Case II are more likely to happen where the authorities in charge of the two sets of rules are closely connected, for example, government departments that do not have competing purposes. France can be seen as an example, particularly of Tax Leads: Case IV being followed by Identity: Case II (Haddou, 1991, p. 56).

For a few topics, the importance of tax law and the overwhelming nature of the tax motivations of companies can lead to contraventions of the general financial reporting principles (i.e. Tax Dominates: Case V; for examples, see Lamb *et al.*, 1998). It has been proposed elsewhere (Haller, 1992; Nobes, 1998) that a good example of tax dominating or leading is the traditional position in Germany.

A competing purpose to tax exists in countries where there are substantial numbers of listed companies with private or institutional shareholders who require financial reporting information in order to make financial decisions. In such countries, the reporting authorities have a motivation to develop rules independently of tax considerations, creating many examples of Disconnection: Case I. A prime example of this is the work of the Securities and Exchange Commission and the Financial Accounting Standards Board in the USA. This also describes the work of the International Accounting Standards Board and its predecessor body, whose *Framework* [2] specifically refers to independence from tax.

The reason why it becomes suitable to develop two independent sets of accounting rules for tax and financial reporting is that the two fields have different purposes in mind. For instance, the tax authorities are concentrating on the measurement of past income that could be fairly taxed and objectively measured. The financial reporting aim is to give useful information to investors to enable them to predict future cash flows. To take the example of financial assets, 'marking to market'[3] might be useful for financial reporting but would represent unrealised and too subjective an 'income' for tax purposes. One motivation of the financial reporting authorities in favour of separation is to avoid the 'pollution' of financial reporting caused by companies attempting to minimise tax. This can be achieved by specifying the financial reporting rules in detail.

There will be well-meaning attempts (e.g. Inland Revenue, 2002, p. 7) to retain tax/reporting linkages because of the administrative convenience of having one set of rules and one set of accounting numbers, but the constant changes to reporting rules and the increasing use of estimations (e.g. current values) will doom this to failure.

In some jurisdictions, such as the USA, the competing purpose for accounting existed early enough (Carey, 1969, p. 6) so that tax rules never dominated financial reporting. In other jurisdictions, the competing purpose has arisen more recently or has not yet arisen. When it does arise, the financial reporting authorities begin the process of disconnecting financial reporting from tax. One way of doing this is to focus on listed companies, as in the USA. The 2002 EU 'IFRS' Regulation[4] can be seen in these terms. This development of financial reporting rules leaves little room for tax influence (Tax Leads or Dominates: Cases IV and V) to operate, although there may still be some room for financial reporting rules to be interpreted with the tax results in mind (Accounting Leads but with reverse effect: Case III[†]). For private companies, in any country, tax considerations might still dominate accounting practice.

A more reliable insulation of financial reporting from tax (and vice versa) is to restrict the use of the investor-related financial reporting rules to consolidated statements only. Aspects of this have been seen in France,[5] Italy[6] and Sweden.[7] Such an approach is available under the EU Regulation, which makes the use of IFRS for unconsolidated statements an option for member states. This allows the possibility of two 'systems' of financial reporting within one jurisdiction.

Unless the new investor-related accounting rules *are* restricted to consolidated statements, the tax authorities respond to them by protecting the tax calculations from estimations and subjectivity. This is done by establishing specific tax rules based on historical costs and other transactions. As a result, many examples of Disconnection: Case I arise.

This model is summarised in Table 2. For countries where corporate tax is introduced after the investor purpose for financial reporting is established,

Table 2. Summary of stages of tax and financial reporting development

Stage 1
Absence of detailed accounting rules. Main purpose of external financial reporting (if any) is to protect creditors.
Stage 2
Corporate income tax is introduced. Calculations are based on assessment or negotiation linked to commercial accounting practices. (Accounting Leads: Cases III and III[†].)
Stage 3
Tax authorities gradually specify rules for topics on which financial reporting rules are vague, permissive or unacceptable.

Stage 3A	**Stage 3B**
A competing purpose to tax exists in jurisdictions where financial reporting is needed for informing investors. This leads to the continuation and further specification of financial reporting rules that are independent from tax rules and tax motivations. (Largely Disconnection: Case I.)	There is no major competing purpose, so tax rules or motivations become the main influence on financial reporting. (Examples of Tax Leads or Dominates: Cases IV and V.)
	Stage 4B
	An investor-related purpose for financial reporting emerges, leading to new financial reporting rules disconnected from tax. (Examples of Disconnection: Case I.)
	Stage 5B
	Unless the investor-related financial reporting is restricted to consolidated statements, the tax authorities further specify tax rules to avoid the estimations of any of the new financial reporting rules that would otherwise be relevant for tax. This specification leads to further disconnections. (Disconnection: Case I becomes typical.)

Stage 3 is accompanied by Stage 3A. Otherwise, Stage 3B occurs, and perhaps eventually Stages 4B and 5B. If so, both types of country end up in a similar position.

4. Case Study: Key Dates

The case of Norway is now introduced. In this section, the key historical developments are outlined. The starting point is the position in Norway before the Companies Law of 1976 and the Accounting Law of 1977 which resulted from the Nordic common company law project (Aisbitt, 2002; Alexander and Schwencke, 2003). The Companies Law of 1957 was in force but contained few detailed requirements. The tax rules were found in the 1911 Tax Law, which was still in force with amendments until 1999. The 1911 Tax Law (§50) specified that normal commercial accounting should generally be used as the basis for the calculation of taxable income. Consequently, for example, depreciation had to be charged in the income statement in order to be tax deductible. Specific tax rules on depreciation[8] and inventory obsolescence allowed high write-offs. Commercial accounting could include such write-offs because, until 1998 (see below), the asset measurement rules in accounting law were written in terms of maximum permissible values. For example, the 1976 Companies Law (§11–9) stated that 'Current assets should not be measured *higher than* the fair value and not *higher than* the cost' (emphases added). This wording did not prohibit a lower measurement than the lower of cost and net realisable value. Similarly, depreciation should be measured at 'at least as high as a reasonable depreciation plan suggests' (§11–10).

A change consequent to the Laws of 1976/7 was that amounts of depreciation caused specifically by following tax rules were included at the bottom of the income statement as a separate line item, enabling readers to see the depreciation expense and the profit figure before this tax effect. This change was brought about not by the law but by a guideline from the NSRF (Institute of Auditors) proposing that the procedure would be necessary to achieve '*god regnskapsskikk*' (good accounting practice). Somewhat similar treatments are required for unconsolidated income statements in Sweden (Heurlin and Peterssohn, 2001, p. 1221) and by the *plan comptable* in France.[9] A disclosure of tax effects was also briefly required in Italy in the early 1990s (Zambon, 2001, p. 584). The Norwegian procedure whereby the tax-related element of a write-off was separately shown at the bottom of the income statement was also applied by some companies to inventory impairments.

These changes of 1976/7 did not affect the balance sheet, in which assets were written down by the full tax-related depreciation or inventory write-off amount. However, in 1984, a statement from the Ministry of Commerce allowed companies to show on the balance sheet an 'untaxed reserve' that contained any depreciation[10] provisions in excess of commercially reasonable amounts. As a result, the fixed asset figures were generally shown, at least by the late 1980s,[11] without deduction of amounts caused by tax-driven depreciation. Again this has analogies with requirements in France[12] and an option in Germany.[13]

In the 1970s and 1980s, there were already some other discrepancies between tax and financial reporting practices in Norway (see Section 5). However, the implied deferred tax was not accounted for (Andenæs, 1985, pp. 140–147 and 195).[14] In 1992, there was a major reform of the Tax Law, moving closer to a transaction basis ('realisation principle') for the tax treatment of certain issues by removing expenses and revenues not substantiated by transactions, for example, those for inventory obsolescence, long-term contracts, financial instruments and provisions. This greatly increased the differences between tax practice and financial reporting. As a result, the Accounting Law was amended in 1992 to require accounting for deferred tax, in both individual and consolidated financial statements. This removed the need for the separate presentation of tax-related depreciation and impairment discussed above.

The Accounting Law was amended again in 1998[15] in order to implement the Fourth and Seventh Directives (Aisbitt and Nobes, 2001; Schwencke, 2002, p. 107; Alexander and Schwencke, 2003), with some major changes to measurement rules that made them more independent of tax practices. Examples of these changes are discussed in Appendix A under the headings of interest capitalisation, long-term contracts and foreign currency.

Eventually, the 1911 Tax Law and all its amendments were re-arranged as the 1999 Tax Law.[16] As had always been the case, this law required (§14–4 (2)) that, in the absence of a specific rule to the contrary, taxable income should be calculated on the basis of the measurements within the financial statements; that is, in accordance with the rules of the 1998 Accounting Law. As detailed in Appendix A, both the Tax Law and other legal sources (i.e. court decisions or long-term administrative practices by the tax authorities) contain many specific tax rules which require a company to measure taxable income in a different manner from the rules of the Accounting Law. There was a further small change to the Tax Law in 2000 which specified that research and development costs are always expensed and that borrowing costs may be capitalised or expensed (in each case, this is irrespective of the financial reporting treatment). In 2005, the law of 9 December (Nr. 116) formally removed the reliance of tax on financial reporting.

This changing relationship between financial reporting and tax is summarised in Table 3. In Section 5, we look more closely at the positions in three years that were chosen to represent the position before or after major changes: 1988 (before the tax reform and introduction of deferred tax accounting in 1992), in 1995 (after the tax reform but before the major amendments in 1998 to accounting rules on several topics) and 2003 (after the 1998 accounting changes).

5. Assessing the Links in Norway

For the three dates chosen, we use the methodology of Lamb *et al.* (1998) to assess the degree of tax/reporting connection in Norway. The 15 topics of

72   *C. Nobes and H. R. Schwencke*

Table 3. Synopsis of major financial reporting and tax changes in Norway, 1970–2005

Period[a]	Tax rules	Reporting rules	Operational link
1. Before 1976/7	1911 Tax Law, as amended from time to time.	1957 Companies Law containing few detailed requirements.	In principle, reporting rules followed for tax, but maximum tax expenses charged in order to minimise profits.
2. 1976/7 to 1991	As above; amendments to depreciation in 1981.	1976/7 Laws; NSRF statement on tax-related depreciation; 1984 statement allowing untaxed reserves.	As above, but tax-driven expenses shown separately; and permission from 1984 to disclose effects on balance sheet as untaxed reserves.
3. 1992 to 1998	Major reform of 1992, stressing the realisation principle.	1992 Amendment requiring deferred tax accounting.	Disconnections in most topics; therefore, many causes of deferred tax.
4. 1998 to 2004	As above; re-arranged as 1999 Tax Law; clarification on deductibility of interest and R&D in 2000.	1998 Law based on Directives.	As above, but further disconnections.
5. 2005+	As above, but formal removal of reliance on financial reporting.	Consolidated statements of listed companies follow IFRS. Other consolidated and all unconsolidated statements allowed to do so or affected by convergence to IFRS.	As above, but yet further disconnections.

[a]For simplicity, we have used the dates of the legal changes. However, the laws generally came into force somewhat after those dates.

Lamb *et al.* were based on the list of International Accounting Standards of the time. These are supplemented here by the topics of impairment and the measurement of financial assets on which there are now standards. This leads to the list of 17 topics shown in Table 4. For each topic, we score the degree of operational tax/reporting connection using the cases of Table 1.

Table 4. Tax linkage in topics of financial reporting

Topic	1988 (net)	1988 (gross)	1995	2003
1 Tangible asset measurement (cost or revaluation)	I		I	II
2 Impairment of tangible assets	I		I	I
3 Depreciation:				
(a) normal	IV	I	I	I
(b) excess tax depreciation	IV	I	n/a	n/a
4 Lease classification	II		II	II
5 Grants and subsidies	I		I	I
6 Research and development costs	III†		III†	I
7 Inventory valuation:				
(a) flow assumptions and cost measurement	II		I	I
(b) other areas (e.g. impairment)	IV	I	I	I
8 Long-term contracts	III†		I	I
9 Interest:				
(a) capitalisation	III†		III†	I
(b) other (e.g. accruals basis)	III		III	III
10 Financial assets	I		I	I
11 Foreign currency receivables/ payables	III, III†		III, I	III, I
12 Amortisation of non-consolidation purchased goodwill	IV	I	I	I
13 Contingencies, provisions	III†, I		III†, I	III†, I
14 Pensions	I		I	I
15 Policy changes and fundamental errors	III		III	I
16 Scope of the group	I		I	I
17 Fines, charitable donations, entertaining expenses	I		I	I

For those topics for which the special tax presentations of 1976/7 to 1992 are relevant, we score the topic in both ways for 1988. The '1988 (net)' column considers the effect on the net profit figure; the '1988 (gross)' column shows any differences from the 'net' column after taking account of the disclosures of the accounting entries specifically made for tax purposes.

The scores in Table 4 for the 17 topics (20 scores in all, including sub-topics) are explained in Appendix A. For all the scoring, we rely on comparing the *rules* of tax and those of financial reporting. For example, the difference between the two 'Accounting Leads' Cases (i.e. III and III†), for both of which there are no specific tax rules, is that Case III† exhibits financial reporting options that would have a tax effect whereas Case III does not. This scoring system does not necessarily record *practice*. For instance, for a topic scored Disconnection: Case I, tax and reporting practice might nevertheless be the same;

for example, untaxable revaluations of tangible fixed assets might be allowed for financial reporting but uncommon, so a cost basis would be used for tax and reporting. Similarly, we do not assess (for Accounting Leads but with reverse effect: Case III†) how common it is for companies to choose an accounting option for tax reasons. First, there are no adequate surveys of financial reporting practice in Norway (or in most countries) at any particular date, let alone at all our chosen dates. Secondly, a survey of practice would not reveal motivation. For example, if it were found that most companies treat development costs as an expense (in a jurisdiction where capitalisation would be allowed but would defer tax deduction), this would not prove a tax influence, because expensing might be the preferred practice (even in a country with disconnected rules) on the grounds of simplicity.

Earlier, the potential for different linkages for different types of companies (e.g. listed and unlisted) was raised. For Norway, for the topics that we measure, there were no differences in either tax or financial reporting rules between these two types of companies. It is possible that certain aspects of *practice* might differ but we are not aware of any examples of this that are relevant here. We come back to this issue in Section 8.

In Appendix A, we give references to the tax and financial reporting laws or standards on which we have relied. In a few cases, we have had to rely for earlier years on such sources as 'administrative tax practice', but nevertheless we have provided references for these.

6.   Interpretation of Norwegian Links

The results of Table 4 are summarised in the four columns relating to Norway in Table 5. The columns for 1988 reflect the position from 1976/7 up to 1992. Although we do not assess in detail the tax/reporting connection *before* 1976, it was approximately the same as the 1988 (net) position, that is, without taking account of the reforms in presentation from 1976 onwards. Inspection of Table 5 shows that the amount of tax/reporting disconnection (Case I) increased over the 30-year period from the early 1970s to 2003, whereas the amount of tax influence (Case IV and potentially Case III†) decreased.

Table 5 also shows the results for the four other countries from Lamb *et al.* (1998). Unlike the summary table in Lamb *et al.*, we record the two Accounting Leads Cases (III and III†) separately, for reasons explained in the next paragraph. The extra topics (impairment[17] and financial assets[18]) have been scored for these countries so that all countries, including Norway, are shown with 17 topics, with three of them split into two parts, adding up to 20 scores. By considering the other four countries, it is possible to put Norway into an international context, although it should be noted that Lamb *et al.*'s measures relate to 1996 and some scores might be different for earlier or later years.

In order to clarify the international comparison, we propose an enhancement of the methodology of Lamb *et al.* by suggesting two indices of the degree of tax

Table 5. International comparison of linkages

Case	Germany 1996	France 1996	Norway 1988 (net)	Norway 1988 (gross)	Norway 1995	Norway 2003	USA 1996	UK 1996
Disconnection: I	2	4.5	7.5	11.5	13	15	13.5	14
Identity: II	0	5	2	2	1	2	2.5	2
Accounting Leads: III	5.5	3.5	2.5	2.5	2.5	1.5	1	1
Accounting Leads: III†	2	1	4	4	2.5	0.5	1	2
Tax Leads: IV	7.5	5	4	0	0	0	1	0
Tax Dominates: V	3	1	0	0	0	0	0	0
n/a	0	0	0	0	1	1	1	1
Total	20	20	20	20	20	20	20	20
Minimum index: Cases IV/V – Case I	+8.5	+1.5	−3.5	−11.5	−13	−15	−12.5	−14
Maximum index: Cases III†/IV/ V–Case I	+10.5	+2.5	+0.5	−7.5	−10.5	−14.5	−11.5	−12

influence on financial reporting, as now explained. Identity: Case II and Accounting Leads: Case III mean that reporting and tax practice are the same, but that this is not caused by an operational influence of tax on reporting. Therefore, for comparison internationally or over time, we concentrate on the other cases: Disconnection: Case I (clear reporting independence) and Cases III†, IV and V (potential or clear operational tax influence on reporting). Our proposed indices of tax influence are a conservative measure (Cases IV/V minus Case I) and a maximum measure (Cases III†/IV/V minus Case I). These indices are presented in the bottom two rows of Table 5. They show that Norway had an intermediate level of tax influence in 1988 and before, unless the separate presentation of tax-driven amounts, introduced in 1976/7, are considered. Taking account of the separate presentation, Norwegian reporting was substantially liberated from tax influence from 1976/7. By 1995, the degree of liberation approximates that of the USA or the UK, and by 2003 exceeds it.

   Lamb *et al.* (p. 174) suggest that their ordering of the Cases is by increasing degree of tax influence (starting at I). They hint (p. 186) at the idea of adding Identity: Case II to Disconnection: Case I when assessing a country. In both Cases, there is no room for current operational tax influence on reporting. As may be seen from Table 5, the only country that would be substantially affected by adding Case II to Case I would be France. On balance, we think that Lamb *et al.* were right to treat the Cases differently and to concentrate on Disconnection: Case I, because Identity: Case II presumably arises as a result of some past influence of tax on the development of reporting rules or vice versa, as suggested in Section 3.

7. How Norway Fits the Development Model

Section 2 noted that the literature on tax/reporting links did not cover Norway and that the accounting literature on Norway was neither detailed nor systematic on this subject. Section 4 identified the landmark developments in the relationship in Norway, summarised in Table 3. Then, Sections 5 and 6 provided a detailed examination (summarised in Table 4) and a synthesis (summarised in Table 5) of the tax/reporting relationship at three dates between these landmarks. This adds to the literature and confirms its hypothesis that the relationship in Norway has changed dramatically since the late 1980s. Indeed, the surprising finding is that Norway's degree of disconnection exceeds that of the USA and the UK.

This contribution is incidental to our main purpose, which is to propose and illustrate a model of the development of tax and financial reporting links. Section 3 proposed the model (summarised in Table 2), and we now interpret the Norwegian data using it.

The model's proposed starting point of sparse regulation of financial reporting describes the position in Norway in the first three-quarters of the 20th century. Johnsen (1993, p. 618) characterises the legislation as not a detailed set of rules but a framework. This framework was used for tax purposes. However, Kinserdal (2001, p. 2052) suggests that there was no strong competition to the tax purpose of accounting until the 1970s. Therefore, given that, from at least 1911 onwards, the tax law, though sparse, contained some rules or maximum deductions, many accounting topics were Tax Leads: Case IV or Accounting Leads but with reverse effect: Case III[†].

Norway was not included in the earliest classification studies (e.g. Mueller, 1967; Frank, 1979; Nair and Frank, 1980; Nobes, 1983). However, Nobes (1984, p. 122) suggests a 'continental' (i.e. tax-dominated) group as opposed to an 'Anglo-American' group for Norway, which is confirmed for the 1970s and earlier by Kinserdal (1994b, p. 149). The developments fit Table 2's Stages 1, 2, 3 and 3B. The next stage (4B) began when, as part of the common Nordic project, specific financial reporting rules for some topics were introduced into Norwegian law in 1976/7 as a competing source of authority to the tax rules. As a result, some topics became Disconnection: Case I, but several examples of Tax Leads: Case IV and Accounting Leads but with reverse effect: Case III[†] remained (see Table 5's '1988 net'). As Section 4 records, the audit profession, with government support in 1984, required the disclosure in financial statements of some tax effects. In a sense, this introduced further disconnections (see Table 5, '1988 (gross)' column).

The investor-related purpose of financial reporting gained importance as the number of listed companies increased[19] by 75% in the decade from 1988. More significantly, the market capitalisation increased by 240% in the same period, and by 1,697% over the two decades from 1983. Kinserdal (1994b, p. 157) dates the increased importance of investors in financial reporting to the late 1980s. By then, not only had the content of financial reporting rules begun to change, but also the way of making the rules. The main rule-makers had been the Ministry (first of Commerce/Trade and then of Finance). There were also some private sector accounting guidelines published, from 1976, by the Accounting Committee of the Institute of Auditors (NSRF). From 1989, the Norsk RegnskapsStiftelse (Norwegian Accounting Standards Board, NASB) took over. Its composition, including representatives of the Oslo Stock Exchange, clearly took account of the importance of the capital market (Johnsen and Eilifsen, 2001, pp. 1295–1296; Schwencke, 2002, p. 109). As suggested in Section 3, the final stage (5B) is that the tax authorities respond to increasing specification of financial reporting rules, especially if such rules seem likely to introduce subjectivity. The Finance Committee of the Norwegian Parliament clarified[20] the reasons for introducing the 'realisation principle' for tax purposes in 1992. Fair valuing of assets was recognised as the correct answer from an economic perspective, but had 'significant practical weaknesses' as a tax basis, particularly because of the unrealised changes in value. Fair values were being considered for financial reporting purposes in the context of adopting international best practice. In particular, the tax legislators considered[21] that:

> the realisation principle has great advantages compared to good accounting practice.... If the realisation principle is enacted as a main principle ..., the tax payers and the tax authorities will have to stick to clear facts to a greater extent than today. This will undoubtedly simplify the tax control significantly.
>
> (our translation)

In immediate response to increasing specification of tax rules, the traditional arrangements that linked financial reporting and tax came to be seen as inappropriate by the financial reporting authorities[22] (NOU, 1992), so that the law on financial reporting introduced the recognition of deferred tax in 1992. The Finance Committee of the Norwegian Parliament focused on the fact that the Norwegian practice of 1976/7 onwards was out of line internationally:[23]

> the traditional 'tax reserve model' only applies in the Nordic countries (except Denmark), and ... Norwegian accounting practices have not been in accordance with the practices of comparable countries on this issue.
>
> (our translation)

Later, a Norwegian government proposal of 1998 refers[24] directly to the competing purpose for accounting:

> The Ministry's objective is that financial reporting regulation shall contribute to informative financial statements which serve the needs of the users.
>
> (our translation)

As a result, the Norwegian implementation of the Fourth and Seventh EU Directives in 1998 introduced several more specific financial reporting rules (Aisbitt and Nobes, 2001; Alexander and Schwencke, 2003). These developments of 1992 and 1998 increased the number of Disconnections: Case I (see Table 5's columns for 1995 and 2003).

We have thus documented the gradual rise from the 1970s onwards in both the importance of the 'competing purpose' for financial reporting and the 'competitive authority' of financial reporting rules. As Appendix A shows, many of the Disconnections: Case I that appear over time in Table 4 resulted from actions of the private sector rule-makers. We have not always proved the causality of changed purpose to changed laws but we suggest that the association is persuasive.

The developments of 2005 onwards can also be fitted into this analysis. As a member of the European Economic Area, Norway has introduced a legal requirement for all listed companies to prepare consolidated statements according to IFRS from 2005. These standards bring further subjectivity[25] into financial reporting. The tax system was not protected from this because IFRS is allowed[26] for unconsolidated financial statements and Norwegian domestic rules may be converged with IFRS. Therefore, new tax disconnections[27] will be necessary in order to protect the tax system from a financial reporting system that is moving further towards the use of current values. As noted earlier, formal disconnection was achieved by an amendment to tax law in 2005.

As may be seen, the model's suggestion of increasing specification by the tax and the reporting authorities (stages 4B and 5B of Table 2) have occurred as several iterations in Norway.

Several writers recognise the importance of 'international influences' throughout these developments (e.g. Johnsen, 1993, p. 624; Kinserdal, 1994b, p. 155). These influences included a German-style system of tax conformity, then a Swedish-influenced system to disclose tax effects (Kinserdal, 1994a, p. 195), then the adoption of US principles by some large Norwegian companies (e.g. Norsk Hydro in the early 1990s), the influence of US and international standards on the NASB (Alexander and Schwencke, 2003, p. 554), the idiosyncratic implementation of the EU Directives (Aisbitt and Nobes, 2001), and finally the probable convergence of Norwegian standards with IFRS. However, the important point is that Norway gradually chose to respond to different international influences, in line with its changing needs as charted above: Norway started by following Germany and Sweden but ended up closer to the USA and the International Accounting Standards Board (IASB).

8.   Further Research

Section 7 attempts to show that the development of tax and reporting links in Norway over the 20th century, and concentrating on the latter part of it, are consistent with the right-hand stream of the model summarised in Table 2. From the literature and from our observations relating to other developed Western countries (several of which are recorded in Section 3), we anticipate that detailed study would confirm such consistency more generally for such countries. For example, we expect that the USA and then the UK would fit on the left-hand side of Table 2. In contrast, Germany and France would be on the right, and the process is not complete except for the consolidated statements of listed companies, and there is no reason to believe that these countries will reach the end of the process in the foreseeable future. These speculations can be the subject of further research.

For many countries outside of the developed West, it has been proposed (e.g. by Nobes, 1998) that the main explanation for financial reporting developments is external influence, such as that of a former colonial power. The same might apply to the tax systems. If so, the model of this paper would not fit such countries. Again, we encourage research in this area.

It would also be valuable if researchers could discover the degree to which financial reporting *practice* is affected by tax motivations for topics where this seems likely (i.e. those scored as Accounting Leads but with reverse effect: Case III[†]). Coupled with this, it would be interesting to try to measure the degree to which tax influence is greater for private companies than for listed companies.

Acknowledgements

The authors are grateful for comments on earlier drafts from Sally Aisbitt, Maria Gee, Ole Gjems-Onstad, Erlend Kvaal, John Christian Langli, Klaus Meyer and Alan Roberts and from two anonymous referees and the editor of this journal.

Appendix A. Explanation of Norway Scores in Table 4

1. Tangible Asset Measurement

Before the enactment of the 1998 Accounting Law, revaluations of fixed assets were specifically allowed in Norway (Companies Law 1976, §11–10.4). However, such revaluations were ignored for tax purposes (1911 Law, §44). This was Disconnection: Case I. Now, revaluation is not allowed for financial reporting (1998 Law, §5–3.1) or taxation purposes. This is Identity: Case II.

2. Impairment of Tangible Assets

Impairment of tangible fixed assets[28] as required under the Companies Law 1976 (§11–10.3) and the Accounting Law 1998 (§5–3) is not deductible for tax purposes (Tax Law 1911, §44 and Tax Law 1999, §6–10). This is Disconnection: Case I.

3. Depreciation

Before 1998, the accounting legislation (Companies Law 1976, §11–10.2) required fixed assets to be depreciated yearly by an amount 'at least' equal to an economically justifiable depreciation. As noted earlier, tax depreciation, based on the 1911 Tax Law (§44), had to be charged in the income statement in order to be tax deductible (§50). This was so until 1992. Therefore, the 1988 (net) column is classified as Tax Leads: Case IV. However, as explained in Section 2, disclosures from 1976/7 to 1992 enabled the effect of tax-driven expenses to be seen. Therefore, the position for 1988 (gross) is Disconnection: Case I. The same conclusion applies from 1992 when deferred tax was introduced.

Until 1992, there was a set of tax rules allowing companies to carry out excess tax depreciation for assets bought in certain areas. The classifications for this should be the same as for 'ordinary' depreciation.

4. Lease Classification

Accounting for leases is based on principles set up by a preliminary accounting standard (of November 2000 and earlier versions),[29] and administrative tax practice is similar (Gjems-Onstad, 1984, pp. 584–602; Wilskow, 1997, p. 70). Given that the two sets of rules are nearly identical, this area should generally be classified as Identity: Case II. However, there may be *slight* differences in the rules and, therefore, all of Cases I, III and IV (i.e. Disconnection, Accounting Leads or Tax Leads) could be applicable under certain circumstances.

5. Grants and Subsidies

The Tax Law (in the case of the 1999 Law, §14–42) includes a specific taxation rule for government grants related to investments in fixed assets, requiring deduction from the asset. Other kinds of government grants are also taxed in accordance with specific tax rules. Financial reporting, however, must be based on a specific accounting standard, NRS 4–Government Grants,[30] which requires a grant to be taken to income over the life of the related asset.[31] Given the difference in the two sets of Norwegian rules, this topic should be classified as Disconnection: Case I.

6. Research and Development Costs

For accounting purposes, there is an option to capitalise research and development costs (Companies Law 1976, §11–11.4; and Accounting Law 1998, §5–6). Until 2000, there was no particular tax rule on this topic. Formally, therefore, the topic should be classified as Accounting Leads: Case III. However, given that capitalisation would postpone a tax deduction, there could have been a tax influence, so we score Accounting Leads but with reverse effect: Case III[†].

Section 14–4 of the 1999 Tax Law was inserted in 2000 and requires that research and development costs should be deducted from taxable income whatever the financial reporting practice. In 2003, therefore, this topic should be classified as Disconnection: Case I.

7. Inventory Valuation

Flow assumption and cost measurement (7a). Flow assumption (FIFO) and cost measurement (variable cost) were traditionally regulated in a similar manner in both financial reporting (Companies Law 1976, §11–9.1.1) and tax regulations (Tax Law 1911, §50). This was Identity: Case II. In the early 1990s, *average cost* was introduced as an alternative acceptable flow assumption for reporting purposes, and *full cost* was introduced as a required principle of cost measurement. However, the 1992 tax reform explicitly clarified that the FIFO method and the variable cost method were required for tax purposes. This suggests Disconnection: Case I in 1995 and 2003.

Impairment (7b). Traditionally, the 1911 Tax Law (§50) implicitly allowed high estimates of inventory impairment which led to a tax measurement below the 'lower of cost and market value' (Andenæs, 1985, pp. 328–332; Handeland and Schwencke, 1985, p. 94). However, the loss included as operating expenses for financial reporting purposes was only the reduction to market value. Therefore, the 1988 (gross) score is Disconnection: Case I. The excess tax-driven loss was charged at the bottom of the profit and loss account, so the 1988 (net) classification should be Tax Leads: Case IV.

The 1992 tax reform no longer accepted any kind of inventory impairment for tax purposes (now 1999 Tax Law, §14–5 (2)). Therefore, in 1995 and 2003, this aspect of inventory measurement should be classified as Disconnection: Case I.

8. Long-Term Contracts

Before the 1998 Accounting Law, profit on long-term contracts could either be accounted for using the percentage of completion method or the completed contract method (Companies Law 1976, §11–9.1.2). As there was no tax rule in this area before 1992, the topic fits into Accounting Leads: Case III[†], because the accounting choice would have affected tax.

As from 1992, the Tax Law (now 1999 Law, §14–5 (3)) generally requires the completed contract method. From that year, this topic should be classified as Disconnection: Case I. This is especially clear in 2003 because the 1998 Accounting Law (§4–1.2) introduced the requirement to use the percentage of completion method.

9. Interest Expense

Capitalisation (9a). Capitalisation of interest cost on a self-produced fixed asset was optional (Companies Law 1976, §11–10.1) until it was required by the 1998

Accounting Law (§5–4). Until 2000, there was no *tax* rule in this area, and, as a consequence, this topic should be classified as Accounting Leads but with reverse effect: Case III[†], for 1988 and 1995.

The Tax Law (now the 1999 Law, §14–4 (7)) has included from 2000 an option whereby a company can capitalise interest for tax purposes. From that year, this topic should be classified as Disconnection: Case I.

Accrual basis (9b). Throughout the period of this paper, the tax system has followed financial reporting in using an accruals basis for interest expense rather than a cash basis, that is, Accounting Leads: Case III.

10. Financial Assets

The Companies Law 1976 (§§11–9.1, 10.1 and 10.3) required a cost basis for financial assets, with impairment as for other fixed or current assets. This was not followed for tax purposes (1911 Tax Law, §44–1). This was Disconnection: Case I.

The Accounting Law 1998 (§§5–2, 5–3 and 5–8) includes rules for financial assets, and specific tax rules are given in the Tax Law (now 1999 Law, §§14–4 (5) and 10–30 f). These rules are different so this topic remains Case I. For example, the Accounting Law requires certain financial assets to be held at fair value. However, the Tax Law does not take account of downward or upward revaluations. Also, the Tax Law (§10–34) requires the cost to be increased by the investor's proportion of the taxable income of the investee (the 'RISK' system). This is relevant for calculating the taxable gain on sale of investments.

11. Foreign Currency Receivables/Payables

Receivables (payables) in foreign currencies were traditionally accounted for by use of the lower (higher) of cost and market principle (Companies Law 1976, §§11–9.1, 10.1 and 10.3). For example, receivables were translated at either the transaction rate or the closing rate, whichever gave the lower asset value. Thus, unsettled gains on foreign currency were not regarded as part of the profit for the year. The 1998 Accounting Law (§5–9) changed this by requiring the application of the current exchange rate.

The Tax Law has no rules regarding *short-term* receivables and payables in foreign currency. These items are regulated in the Accounting Laws (1976 Law, §11–9 and 1998 Law, §5–9) and should therefore be classified throughout as Accounting Leads: Case III.

Before 1992, there was no tax rule regarding *long-term* receivables in foreign currency. The flexibility inherent in the then existing accounting rule (Accounting Law 1976, §11–10) led to a potential tax influence on accounting practices, similar to the positions explained in items 6, 8 and 9 above. We therefore suggest Accounting Leads but with reverse effect: Case III[†] for 1988. From 1992, the Tax Law (now 1999 Law, §14–5.5) includes a specific regulation on measurement of long-term receivables and payables in foreign currency. Therefore, this should be classified as Disconnection: Case I in 1995 and 2003.

12. Amortisation of Non-consolidation Purchased Goodwill

The position regarding the amortisation of goodwill is the same as that for depreciation of tangible assets. Therefore, we refer to (3) above.

13. Contingencies, Provisions

Provisions for financial reporting purposes are based on the general recognition and measurement principles of the 1976 Companies Law (§11−4.1) and the 1998 Accounting Law (§§4−1 and 4−6). This implies the possibility that companies would wish to exaggerate provisions in order to gain tax relief (Accounting Leads but with reverse effect: Case III[†]). However, some provisions are not deductible for tax purposes (Tax Law 1911, §50; Tax Law 1999, §14−4 (3)). These should be classified as Disconnection: Case I.

14. Pensions

There was no requirement to account for pension liabilities in 1988, although companies could do so and, from 1984, there was a requirement for note disclosure of uninsured liabilities (Handeland and Schwencke, 1985, p. 91). However, for 1995 and 2003, NRS 6 − Pensions, applies. This standard is generally similar to IAS 19 − Employee Benefits, and requires the accrual of pension obligations.

Tax deductions for pensions are measured on a cash basis (now Tax Law 1999, §6−46). Therefore, this topic clearly qualifies as Disconnection: Case I for 1995 and 2003, and should probably also be seen as Disconnection for 1988.

15. Policy Changes and Fundamental Errors

Until the 1998 Accounting Law, policy changes and corrections of errors were recorded as extraordinary income or expense (the 1989 revision of NRS 5).[32] This was followed for tax purposes, in the absence of a specific tax rule (Accounting Leads: Case III).

The 1998 Law (and a new version of NRS 5) require retrospective correction with an adjustment to equity. However, administrative tax practice requires correction through income (Gjems-Onstad, 1999, p. 1351f). This topic is therefore now classified as Disconnection: Case I.

16. Scope of the Group

For accounting purposes, a group is defined by the Companies Law 1976 (§1−2) and the Accounting Law 1998 (§1−3). The Tax Law (now the 1999 Law, §§10−2,

84   *C. Nobes and H. R. Schwencke*

10–3 and 10–4) includes rules for group taxation. The definition of a tax group is different[33] from the accounting definition, and the topic should therefore be classified as Disconnection: Case I.

17. Fines, Charitable Donations, Entertaining Expenses

Specific tax rules on the non-deductibility of these items are given in the Tax Law (now the 1999 Law, §§6–1, 6–21 and 6–50). This topic qualifies as Disconnection: Case I.

Appendix B. Tax Linkages for Financial Assets

In Table 5, scores are added for financial assets for the four countries covered by Lamb *et al.* (1998). These scores are France (III[†]), Germany (V), the UK (I) and the USA (I). The rules of 1996 are used in order to be consistent with the rest of Lamb *et al.* The justifications follow.

In France, investments were generally carried at the lower of cost or market whether they were fixed or current. In principle, losses on fixed asset investments should only be recorded if irreversible. The exact rules in the Commercial Code and the accounting plan are detailed (Griziaux, 1995, pp. 1222, 1226). The tax rules are less detailed, although there may be a tax effect in encouraging companies to recognise falls in value on fixed asset investments by interpreting 'irreversible' prudently. So, this can be characterised as Accounting Leads but with reverse effect: Case III[†].

In Germany, investments were generally held at the lower of cost or market. However, provisions were also allowed for possible future losses, and it was also possible to retain former lower market values even if market value returned to above cost (Ballwieser, 1995, pp. 1506–1510). This use of a value even below cost or market overrides normal commercial rules and can be seen as Tax Dominates: Case V (tax dominance).

In the UK, there was (and is) no accounting standard on financial assets but the Companies Act 1985 (Schedule 4, para. 31) allows several methods of valuation. These are more detailed than the tax law. If a company values investments above cost, the gain is not taxable until realisation. This suggests Disconnection: Case I.

In the USA, the tax system uses historical cost rules but the financial reporting rules are complex. They include a variety of standards (e.g. SFAS 115) that require revaluations. These are all ignored for tax purposes, which suggests Disconnection: Case I.

Notes

[1]By 'tax system' is meant the rules and practice of the calculation of corporate taxable income at a particular time in a particular jurisdiction.
[2]The IASB's *Conceptual Framework*, issued by the IASC in 1989 (para. 6).

[3]That is, continuous revaluation to current market values, with the implied gains and losses taken immediately to the income statement.

[4]Regulation 1606/2002.

[5]The 1986 revision of the *plan comptable général* extended the plan to cover consolidated reporting in response to the EU Seventh Directive. For several accounting issues, particular optional valuation rules are allowed for consolidated statements only (Richard, 2001).

[6]Until the 1991 law, consolidated statements were not generally required in Italy. However, from the 1970s, the stock market regulator (CONSOB) was in charge of a special regime (mainly for listed companies) that did require consolidation. Special rules, including accounting standards (*principi contabili*) applied (Zambon, 2001, pp. 536, 568).

[7]For consolidated, but not unconsolidated, statements in Sweden, untaxed reserves must be removed (Heurlin and Peterssohn, 2001, p. 1221).

[8]From 1981, a regime based on the reducing balance method was allowed.

[9]Special depreciation is included under the heading '*exceptionnel*' expense.

[10]This did not specifically apply to inventory impairment, so practice was mixed.

[11]It became 'good accounting practice' and was therefore seen as required by law.

[12]These amounts are shown as '*provisions réglementées*'.

[13]The credit can be shown as '*Sonderposten mit Rücklageanteil*'.

[14]A deferred tax liability relating to an upward revaluation could have been accounted for but generally was not.

[15]July, 17, 1998, no. 56.

[16]March, 26, 1999, no. 14.

[17]As noted earlier, the topic of impairment has also been split out from the topic of fixed asset measurement, with scores added for the other four countries. However, for each country, the scores are the same for the two topics.

[18]See Appendix B.

[19]www.oslobors.no

[20]Innst. O. nr. 80 (1990–91), p. 123.

[21]Ot. prp. nr. 35 (1990–91), p. 60.

[22]That is, as suggested above, the Ministry of Finance, advised by the Oslo Stock Exchange, the NASB and the NSRF.

[23]Innst. O. nr. 77 (1991–92), p. 8.

[24]Ot. prp. nr. 42 (1997–98), p. 16.

[25]For example, the use of fair values for investment properties and biological assets in IASs 40 and 41.

[26]Ot. prp. nr. 89 (2003–2004), p. 26.

[27]Innst. O. nr. 17 (2004–2005).

[28]In respect of intangible assets, the Tax Law (§6–10) includes impairment rules similar to the Accounting Law (§5–3). This would be Identity: Case II, but we follow Lamb *et al.* in assessing only tangible assets and non-consolidation goodwill (see 12).

[29]The earliest version was issued by the Norwegian Institute (DnR) in 1988 and could have been applied in that year. Otherwise, 'good accounting practice' up to that date would be to treat all leases as operating leases which coincided with the tax practice that ruled until the new accounting rules came into force.

[30]This standard was issued in 1996 but was preceded by a similar recommendation issued in 1979.

[31]As for IAS 20, the initial credit entry for the grant is either deferred income or a reduction in the cost of the asset.

[32]'Extraordinary income and expenses, correction of errors and effects of change in principles and estimates'.

[33]For example, subsidiaries must be held by 90% or more. For such 'groups', there is a mechanism for transferring taxable income from one company to another.

86   *C. Nobes and H. R. Schwencke*

References

Aisbitt, S. (2002) Harmonisation of financial reporting before the European Company Law Directives: the case of the Nordic Companies Act, *Accounting and Business Research*, 32(2), pp. 105–117.

Aisbitt, S. and Nobes, C. W. (2001) The true and fair requirement in recent national implementations, *Accounting and Business Research*, Spring, pp. 83–90.

Alexander, D. and Schwencke, H. R. (2003) Accounting change in Norway, *European Accounting Review*, 12(3), pp. 549–566.

Andenæs, T. (1985) *Årsoppgjøret i praksis* (Oslo: Forlag Andenæs).

Ballwieser, W. (1995) Germany – individual accounts, in: D. Ordelheide and KPMG, *Transnational Accounting* (London: Macmillan).

Carey, J. L. (1969) *The Rise of the Accounting Profession: From Technician to Professional 1896–1936* (New York: American Institute of Certified Public Accountants).

Choi, F. *et al.* (2002) *International Accounting* (Englewood Cliffs, NJ: Prentice Hall).

Doupnik, T. and Salter, S. (1995) External environment, culture, and accounting practice: a preliminary test of a general model of international accounting development, *International Journal of Accounting*, 30(3), pp. 189–207.

Frank, W. G. (1979) An empirical analysis of international accounting principles, *Journal of Accounting Research*, Autumn, pp. 593–605.

Freedman, J. (1993) Ordinary principles of commercial accounting – clear guidance or a mystery tour, *British Tax Review*, 6, pp. 468–478.

Gjems-Onstad, O. (1984) *Depreciation* (Oslo: Tanum Norli).

Gjems-Onstad, O. (1999) *Norsk bedriftskatterett* (Oslo: Ad Notam Gyldendal).

Griziaux, J.-P. (1995) France – individual accounts, in: D. Ordelheide and KPMG, *Transnational Accounting* (London: Macmillan).

Haddou, G. (1991) Fiscalité et comptabilité: évolution législative depuis 1920, *Revue Française de Comptabilité*, July–August, pp. 55–64.

Haller, A. (1992) The relationship of financial and tax accounting in Germany: a major reason for accounting disharmony in Europe, *International Journal of Accounting*, 27, pp. 310–323.

Handeland, O. and Schwencke, H. R. (1985) *Regnskapsloven og aksjelovens årsoppgjørskapittel* (Oslo: Universitetsforlaget).

Heurlin, S. and Peterssohn, E. (2001) Sweden, in: D. Alexander and S. Archer (Eds) *European Accounting Guide* (Gaithersburg, MD: Aspen).

Hoogendoorn, M. (1996) Accounting and taxation in Europe – a comparative overview, *European Accounting Review*, 5(Suppl.), pp. 783–794.

Inland Revenue (2002) *Reform of Corporation Tax: A Consultative Document* (London: Inland Revenue).

Johnsen, A. (1993) Accounting regulation in Norway, *European Accounting Review*, 2(3), pp. 617–626.

Johnsen, A. and Eilifsen, A. (2001) Norway, in: D. Alexander and S. Archer (Eds) *European Accounting Guide* (Gaithersburg, MD: Aspen).

Kinserdal, A. (1994a) The history of financial reporting in Norway, in: P. Walton (Ed.) *European Financial Reporting: A History* (London: Academic Press).

Kinserdal, A. (1994b) Norway, in: J. Flower (Ed.) *The Regulation of Financial Reporting in the Nordic Countries* (Publica).

Kinserdal, A. (1995) Norway – individual accounts, in: D. Ordelheide and KPMG, *Transnational Accounting* (London: Macmillan).

Kinserdal, A. (2001) Norway – individual accounts, in: D. Ordelheide and KPMG, *Transnational Accounting* (Houndmills, Basingstoke: Palgrave).

Lamb, M. (1996) The relationship between accounting and taxation: the United Kingdom, *European Accounting Review*, 5(Suppl.), pp. 933–949.

Lamb, M. *et al.* (1998) International variations in the connections between tax and financial reporting, *Accounting and Business Research*, Summer, pp. 173–188.

Lemarchand, Y. (1995) 1880–1914, L'échec de l'unification des bilans. Le rendez-vous manqué de la normalisation, *Comptabilité-Contrôle-Audit*, March, pp. 7–24.

Mueller, G. G. (1967) *International Accounting*, Part I (London: Macmillan).

Nair, R. D. and Frank, W. G. (1980) The impact of disclosure and measurement practices on international accounting classifications, *Accounting Review*, July, pp. 426–450.

Nobes, C. W. (1983) A judgmental international classification of financial reporting practices, *Journal of Business Finance and Accounting*, 10(1), pp. 1–19.

Nobes, C. W. (1984) *International Classification of Financial Reporting* (London: Croom Helm).

Nobes, C. W. (1998) Towards a general model of the reasons for international differences in financial reporting, *Abacus*, 34(2), pp. 162–187.

Noguchi, M. (2005) Interaction between tax and accounting practice: accounting for stock-in-trade, *Accounting, Business & Financial History*, 15(1), pp. 1–34.

NOU (1992) Section 13, Accounting for Taxes of NOU (Norwegian Government Paper), p. 11.

Radebaugh, L. and Gray, S. (2002) *International Accounting and Multinational Enterprises* (New York: Wiley).

Richard, J. (2001) France – group accounts, in: D. Ordelheide and KPMG, *Transnational Accounting* (Houndmills, Basingstoke: Palgrave).

Roberts, A. D. (1995) The very idea of classification in international accounting, *Accounting, Organizations and Society*, 20, pp. 639–664.

Schwencke, H. R. (2002) *Accounting for Mergers and Acquisitions in Europe* (Amsterdam: International Bureau of Fiscal Documentation).

Wilskow, P. C. (Ed.) (1997) *Bedriftsbeskatning i praksis* (Oslo: Cappelen Akademisk Forlag).

Zambon, S. (2001) Italy, in: D. Alexander and S. Archer (Eds) *European Accounting Guide* (Gaithersburg, MD: Aspen).

[3]

J. Account. Public Policy 28 (2009) 148–153

Observations on measuring the differences between domestic accounting standards and IAS

Christopher W. Nobes *

University of London, Royal Holloway, Egham Hill, Egham, Surrey TW20 0EX, United Kingdom

ARTICLE INFO

Keywords:
International accounting differences
Rules versus practices
Biases in data

ABSTRACT

In an earlier edition of this journal, Ding et al. use data in *GAAP 2001* to assess determinants and effects of differences between domestic and international standards. This paper examines whether those data are suitable for the purposes of academic research by outlining the biases and particular features of *GAAP 2001*. The main problem with the data for research is that the differences from IAS that it records, which focus on rules, are of varying importance for accounting *practice*. This raises questions about the equal weighting applied by Ding et al. This paper also questions their distinction between absence of IAS requirements and divergence from those requirements. Some doubts are also raised about the independent variables.

© 2009 Elsevier Inc. All rights reserved.

1. Introduction

Ding et al. (2007) use the data of Nobes (2001) in order to assess the determinants and effects of differences between domestic and international accounting standards (IAS). Many other authors[1] refer to the same data for various purposes. As Ding et al. report, the data relate to the accounting rules in force at the end of 2001 in 62 countries, of which they choose 30 countries. The original data for each country were divided into four categories: absence of recognition/measurement rules (compared to IAS), absence of disclosure requirements, inconsistencies in rules (compared to IAS) affecting many enterprises, and inconsistencies affecting certain enterprises. Ding et al. add the first two categories together as "absence", and the second two as "divergence".

---

* Tel.: +44 1784 276213; fax: +44 1784 276100.

E-mail address: Chris.Nobes@rhul.ac.uk

[1] Google Scholar (accessed on 7 September 2007) shows 549 results for "GAAP 2001 Nobes", most of which are for this publication.

0278-4254/$ - see front matter © 2009 Elsevier Inc. All rights reserved.
doi:10.1016/j.jaccpubpol.2009.01.003

C.W. Nobes/J. Account. Public Policy 28 (2009) 148–153   149

As the preparer of the data (called hereafter '*GAAP 2001*'), I comment here on its nature and on its use in academic research, such as that of Ding et al. I do so under five headings in Section 2. I then make some observations about their particular paper in Section 3. Conclusions are reached in Section 4. As well as adding some caveats to the findings of Ding et al., this paper might be helpful to future users of the data in *GAAP 2001*.

2. The data

2.1. Fit for purpose?

Ding et al. (2007, p. 3) refer to the use of Price Waterhouse (PW) data in prior research, which includes that by da Costa et al. (1978), Frank (1979), and Nair and Frank (1980). Nobes (1981) had earlier noted that it is dangerous to use these data for academic research because, among other problems, they were not designed for the purpose. Does use of the data in *GAAP 2001* suffer from this problem?

Although it is not reported in *GAAP 2001*, the motivation for that survey was to protect large accounting firms from criticism (by the World Bank and others) resulting from the then recent collapse of companies and economies in the Far East. The survey aimed to reveal the existence of the large differences from IAS (or absences of requirements compared to IAS) in the accounting rules of many countries so that poor reporting would not be blamed on poor auditing. The objective was to focus the attention of regulators in any particular country on improving accounting rules rather than on attacking the audit profession. As such, the survey's purpose was not to enable international comparisons, let alone to provide data for academic research.

Nevertheless, as long as there are no systematic biases in the data, it might be reasonable to use them for research. For example, whereas the PW data started from a questionnaire that focused on differences between US and UK accounting (thus highlighting differences between these two countries), I am not aware of any such *national* bias in *GAAP 2001*. The reference point for comparisons was International Accounting Standards (IAS), which *is* a bias, but this need not affect the purpose of Ding et al. This bias is discussed later (see Section 2.3).

2.2. Rules not practices

In addition to the national bias in the PW data, a further problem noted in Nobes (1981) is that differences in the rules (*de jure* differences) are mixed with those relating to practices (*de facto* differences). How does the *GAAP 2001* data compare?

GAAP 2001 does not suffer from this problem. It records only *de jure* differences between national and IAS rules, not *de facto* differences between national and IAS practice. Although not so serious a limitation as would be created by mixing rules and practices, the concentration in *GAAP 2001* on rules rather than practices could cause problems for research, which Ding et al. do not discuss. For example, if a nation's rules do not require a particular item to be disclosed but companies often disclose it in practice, then this "absence" of a rule should perhaps be ignored. Or, if a national system (unlike IAS 38) allows internally-generated research costs to be capitalized but in practice companies do not capitalize, then the "divergence" in rules is perhaps irrelevant.

Another aspect of this is that some *de jure* differences do not lead to *de facto* differences in a particular country because the issue is irrelevant. For example, the absence of rules on pension accounting is of little importance in China because Chinese companies do not generally run defined benefit pension plans.

More subtly, both "inconsistency" categories in *GAAP 2001* (see the first paragraph of this paper) contain two types of inconsistency with IAS: (i) where the national rule and the IAS is incompatible (e.g. if the national rule required LIFO but IAS required FIFO), and (ii) where the national rule would not ensure IAS compliance (e.g. if the national rule allowed either LIFO or FIFO, but IAS required FIFO). The former inconsistency is more serious. Indeed, the latter may be of no practical importance (e.g. if companies using the national rule choose not to use LIFO).

Whether *de jure* differences that are not *de facto* differences should be set aside depends upon the purpose of the research. A discussion of this issue by future researchers would be helpful. In the context of Ding et al. it would be worth discussing whether good quality reporting needs good quality regulation or whether good reporting can develop without good regulation if a strong equity market demands it. If the latter is the case, then a study of *de jure* differences from IAS is less relevant.

2.3. An IAS bias

The *GAAP 2001* data were based on looking at accounting rules from one direction: the content of IAS. So, if a national system had more rules or more restrictive rules than IAS had, this did not show up. For example, US GAAP covered many issues on which IAS was silent (e.g. oil and gas accounting); and UK GAAP did not allow LIFO whereas IAS did. Since these types of difference are not covered by *GAAP 2001*, they were not included by Ding et al. (as they note in their Appendix A). If these differences were included, it would make the US and the UK look more different from IAS than the "absence" and "divergence" measures suggest, but it would not much affect the position of the Netherlands, where the rules were generally less detailed or less restrictive than IAS.

2.4. 111 topics but 79 survey questions

Ding et al. (in Appendix A) notice that some topics in the survey do not correspond with the original survey questions asked. This is because the survey results were prepared after an interactive process. First, I prepared the questions by analysing the whole of IAS, assessing which were its key requirements. Country teams of senior technical staff replied to the questions. I asked for clarifications, often disputing country answers. Sometimes, new issues turned up. Consensus was eventually reached, and the country teams signed off on the lists of differences.

This also explains another feature of *GAAP 2001* upon which Ding et al. comment: that the country lists of differences are not in exactly the order of the original questions. They are broadly in the order of: (i) consolidation issues, (ii) assets, and (iii) liabilities. However, an exact order is less important if there is no intention to compare countries.

Incidentally, researchers using other data might consider contacting the preparers of the data in order to ask questions such as these.

2.5. Respondent behavior

Another possible bias in the data is behavioral. Some countries like to be seen to be "international" and therefore to be complying with IAS. This includes many developing countries. By contrast, in 2001 (before the Enron/Andersen debacle), the US was emphasizing that its accounting was different from (i.e. better than) IAS (e.g. Bloomer, 1999). There was thus pressure from some countries to minimize the list of differences and from a few others to maximize it. I believe that we did not give way in the former case, but readers of the US entry in *GAAP 2001* might notice that some of the "divergence" from IAS is abstruse, meaning that US divergence is exaggerated.

3. Methodology

This section contains some specific observations on the paper by Ding et al. (2007), under three headings.

3.1. Additivity

Ding et al. need to add items together so as to create scores for countries in order to perform numerical analyses. In *GAAP 2001*, we resisted the temptation to add items together because the items are clearly of differing importance. The above Sections 2.2 and 2.5 mention some examples of this. It

C.W. Nobes/J. Account. Public Policy 28 (2009) 148–153   151

would require a great deal of work and subjectivity to weight items according to importance. Not surprisingly, Ding et al. did not do it.

However, this might introduce systematic biases. First, because less financially complex countries do not need the most complex rules, several of the "absences" in developing countries might be of no practical importance. So, the "absence" scores for those countries are exaggerated.

Secondly, as noted earlier, Ding et al. reduce the problem of additivity by creating two distinct totals: absence and divergence. Nevertheless, they add the two "inconsistency" categories together, despite the attempt in *GAAP 2001* to suggest that the second category was of less widespread practical importance. This might constitute a further systematic bias because, for example, many of the abstruse points of US divergence (see 2.5 above) were deliberately put into the second category. Future researchers could calculate whether their results are robust to, for example, a double weighting of the first category's items compared to those in the second.

3.2. Are there really two separate dimensions?

As noted above, Ding et al. construct measures of two separate "dimensions" of difference from IAS: absence and divergence. They say (p. 4) that this is their paper's first contribution to the literature.

However, I suggest that the distinction between the measures might not be useful. In the end, the important issue is whether accounting *practices* are "good"[2] or are comparable among firms nationally or internationally. The purpose of *GAAP 2001* was to catalog various aspects of deficiency in rules that could contribute towards poor or non-comparable accounting. In that context, the absence of rules is not a separate dimension from divergence of rules, as now explained.

Suppose that IAS requires FIFO for inventory valuation, Country X requires LIFO, Country Y allows FIFO or LIFO, and Country Z has no rules. Countries X and Y will turn up in Ding et al.'s "divergence" from IAS, whereas Country Z will exhibit "absence". However, whereas companies in Country X will indeed diverge from IAS practices (assuming that companies obey the rules), companies in Country Y (and in Z) might mostly be consistent with IAS (i.e. use FIFO). In other words, some examples of *de jure* divergence lead to the same result as absence, and some do not.

Most of the *de jure* absences recorded in *GAAP 2001* relate to whole accounting topics (e.g. impairment or pensions), so are likely to be greater causes of *de facto* divergence than some of the detailed *de jure* divergences.

For researchers who are interested in accounting practice or in the effect of *de jure* differences on accounting practice, I suggest that there are not two dimensions. The *absence* of rules on whole accounting topics is likely to be a particularly major cause of *divergence* in practice.

By creating two dimensions, as dependent variables, Ding et al. have to double up all their generating of hypotheses. That is, for each of their five independent variables (determinants), they create hypotheses for both absence and divergence. I suggest that this is artificial, as illustrated in 3.3 below which notes that Ding et al.'s hypothesis relating to how equity weakness causes *divergence* is wholly expressed in terms of how equity weakness might affect *absence* of disclosures.

3.3. Independent variables

3.3.1. Accounting profession

Ding et al. make "the importance of the accounting profession" an independent variable for difference between national standards and IAS. They list it as a "determinant". However, in their discussion (e.g. Section 3.1.4), they more carefully say that the two are "associated".

I suggest that the direction of influence is more likely to be *from* accounting *to* the profession. Nobes (1998) discusses this, and concludes that the amount and style of financial reporting affects the quantity and role of auditors. For example, the presence of large numbers of listed companies in the USA and the requirements for quarterly reporting, extensive disclosure and some use of fair values led to a need for more auditors in the USA in 2001 than in countries where these things were absent (e.g. in Germany).

---

[2] For example, whether they enable investors to make successful economic decisions.

Later, in their 3.2.4, Ding et al. talk of the importance of the profession in the context of setting standards. However, in most countries, the accounting rules are largely controlled by the public sector (e.g. in Belgium, China, France or Germany) or by independent private-sector trusts (e.g. the UK or the US). Japan has moved from the former to the latter. So, again, the profession is not directly relevant as an independent variable.

However, there is probably some "feedback". For example, because the accounting profession becomes large, it is willing and able to take the lead in standard-setting (e.g. in the US until 1973, in the UK until 1990, and internationally until 2001).

3.3.2. Equity markets

When formulating an hypothesis for the variables affecting divergence from IAS (in their 3.2.5), Ding et al. discuss the need for an IAS-like quantity of disclosures in strong equity countries. This, they suggest, should lead to smaller divergence from IAS in such countries than in weak equity countries. However, none of the survey topics included in their measures of divergence (the "inconsistency" categories of *GAAP 2001*) were related to disclosure. That is, their hypothesizing relates to the causation of a high quantity of disclosure but their dependent variable is not related to the quantity of disclosure. So, their whole sub-section is of doubtful relevance.

My hypothesis would be that strong equity markets need a certain style of recognition and measurement, and comparability of it (broadly IAS style). Therefore, there will be a negative association between equity strength and divergence from IAS.

4. Conclusion

Ding et al. (2007) provide a clear and interesting paper. Their conclusion that the absence of accounting rules on IAS topics in many countries is associated with weak equity markets and with concentrated ownership is convincing, and is indeed the main proposal in the general model of the development of accounting rules in Nobes (1998).

In this paper, I provide explanations for various features of *GAAP 2001* that had been commented on by Ding et al. I also ask whether those data are suitable for the purposes of academic research, including that by Ding et al. I conclude that they might be, although there are some systematic biases in the data. In particular, (i) the data leave out the aspect of "divergence" caused by certain national rules (e.g. US or UK) being more detailed or more restrictive than IAS in 2001, (ii) against that, one or more of these countries might have wanted to exaggerate their divergence from IAS, (iii) the equal weighting of widespread and less widespread divergences is questionable, and (iv) the "absence" scores for developing countries are overstated because some topics are not relevant in those countries. Other potential problems might not be systematic, e.g. the concentration on rules rather than on practices.

A question concerning Ding et al.'s methodology is whether the *GAAP 2001* data have meaningful additivity. While accepting that the research requires scores to be created for each country, major problems of weighting need to be considered.

More fundamental to Ding et al.'s paper is the question whether their separate dimensions of absence and divergence are valid. I suggest that, in terms of their effects on differences from IAS practice, some *de jure* absences are more serious than some *de jure* divergences, and vice versa. Some of the absences are just extreme forms of divergence, others might be of little practical importance. The separation of the two dimensions creates a cumbersome and artificial doubling up of hypotheses.

This paper also questions the direction of causality for the association between accounting rules and the accounting profession. Further it questions the explanation of the hypothesis concerning the effect of equity markets on divergence, given that the dependent variable in the hypothesis concerns disclosure but the data for it does not.

Acknowledgements

The author is grateful for comments on an earlier draft from Erlend Kvaal and R.H. Parker. He is also grateful to PricewaterhouseCoopers for sponsorship of research.

References

Bloomer, C., 1999. The IASC-US Comparison Project, FASB.

Da Costa, R.C., Bourgeois, J.C., Lawson, W.M., 1978. A classification of international financial accounting practices. International Journal of Accounting 13 (2), 73–85.

Ding, Y., Hope, O.-K., Jeanjean, T., Stolowy, H., 2007. Differences between domestic accounting standards and IAS: measurement, determinants and implications. Journal of Accounting and Public Policy 26, 1–38.

Frank, W.G., 1979. An empirical analysis of international accounting principles. Journal of Accounting Research, Autumn, 593–605.

Nair, R.D., Frank, W.G., 1980. The impact of disclosure and measurement practices on international accounting classifications. Accounting Review 55 (3), 426–450.

Nobes, C.W., 1981. An empirical analysis of international accounting principles – a comment. Journal of Accounting Research 19 (1), 268–270.

Nobes, C.W., 1998. Towards a general model of the reasons for international differences in financial reporting. Abacus 34 (2), 162–187.

Nobes, C., (Ed.), 2001. *GAAP 2001*. A Survey of National Accounting Rules Benchmarked Against International Accounting Standards. Arthur Andersen and other Firms.

[4]

Accounting Historians Journal
Vol. 28, No. 2
December 2001

COMMENT

Christopher W. Nobes
UNIVERSITY OF READING

WERE ISLAMIC RECORDS PRECURSORS TO ACCOUNTING BOOKS BASED ON THE ITALIAN METHOD? A COMMENT

Abstract: Some readers might have interpreted Zaid [2000] as claiming that the accounting practices of the Islamic State already used or directly led to double entry. This comment puts Zaid's paper into the context of prior literature and points out that no evidence is offered in that literature or by Zaid to dispute an Italian origin for double entry. Nevertheless, there are clear influences from the Muslim world on some antecedents to Western accounting developments and on some features of pre-double-entry accounting in the West.

INTRODUCTION: ZAID'S HYPOTHESIS

Zaid [2000, p. 89] argues that "the development of accounting records and reports in the Islamic State have most likely contributed to the development and practice of accounting in the Italian Republics as documented by Pacioli in 1494". Zaid would seem to be seeking to identify the influence of the practices of the Islamic State on one or other of the following Italian developments:

1. various pre-double-entry accounting records and reports, or
2. the accounting records and reports specifically related to the practice of double entry.

Readers might well infer from the reference to "as documented by Pacioli" that Zaid is suggesting Interpretation 2. Such an

Acknowledgments: The author is grateful for help from Brian Rutherford and for comments on an earlier draft from Richard Macve, R.H. Parker, Alan Roberts, Michael Scorgie, Basil Yamey, Omar Zaid and the editor of this journal.

Submitted October 2000
Revised March 2001
Accepted March 2001

inference might be confirmed when Zaid [p.74] states, without questioning it, that (according to ten Have) it is "received wisdom" that Italians borrowed the concept of double entry from the Arabs. Zaid also refers to "the Italian Method" [title]. The main feature that distinguishes "the Italian Method" of recording described by Pacioli [1494] from that of previous Western systems is double entry.

Zaid has confirmed[1] that he has no evidence that Islamic records were kept in double entry in the period examined in his paper and that, despite the above references, he did not intend to claim Islamic influence over the development of the system. It is vital to establish this because a mass of literature would be overturned if Zaid had proposed and provided support for Interpretation 2. Not only do standard texts [e.g. Edwards, 1989, p.48; Chatfield and Vangermeersch, 1996, p.218] now assume an Italian origin for double entry, but scholars have expended great effort on explaining why it developed there when it did and how it spread from these origins [e.g. Bryer, 1993;[2] Mills, 1994].

The purposes of this comment are to try to summarise the literature relating to the Islamic influence on accounting in order to put Zaid's paper into that context and to correct any misinterpretation of the paper that some readers may have reasonably made.

PRIOR LITERATURE

Double-entry bookkeeping (or, at least, substantial elements of it) can be found in use by Italian merchants in Provence in 1299-1300 [Lee, 1977] and in London in 1305-8 [Nobes, 1982] and in the records of the commune of Genoa in 1340 [de Roover, 1956]. It can be seen evolving in Italy in records earlier than this [Yamey, 1947; de Roover, 1956; Lee, 1973]. It is the later Venetian version of the system that Pacioli describes in a small section of his *Summa*.

There is widespread acceptance that many of the necessary conditions for the development of double entry (as suggested by Littleton, 1966) were established in the Muslim world earlier than in Italy and that they probably moved from the former to the latter. Parker [1989] examines this in detail. Incidentally, the suggestion that Hindu/Arabic numbers are important for

---

[1]Correspondence between O.A. Zaid and the author of 14 March 2001.

[2]As Macve (1996, footnote 14) notes, Bryer argues that double-entry reflects things about Northern Italy other than the needs of capitalism.

double entry (as in many references noted by Parker, 1989, p.110) can be countered by referring to the use of Roman numerals in the Farolfi and Gallerani records [Lee, 1977; Nobes, 1982].

Parker [1989] identifies medieval Jewish traders as the major intermediaries for taking Muslim ideas to Italy. He leaves open the question [p.112] of whether there was direct influence on accounting practices rather than on the antecedents of those practices (such as paper, arithmetic and money). Commenting on this, Scorgie [1994, p.141] refers to evidence that Jewish bankers in Cairo used a bilateral form of accounts in the eleventh and twelfth centuries, thus predating Italian use.

Albraiki [1990] provides some evidence that certain bookkeeping features needed for the development of double entry were invented in the Islamic world, but no evidence of direct transfer to suggest that they were not also separately invented in Italy. Albraiki examines sources relating particularly to tax records in the Islamic world from the ninth to twelfth centuries. They show the development of bilateral accounts and of dual entries for certain transactions. There is also balancing of accounts. However, there seem to be no trial balances of the whole system, nor balance sheets.

Hamid et al. [1995] also describe in detail the registers of a tax department of a 10th-century Muslim administrative office. They conclude that the environment was suitable for the development of double entry but that "[i]t cannot be concluded from this tentative enquiry that double-entry was practised" [p.331].

ZAID'S EVIDENCE

Like Hamid et al. [1995], Zaid [2000] describes (from secondary sources) some of the accounting records of the Islamic state. He identifies four types of journal, three types of other accounting book and two types of report. Some of these can be identified in Hamid et al.'s list [p.325] of nine "registers". Zaid's categorisation of the records adds some clarity, but it would have been useful to readers if Zaid had acknowledged and commented on the similarities and differences between the two outlines.

As noted above, Zaid does not suggest that he is offering evidence that any of the Islamic records were kept in double entry. The fact that certain accounts had two columns (e.g. for tax liabilities and tax payments) [p.82], classified expenses according to type [p.84] or totalled revenues and expenses by month [p.85] would neither confirm nor deny the existence of double entry.

Zaid notes [p.86] that "the concept of the balance sheet as a separate statement . . . was not common". There seems to be no evidence of the balance sheet in the sense of a periodic balancing list of debit balances and credit balances from a recording system (including some form of owner's equity). By contrast, Zaid reports [p.86] that for particular purposes "some balance sheet items were included".

The most specific of Zaid's suggestions [p.81] of borrowing by Italian merchants from Islamic merchants concern Pacioli's admonition to start accounts with "In the Name of God" and his use of the term "journal". However, pious inscriptions can be found in Italy throughout the centuries leading up to the appearance of double entry [Lopez and Raymond, 1955, pp. 146, 170-178, 188, etc; Yamey, 1974, pp. 143-144]; they were applied to other documents, not just to accounting.

As for the word "journal" (or Venetian "*zornal*"), Zaid suggests [p.81] that this "may be based on the translation of the Arabic word *Jaridah*", although later [p.89] the suggestion becomes a statement that the word "is the literal translation of the Arabic word "*Jaridah*"". However, the English word "journal" has, as one of its meanings, the same meaning as the English word "diurnal"; and a large dictionary of English [e.g. OED, 1970, p.1069] will show that the English word "journal" derives from the French "*journal*", related to the Italian "*giornale*", and that it goes back (like the English word "diurnal") to the late Latin adjective "*diurnalis*" and the ancient Latin adjective "*diurnus*" (both meaning diurnal or daily). In ancient Rome, a diary or day-book was a "*diurnum*". This pre-dates Islam by many centuries.

ZAID'S USE OF OTHER AUTHORS

Zaid's introductory reference to ten Have (see above) might mislead readers into thinking that it is now generally accepted by scholars that double entry was borrowed by the Italians. However, ten Have himself [1976, p.11] rejects the idea of any proof:

> It cannot be demonstrated that the Arabs in this period had already developed the double-entry system; thus there is no proof the Italians borrowed from the Arabs. Nevertheless, the possibility cannot be ruled out completely.

Zaid [p.74] cites Woolf [1912, p.54] as a further reference for the unlikelihood of accounting progress in Italy "at the time". Since this reference comes in the same paragraph as Zaid's quotation from ten Have, readers might infer that Woolf was referring to the period leading up to the appearance of double-entry in Italy. However, Woolf is referring to the period from 500 AD to 1000 AD. Woolf himself [pp.105-106] ascribes developments in accounting (up to the appearance of double entry) to the Italians.

Zaid [p.81] also tries to support the idea of Islamic influence by suggesting that Ball [1960, p.209] saw Pacioli's *Summa* as based on the work of Leonardo of Pisa who had translated Arabic writings, and that Chatfield [1968, p.45] saw Pacioli as "a translator of what existed in other cultures". Of course, these references by Zaid to Pacioli are not really relevant to his thesis. Examination of the content of a book of 1494 cannot help us much in determining the foreign influences on the development in Italy of accounting records and reports which occurred 200 or more years earlier.

Anyway, Zaid's references are likely to mislead readers again. Ball referred to Pacioli relying particularly on Leonardo of Pisa for other arithmetic matters, not for accounting. When it comes to accounting (both before and after the appearance of double entry), Ball [1960, p.187] is quite clear:

> The history of modern mercantile arithmetic in Europe begins then with its use by Italian merchants, and it is especially to the Florentine traders and writers that we owe its early development and improvement. It was they who invented the system of book-keeping by double entry.

There is nothing in the Chatfield [1968, p.45] reference which corresponds to Zaid's description. However, on p.45 of another Chatfield [1974] book, there is a reference to Pacioli drawing on the work of other Italian writers, but no reference to other cultures. Elsewhere, Chatfield [1974, pp. 32 and 34] specifically refutes the idea of non-Italian invention of various accounting practices (again both before and after double entry):

> Bilateral accounts developed in northern Italy between 1250 and 1440 ... They were not the product of any earlier civilization ... [p.32]. Though claims are made for an earlier invention of double entry in other places ... in fact the Italian system was from the beginning essentially different from any which preceded it [p.34].

Perhaps the more recent scholarship cited earlier in this comment casts some doubt on the certainties of Ball and Chatfield, but this merely reinforces the point that Zaid should not have used them in support of his thesis.

CONCLUSION

Zaid's paper could be interpreted as suggesting Islamic influence on pre-double-entry Italian accounting records and reports (Interpretation 1) or directly on double-entry itself (Interpretation 2). Elsewhere Zaid refutes the latter.

Assuming Interpretation 1, Zaid offers no new evidence about the state of Islamic accounting in the period before Italian double entry, and does not link his description to prior descriptions. He offers no evidence of actual transfer of accounting technology to Italy. The most precise suggestions of borrowings (notably the word "journal") seem to be clearly unfounded.

Three authors (ten Have, Ball and Chatfield) called in aid by Zaid make it clear that they would either have been opposed to or could not have offered any evidence to support either Interpretation.

In sum, influences from Arabia on mathematics and on some other antecedents of accounting developments in the West are undoubted. It has also been clear for many years that several features of pre-double-entry accounting were used in the Muslim world before they were used in the West. Further, direct influences on some elements of Western accounting are plausible, although no evidence is offered by Zaid or others on this. Finally, there is still no evidence that double entry was first developed outside Italy. At present, it still seems that it was Italians who were the authors of the earliest surviving records kept as full double-entry systems; Italians who wrote the earliest surviving descriptions of double entry; and, above all, it is in sets of Italian records that the gradual evolution of the elements of double entry, towards a full system, can be seen in the 13th and 14th centuries.

REFERENCES

Albraiki, S.S. (1990), *The Muslim Contribution to the Development of Accounting* (University of Kent, unpublished PhD thesis).
Ball, W.W.R. (1960), *A Short Account of the History of Mathematics* (New York: Dover Publications), as reprinted from earlier editions, e.g. that by Macmillan, London, 1908.

Bryer, R.A. (1993), "Double-entry bookkeeping and the birth of capitalism: accounting for the commercial revolution in medieval Northern Italy," *Critical Perspectives on Accounting*, Vol. 4: 113-140.

Chatfield, M. (1968), *Contemporary Studies in the Evolution of Accounting Thought* (Belmont, CA: Dickenson Publishing Company).

Chatfield, M. (1974), *A History of Accounting Thought* (Hinsdale, Illinois: Dryden Press) reprinted in 1977 by Robert E. Krieger, New York.

Chatfield, M. and Vangermeersch, R. (1996), *The History of Accounting: An International Encyclopedia* (New York: Garland).

de Roover, R. (1956), "The Development of Accounting prior to Luca Pacioli according to the Account-Books of Medieval Merchants," in A.C. Littleton and B.S. Yamey (eds), *Studies in the History of Accounting* (London: Sweet & Maxwell).

de Ste Croix, G.E.M. (1956), "Greek and Roman Accounting," in A.C. Littleton and B.S. Yamey (eds), *Studies in the History of Accounting* (London: Sweet & Maxwell).

Edwards, J.R. (1989), *A History of Financial Accounting* (London: Routledge).

Hamid, S., Craig, R. and Clarke, F. (1995), "Bookkeeping and accounting control systems in a tenth-century Muslim administrative office," *Accounting, Business and Financial History*, Vol.5, No.3: 321-333.

Have, O. ten (1976), *The History of Accounting* (Palo Alto, CA: Bay Books).

Lee, G.A. (1973), "The Development of Italian Bookkeeping, 1211-1300," *Abacus*, December : 137-155.

Lee, G.A. (1977), "The Coming of Age of Double Entry: The Giovanni Farolfi Ledger of 1299-1300," *The Accounting Historians Journal*, Fall: 79-95.

Lopez, R.S. and Raymond, I.W. (1955) *Medieval Trade in the Mediterranean: Illustrative Documents* (New York: Columbia University Press).

Macve, R.H. (1985), "Some Glosses on "Greek and Roman Accounting"", *History of Political Thought*, Spring [reprinted in Edwards, J.R. (ed.) (2000) *The History of Accounting: Critical Perspectives on Business and Management*, London & New York: Routledge, Vol.II: 66-97].

Macve, R.H. (1996), "Pacioli's Legacy," in Lee, T.A., Bishop, A.C. and Parker, R.H. (eds.) *Accounting History from the Renaissance to the Present: A Remembrance of Luca Pacioli* (New York: Garland): 3-30.

Mills, G.T. (1994), "Early accounting in Northern Italy: the role of commercial development and the printing press in the expansion of double-entry from Genoa, Florence and Venice," *The Accounting Historians Journal*, Vol.21, No.1: 81-96.

Nobes, C.W. (1982), "The Gallerani Account Book of 1305-1308," *The Accounting Review*, Vol. 57, No. 2: 303-310.

OED (1970), *The Shorter Oxford English Dictionary* (London: Oxford University Press).

Pacioli, L. (1494), *Summa de Arithmetica, Geometria, Proportioni e Proportionalita* (Venice: Paganinus de Paganinis).

Parker, L.M. (1989), "Medieval traders as international change agents: a comparison with twentieth century international accounting firms," *The Accounting Historians Journal*, Vol.16, No.2: 107-118.

Scorgie, M. (1994), "Medieval traders as international change agents: a comment," *The Accounting Historians Journal*, Vol.21, No.1: 137-143.

Woolf, A.H. (1912), *A Short History of Accountants and Accounting* (London: Gee).

Yamey, B.S. (1947), "Notes on the Origin of Double-entry Bookkeeping," *The Accounting Review*, Vol. 22: 263-272.

Yamey, B.S. (1974), "Pious inscriptions; confused accounts; classification of accounts: three historical notes," in H. Edey and B.S. Yamey, *Debits, Credits, Finance and Profits* (London: Sweet & Maxwell).

Zaid, O.A. (2000), "Were Islamic Records Precursors to the Accounting Books Based on the Italian Method?," *The Accounting Historians Journal,* Vol. 27, No.1: 73-90.

5

ABACUS, Vol. 38, No. 1, 2002

CHRISTOPHER NOBES

An Analysis of the International Development of the Equity Method

The equity method was used as an early form of consolidation for all sub-sidiaries in the U.K. and for certain subsidiaries in the U.S. Another use of the method in some countries, even in the era of full consolidation, has been in the financial statements of investor legal entities. This seems to result from using the equity method as a technique for valuation or as an aid in the preparation of consolidated statements rather than as a form of consolidation. The method has also been used as a substitute for consolida-tion for excluded subsidiaries or for controlled companies not included in the definition of subsidiaries. Later, the equity method was introduced for joint ventures and then for other forms of 'strategic alliance', but the latter bring definitional problems, which have led to a consensus around an arbitrary threshold of 20 per cent of voting rights. This article traces these developments across time and space, and criticizes several of the past and present applications of the equity method. There is also an examination of the development of the terms 'equity method' and 'associated company'.

Key words: Accounting; Equity; International.

Across time and across countries, the equity method has been used for different types of investees, and it has also been used in both unconsolidated and con-solidated statements. The present international consensus about its use in con-solidated statements for certain non-subsidiary investees is hard to defend on the basis of extant accounting conceptual frameworks or of legal concepts. The consensus about the threshold (20 per cent shareholding) connected to the use of the equity method seems to have arisen by accident. The spread of the equity method is another example of the international transfer of accounting technology, as

CHRISTOPHER NOBES is PricewaterhouseCoopers Professor of Accounting at the University of Reading. The author is grateful for comments on an earlier draft and for other assistance from David Cairns, Janie Crichton (Accounting Standards Board, London), Sigvard Heurlin (Öhrlings Coopers & Lybrand, Stockholm), Jan Klaassen (KPMG and Free University, Amsterdam), Liesel Knorr (Deutsches Rechnungslegungs Standards Committee), Pat McConnell (Bear Stearns and Co., New York), Malcolm Miller (University of New South Wales), Michael Mumford (University of Lancaster), Christopher Napier (University of Southampton), Dieter Ordelheide (formerly of Goethe University, Frankfurt), Paul Pacter (IASC), Bob Parker (University of Exeter), Alan Roberts (University of Reading), Rolf Rundfelt (KPMG, Stockholm), Michael Wallace (Listing Department, London Stock Exchange), Stefano Zambon (University of Ferrara), Peter van der Zanden (Moret Ernst & Young, Eindhoven), Steve Zeff (Rice University), and to the editor and a referee of this journal. The author is particularly indebted to Malcolm Miller for information on Australia and on empirical studies, to Alan Roberts for information on European regulations, and to Steve Zeff for suggesting a study of early textbooks and for providing photocopies of some relevant parts of them.

INTERNATIONAL DEVELOPMENT OF THE EQUITY METHOD

outlined by Parker (1989) for double-entry bookkeeping and for the true and fair view requirement (see also Nobes, 1993, for the spread of the latter in Europe).

There are several forms of the equity method (e.g., see Ma *et al.*, 1991, p. 188), but the common feature is the inclusion in the investor's income statement of the appropriate proportion of the investee's earnings rather than merely the dividends flowing to the investor or, at the other extreme, rather than the investee's detailed revenues and expenses. In the investor's balance sheet, there is also 'one-line consolidation' of the net assets of the investee rather than merely the cost of the investment and rather than line-by-line consolidation of assets and liabilities. As will be clear to users of American English, the term 'equity method' implies a measurement at the investor's proportion of equity (subject in some versions to adjustment for goodwill), which is equal to net assets. This article does not deal with the technical details of the equity method except when there are underlying theoretical issues of relevance to the paper's theme.

To begin, there is a description of the use of the equity method early in the twentieth century as a form of consolidation used before full consolidation had developed (called 'proto-consolidation', below). Its use in parent company statements (pseudo-consolidation) is also a long established treatment of subsidiaries. Another early use was in consolidated statements for excluded subsidiaries (substitute-consolidation). The next three sections below deal with these uses relating to subsidiaries.

In the 1960s, the equity method began to be recommended also for investments in certain non-subsidiaries: as a form of pseudo-consolidation in investor statements and as a form of semi-consolidation in consolidated statements. It is possible to see pseudo-consolidation and semi-consolidation as techniques of valuation rather than of consolidation. For all these uses, there has been opposition, concentrated in a few countries.

This article pieces together the above history, analyses the reasons for the rise of the equity method and assesses the strength of the criticisms. The threshold for the use of the equity method is also examined. One conclusion is that the forces of accounting harmonization might have overcome logic and law, and that the equity method is inappropriate for most, if not all, of its present uses; a point noted earlier by, for example, Chambers (1974) and Miller and Leo (1997). There is also a summary of previous academic research and a look at the development of the terms used in the context of the equity method in various countries.

Thus, the aim is to contribute to the literature on the international transfer of accounting technology, but there are also major policy implications for standard setting in an area of financial reporting where further developments can be expected soon (Milburn and Chant, 1999). The concentration is on major countries in the English-speaking world and Continental Europe. In the topic areas considered here, the rest of the world has probably derived its practices from these countries. For example, for Japan, there are many consolidation practices similar to those of the U.S.A., including the 20 per cent threshold for equity accounting (Sawa, 1998). Issues of special relevance to group structures in the Far East (e.g., the Keiretsu in Japan or the Chaebol in Korea) are not examined here.

PROTO-CONSOLIDATION

In the U.K., the earliest use of the equity method appears to be for the purposes of including subsidiaries in the financial statements of investors as an alternative to consolidation. This method was more common than full consolidation in the 1910s and was still used in the 1920s (Edwards and Webb, 1984, Table 1); for example by Lever Brothers (Edwards, 1989, p. 229). On the whole, the equity method was superseded, in the 1930s, by full consolidation or no consolidation; predominantly the latter (Bircher, 1988, p. 7). Another approach was to treat subsidiaries as though they were branches of the parent. This was still practised in the 1930s in such companies as Unilever (Hodgkins, 1979, p. 45). Only with the Companies Act 1947 did 'branching' finally disappear.

Walker (1978a, pp. 99, 117) suggests that the equity method became less popular because, in the context of the conservative mood following the Royal Mail case, it was interpreted as recognizing unrealized profit. However, Edwards and Webb (1984, p. 40) point out that the equity method is more conservative in the sense that it does not ignore losses of subsidiaries as the cost-based method can. As another part of the explanation, they note that the Greene Committee on law reform and the Companies Act 1928 provided no support for the equity method. The Act required holding companies to show shares in subsidiaries, which would not be shown naturally by the equity method. Counsel's opinion[1] suggested that the balance sheet of the legal entity should be the one filed and presented to the shareholders.

In the U.S., a more full-blooded approach to consolidation was taken at the beginning of the century, without much need for partial steps such as the equity method. This seems to be due to fewer legal problems in the U.S., less conservatism of practice, and to acceptance of consolidation for certain purposes by the tax authorities and the New York Stock Exchange (Edwards and Webb, 1984, pp. 41–7; Walker, 1978a, Section III). Nevertheless, the equity method was used in parent company statements for certain subsidiaries. For example, Kester (1918, p. 261) distinguished between parents which had 'substantially full ownership' of subsidiary companies and cases where 'ownership is not complete but still controlling'. For the latter, the equity method in parent statements was seen as a reasonable alternative to the preparation of consolidated statements.

PSEUDO-CONSOLIDATION

The early use of the equity method for subsidiaries in the financial statements of holding companies before the full development of consolidation is considered above under 'proto-consolidation'. However, its use has continued in parent statements in some jurisdictions despite inclusion of the subsidiaries in consolidated statements. In the U.S., a long line of textbooks describe and recommend the use of the

Edwards and Webb (1984) refer to *The Accountant*, 31 August 1929, p. 281.

INTERNATIONAL DEVELOPMENT OF THE EQUITY METHOD

equity method in this context. Until the 1960s, there was little promulgated GAAP[2] in this area, so textbooks and monographs contributed to unpromulgated GAAP.

As noted above, Kester (1918) recommended use of the equity method in parent statements early on for certain purposes, but was still recommending it in his 1933 edition and the 1945 reprint of that (pp. 194–5), when consolidated statements had become fully developed. Perhaps because of the comparative lack of legal restraints, Kester (1918, p. 262) had no qualms about the resulting profit, suggesting that 'the profit taken onto the books of the holding company by the above method is a real, not a book, profit', given that the parent controls the subsidiary's dividend policy. A similar view was taken by Finney (1922, p. 42) for the investment account in the holding company's books, even though there would also be a consolidated balance sheet.

Moonitz (1944, p. 49) also advocated the use of the equity method in the parent's books for several reasons:

1. The cost method makes sense when there is uncertainty but that does not apply to subsidiaries (p. 48) over which there is full control of dividend policy (p. 49).
2. The status of the investments varies with the fortunes of the investees not with the movements of cash (p. 49). Income accrues as the investments increase in value. Income accrues to the parent when it accrues to the subsidiary (p. 52).
3. The validity of the subsidiary's profit calculation is as well established as the parent's (p. 49).
4. Because companies plough back part of their profits, the cost rule will probably understate parent income in prosperous periods (p. 53).

Incidentally, Carman (1932, p. 103) and Dickerson and Weldon Jones (1933, p. 200) also propose the method for the treatment of subsidiaries in the investment account of the parent. However, they see it as a useful arithmetic device for preparing consolidated balance sheets when there are several layers of subsidiaries. They seem to regard the resulting balance sheet of the parent as not important in its own right, so that they should not be seen as proposers of pseudo-consolidation.

The contrary point of view to that of Kester and Moonitz is argued by Kohler (1938) who suggests that 'no practical benefits are derived from accruing profit and loss of subsidiaries on the books of the controlling company'. This is strongly supported by Paton (1951), who specifically opposes Moonitz' arguments: 'He is recommending, in effect, that the parent company keep its own accounts from the consolidated point of view, and were his recommendation adopted there would be little excuse left for preparing consolidated statements' (p. 46).

Despite this disagreement, it is clear that the method was acceptable where it really mattered. Kester (1945, pp. 211–12) wrote that: 'The Securities and Exchange Commission considers the equity of a holding company in subsidiary profits and losses sufficiently important to require disclosure . . . if such equities are not taken up on the books of the holding company'.

---

[2]   That is, 'generally accepted accounting principles' as adopted by a body approved by the SEC (e.g., currently, the Financial Accounting Standards Board).

Finney (1946) illustrates the use of the equity method and calls it the 'economic basis' of parent company accounting, but notes that it does not conform 'strictly to the legal realities' (p. 299). As a compromise, Finney recommends the equity method with the undistributable earnings shown separately in shareholders' equity (p. 301). The matter of whether equity-accounted profit was distributable seems not to have constrained the debate.[3]

When GAAP was promulgated in 1971 by APB Opinion 18 (para. 14), the equity method was required in parent statements. Although the requirement was subsequently removed by SFAS 94 (of 1987, para. 15), there is no replacement instruction, so the equity method can still be used in parent statements. The lack of U.S. interest in this area is because parent statements are not generally required to be filed. This is unlike the position in most countries, where the law deals with parent statements, sometimes clearly as less important than consolidated statements (as in the U.K.) and sometimes as more important (as traditionally in some other European countries).

There was no equivalent U.K. discussion, let alone advocacy, of the equity method for use in parent statements in the days before accounting standards, presumably for the legal reasons noted earlier. For example, Cropper's *Accounting* (Cropper *et al.*, 1932, p. 316) recommends that subsidiaries should be accounted for either at cost with attached statements or by consolidation. Similar recommendations come from Garnsey (1923 and 1931, ch. VI); and others are silent on the issue (e.g., Pixley, 1910; Dicksee, 1927; Dicksee and Montmorency, 1932; Bogie, 1949, 1959; Castle and Grant, 1970). Subsequently, the method was prohibited in the U.K. by accounting standard.[4] It is also not allowed for this purpose in Australia[5] (AASB 1016).

However, in the Netherlands, subsidiaries (and joint ventures and associates; see later) are reported by using the equity method in the unconsolidated financial statements of the investor (Art. 389 (1–3) Book 2, Title 9 of the Civil Code; Dijksma and Hoogendoorn, 1993, p. 132). This use of the equity method in parent statements is long-standing practice. For example, it can be found in the parent statements which accompanied one of the earliest examples of Dutch consolidation: that by Philips[6] in 1931. The treatment generally enables the equity of the parent to be equal to that of the group. The equity-accounted share of profit (in excess of dividends) is, under certain conditions,[7] shown as undistributable reserves (Art. 389 (4)). In order to allow such practices, an option was written into

---

[3] The notion of distributable profit was discussed early on (e.g., Hatfield, 1918, pp. 205–31) but the rules vary from state to state (e.g., Littleton, 1934, pp. 140–8).

[4] SSAP 1, para. 18; FRS 9, para. 26.

[5] Except where there are no consolidated statements.

[6] I am grateful, for this information, to Professor H. L. Brink, a former Philips executive. He writes, on 20 March 1999 to Peter van der Zanden, that 'The equity per the company only and the consolidated balance sheets was exactly the same' (translation by Peter van der Zanden).

[7] The elements for which the parent cannot control the distribution of profits.

INTERNATIONAL DEVELOPMENT OF THE EQUITY METHOD

the EC Fourth Directive (Article 59, as amended by Article 45 of the Seventh Directive). Consequently, the Netherlands and some other member states have enacted legal permission for this practice. For example, it is allowed and common in Denmark (Christiansen and Elling, 1993, p. 136), where the practice began in the 1970s (before the Directive). It is also allowed in France (Art. L340–4, Law of 3.1.1985) and in Italy (Civil Code, Art. 2426(4)), but is seldom used. Such permission is not granted in law in the U.K. or in Germany, where equity accounting is restricted to consolidated statements. Given this international difference, it is not surprising that IAS 3 deliberately excluded this issue (para. 3), and that its replacement (IAS 27) allows, but does not require, equity accounting for subsidiaries in an investor's financial statements (para. 29).

This use of the equity method in investor financial statements could be seen as an example of attempts by accountants to express commercial substance over legal form. Since an investor could usually obtain its share of profits in a subsidiary merely by requesting them, to recognize only dividends might seem like a legal nicety. A clue to another rationale for the use of equity accounting in investor statements can be found in the Dutch term for the method: *intrinsieke waarde* (intrinsic value). That is, this may be seen as a method of valuation rather than as a method of consolidation. Further, the consolidated statements are treated in Dutch law (Art. 406) as a note to the legal entity's statements, which raises an expectation of consistency of valuation, which is also encouraged by the Seventh Directive (Art. 292 (a)). These rationales are examined later.

SUBSTITUTE-CONSOLIDATION

Another use of the equity method, this time in consolidated statements, was as a back-up in cases where certain subsidiaries were not consolidated. For example, in the U.S., Accounting Principles Board Opinion No. 18 (of 1971) required the equity method for unconsolidated subsidiaries. The reasons for lack of consolidation in the rules of the 1950s onwards (Accounting Research Bulletin No. 51, para. 2; Accounting Research Bulletin No. 43, ch. 12, para. 8) include temporary control, control being with non-majority owners, large minority interest and foreign subsidiaries (particularly those subject to restrictions on the transfer of funds).

However, the AICPA proposed that, in those cases where there was lack of control or there were foreign exchange restrictions, the cost method would be more suitable (AISG, 1973, para. 50). More recently, SFAS 94 (of 1987) requires all subsidiaries to be included except when control is temporary or when significant doubt exists about ability to control. SFAS 94 removes the APB 18 requirement to use equity accounting for unconsolidated subsidiaries, although such treatment seems still to be allowed (Williams, 1996, p. 6.05).

One important piece of context is that the U.S. definition of a subsidiary seems to be based in practice on ownership of a majority of voting shares rather than on *de facto* control. Although ARB 51 refers to 'controlling financial interest', the usual condition for this is said to be a majority voting interest, and no other examples are given (paras 1 and 2). This is reinforced by the title of SFAS 94,

Consolidation of All Majority Owned Subsidiaries. As a result, certain[8] controlled investees are not seen as entities to be consolidated. Here, the equity method seems a useful fallback position.

In Australia, the matter of equity accounting was first officially raised by the accountancy bodies in 1970 in the context of the de-consolidation of loss-making subsidiaries (Zeff, 1973, p. 39; Walker, 1978b, p. 107; Gordon and Morris, 1996, p. 161). The equity method is not now used as a substitute for consolidation, because no exclusions from consolidation are allowed[9] (AASB 1024). Its use for other purposes in Australia is examined later.

The original International Accounting Standard in this area (IAS 3 of 1976) derives from a study by the Accountants' International Study Group (1973) which noted (para. 47) the use of the equity method for excluded subsidiaries. The IASC's E3 (of 1974) had proposed (para. 31) to require the method for exclusions on the ground of temporary control, but IAS 3 required its use instead as a substitute for consolidation where dissimilar subsidiaries were optionally not consolidated (para. 40). The current standard (IAS 27) no longer allows dissimilar subsidiaries to be unconsolidated. However, it does continue to require (para. 13) exclusion from consolidation when (and only when) control is temporary (and the investee has never been consolidated) or when there are severe long-term restrictions on the transfer of funds to the parent. In such cases, reference should be made to IAS 25 on investments (or from 2001 to IAS 39), which does not allow the equity method. Perhaps this is reasonable, as there is no long-term significant influence.

In the U.K., SSAP 14 (of 1978) contained the earliest requirement for the use of the equity method for subsidiaries excluded from consolidation for reasons of dissimilarity or lack of effective control (paras 23 and 24). Subsequent law[10] confirmed this. Thus, the equity method acted as a safety net for the partial inclusion of companies that were controlled but were 'off balance sheet' due to the lax U.K. definition[11] of a subsidiary in the U.K. until the Companies Act 1989. The requirement is retained by FRS 2 (of 1992) for subsidiaries excluded on the grounds of dissimilarity (para. 30), although such cases are said to be exceptional (para. 25(c)). Support for this exclusion and for the concomittant use of the equity method seems to come from the EC Seventh Directive.[12] Consequently, it can be found in

---

[8] The SEC has a somewhat broader notion, including special purpose entities. EITF 90–15 also goes somewhat further.

[9] 'Temporary' exclusions are not allowed; the existence of severe restrictions on ability to control implies that the investee is not a subsidiary.

[10] Companies Act 1981; re-enacted as Sch. 4, para. 65(1) to the 1985 Act; then, in 1989, relating to dissimilarity, as Sch. 4.A, para. 18.

[11] The definition was expressed (Companies Act 1985, s. 736) in terms of control of the composition of the board (not votes on the board), or ownership of the majority of equity (not of voting equity). This gave rise to the possibility of 'controlled non-subsidiaries'.

[12] Reference in Article 14 (1) (on exclusion) is made to Article 33 (on the equity method).

the laws of other member states (e.g., Germany: *HGB*, §295 (1)[13]; Italy: *Decreto Legislativo 127*, Art. 36; Sweden: Annual Accounts Act 1995, Chapter 7, Section 23).

SEMI-CONSOLIDATION

So far, there has been concentration on three types of use of the equity method for the treatment of subsidiaries, as summarized in the first column of Table 1. Another use of the equity method is in consolidated statements (and sometimes in investor statements) for certain investees other than subsidiaries. Here the rationale for the equity method as a form of semi-consolidation or of valuation is less clear than above, as will be explored in a later section, after a discussion of some definitional points and an outline of international practice.

Scope
The major issue here is to identify the nature of the non-subsidiary investees for which equity accounting would be a suitable treatment. It is clear that, in the U.K. and the U.S., joint ventures were originally much in mind. The first exposure draft (in 1970) of the U.K.'s Accounting Standards Steering Committee (ASSC)[14] was on the subject of equity accounting, for reasons explored below. It defined an associated company as a joint venture or a company in which there is a substantial interest '(i.e. not less than approximately 20 per cent of the equity voting rights)' (para. 6).

TABLE 1

USES OF EQUITY METHOD

	Subsidiaries	Joint ventures	Associates
Investor statements	I *Proto-consolidation* (e.g., U.K. and U.S., early 20th century) II *Pseudo-consolidation* (e.g., Netherlands)	III *Pseudo-consolidation* (e.g., Netherlands)	IV *Pseudo-consolidation* (e.g., Netherlands)
Consolidated statements	V *Substitute consolidation* (e.g., U.S. if no majority votes; formerly for foreign subsidiaries and dissimilar subsidiaries)	VI *Semi-consolidation* (e.g., U.S.; and EU Directive and IAS 31 when not using proportional consolidation) (Note the use of gross equity method in U.K.)	VII *Semi-consolidation* (e.g., U.S. and EU) (Note former Australian use of disclosures based on equity method for this Case and Case VI)

---

[13] Ordelheide and Pfaff (1994, p. 177) suggest that it is also appropriate for optionally excluded subsidiaries (e.g., limitations on control).

[14] Established in 1970 and later re-named the Accounting Standards Committee.

Commenting on the development of the U.K. standard, Leach (1981, p. 6) states that 'the existence of consortium companies, controlled by no single corporate body, was very much in point' and that the definition 'emerged as the concept of partnership, recognition of substantial interest . . . and ability to exercise substantial influence'.

The U.S. statement of 1971 on the equity method referred to 'joint ventures and certain other investments in common stock' (APB Opinion 18, para. 1). Thus, there are two categories in the original U.K. and U.S. statements, but joint ventures come first, and the others are to be treated in the same way.

In some other jurisdictions (e.g., Australia, France and now in the U.K.), a clear separation of joint ventures from associates is made. It leads to the possibility or the requirement that joint ventures and associates are treated differently. The rest of this section considers the use of the equity method for associates in consolidated and investor statements. In the following two sections, more detail is added to the above outline of the definition of an associate, and the special treatments for joint ventures are considered.

Recommendations and Requirements for Consolidated Statements
This subsection looks at the treatment of associates in consolidated financial statements. It is followed by a note on treatments in investor statements. The requirement to use the equity method for associates (defined then as including joint ventures) in consolidated statements can be found in the U.K.'s SSAP 1 (of January 1971). This followed 'extensive developments' in the 1960s of holdings in associates (Shaw, 1973, p. 176) and a brief period of experimentation with the method by some British companies (Accountancy, 1970b). Tweedie (1981, p. 171) reports that the ASSC stated that only nine out of a survey of 300 major companies for 1968[15] went beyond accounting for dividends received. However, this had risen to twenty for 1969 (ICAEW, 1971); and it included some very important companies (e.g., GEC and Dunlop). Incidentally, Tweedie suggests that the equity method was therefore 'not a subject of great controversy' (p. 171) and that it was chosen as the ASSC's first topic partly because the ASSC had inherited work-in-progress for a draft Recommendation from the Institute of Chartered Accountants in England and Wales. By contrast, the first chairman of the ASSC suggested that the topic was 'a highly controversial one', chosen because of varied practice (Leach, 1981, p. 6). The controversial aspect is backed up by an editorial in *The Accountant* (1970) and, in retrospect, by Sharp (1971). Perhaps these views are reconcilable by noting that the subject was not controversial *before* ED 1 but that the ASSC's proposal *caused* a controversy.

Of relevance here are several observations by Napier (1999). There are at least two reasons why the ASSC's first chairman (Sir Ronald Leach) would have been interested in this topic. First, Leach was one of the inspectors appointed by the government in September 1969 to investigate Pergamon Press which had not shown

---

[15] Tweedie and the survey's title refer to 1968–9, but that is largely to include a few companies with year ends in early January 1969.

INTERNATIONAL DEVELOPMENT OF THE EQUITY METHOD

its share of a large 1968 trading loss in its consolidated profit and loss account because it was not using equity accounting for its 50 per cent interest in a company (Napier, 1999, pp. 6, 12, 14, 17). Second, Leach's most important audit client, Rank Organisation, had a 49 per cent interest in a company that carried out the group's most important operations, Rank Xerox.

Similar U.S. requirements on equity accounting date from very slightly later: APB Opinion 18 of March 1971. In some other countries, recommendations can be found in the 1960s. In France, a ministerial decree of 20 March 1968 (Beeny, 1976, p. 147) referred to methods used in group accounts, including full consolidation (*intégration globale*), proportional consolidation (*intégration proportionnelle*) and equity accounting (*mise en équivalence*). The equity method was recommended for companies in which the investee held more than 33.3 per cent of the equity and which were neither subsidiaries nor joint ventures. There was further official encouragement from the Conseil National de la Comptabilité (CNC, 1973).

In the Netherlands, the non-governmental[16] Hamburger Report of 1962 recommended a version of the equity method ('intrinsic value', see above) for 'participations' (*deelnemingen*), which are long-term significant holdings where the business of the investor and investee are similar (Zeff *et al.*, 1992, p. 135). This would include joint ventures. The governmental Verdam Commission reported in 1964, recommending particular disclosures (although no particular accounting method) for such investments, defined as holdings of 25 per cent or more (Zeff *et al.*, 1992, p. 154). The first exposure draft of the Tripartiete Overleg[17] in 1971, following soon after U.K. and U.S. drafts, also preferred a version of the equity method for participations (Zeff *et al.*, 1992, p. 207).

This growing international consensus led to the inclusion, in the IASC's E3 (of 1974) and IAS 3 (of 1976) and in the EC Seventh Directive (drafts of 1976 and 1978, and Article 33 of the final version of 1983), of requirements for the use of equity accounting for associates in consolidated statements. The requirement in the Directive also explicitly covers joint ventures unless proportionally consolidated (see later). Some European countries had held out against the equity method until they were overwhelmed by the Seventh Directive. For example, in Germany, the concept of the group in the 1965 *Aktiengesetz* was based on uniform direction (*einheitliche Leitung*), which survives as an optional basis for the definition of a subsidiary in the Seventh Directive (Art. 1 (2)). On this conceptual basis, since associates are not managed on a unified basis with the investor (because they are not controlled) and so they are not group companies, they had to be accounted for on a cost basis. Although German influence was clear on many issues in the first draft of the Seventh Directive, the Germans had little support on this point and the equity method for associates was proposed as compulsory from the beginning (Diggle and Nobes, 1994, p. 324).

---

[16]   Set up by the Council of Dutch Employers' Federations.

[17]   Tri-partite committee; the predecessor of the Council for Annual Reporting (Raad voor de Jaarverslaggeving).

In Sweden, the equity method was regarded with suspicion from a legal stand-point in the early 1980s. The doubt concerned whether the equity method was a legally acceptable valuation method.[18] A few large groups used it in consolidated statements but most did not (Cooke, 1988, p. 62). Legal doubts were partially resolved by considering the equity method as a form of consolidated rather than as a valuation method. The equity method was proposed for consolidated statements by the then standard-setting body (FAR) in 1986 (Heurlin and Peterssohn, 1995, p. 1997) before becoming legally required on implementation of the Seventh Directive in the Swedish Annual Accounts Act of 1995 (Chapter 7, Article 24).

Outside of Europe, the most sceptical country has been Australia. A series of exposure drafts (1971, 1973 and 1979) recommending equity accounting began to be issued soon after those in the U.K. and the U.S. However, these met problems. First there was an impediment arising from a legal interpretation of the Victorian Companies Act 1971 that group accounts should encompass only the holding com-pany and subsidiaries and therefore not equity-accounted earnings. Gordon and Morris (1996, p. 166) explain how the legal debate began in 1972 and continued for years. The legal impediment is also discussed by Eddey (1995, p. 303) and Vallely *et al.* (1997, p. 17). There were also, in the 1980s, abuses of the equity method. For example, some effectively controlled entities were equity-accounted instead of being consolidated, and some investees not subject to significant influence were equity-accounted (Ma *et al.*, 1991, pp. 204–8). Consequently, the standard setters eventually limited the use of the equity method to disclosures based on it (Ma *et al.*, 1991, p. 191). Some Australian groups showed an extra column in their consolid-ated financial statements on an equity-accounted basis (Deegan *et al.*, 1994).

Just as the legal and conceptual doubts of Germany and Sweden seem to have been swept aside by majority international practice rather than by clear arguments, even Australia amended AASB 1016 in 1998 to require equity accounting, following the removal of the legal impediment and a commitment to harmonization with IASC standards (Peirson and McBride, 1997). To avoid a conflict with the Australian con-ceptual framework (which clearly places associates outside the group reporting entity) and the consolidation standard, equity accounting is said to be a valuation method rather than a consolidation technique (Miller and Leo, 1997). This is up-side down compared to the reasoning in Sweden (noted above), although it fits the Dutch view.

Associates in Investor Statements

In most countries examined here, associates (like subsidiaries) are valued at cost in investor financial statements. However, in those countries where pseudo-consolidation (or valuation) is used for subsidiaries in an investor's statements, it is generally extended to associates and joint ventures. Otherwise, the objective of making the group equity equal to the investor's equity is not achieved.

For example, in Denmark and the Netherlands, the equity method is used in the investor's statements for associates and joint ventures. This appeared to be in conformity with the Fourth Directive, where Article 59 allowed such treatment for

---

[18] I am grateful, here, to Rolf Rundfelt of KPMG, Sweden.

an undefined category of 'affiliated undertakings'; and this was clarified by an amendment in Article 45 of the Seventh Directive which refers to significantly influenced undertakings. In the U.S., the equity method was also originally required in parent statements for those investments that were equity accounted in consolidated statements (APB Opinion 18, para. 17). It is presumably now allowed despite the amendments to SFAS 94 (see the earlier section on pseudo-consolidation). It is also allowed by IAS 28 (paragraph 12). In the same way as for subsidiaries, the method is allowed for associates in France and Italy (but not used), and is not allowed in the U.K. or Germany.

MORE ON THE DEFINITION OF AN ASSOCIATE

The UK Origins of the 20 Per Cent Threshold

U.K. and U.S. rules (SSAP 1 and APB Opinion 18, both of 1971) basically defined associates[19] as those over which the investor exercises a significant influence over operating and financial policies (SSAP 1, para. 13; APB Opinion 18, para. 17). This is the definition followed by the EC Seventh Directive of 1983 (Article 33 (1)), and therefore found in many European national laws.

However, this is a much vaguer concept (and more difficult to audit) than even the concept of 'control' which is the basis of the definition of a subsidiary in many jurisdictions. Consequently, it is difficult to operationalize (Chambers, 1974) and guidance is needed if standardized practice is to result. Part of the guidance comes in the form of a numerical threshold of the percentage of shares (or voting shares) to be held. In some jurisdictions, the threshold appears to be of a mechanical nature; in others it is hedged around with rebuttable presumptions. This point will be considered after the *size* of the threshold has been examined. The emergence of an internationally agreed threshold of 20 per cent of voting shares seems to have been accidental, as will now be charted.

There is a long history of separately identifying non-subsidiary investments above a certain size of holding. For example, in the U.K., the Companies Act 1947[20] designated certain holdings as 'trade investments'. According to Shaw (1973, p. 175), these: 'may be taken to be investments made to cement a trading relationship or for specific purposes associated with the trade of the investing company'.

Recommendation N 20 (ICAEW, 1958, para. 41) also required disclosures relating to material, but undefined, 'associated companies'. The Companies Act 1967 (s. 4) was more precise and required some non-financial disclosures where an individual investor held more than 10 per cent of equity[21] in an investee. Also, the London Stock Exchange Listing Agreement required, at least from the first 'Yellow Book' of 1966, disclosures about so called 'associated companies', defined

---

[19]   APB Opinion 18 does not use this term, although it can be found in U.S. literature (e.g., Neuhausen, 1982, p. 55).

[20]   Consolidated as paras 8(1)(a) and 12(1)(g) of Schedule 8 to the 1948 Act.

[21]   Or where the book value of the shares was more than 10 per cent of total assets.

originally as those in which the investing group held more than a certain threshold level of equity. Shaw (1973, p. 176) suggests that this was a significant precedent for the ASSC's work because of the use of the term 'associated company' and the reference to total group holdings rather than to investor holdings. These two points distinguish the Stock Exchange's requirement from previous company law or tax law. Shaw (1973, p. 176) also states that the Listing Agreement uses a 20 per cent threshold, which would seem to clinch the argument about the source of the definition. However, the Yellow Books of June 1966 and of April 1969 use 25 per cent in their definitions.[22] This threshold is noted in the ICAEW's survey of 1970–71 (ICAEW, 1972, p. 13). An amendment to the Yellow Book, to reduce the threshold from 25 per cent to 20 per cent holdings, was published in June 1972, which puts it *after* SSAP 1, suggesting that the latter influenced the stock exchange, rather than the other way round.

In the U.K., the ASSC's first exposure draft (ED 1) of June 1970 had already used a threshold of 20 per cent (para. 7). No explanation is given for this level in the exposure draft.[23] There are no references to the origins of the 20 per cent threshold in the archives[24] of the ASSC or in the current memories of participants[25] in the debates. There are several comments on equity accounting in the accountancy journals[26] of the day (Titcomb, 1970; Goch, 1972), but only one can be found with any explanation of the 20 per cent: MacNair (1970, p. 367) notes that, under tax law of the time, a consortium that could share tax losses was one where equity participation was held by five or fewer companies. It was suggested that 'common interest' would be implied where such consortium relief was used.

A survey of tax and company law literature fails to reveal any other convincing source of the 20 per cent threshold. In U.K. tax law, thresholds of 10, 50 and 75 per cent can be found (Lamb, 1995, p. 37). The Companies Act 1948 had contained various thresholds other than 20 per cent; for example, 10 per cent relating to an extraordinary general meeting (s. 132(1)), 15 per cent relating to variation in rights and alteration of memorandum (ss. 72(1) and 5(2)), and 75 per cent for special resolutions (s. 141(1)).

The practices of the few British companies who used equity accounting before ED 1 may have been influential. Grand Metropolitan in its 1967 accounts reported on a number of associates held from 28 per cent to 50 per cent. A comment in

---

[22] Schedule VIII, part A, para. 6(c), note (i): 'For the purpose of this Undertaking "associated company" means a company which is not a subsidiary but in which 25% or more of the equity is held by the company or, if the company has subsidiaries, by the group companies collectively (i.e. before excluding any proportion attributable to interests of outside shareholders in the subsidiaries).'

[23] Reprinted in *Accountancy*, July 1970, pp. 496–8.

[24] I am very grateful to Michael Mumford (letter to me of 29 June 1998) for examining the relevant minutes of the ASSC in the John Rylands Library.

[25] I have corresponded with Harold Edey, Michael Renshall and Chris Westwick.

[26] The author has examined contemporary issues of *Accountancy*, *The Accountant's Magazine*, *The Accountant* and *The Journal of Accountancy*.

INTERNATIONAL DEVELOPMENT OF THE EQUITY METHOD

Accountancy (1970a) presumed a threshold of 25 per cent, which had been used by Dunlop and by William Cory in their 1969 accounts. Other companies stressed a relationship rather than a specific threshold (Holmes, 1970, pp. 514–18). However, British Ropes adopted a specific 20 per cent threshold for the first time in its accounts issued in early 1970, before ED 1 (Holmes, 1970, p. 515). Other companies (e.g., Delta Metal; see ICAEW, 1971) used the term 'associated' for holdings of above 10 per cent, but only for disclosures not for equity accounting. It seems that the ASSC chose the lowest threshold actually used in practice for equity accounting, beginning its tradition of accommodating companies' wishes.

The Spread of the Threshold

In the U.S., the APB's sub-committee on this subject initially favoured a 10 per cent threshold on the basis of what it called an 'economic interest' interpretation.[27] Some members of the sub-committee[28] and the SEC staff preferred a 25 per cent threshold on the basis of 'presumption of control', particularly over dividend payments. The board, at its meeting of March 1970, changed its position from favouring 10 per cent to 25 per cent. However, at the July meeting, it was noted[29] that the U.K.'s ED 1 proposed 20 per cent and that international coordination would be beneficial (Defliese, 1981, p. 110; Journal, 1970, p. 12). It seems that, even in the first year of operations of the U.K. standard-setter, there was an exchange of exposure drafts with the APB; and in the following year, the APB chairman was in London for discussions (Accountancy, 1971). In October 1970, the board decided on 20 per cent as an internationally coordinated compromise between its two previous views, although the SEC still did not agree.

Thus, on the basis of no clear arguments, the foundations for the eventual worldwide triumph of 20 per cent were laid. In January 1971, SSAP 1 was issued, retaining the 20 per cent. In March 1971, APB Opinion 18 (also containing 20 per cent) was issued. The U.K. press had noted[30] the earlier U.S. change to 25 per cent and then noted[31] the change to 20 per cent. However, in neither case was there any comment about the comparison with the British exposure draft's 20 per cent. This Anglo-American agreement is mirrored in a reference to a 20 per cent threshold in IAS 3 (para. 4) of 1976.

In the meantime, many other thresholds were in use internationally. As explained earlier, 25 per cent was to be found in Dutch proposals from at least 1964, and 33.3 per cent was preferred in France from 1968. However, another strand of

---

[27] I am most grateful to Steve Zeff for the information in this paragraph. Professor Zeff writes in a letter to me of 8 July 1996 that he has based the information on minutes of the APB sub-committee and reports of Big 8 firms to partners after meetings of the sub-committee.

[28] The sub-committee was chaired by George R. Catlett of Arthur Andersen, but those preferring 25 per cent included representatives from Arthur Young and from Lybrand.

[29] See note 26.

[30] News section of *Accountancy*, November 1970, p. 759.

[31] News section of *Accountancy*, August 1971, p. 431.

French thinking relevant to this issue is the concept of participating interests (*participations*). From the 1966 Companies Law, these are investments of 10 per cent and above, which reminds one of the 10 per cent threshold in the U.K.'s 1967 Act noted earlier. Such investments were, and still are, to be shown separately in an investor's balance sheet in France, and one of the *régimes*[32] for group taxation treats income from such investments favourably. In Italy, a remnant of this survives, in that investments of 10 per cent or more in *listed* companies are treated as associates (Civil Code, Article 2359). This seems to accord with the APB's 'economic interest' concept.

Given the diversity of European views and the ascendancy of Anglo-American practices in the field of consolidation (Diggle and Nobes, 1994), it is not surprising that the EC Seventh Directive contained a 20 per cent threshold from its earliest published version (Article 1 (2) of the 1976 draft). This threshold has now been implemented into the laws of most of the 15 EU member states, and elsewhere in Europe (e.g., Norway, as a member of the European Economic Area). In these cases, previous thresholds for other issues have been ignored. For example, many thresholds are found in tax legislation in Europe, including 5, 10, 25 and 95 per cent (Lamb, 1995, pp. 62–73). The predominant thresholds are 10 and 25 per cent, with 20 per cent appearing rarely.[33] On other issues, German law contained a threshold of 25 per cent for blocking changes to a company's constitution and for the existence of a mutual participation (*wechselseitige Beteiligung*).[34] However, as noted above, the Italian implementation (of 1991) refers to holdings of 10 per cent in the case of listed investees. The Spanish implementation (of 1989) refers to holdings of 3 per cent in the case of listed investees (Article 185 (2), Decree 1564/1989; Gonzalo and Gallizo, 1992, p. 167). These lower thresholds are not mentioned in the Seventh Directive. However, since the Directive states that significant influence is presumed where the investor 'has 20% or more of the . . . voting rights' (Article 33 (1)), a lower threshold is not specifically ruled out.

Further afield, 20 per cent is recommended in Switzerland by the standard-setters (ARR 2 of FER), and it is required in Japan by the rules of the Ministry of Finance (Financial Accounting Standards, IV, 5, 2) and in Korea (Financial Accounting Standards App. II, Art. 15(a)). Although Australia held out for years against the use of the equity method as a valuation or consolidation practice, the 20 per cent threshold was in the first exposure draft of 1971 and continued through to the eventual disclosure standard of 1988 (ASRB 1016). Turning to international standards, IAS 28 (originally of 1988) naturally followed the international consensus of 20 per cent (now in IAS 28, para. 4). Table 2 summarizes the exceptions from the 20 per cent threshold; the last two of which are extant.

---

[32] The *régime des sociétés mères et filiales*.

[33] For example, the draft EC Parent/Subsidiary Directive of 1969 would relieve withholding taxes at a 20 per cent threshold, although this was changed to 25 per cent in the directive of 1990.

[34] I am grateful to Dieter Ordelheide for pointing out the blocking percentage. The mutual participation is to be found in s. 19 of Aktiengesetz 1965.

INTERNATIONAL DEVELOPMENT OF THE EQUITY METHOD

TABLE 2

SOME EXCEPTIONS FROM THE 20% FOR THE DEFINITION OF ASSOCIATES

Netherlands	25% in a government report of 1964
France	33¹/₃% in CNC recommendation of 1968
U.S.	10% and 25% in APB discussions in early 1970
Spain	3% for listed holdings in 1989 law
Italy	10% for listed holdings in 1991 law

Rebuttable Presumption

As noted above, the numerical threshold is stated baldly in some rules, particularly those flowing from the Seventh Directive. For example, in Germany (HGB §311 (1)) and in Italy (Civil Code, Art. 2359 (3)), the assumption of significant influence rests squarely on the numerical thresholds, and no qualitative indications are given. In other jurisdictions, the rule-makers appear to have attempted to ensure that financial reporting choices rest on something less mechanical. As noted later, the problem then becomes the vagueness of the rationale for equity accounting. Some rule-makers are clear, at least, that an investor should not be able to treat an investee differently from year to year by buying and selling a few shares around the 20 per cent threshold. Consequently, in the U.S., APB Opinion 18 discusses this in terms of 'considerations' (e.g., representation on the board, and the concentration of other shareholdings) and 'presumptions' (para. 17). The same applies to IAS 3 (para. 4) and IAS 28 (para. 4).

Despite the U.S. attempt to make the threshold less stark, Mulford and Comiskey (1985) found a high concentration of investments in the 16–24 per cent range. Further, affiliates in the 19–19.99 per cent range of ownership reported losses far more often than those in the 20–20.99 per cent range.

The U.K.'s ED 1 (para. 6) contained the threshold of 'approximately 20 per cent'. The 'approximately' was removed for the original SSAP 1 (para. 6), presumably on the grounds of reducing vagueness. However, the 'rebuttable presumption' basis was introduced later (in 1982, para. 14), along U.S. lines. This was strengthened in FRS 9, where there is an extensive discussion of 'significant influence' and it is made clear that this overrides the numerical threshold (paras. 4 and 14–19). Indeed, the 20 per cent is referred to as part of 'companies legislation', suggesting that the reference to a numerical threshold would have been removed but for this. The irony here is that the 20 per cent threshold in the British law was based on the Seventh Directive which was based on the Anglo-American practice which can be traced to a British exposure draft of 1970.

WHAT'S IN A NAME?

It is now appropriate to address a related issue: the origins of the terms 'equity method' and 'associated company'.

31

Equity Method

'Equity method' is clearly an American coinage, and can be traced back at least to the early 1930s in the context of the arithmetic used for the preparation of consolidated balance sheets (Carman, 1932, p. 103; Dickerson and Weldon Jones, 1933, p. 200). The term can also be found later in the context of 'pseudo-consolidation' in investor statements. This is the case in Noble *et al.* (1941, p. 581) and in Finney and Miller (1952, pp. 343–5); although not in the previous edition of the latter book (Finney, 1946, p. 297). Other terms for the equity method in this context were also in use: for example, 'book value' (Paton, 1943, p. 1073; and Moonitz, 1994, p. 51), 'economic basis of accounting' (Finney, 1946, p. 297); 'book value change basis' (Moonitz and Staehling, 1950, p. 184).

In promulgated GAAP, the term was not initially used; that is, it cannot be found in ARB No. 51 of 1959 (see para. 19). However, it was employed in APB Opinion 10 of 1966: 'This practice is sometimes referred to as the "equity" method' (para. 3). By APB Opinion 18 of 1971 (para. 6), the quotation marks have disappeared. The term was then frequently used by the IASC in IAS 3 of 1976.

In the U.K., acceptance of the term is much more recent. It was not to be found in SSAP 1 (of 1971 and subsequent amendments to 1990). It does, however, appear in the EC Fourth Directive (Article 59 of the 1978 final version, but not the drafts of 1971 and 1974). Since, as noted earlier, the U.K. did not take up the Directive's option in Article 59 to use the equity method in the investor's accounts, the term was not used in the Companies Act 1981 which implemented the Directive. It is used in the Companies Act 1989,[35] though not in the EC Seventh Directive which preceded it (see Article 33). In FRS 9 of 1997 it is well established (e.g. para. 4). In Australia, the term appeared in the two exposure drafts in 1971 and 1974 (see Chambers, 1974).

The terms in French (*mise en équivalence*) and in Dutch (*intrinsieke waarde*) appear to have other origins. The French term seems to refer to the fact that the parent's and group's equity are made equal. The Dutch term refers to the valuation aspect of the method, as noted earlier. Terms in some other languages seem likely to be derived from the American (e.g., the unofficial German terms, *Equitykonsolidierung* and *Equitymethode*).

Associated Company

The term 'associate' (used here to include 'associated company' and similar expressions) is not in universal use in the English-speaking world. For example, it is not to be found in U.S. authoritative literature, which refers to such enterprises elliptically.[36] The term seems to be of British origin but was originally undefined. For example, it was used by Lever Brothers in the 1920s to include subsidiaries. It also has such a meaning in British tax law.[37] It was used vaguely in the ICAEW's

---

[35] Now paragraph 22 of Schedule 4A to the 1985 Act.

[36] For example, APB Opinion 18 (para. 17) refers to significant influence over an investee. In practice, the equivalent to 'associated undertaking' is an expression such as 'equity accounted investee'.

[37] For example, in the Income and Corporation Taxes Act 1970, s. 302(1), a company is associated with another if one of the two controls the other or both are under the control of the same person.

INTERNATIONAL DEVELOPMENT OF THE EQUITY METHOD

Recommendation N 20 and precisely (for disclosures) in the Stock Exchange listing requirements of 1966 (see earlier discussion). Companies used the term; for example, Grand Metropolitan in its 1967 accounts (*Accountancy*, 1968) and several others by 1970 (Holmes, 1970; ICAEW, 1971). The term then arrived in accounting standards in 1971 (international standards in 1976) and law in 1989.[38]

The term is not to be found in the Fourth Directive (where the vague 'affiliated undertakings' includes subsidiaries; and 'participating interests' includes those not significantly influenced), but 'associated undertaking' does appear in the Seventh Directive (Art. 33). The English origin seems clear enough in other language versions of the Directive; for example, *geassocieerde onderneming* in Dutch, *enterprise associée* in French, *assoziertes Unternehmen* in German, *impresa associata* in Italian and *sociedad asociada* in Spanish.

The Directive's terms survive into some EU national laws (e.g., German[39] and Spanish[40]) but not all. For example, the Italian code[41] uses *società collegata*, and no terms are used in Dutch[42] or French[43] law, merely references to significant influence.

JOINT VENTURES

Definition
It was noted above that 'semi-consolidation' was initially seen in the U.S. and the U.K. as particularly appropriate for joint ventures, with other associated investees also mentioned. Originally in the U.K. the category 'associate' included the joint venture. However, most jurisdictions now define the terms exclusively, even where the accounting treatment is to be the same.

Early French definitions of the joint venture, including that in a report of the CNC of March 1968 (CNC, 1973; Beeny, 1976, p. 47) refer to a *société fermée* (i.e., one where no shares are held outside of a group of venturers). For an investee to be a joint venture, the investor would have to hold a *participation* (i.e., at least 10 per cent of the shares). Once more, the 10 per cent threshold arises. In APB Opinion 18 (para. 3) the relevant joint venture is 'a corporation owned and operated by a small group of businesses . . . as a separate and specific business or project for the mutual benefit of the members of the group'.

The EC Seventh Directive depicts joint ventures as separate from associates, partly because different treatments are allowed (see below). The Directive's definition of joint venture (Article 32) rests on 'jointly managed'. British law (1985 Act,

---

[38]   The Companies Act 1981 used 'related companies' (e.g., Schedule 4, part I, B) whereas the 1989 Act has 'associated undertakings' (now para. 20 etc. of Schedule 4A to the 1985 Act).

[39]   HGB § 311.

[40]   Real Decreto 1815/1991, Cap. 1, art. 5.

[41]   Codice civile, Art. 2359.

[42]   Art. 389.

[43]   Art. L357–1.

Sch. 4A, para. 19) follows these words but in FRS 9 'jointly controlled' is used, as follows: 'An entity in which the reporting entity holds an interest on a long-term basis and is jointly controlled by the reporting entity and one or more other venturers under a contractual arrangement' (para. 4).

A similar interpretation has occurred in France, where the Directive says *dirige, conjointement* but the law refers to *contrôle conjoint* (amendment in 1985 to Article 357-1 of the Law of 1966).

In what follows, joint ventures will be assumed to be entities separate from the venturers. For example, IAS 31 (para. 3) distinguishes between jointly controlled 'entities', 'operations' and 'assets'. The latter two categories create few accounting problems because the various assets and liabilities belong to the venturers, so they are included in the financial statements of the venturer (both in the individual entity statements and in the consolidated).

Treatment of Joint Ventures
As noted earlier, in cases where equity accounting is used in an investor's unconsolidated financial statements for subsidiaries and associates (e.g., in Denmark and the Netherlands), then it is also used for joint ventures. This seems to create no difficulty for the Fourth Directive and various laws in the EU because joint ventures fall within the broad categories of 'affiliated' or significantly influenced undertakings. However, there is a difficulty in IAS 31, which specifically deals with joint ventures rather than associates. Strangely, IAS 31 gives no direct consideration[44] to the treatment of joint ventures in the unconsolidated statements of a venturer. That is, there is no equivalent of paragraph 29 of IAS 27 or paragraph 12 of IAS 28. Consequently, although IASs allow subsidiaries and associates to be held by the cost method in investor statements, it appears[45] that IAS 31 does not allow this for joint ventures. This seems to be an oversight.[46]

In consolidated financial statements, the treatment of joint ventures now differs internationally. U.S. and U.K. practice[47] (at least for joint ventures that are incorporated entities) is to use equity accounting on the grounds that there is significant influence but no control. In effect, joint ventures are still seen as a special case of associates, or associates are seen as a less formal type of joint venture. Consistently with this, the equity method is allowed in consolidated statements by the Seventh

---

[44] Paragraph 38 is deliberately non-committal. David Cairns (IASC Secretary General at the time of IAS 31) confirms that the IASC could not agree on a single practice (letter to me of 7 July 1999). Paragraph 41, despite its heading, relates to particular joint ventures where an investor is not a venturer.

[45] Paragraph 39 requires profit made by selling from an investor to a joint venture (including a joint venture entity) to be eliminated. In practice, this requirement means that the cost method cannot be used. There is no similar requirement in IASs 27 or 28 for an investor selling to a subsidiary or an associate.

[46] The author contacted the IASC on this (9 February 1999), and there is informal acceptance of the problem. But as yet there is no action to amend the IASs.

[47] APB Opinion 18 (para. 16); the Companies Act 1985 (as amended in 1989), Sch. 4A, paras 19–22; and FRS 9 (para. 20) cover this.

INTERNATIONAL DEVELOPMENT OF THE EQUITY METHOD

Directive and by IAS 31. However, proportional consolidation is also allowed by the Directive (Article 32); and in IAS 31 (paras 25 and 33) it is *preferred* on the grounds that it 'better reflects the substance and economic reality of a venturer's interest in a jointly controlled entity, that is control over the venturer's share of the future economic benefits'. This is despite the fact that the IASC's Framework (para. 49) defines assets in terms of control over the resources not control over the benefits from the resources. It is clear that the venturer does not *control* any of the resources. Consequently, neither the resources nor part of them are assets of the venturer. The same conclusion would be arrived at even if the definition of asset had referred to control over benefits.[48]

The response to the Seventh Directive in France was to *require* proportional consolidation, which was previous French practice. In most EU member states proportional consolidation is allowed. However, this is not the case in Greece, nor in Ireland and the U.K. for corporate joint ventures. It is also not allowed for joint venture entities in Australia (AASB 1006 and 1024 and AAS 19).

In some jurisdictions where proportional consolidation is not allowed, there is nevertheless some concern about the potentially misleading nature of equity accounting for joint ventures. For example, a group would not be required to recognize its share of the liabilities of a 50 per cent held joint venture. One way of responding to this is now used in the U.K., where FRS 9 requires the use of the 'gross equity method' for joint venture entities (paras 20–1). This method, which has a precedent in FASB discussion papers,[49] involves extra disclosures on the face of the consolidated financial statements, including the investor's share of the joint venture's turnover, gross assets and gross liabilities.

The Reporting Entity
This international lack of agreement on the treatment for joint ventures illustrates the need for greater clarity in some conceptual frameworks. The EC Seventh Directive has no explicit framework. The U.S. and IASC frameworks do not discuss the boundary of the reporting entity, and therefore have nothing directly to offer on consolidation issues, although the definition of asset seems relevant, as noted above. By contrast, the U.K.'s later *Statement of Principles* covers the 'reporting entity'. The boundary of the group rests on control (para. 2.6) which puts joint venture entities outside the group and therefore proportional consolidation should not be used (para. 8.9). There was a similar conclusion on the status of joint venture entities in the earlier Australian concepts statement, SAC 1.

RATIONALES FOR THE EQUITY METHOD

Although the equity method is now used for various purposes in much of the world, the rationales for this are not well explained. The seven cases in Table 1 are examined here.

---

[48] Because the definition would mean control over the services provided by the asset, not control over a share of net profit. A venturer does not control these services.

[49] I am grateful to Janie Crichton (the ASB's project director on FRS 9) for this information.

In the context of the treatment of subsidiaries in an investor's unconsolidated financial statements, the rationale for proto-consolidation (Case I) has been over-taken by the development of full consolidation. Possible rationales for pseudo-consolidation (Case II) include that the equity method is a form of accruals accounting rather than the cash accounting used by the cost method (Neuhausen, 1982, p. 62). This seems inconsistent with the realization convention but, given that Case II relates to subsidiaries, one could try to support it with a substance over form argument. Several such arguments of U.S. writers were examined earlier. A doubt, which did not concern early U.S. writers, could be raised for foreign investees where there might be uncertainties connected to the transfer of funds and the exchange rate.

A similar rationale for the equity method is that it is a form of valuation. The link is made in an Australian exposure draft where equity accounting is seen as 'a method of accounting, on an accrual basis, . . . thereby ensuring improved report-ing on the worth of particular investments to the investor' (ASA/ICAA, 1973, para. 19). This seems to be inconsistent with the historical cost convention used in most countries, though not uniformly in some countries (e.g., Australia and the Netherlands).

For investees other than subsidiaries, pseudo-consolidation in investor state-ments (Cases III and IV) seems even less convincing. The substance over form argument no longer applies, as the investor controls neither the assets of the investee nor its dividend decisions. The profits of the investee (in excess of dividends) are not within the control of the investor. The basis for a threshold at 20 per cent is also unclear, particularly since the 'intrinsic value' of all investments changes as profits are made. Further, as pointed out by Paton (1951, p. 46) and discussed (along with other criticisms of the equity method) by Zambon (1996, pp. 220–5), there seems little economic significance in the 'values' arrived at by the equity method. So, the method is not a conceptually impressive way of valuing, and 'fair value' would now seem more relevant (e.g., IASC, 1997). Nevertheless, a possible defence of the method in the context of the general use of fair values would be that fair value cannot always be reliably measured (e.g., for some unlisted securities) and that large blocks of shares could not be sold at apparent market value. Of course, a large block of shares does have a fair value, although it may be more difficult to identify.

For the above Cases II to IV, the usefulness of making the parent's income and equity the same as the group's is unclear, unless the parent statements are merely unpublished worksheets.

Turning to consolidated statements, the rationale for substitute-consolidation (Case V) has also been overtaken by events in jurisdictions where all controlled investees must be consolidated. For uncontrolled investees (Cases VI and VII), the equity method could be seen again as a method of valuation, whereupon the above points on that topic apply. It could also be seen as a form of semi-consolidation. However, just as the investor does not control the investee's assets, profits or dividend decisions, neither does the group. A basic question here is: Are such investees part of the investor's group? As noted above for joint venture entities,

36

the answer in the Australian and British frameworks is that they are clearly not. Elsewhere, the answer should be the same if the scope of the group is either based on control or majority ownership, as is the case in the U.S. (ARB 51, para. 2), the European Union (Seventh Directive, Article 1) or the IASC (IAS 27, para. 6). It seems difficult, then, to support the equity method as semi-consolidation on the basis of substance over form.

However, perhaps a rationale can be built around the idea that, above a certain threshold level of interest, the investor is in some form of special relationship with the investee. This approach, which regards associates and joint ventures as much the same, survived into the U.K. Discussion Paper in this area (ASB, 1994) which treated them both as 'strategic alliances' (para. 2.3) to be accounted for by the equity method. Later, FRS 9 (of 1997) rephrases this as follows:

> The investor needs an agreement or understanding, formal or informal, with its associate to provide the basis for its significant influence. An investor exercising significant influence will be directly involved in the operating and financial policies of this associate. Rather than passively awaiting the outcome of its investee's policies, the investor uses its associate as a medium through which it conducts a part of its activities.... Over time, the associate will generally implement policies that are consistent with the strategy of the investor and avoid implementing policies that are contrary to the investor's interests. (para. 14)

This clearly interprets the equity method as semi-consolidation, and it rests on joint control of the dividend decision even in those cases where there is not joint control of the individual assets and liabilities. It seems to suit Case VI the best, but might be extended to some associates in Case VII.

TECHNICAL PROBLEMS RAISED BY LACK OF FRAMEWORK

Since the concept behind the equity method and the purpose of its use are unclear, it also becomes difficult to resolve technical issues. Three examples are examined: elimination of profits, presentation in income and cash flow statements, and discontinued operations.

First, when an investor makes a profit by selling to an associate which retains the goods (downstream sales), should some or all of the profit be eliminated from the investor's and the consolidated statements? The profit in the hands of the investor results form an arm's length transaction. It is realized and legally distributable, and therefore should presumably not be eliminated. The same could be said of a profit arising from a sale from a parent to a subsidiary. On consolidation, this latter profit would be eliminated because the subsidiary is part of the group, and the price (and therefore profit) of the sale was controlled by the group. Neither of these points applies to a sale to an associate, which might suggest no elimination, even in consolidated statements.

The Seventh Directive (Article 33 (7)) appears to require elimination but either total or proportional elimination seem to be allowed. In the U.K., FRS 9 (para. 31) states that there should be proportional elimination. The IASC has also recently concluded (SIC Interpretation No. 3) that there should be proportional elimination.

The problem is that, since the theory supporting the equity method is unclear, the theoretical answer on elimination is also unclear.

Another technical point is the location of the equity-accounted elements in income and cash flow statements. The basic issue is whether the amounts are to be classified as operating or as financial. In the EC Fourth Directive (e.g., Article 23, line 9), the profit from participating interests is shown after operating items and as the first financial item. This allows companies to draw the operating line above or below equity-accounted profits. In the U.K., for example, SSAP 1 did not specify the treatment, but FRS 9 (para. 27) requires equity-accounted operating profits to be shown immediately after group operating profit. For U.K. cash flow statements, dividends from associates were originally to be shown as returns on investments (FRS 1 of 1991, para. 19), then as operating activities (FRS 1 as revised in 1996, paras. 11, 14), then as a separate item between the two (FRS 1 as revised again by para. 61 of FRS 9).

The EC Seventh Directive (Article 33 (6)) could be interpreted as allowing a different position for equity-accounted income in consolidated income statements from that required under the Fourth Directive. In France, advantage has been taken of this, so that such amounts are shown after consolidated profit and before minority interests (*Plan comptable général*, p. 11.168). This suggests that such profit is neither operating nor financial.

In the U.S., APB Opinion 18 (para. 19 (c)) is unclear on the location of equity-accounted income. Burnett *et al.* (1979) found that, for twenty-two finance subsidiaries excluded from consolidation, there were five different presentations of the equity-accounted income in consolidated income statements. Modern practice still ranges from presentation as 'other income' before various operating expenses to presentation after minority interests.[50] In U.S. cash flow statements, dividends received form equity-accounted companies are generally included in operating activities (Williams, 1996, p. 4.23).

IAS 1 (para. 75, and appendix) shows equity-accounted profits after operating and financial items in income statements, whereas IAS 7 (paras 31 and 37) allows dividends from equity accounted companies to be treated as either operating or investing items in cash flow statements.

A third technical issue is the presentation of discontinued operations. There are U.S., U.K. and IASC rules in this area. The relevant issue relates to the disposal of some shares in a major subsidiary such that it becomes an associate. Assuming that the subsidiary were large enough to satisfy the size criterion for being a discontinued operation (e.g., FRS 3, para. 4), would the disposal of the shares amount to a discontinuance of the operation by the reporting entity? This issue was a matter for international debate[51] when IAS 35 was agreed in 1998. Since the reporting

---

[50] For example, General Electric (1996, p. 49) do the former, and General Motors (1997, p. 50 in a supplementary statement) do the latter.

[51] The author was the chairman of the IAS 35 steering committee, and chaired the IASC Board discussion leading to approval of IAS 35 in April 1998.

38

entity is the group, it would seem that the group has disposed of the operation, and it no longer consolidates any individual assets, liabilities, revenues or expenses. However, the IASC Board decided that is would be consistent with other equity accounting practices to regard the operation as continuing within the sphere of the group's interests. The issue is not directly addressed in IAS 35.

SOME EMPIRICAL FINDINGS

In addition to the many writings referenced above, there has been some empirical research related to the use of the equity method. Mulford and Comiskey (1985) and Burnett *et al.* (1979) have already been mentioned. Another U.S. paper is by Ricks and Hughes (1985) who found a positive market reaction to the first publication of U.S. financial statements using the equity method. The reaction was positively correlated with size of equity earnings and degree of previous underestimate by analysts. This suggested that 'the equity method provided information concerning affiliate earnings not previously available from other sources' (p. 50).

Vallely *et al.* (1997) survey eight studies on equity accounting in Australia. Most of these examine whether management adopts aspects of equity accounting for particular reasons (e.g., attempting to increase management compensation). Mazay *et al.* (1993) suggest that the equity method may be useful in controlling management's behaviour where a material proportion of a firm's assets is in the form of investments in associates. Without the equity method, management might be able to manipulate profit by influencing dividend decisions or by non-arm's length transactions with investees. Similarly, lenders cannot reliably assess borrowers who have material investments in unlisted associates.

Another Australian paper (Czernkowski and Loftus, 1997) suggests that, in the period 1983 to 1990, the equity method provided useful information, particularly when cost-based information was also available.

SUMMARY AND POLICY IMPLICATIONS

The equity method arose as a form of proto-consolidation for inclusion of subsidiaries (or less than fully owned subsidiaries) in parent's financial statements before the practice of consolidation was fully established. Later, the equity method was seen to be unnecessary in some jurisdictions for parent statements. However, in other jurisdictions its sporadic or generalized use is still found, such that the parent's statements contain technically unrealized profits. This pseudo-consolidation can be seen instead as a method of valuation. The term 'equity method' is an American coinage used originally in this context of investor statements. Another formerly widespread use (substitute-consolidation) relates to the treatment in consolidated statements of certain subsidiaries or controlled non-subsidiaries excluded from full consolidation.

These three uses of the equity method for the treatment of subsidiaries (Cases I, II and V of Table 1) seem to be unnecessary or unsuitable:

1. proto-consolidation, because it has been replaced by consolidation;

2. pseudo-consolidation in investor's financial statements, because any form of consolidation seems inappropriate or unhelpful and because there are convincing arguments against using the equity method as a valuation method; and
3. substitute-consolidation, because a control-based concept of the group means that all controlled enterprises should be fully consolidated.

The equity method has also been used for inclusion of joint ventures and associates in investor statements (Cases III and IV: more pseudo-consolidation or valuation) or in consolidated statements (Cases VI and VII: semi-consolidation or valuation). These uses seem to have arisen with little theoretical justification and no prior research into their usefulness. Cases III and IV seem inappropriate for the same reasons as apply to pseudo-consolidation of subsidiaries, and for some extra reasons related to lack of control. This leaves semi-consolidation, which can be divided into two categories: joint ventures (Case VI) and less formal partnerships and other holdings of 20 per cent or more (Case VII). In the U.K. and the U.S., the context for the method originally stressed joint ventures, but other associated enterprises were also included, leading to definitional problems. Terms such as 'associated company' were U.K. inventions of the 1920s onwards.

The arguments for Case VII seem the weaker of the two, particularly where there is no sense of partnership. The concept of 'significant influence' is vague and not easily operationalized; and the 20 per cent threshold is unsupported by argument, having apparently arisen pragmatically in the U.K. and been accepted in the U.S. as a compromise. Where an arbitrary threshold has to be invented in order to operationalize an accounting rule, two features generally occur in conjunction. First, there is a lack of convincing theory and, second, management will try to avoid unattractive financial reporting by making arrangements that fall above or below the threshold, as noted earlier.

An analogy to this aspect of equity accounting for associates is the capitalization of finance leases. The U.S. and U.K. rules[52] contain, *inter alia*, a threshold of 90 per cent of fair value. The German tax rules[53] (and therefore accounting practice) also contain numerical thresholds. These various rules enable management to select leases below the thresholds, which the leasing industry is happy to provide. The U.S. and U.K. thresholds can be seen as an attempt to operationalize the 'substantially all of the risks and rewards of ownership of an asset to the lessee' concept (e.g., SSAP 21, para. 15). However, this has no theoretical basis in any published conceptual framework. When the frameworks' definitions of asset and liability are applied, it becomes clear that all non-cancellable leases meet the definitions, so the arbitrary thresholds are not needed (McGregor, 1996). The U.K. standard setter, in conjunction with others, has begun a project to move in this direction (Nailor and Lennard, 1999).

Applying this analogy to equity accounting, the 'significant influence' concept is difficult to operate, which is why an arbitrary threshold (of 20 per cent) arose.

[52] SFAS 13 (para. 7) and SSAP 21 (para. 15).

[53] See Nobes (1997, p. 64).

INTERNATIONAL DEVELOPMENT OF THE EQUITY METHOD

However, the concept is not found in the frameworks (except for the U.K.'s recent *Statement of Principles*). Further, it is clear that an application of the frameworks' definitions suggests that an associate is not part of the group and that its profits (in excess of dividends) are not group profits. This all suggests that equity accounting has little theoretical support. If equity accounting were not allowed, we would not need non-operational concepts or arbitrary thresholds. We would also not need to worry about technical problems such as the treatment of profits made on selling to associates.

Overriding all this must be a consideration of the objectives of financial statements. If one accepts the frameworks' objectives, then the issue becomes largely an empirical matter of the best prediction of future cash flows (subject to reliability). In academic writings, there is some justification for the equity method as an approximate valuation method, as a way of reducing agency problems or as a way of providing more information on earnings. However, more research is needed here.

One conclusion is that standard setters should not perpetuate operationally difficult concepts and arbitrary thresholds or group concepts which seem inconsistent with their frameworks unless they can produce evidence that the prediction of future cash flows is enhanced. One way forward would be to require all investments to be shown at fair value, taking gains and losses to comprehensive income.[54] This would replace the equity method with a more honest valuation approach and would remove arbitrary thresholds.

In practice, recent moves towards the use of fair value for investments have deliberately excluded investments in subsidiaries, joint ventures and associates (e.g., SFAS 115, para. 4; and IAS 39, para. 1a). This leads to such delicious ironies as that, under IAS accounting, a 10 per cent holding in a listed company would be held at fair value in the investor's statements, whereas a 25 per cent holding would generally[55] be valued at cost. In the group's statements, the 10 per cent holding would again be fair valued, whereas the 25 per cent holding would be equity accounted. If the latter were seen as a valuation method, it would not be a serviceable one.

Most of the above arguments also apply against using the equity method in the final remaining case: for the treatment in consolidated statements of joint ventures (Case VI) and perhaps other 'partnerships' (those associates most like joint ventures). Theoretical support has to rest on the idea that the investor exercises long-run control over its share of the profits. Another form of support comes from concern that any alternative to the equity method is worse. For example, full consolidation or proportional consolidation of individual assets of a 20 per cent holding in a joint venture or other partnership would be inconsistent with the frameworks' concept of control. At the other extreme, a cost-based method seems to be misleading as a group presentation of an interest in a 50 per cent-held joint venture. Consequently, this last case seems to be the least objectionable use of

---

[54] 'Comprehensive income' is the term now to be found in SFAS 130. In U.S. terms, whether such gains and losses should be shown in 'income' or 'other comprehensive income' may become a relatively trivial issue as moves are made towards a single income statement.

[55] Assuming, as in many countries, that equity accounting is not used in investors' statements.

equity accounting, and could be seen as semi-consolidation rather than valuation. The U.K.'s 'gross equity method' addresses some of the disclosure problems caused by the netting off involved in the equity method. A report of six English-speaking standard setters (the G4 + 1) concluded in a similar way about the treatment of joint ventures (Milburn and Chant, 1999, p. 25) and makes a supporting reference[56] to an earlier (1998) draft of this article.

The spread of the equity method from one use to another can be seen as part of the response of pragmatic accountants to a series of technical problems: the lack of consolidated statements, then the complications of preparing such statements, then the lack of consolidation of certain subsidiaries, then the lack of consolidation of those jointly controlled investees that were rather like subsidiaries, and so on. The spread of the equity method internationally, despite good arguments against it in several countries, should warn us that the pressures for international harmonization (that are now even stronger than in the period covered in this article) can lead to world-wide use of bad methods as well as good ones. Similarly, the international spread of the 20 per cent threshold illustrates how a pragmatically neat number, once it is supported by the two strongest accounting nations, can prosper in a theoretical vacuum.

REFERENCES

Accountancy, 'Editorial Comment', *Accountancy*, March 1968.

——, 'Editorial Comment', *Accountancy*, June 1970a.

——, 'First Proposal from Accountancy [*sic*] Standards Committee', *Accountancy*, July 1970b.

——, 'APB Chairman in London', *Accountancy*, July 1971.

Accountant, 'A Revolutionary Proposal', *The Accountant*, 25 June 1970.

Accountants International Study Group, *Consolidated Financial Statements*, AISG, 1973.

Accounting Standards Board, *Associates and Joint Ventures*, Discussion Paper, Accounting Standards Board, 1994.

ASA/ICAA, Second Exposure Draft, ASA and ICAA, 1973.

Beeny, J. H., *European Financial Reporting: France*, Institute of Chartered Accountants in England and Wales, 1976.

Bircher, P., 'The Adoption of Consolidated Accounting in Great Britain', *Accounting and Business Research*, Winter 1988.

Bogie, D. J., *Group Accounts*, Jordon & Sons, 1949.

——, *Group Accounts*, 2nd ed., Jordon & Sons, 1959.

Burnett, T., T. E. King and V. C. Lembke, 'Equity Method Reporting for Major Finance Company Subsidiaries', *Accounting Review*, October 1979.

Carman, L. A., 'Intercorporate Relationships', *American Accountant*, April 1932.

Castle, E. F., and A. J. C. Grant, *Practical Bookkeeping and Accounts (Advanced Stage)*, University Tutorial Press, 1970.

Chambers, R. J., 'The Use of the Equity Method in Accounting for Investments in Subsidiaries and Associated Companies', *The Chartered Accountant in Australia*, February 1974.

---

[56]   See Milburn and Chant (1999), note 21. This refers to the 1998 draft in the form of a University of Reading discussion paper in accounting, No. 59.

INTERNATIONAL DEVELOPMENT OF THE EQUITY METHOD

Christiansen, M., and J. O. Elling, *European Financial Reporting: Denmark*, Routledge, 1993.

Conseil National de la Comptabilité, *Consolidation des Bilans et des Comptes*, CNC, 1973.

Cooke, T. E., *European Financial Reporting—Sweden*, Institute of Chartered Accountants in England and Wales, 1988.

Cropper, L. C., F. D. Morris and A. K. Fison, *Accounting*, 5th ed., Macdonald and Evans, 1932.

Czernkowski, R., and J. Loftús, 'A Market-Based Evaluation of Alternative Methods of Reporting on Investments in Associated Entities', paper presented at the European Accounting Association annual congress, Graz, 1997.

Deegan, C., P. Kent and C.-J. Lin, 'The True and Fair View: A Study of Australian Auditors' Application of the Concept', *Australian Accounting Review*, Vol. 4, No. 1, 1994.

Defliese, P., 'British Standards in a World Setting', in Leach and Stamp (1981).

Dickerson, W. E., and J. Weldon Jones, 'Observations on "the Equity Method" and Intercorporate Relationships', *The Accounting Review*, September 1933.

Dicksee, L. R., *Published Balance Sheets and Window Dressing*, Gee, 1927.

Dicksee, L. R., and J. E. G. Montmorency, *Advanced Accounting*, 7th ed., Gee, 1932.

Diggle, G., and C. W. Nobes, 'European Rule-Making in Accounting: The Seventh Directive as a Case Study', *Accounting and Business Research*, Autumn 1994.

Dijksma, J., and M. N. Hoogendoorn, *European Financial Reporting: The Netherlands*, Routledge, 1993.

Eddey, P., *Accounting for Corporate Combinations and Associations*, Prentice-Hall, 1995.

Edwards, J. R., *A History of Financial Accounting*, Routledge, 1989.

Edwards, J. R., and K. M. Webb, 'The Development of Group Accounting in the UK to 1933', *Accounting Historians Journal*, Spring 1984.

Finney, H. A., *Consolidated Statements*, Prentice-Hall, 1922 (reprinted, Arno Press, 1982).

——, *Principles of Accounting, Advanced*, 3rd ed., Prentice-Hall, 1946.

Finney, H. A., and H. E. Miller, *Principles of Accounting, Advanced*, Prentice-Hall, 1952.

Garnsey, G., *Consolidated Accounts*, Gee, 1923.

——, *Consolidated Accounts*, 2nd ed., Gee, 1931.

Goch, D., 'Accounting for Associated Companies', *The Accountant*, 1 June 1972.

Gonzalo, J. A., and J. L. Gallizo, *European Financial Reporting: Spain*, Routledge, 1992.

Gordon, I., and R. D. Morris, 'The Equity Accounting Saga in Australia: Cyclical Standard Setting', *Abacus*, September 1996.

Hatfield, H. R., *Modern Accounting*, Appleton, 1918.

Heurlin, S., and E. Peterssohn, 'Sweden', in D. Alexander and S. Archer (eds), *European Accounting Guide*, Harcourt Brace, 1995.

Hodgkins, P., 'Unilever—the First 21 Years', in T. A. Lee and R. H. Parker (eds), *The Evolution of Corporate Financial Reporting*, Nelson, 1979.

Holmes, G., 'Associated Companies', *Accountancy*, July 1970.

International Accounting Standards Committee, *Accounting for Financial Assets and Financial Liabilities*, Discussion Paper, IASC, 1997.

Institute of Chartered Accountants in England and Wales, *Recommendation N 20, Treatment of Investments in the Balance Sheets of Trading Companies*, ICAEW, 1958.

——, *Survey of Published Accounts, 1969-70*, ICAEW, 1971.

——, *Survey of Published Accounts, 1970-71*, ICAEW, 1972.

Journal, 'Three Nations Join in Common Standards', *Journal of Accountancy*, October 1970.

Kester, R. B., *Accounting Theory and Practice*, Vol. II, Ronald Press, 1920 (year of printing; 1918 year of copyright and publication).

Kohler, E. L., 'Some Tentative Propositions Underlying Consolidated Reports', *Accounting Review*, March 1938.

43

Lamb, M., 'When is a Group a Group? Convergence of Concepts of "Group" in European Union Corporation Tax', *European Accounting Review*, Vol. 4, No. 1, 1995.

Leach, Sir R., 'The Birth of British Accounting Standards', in Leach and Stamp (1981).

Leach, Sir R., and E. Stamp (eds), *British Accounting Standards: The First 10 Years*, Woodhead-Faulkner, 1981.

Littleton, A. C., 'The Dividend Base', *The Accounting Review*, June 1934.

MacNair, H. S. A., 'A Practitioner's View', *The Accountant's Magazine*, September 1970.

McGregor, W., *Accounting for Leases: A New Approach*, Financial Accounting Standards Board, 1996.

Ma, R., R. H. Parker and G. Whittred, *Consolidation Accounting*, Longman Cheshire, 1991.

Mazay, V., T. Wilkins and I. Zimmer, 'Determinants of the Choice of Accounting for Investments in Associated Companies', *Contemporary Accounting Research*, Vol. 10, No. 1, 1993.

Milburn, J. A., and P. D. Chant, *Reporting Interests in Joint Ventures and Similar Arrangements*, Financial Accounting Standards Board for the G4 + 1, 1999.

Miller, M. C., and K. Leo, 'The Downside of Harmonisation Haste: The Equity Accounting Experience', *Australian Accounting Review*, Vol. 7, No. 2, 1997.

Moonitz, M., *The Entity Theory of Consolidated Statements*, American Accounting Association, 1944 (reprinted, Foundation Press, 1951).

Moonitz, M., and C. C. Staehling, *Accounting: An Analysis of its Problems*, Foundation Press, 1950, (printed in 1952).

Mulford, C. W., and E. Comiskey, 'Investment Decisions and the Equity Accounting Standard', *The Accounting Review*, July 1985.

Nailor, H., and A. Lennard, *Leases: Implementation of a New Approach*, Accounting Standards Board, 1999 (and published by other G4 + 1 bodies in 2000).

Napier, C. J., 'Scandalous Accounts: Robert Maxwell and the British Accounting Crisis of 1969', paper revised after *Accounting History* conference, Melbourne, August 1999.

Neuhausen, B. S., 'Consolidation and the Equity Method—Time for an Overhaul', *Journal of Accountancy*, February 1982.

Nobes, C. W., 'The True and Fair View Requirement: Impact on and of the Fourth Directive', *Accounting and Business Research*, Winter 1993.

——, *German Accounting Explained*, Financial Times Reports, 1997.

Noble, H. S., W. E. Karrenbrock and H. Simons, *Advanced Accounting*, South-Western Publishing Co., 1941.

Ordelheide, D., and D. Pfaff, *European Financial Reporting: Germany*, Routledge, 1994.

Parker, R. H., 'Concepts of Consolidation in the EEC', *Accountancy*, February 1997.

——, 'Importing and Exporting Accounting: The British Experience', in A. G. Hopwood (ed.), *International Pressures for Accounting Change*, Prentice-Hall, 1989.

Paton, W. A., 'Editorial Note' in Moonitz (1951).

Peirson, G., and P. McBride, 'More on International Harmonisation in Australia', *CPA Communiqué*, 75, 1997.

Pixley, F. W., *Auditors' Duties and Responsibilities*, Henry Good, 1910.

Ricks, W. E., and J. S. Hughes, 'The Case of Long-Term Investments', *The Accounting Review*, January 1985.

Sawa, E., 'Accounting in Japan', in P. Walton, A. Haller and B. Raffournier (eds), *International Accounting*, Thomson, 1988.

Sharp, K., 'Accounting Standards After 12 Months', *Accountancy*, May 1971 (reprinted and added to in S. A. Zeff, *Forging Accounting Principles in Five Countries*, Stipes, 1972).

Shaw, J. C. (ed.), *Bogie on Group Accounts*, 3rd ed., Jordon & Sons, 1973.

Titcomb, S. J., 'A Stockbroker's View', *The Accountant*, 17 September 1970.

Tweedie, D. P., 'Standards, Objectives and *The Corporate Report*', in Leach and Stamp (1981).

INTERNATIONAL DEVELOPMENT OF THE EQUITY METHOD

Vallely, M., D. Stokes and P. Liesch, 'Equity Accounting: Empirical Evidence and Lessons From the Past', *Australian Accounting Review*, Vol. 7, No. 2, 1997.

Walker, R. G., *Consolidated Statements*, Arno Press, London, 1978a.

——, 'International Accounting Compromises: The Case of Consolidation Accounting', *Abacus*, December 1978b.

Williams, J. R., *GAAP Guide 1996*, Harcourt Brace, 1996.

Zambon, S., *Entità e Proprietà nei Bilanci di Esercizio*, Cedam, 1996.

Zeff, S. A., *Forging Accounting Principles in Australia*, Australian Society of Accountants, 1973.

Zeff, S. A., F. van der Wel and K. Camfferman, *Company Financial Reporting: A Historical and Comparative Study of the Dutch Regulatory Process*, North Holland, 1992.

PART II

CLASSIFICATION

6

Pergamon

The International Journal of Accounting
38 (2003) 95–104

The
International
Journal of
Accounting

On the myth of "Anglo-Saxon" financial accounting: a comment

Christopher Nobes

School of Business, University of Reading, P.O. Box 218, Whiteknights, Reading, RG6 6AA, UK

Abstract

Alexander and Archer (AA) in this journal suggest that the existence of Anglo-Saxon accounting (ASA) is a myth. They identify four hypotheses that might be thought to underpin ASA and seek to show that they are false. This comment suggests that two of the hypotheses are not central to AA's definition of ASA, and that the other two are more complex but do contain some support for the existence of ASA. More importantly, strong support for the existence of ASA can be found elsewhere in similar conceptual approaches and accounting practices and in international cooperation. It is suggested that the identification of ASA does have explanatory and predictive power for recent and forthcoming international developments.
© 2003 University of Illinois. All rights reserved.

Keywords: Anglo-Saxon; Financial reporting; Myth; IASC

1. Introduction

Alexander and Archer (2000) in a clear and interesting paper seek to establish that the existence of Anglo-Saxon accounting (ASA) is a myth in the sense of "similar conceptual and technical approaches, but also a hegemonic alliance in the international politics of accounting regulation" (p. 539). As they say (pp. 541–543), the concept of ASA is well established in the literature. Therefore, their claim, if founded, is a major one.

Alexander and Archer (hereafter AA) identify four hypotheses that might be thought to support the existence of ASA but conclude that there is no support. This comment asks whether the four hypotheses are relevant to AA's claims and, if so, whether AA prove the lack

E-mail address: c.wright@reading.ac.uk (C. Nobes).

0020-7063/03/$ – see front matter © 2003 University of Illinois. All rights reserved.
doi:10.1016/S0020-7063(02)00213-3

of support for the existence of ASA. It is useful to distinguish between conceptual approaches, accounting practices, international alliances, and regulatory systems. For the first three, it is suggested here that ASA does exist.

AA also discuss the politics of the International Accounting Standards Committee (IASC). Contrary to AA's claim (p. 533), this comment suggests that the identification of ASA does help to explain the IASC's past and to predict its future.

2. Similarities and differences

The identification of a group of similar objects only gains relevance in the context of a wider classification. Thus, ASA could only be a useful category when put in the context of other accounting systems. AA (p. 541) sensibly begin their analysis in the context of broader classifications. However, they then concentrate almost exclusively on two countries (the United Kingdom and the United States). To show that there are differences between the two countries does not tell us whether or not the two can usefully be seen as members of the same group. There are generally differences between members of a group. The question is whether the group members share features in a way that distinguishes them from members of other groups. On the subject of similarities between things, Wittgenstein (1953) notes:

> ...we see a complicated network of similarities overlapping and criss-crossing: sometimes overall similarities, sometimes similarities of detail ... I can think of no better expression to characterize these similarities than "family resemblances"; for the various resemblances between members of a family: build, features, colour of eyes, gait, temperament, etc. etc. overlap and criss-cross in the same way. (paragraphs 66 and 67)

In order to assess the existence of ASA, it is necessary to see whether the differences between members of the proposed group are dwarfed by differences between the shared pool of group traits and the traits of individuals outside the group. For this, it would be necessary to study other proposed groups, and also preferably more than two members of the ASA group.

3. AA's hypotheses

Although concentrating on two members in a proposed group is not sufficient, it can be part of assessing the existence of the group. In this context, AA's four hypotheses are now examined. For each, it will be noted whether they seem to concern conceptual approaches, accounting practices, international alliances, or regulatory systems. It is suggested here that the last of these four is not central to the definition of ASA, and is indeed omitted from AA's initial definition (p. 539). That is, companies from two countries might practice very similar accounting even if their regulatory systems are noticeably different. Similarly, two sets of companies in the same country might use similar accounting practices even though they are subject to different regulatory systems. For example, United States generally accepted

C. Nobes / The International Journal of Accounting 38 (2003) 95–104 97

accounting principles are used by many European companies that are not within the regulatory control of the Securities and Exchange Commission (SEC), and also by many United States companies that are not SEC-registered and have no auditing or reporting requirements.

3.1. True and fair view (TFV)/fair presentation (FP)

AA seek to show that there are more differences than similarities in Anglo-Saxon countries (particularly the United Kingdom and the United States) under this heading. I think that AA and I agree on the following:

(i) There is a TFV or FP requirement for preparers and auditors in both the UK and the US.
(ii) The TFV does not mean in practice the same thing as FP.
(iii) There is an override in the United Kingdom but not in the United States.

Two expansions of these points need to be made here. First, although the TFV is a legal requirement for preparers in the United Kingdom (with no equivalent legal requirement in the United States), this requirement is generally fulfilled by complying with standards (Arden, 1993). Secondly, the override in the United Kingdom is mainly used now by the standard setters (and then preparers and auditors) to enable standards to override the law (Alexander, 1999; Nobes, 2000). In this sense, the override is not needed in the United States because there is no accounting law. Consequently, the UK/US differences are less important in practice than in concept.

I disagree with AA that the United States is different from the United Kingdom because "there is no requirement that any U.S. standard-setting body should use the FP criterion" (p. 548). AA try to support this suggestion with two published references (p. 549). First there is Zeff (1995), but he talks of auditors, preparers, and the regulators (the SEC) not the standard setters (the FASB). Secondly, they refer to the U.S. position during the IAS 1 discussions, but again there is no mention of the standard setter in this section of their paper. The U.S. member of the IASC Board was the AICPA and their reference is to the SEC. Although the FASB might agree with the AICPA and the SEC, the U.S. opposition to IAS 1 was, as AA make clear, concerned with the override not with the use of FP by preparers, auditors, or standard setters.

In sum, AA offer no evidence concerning the FASB and FP. The FASB's Statements of Financial Accounting Concepts refer to such notions as understandability, relevance, and representational faithfulness which are said by the IASC's *Framework* (paragraph 46) to lead to TFV/FP. The criterion is sufficiently vague that absence of the exact words in the U.S. framework does not tell us that the content is different in substance from the IASC or U.K. frameworks. There is no U.S. requirement in law concerning use by standard setters of FP because, as noted above, there is no direct equivalent of the Companies Act in the United States. The situation seems little different from the United Kingdom, where the ASB is not directly given instructions by law. It operates (as does the FASB) by reference to its own framework and to the requirements for TFV/FP imposed on preparers or auditors. It would be easy, in both countries, to find cases where the TFV/FP criterion seems to have been overcome by politics or other factors, but that is not the same as saying that it is not required to be used by standard setters.

If we are to identify a relevant TFV/FP feature that distinguishes ASA, it would not be the override (which, as in the United States, is now little used[1] by listed companies in the United Kingdom except to comply with standards); nor would it be any general use of TFV by preparers (because, as in the United States, it seems of little importance to them in practice in the United Kingdom; Nobes & Parker, 1991). Of course, versions of the TFV and the override have been exported to many continental European countries (Aisbitt & Nobes, 2001; Nobes, 1993), so a TFV requirement for preparers or auditors can now hardly be seen as a defining feature of ASA. The distinguishing feature of ASA would be the general purpose of financial statements according to the standard setters. This takes us to the second hypothesis.

3.2. Conceptual frameworks

AA seem to be arguing here that, although the ASA countries share a propensity to develop frameworks, there are two myths: (i) self-regulation, and (ii) actual use of the frameworks. The first point is taken up again in Section 3.4 (below). As for use by the standard setters of the frameworks, my own lengthy experience on two standard-setting bodies[2] is of very extensive use of the frameworks (in draft or otherwise). In standard-setting discussions, references to the purpose of accounting and to the definitions of "asset" and "liability" are continual. The main relevant point here is that the ASA standard setters closely share these purposes and definitions, but that these differ for continental European rule-makers. As noted earlier, I agree with AA (p. 549) that frameworks are not always complied with by the standard setters, a point discussed elsewhere (Nobes, 2000, p. 311).

A relevant body, not mentioned by AA, is the "G4 + 1" group of standard setters which operated from 1992 until early 2001. It comprised the standard setters from exactly the countries that AA identify (p. 539) as ASA countries.[3] Why did these standard setters bother to meet, and why did they not invite non-ASA standard setters? It was because they all (including the IASC)[4] shared a conceptual framework and that they wanted to move faster than the IASC Board (some of whose countries did not share the framework). In other words, there is evidence of "similar conceptual and technical approaches" in ASA (part of the definition of ASA in AA, p. 539). This is considered further later.

---

[1] See, for example, AA's Fig. 2 (p. 548). Most of the departures are to enable compliance with SSAP 19 on investment properties.

[2] The Accounting Standards Committee of the United Kingdom and Ireland (1987–1990), and the IASC (1993–2001). In the case of the former committee, the U.S. framework was occasionally referred to and the IASC's framework was formally noted on its release.

[3] The United Kingdom (which also covers standard setting for Ireland), the United States, Canada, Australia, and New Zealand, with IASC staff (the " + 1") as observers.

[4] The staff of the IASC (observers at G4 + 1) were accustomed to arguing on the basis of the *Framework*, even if some board members were not.

C. Nobes / The International Journal of Accounting 38 (2003) 95–104   99

3.3. Codified versus common law

The relationship of common law and ASA is discussed only briefly by AA, but I agree with them in principle that causality is not proven. Elsewhere, more detailed treatments see some relevance in the association (e.g., La Porta, Lopez-de-Silanes, Shleifer, & Vishny, 1997; Nobes, 1998a; Nobes & Roberts, 2000). However, for the purposes of this comment, no more need be said because this is an issue of ASA regulatory systems which is not central to AA's theme of conceptual/technical approaches and hegemonic alliances.

3.4. How private-sector is U.S. regulation?

AA's treatment of this feature overlaps with the second feature (Section 3.2). I can agree with their conclusion that government bodies may have a stronger influence in the United States than in the United Kingdom. However, this is again about the peripheral issue of regulatory systems.

3.5. Summary so far

AA have illustrated that certain features related to regulatory systems differ among ASA countries. However, this is not central to the existence or otherwise of ASA as defined. They have also shown that TFV and FP are different and so is the override, although this has little practical effect on compliance with standards. However, to show differences between two countries does not prove that they are not in the same group. More importantly, AA have not shown that the conceptual and technical approaches of ASA standard setters differ.

4. ASA approaches and practices

AA say (p. 541) that the above four hypotheses "could be taken" to support the validity of ASA. Consequently, they leave open the possibility that other hypotheses are more relevant. I suggest the hypothesis that ASA does exist and can be seen in shared conceptual approaches and accounting practices. In terms of approaches, the hypothesis can be formulated as follows:

> ASA (compared to other forms of accounting) is oriented towards decision-making by investors; it plays down the measurement of taxable income and distributable income; it is less worried about prudence; it is more willing to go beyond superficial legal form.

Of course, it will be possible to find certain features of U.S. accounting (for example) which do not fit the above, or certain features of conventional[5] German accounting (for example) which do. However, taken as a package, it is suggested that the above is a fair description of U.S. and U.K. accounting compared to conventional German accounting. It is

---

[5] That is, accounting as set out in the HGB, rather than as now practiced by some listed companies in their consolidated statements whereby §292 enables use of international rules instead.

Table 1
Specific accounting practices

Anglo-Saxon	Some Continental European[a]
Percentage of completion method	Completed contract method
Depreciation over useful lives	Depreciation by tax rules
No legal reserves	Legal reserves
Finance leases capitalized	Lease capitalization rare
Cash flow statements	Cash flow statements rare
No secret reserves	Secret reserves
No tax-induced provisions	Tax-induced provisions
Preliminary expenses expensed	Preliminary expenses capitalizable
Taking gains on unsettled foreign currency monetary items	Deferring gains on unsettled foreign currency monetary items

[a] This heading is used to cover conventional accounting in Belgium, France, Germany, and Italy, which concentrates on individual companies.

clear that AA fundamentally agree with the above characterization of ASA because they too identify its "investor-oriented approach" (p. 553).

Incidentally, France, Germany, and Japan have recently established private sector standard setters who may share some aspects of the above approach. This would not undermine the existence of an ASA approach, it would show that it was being exported.

In terms of detailed accounting practices, I suggest that, here also, ASA can be identified. A second hypothesis can be set out as in Table 1. Again, not all companies in all ASA countries have always to exhibit all the features on the left of the table for ASA to exist as a recognizable body of practices. Table 1 concerns accounting policies related to the financial statements of individual legal entities. The reason for choosing this scope is that the laws of certain countries (e.g., Germany) allow the use of U.S. or IASC rules for consolidated statements under certain conditions; and the laws of others (e.g., France) allow certain ASA features as options in consolidated statements. Consequently, it is complicated to include consolidated statements and therefore to include consolidation issues. The fact that some German or French listed companies can adopt features on the left of Table 1 for their consolidated statements does not threaten the existence of ASA. This debate has also been played out elsewhere (e.g., Cairns, 1997; Nobes, 1998b).

5. The politics of the IASC

Roberts (1995) suggests that there are no real, objective, or natural classifications (p. 661) so that a "good" classification is one that is useful for its purpose. Here, one can agree with AA that it is important whether ASA has "explanatory power for today's developments and ... predictive power for tomorrow's" (p. 543). AA's claim that ASA lacks such power will be refuted below by assessing their arguments about the IASC.

AA examine the membership of the IASC in 1999 and show that ASA countries did not make up the then necessary 75% majority to pass a standard. However, they note that the

ASA's investor-oriented approach has dominated international standard setting. I agree with them on these points. Of course, there were frequent disagreements between and within ASA delegations on the IASC Board, and they did not vote as a group. However, this does not prove AA's major theses, as now explained.

One of AA's purposes (p. 540) is to suggest that the ASA countries had no hegemony over the IASC, and that in the future (after 1999) "internecine warfare is inevitable" (p. 554). In assessing these claims, it is useful to refer again to the "G4 + 1." The fact that it was needed by the ASA standard setters supports AA's conclusion about lack of voting hegemony.

The G4 + 1 sets the agenda for international harmonization by discussing and publishing papers on such topics as provisions, lease accounting, and comprehensive income (Johnson & Lennard, 1998; Lennard & Thompson, 1995; McGregor, 1996). In this way, the ASA standard setters have dominated the IASC's agenda. Also, for all the standards from IAS 33 to IAS 41, only ASA countries had (or were developing) detailed accounting rules. The IASC always began projects with studies of existing rules, so there was little competition from non-ASA countries. In these ways, there was ASA hegemony of ideas, if not, of voting power.

It should be noted that AA would have more difficulty countering the idea of ASA voting hegemony with the new Board of the IASC (i.e., the IASB; see Table 2, which suggests 10 ASA votes out of 14), especially as only a simple majority is now needed to pass a standard. The G4 + 1 was wound up in February 2001 (*IASC Insight*, 2001), and a glance at Table 2 shows why it is no longer needed, given the importance on the IASB not only of ASA *countries* but particularly of ASA *standard setters*.

However, I agree with AA that ASA hegemony is not a useful way of looking at it. The non-ASA board members probably also share the framework's philosophy that the purpose of IAS accounting is to give useful information to investors.

Table 2
IASB members from April 2001

Country	Number	Comment
United States	5 (or 3)[a]	2 former FASB + 1 former FASB trustee (and former IASC chairman) + 2 part-time
United Kingdom	2 (or 4)[a]	Both former ASB
Australia	1	Former AARF executive director
Canada	1	Former AcSB chair
South Africa	1	–
France	1	Former IASC Board
Germany	1	Former Daimler-Chrysler, which uses U.S. GAAP
Japan	1	Former IASC Board
Switzerland	1	Former IASC Board
Total	14	

AcSB = Accounting Standards Board of Canada.
ASB = Accounting Standards Board of the United Kingdom.
AARF = Australian Accounting Research Foundation, which provided the secretariat for the Australian standard setter, the AASB.
FASB = Financial Accounting Standards Board of the United States.
 [a] Two board members have United States work backgrounds but United Kingdom nationality.

The previous two paragraphs show that the existence of ASA is helpful in explaining the IASC developments covered. It is also useful for predictions. For example, will there be "internecine warfare" among ASA standard setters?

One of the objectives of the IASB arrangements is that the national standard setters and the IASB should all move together on projects. The G4 + 1 began this process. The IASB seems set to accelerate it. Seven of the board members have liaison responsibilities with eight national Boards. These seven are the countries of Table 2, except for South Africa and Switzerland. The New Zealand standard setter is added to the Australian liaison to complete the coverage of the former G4 + 1.

Just as there are disagreements within a country, so there are among ASA standard setters. However, there seems to be a broad measure of agreement over a wide spectrum of dramatic proposals, such as:

- all noncancellable leases are capital leases,
- the income statement needs to be replaced by a comprehensive statement,
- share options are an expense when granted,
- government grants are income when all their conditions are met,
- financial assets and liabilities should be fair valued with gains/losses treated as income,
- hedge accounting should not be allowed as an exception from the above,
- actuarial gains and losses should be recognized immediately,
- proportional consolidation should not be allowed.

These conclusions, which would lead to major changes in US/UK/IASB requirements (and even larger changes elsewhere) are now part of a consensus of ASA standard setters. Contrary to AA's conclusion, this enables predictions of change, based on agreement among ASA standard setters which is itself based on the framework. On most issues, I see no sign of the fulfillment of AA's prediction (p. 554) of a possible IASB/EU/UK combination against the United States. Time will tell.

6. Conclusion

AA define ASA in terms of similar conceptual and technical approaches and an international alliance for standard setting. For the purposes of this comment, I accept this definition and the countries that they identify as Anglo-Saxon.

AA claim that the existence of ASA is a myth. They then choose four hypotheses connected to ASA and try to show that they do not support its existence. However, two of these (on law and on regulation), while treated plausibly by AA, are not central to their definition of ASA so can offer little support to their claims of nonexistence of ASA.

The other two are more complex. On TFV/FP, AA do not prove that there is much difference between the United Kingdom and the United States in terms of the practical effect of the override on compliance with standards or on the use of TFV/FP by standard setters or by preparers and auditors. On conceptual frameworks, they do not show that the ASA standard setters fail to *use* the frameworks (as opposed to always complying with them), and they do not consider the relevance of the existence of the G4 + 1.

Further, to show that there are some differences between two members of a proposed group does not tell us that the group does not exist. It is useful to look at more members and it is necessary to look at nonmembers for all the features examined. Luckily, it is easier to prove existence than nonexistence. This comment has suggested two hypotheses that are more central to AA's definition of ASA than their own four hypotheses are. That is, in terms of both shared conceptual approaches and accounting practices, it is proposed here that ASA does exist and can easily be identified by comparison with other countries. On the topic of international alliance, it is also suggested that an ASA hegemony of ideas can be identified, particularly during the 1990s, and that it is set to intensify.

The key point is whether the identification of an ASA family is useful. Using AA's own discussion of the IASC, I have suggested that there are several features for which ASA is helpful for explanation and prediction.

7. Codicil

Given the increasing use of U.S. and international standards for certain purposes in such countries as Germany, it might be helpful to move from such labels as ASA and continental accounting towards such descriptors as investor/decision accounting compared to creditor/tax accounting. AA are pointing us in this direction. However, this would not imply that ASA did not or does not exist. Rather the reverse; it would acknowledge that, for example, most German listed companies have chosen to use ASA for their consolidated statements.

Acknowledgements

The author is grateful for comments on an earlier draft from David Alexander, Simon Archer, R.H. Parker, Alan Roberts, and Stephen Zeff.

References

Aisbitt, S., & Nobes, C. W. (2001 Spring). The true and fair requirement in recent national implementations. *Accounting and Business Research*, 83–90.

Alexander, D. (1999 Summer). A benchmark for the adequacy of published financial statements. *Accounting and Business Research*, 239–253.

Alexander, D., & Archer, S. (2000). On the myth of Anglo-Saxon financial accounting. *International Journal of Accounting*, *35*(4), 539–557.

Arden, M. (1993). The true and fair requirement. (Appendix) *Foreword to Accounting Standards*. London: Accounting Standards Board.

Cairns, D. (1997). The future shape of harmonization: a reply. *European Accounting Review*, *6*(2), 305–348.

IASC Insight (2001, March). G4 + 1 to disband. *IASC Insight*, 18.

Johnson, L. T., & Lennard, A. (1998). *Reporting financial performance: current developments and future directions.* FASB for the G4 + 1.

La Porta, R., Lopez-de-Silanes, F., Shleifer, A., & Vishny, R. W. (1997, July). Legal determinants of external finance. *Journal of Finance,* 1131–1150.

Lennard, A., & Thompson, S. (1995). *Provisions: their recognition, measurement, and disclosure in financial statements.* FASB for the G4 + 1.

McGregor, W. (1996). *Accounting leases: a new approach.* FASB for the G4 + 1.

Nobes, C. W. (1993 Winter). The true and fair view requirement: impact on and of the fourth directive. *Accounting and Business Research,* 35–48.

Nobes, C. W. (1998a). Towards a general model of the reasons for international differences in financial reporting. *Abacus, 34*(2), 162–187.

Nobes, C. W. (1998b). The future shape of harmonization: some responses. *European Accounting Review, 7*(2), 323–333.

Nobes, C. W. (2000). Is true and fair of over-riding importance?: a comment on Alexander's benchmark. *Accounting and Business Research,* 307–312.

Nobes, C. W., & Parker, R. H. (1991, April). True and fair: a survey of U.K. financial directors. *Journal of Business Finance and Accounting, 18*(3), 359–375.

Nobes, C. W., & Roberts, A. D. (2000). Towards a unifying model of systems of law, corporate financing, accounting and corporate governance. *Australian Accounting Review,* 26–34.

Roberts, A. D. (1995). The very idea of classification in international accounting. *Accounting Organizations and Society, 20*(7/8), 639–664.

Wittgenstein, L. (1953). *Philosophical investigations.* Oxford: Basil Blackwell (G. E. M. Anscombe, Trans.).

Zeff, S. A. (1995). A perspective on the U.S. public/private approach to the regulation of financial reporting. *Accounting Horizons, 9*(1), 52–70.

7

Available online at www.sciencedirect.com

SCIENCE @ DIRECT•

PERGAMON   Accounting, Organizations and Society 29 (2004) 189–200

Accounting,
Organizations
and Society

www.elsevier.com/locate/aos

On accounting classification and the international harmonisation debate

Christopher Nobes*

School of Business, University of Reading, Reading RG6 6AA, UK

Abstract

In an earlier issue of this journal, d'Arcy presents a classification of accounting systems that shows the UK and the US in separate groups and Australia as an outlier. It is suggested here that the classification is unsound because the data were unsuitable in nature and contained errors.
© 2003 Elsevier Ltd. All rights reserved.

Introduction

In an earlier issue of this journal, d'Arcy (2001) uses data derived from Ordelheide and KPMG (1995) to prepare a classification of the accounting rules of 14 countries plus the IASC. A major conclusion is that 'it is not at all possible to find an Anglo-American cluster' (p. 345). As d'Arcy suggests (p. 330), this runs counter to some previous research (e.g. Nobes, 1983). It is not intended here to offer support for previous classifications. It is accepted (e.g. Nobes, 1998, 2003) that the 'Anglo-Saxon v. continental European' classification needs amendment and is, to some extent, historical. Instead, the purpose of this comment is to suggest that the data used by d'Arcy are sufficiently unreliable as to render her own classification misleading.

D'Arcy's results include cluster analysis leading to a dendrogram (Fig. 1 in d'Arcy, 2001) in which an 'Anglo-American cluster, including the UK

and the US cannot be found' (p. 341). There is also a two-dimensional diagram derived from multidimensional scaling (Fig. 2 in d'Arcy, 2001). This shows that 'Switzerland and UK are very close' (p. 343), but that Australia is far removed from the UK: 'the Australian system enforces its outsider position by certain requirements and prohibitions' (p. 345).

Having arrived at this counter-intuitive result concerning Australia, d'Arcy does not question the data but accepts the result and seeks to explain it. Although d'Arcy uses superior methods,[1] this reminds one of previous classifications based on data that had not been prepared for that purpose. For example, da Costa, Bourgeois, and Lawson (1978) justify why, in their classification, Germany was in the same group as the US but Canada was not, and why UK accounting was less like US accounting than any other in the world (see Nobes, 1992, p. 49). Also, the Goodrich (1982)

---

[1] Anne d'Arcy points out (letter of 9 August 2002) that she only seeks to explain those results derived from cluster analysis that was tested by multidimensional scaling. She does not rely on factor analysis.

---

* Tel.: +44-118-93-18-228; fax: +44-118-93-16-350.
  E-mail address: c.wright@reading.ac.uk (C. Nobes).

0361-3682/$ - see front matter © 2003 Elsevier Ltd. All rights reserved.
doi:10.1016/S0361-3682(03)00045-X

190 *C. Nobes / Accounting, Organizations and Society 29 (2004) 189–200*

classification included a group headed by Jersey which contained Germany, the Netherlands, Italy, Senegal and Ecuador (see Nobes, 1982). Once again, this was not dismissed as a statistical freak but justified.

The data

Its nature

D'Arcy (2001) uses data from d'Arcy (1999, pp. 252–255) which were based on Ordelheide and Semler (1995) (hereafter O&S), which were themselves derived from Ordelheide and KPMG (1995) (hereafter, OKPMG). It is relevant to note here that Anne Semler changed her name to Anne d'Arcy in 1997. In the discussion in this section, there are inevitably many references to these sources because d'Arcy (2001) does not itself contain the data that it is based on. In d'Arcy (1999), there are codes for the rules of 15 countries[2] on 129 variables based on accounting topics drawn from O&S. D'Arcy reports (2001, p. 335) that topics are scored in O&S for each country as R (required), A (allowed) or F (forbidden), and that these topics took up two variables in her research, with a coding of $1.0 = R$; $0.0 = A$; and $0.1 = F$. Some (yes/no) topics in O&S needed only one variable and were coded on a 0/1 basis. In total, d'Arcy used 88 topics: 41 dealt with by two variables each and 47 by one variable each (i.e. 129 variables in total). The many remaining issues in O&S were deemed not to be susceptible to coding, for example because there was not sufficient detail in OKPMG.

D'Arcy (2001, pp. 333–334) discusses the weaknesses in the data obtained from surveys by Price Waterhouse which were used for several previous classifications, such as the two mentioned in the first section. However, she does not mention that her own data may suffer from two of the same problems (see "Swamping of important issues" and "Errors on contestable interpretations" below) and from some others. These are now examined.

Swamping of important issues

As d'Arcy notes, Nobes and Matatko (1980, p. 70) point out that important issues in a data set may be swamped by trivial ones. This is a problem for d'Arcy (2001) because, for example, six variables are used for negative goodwill but only two for positive goodwill. Five variables are used for the treatment of hyperinflationary subsidiaries but none for lease accounting. Again, eight variables are used for the equity method, but none of them deals with whether the method is compulsory for the inclusion of associates in consolidated statements (as it was not in Australia, for example; see Gordon and Morris, 1996).

In an attempt to avoid subjectivity, d'Arcy used all the codable data rather than selecting the important topics from the mass of data. However, it would have been no more subjective to have identified important topics than to have chosen to use all topics that happened to be codable from a list selected by O&S for a purpose other than classification. In this case, the impression of objectivity in d'Arcy (1999, 2001) is misleading for an additional reason: d'Arcy/Semler was the co-author of the publication which selected the topics in O&S. Although d'Arcy restricts herself to the topics in O&S (and to codable topics within that), she did use judgement in deciding which topics were codable and in deciding on what exactly to code (e.g. of the various issues in 'simplified valuation methods for stock' on page 26 of O&S, she focussed on the single issue of whether LIFO is forbidden). In my view, these judgements were made well, helped by involvement with the preparation of the database.[3] This suggests that less constraint should have been put on the exercise of judgement.

Another issue is that all 129 variables are given equal weight (although this includes 41 topics given a double weight of variables for reasons of coding rather than importance). It would have been no more subjective to assign weights than to choose to give all variables equal weight and to allow some topics to have two variables. This issue is not covered in d'Arcy (2001) but d'Arcy (1999,

---

[3] Unlike the position of those researchers who used the earlier Price Waterhouse data.

C. Nobes / Accounting, Organizations and Society 29 (2004) 189–200 191

pp. 168–171) reports that her results were robust to different weightings. Roberts (1995, p. 647) notes the arguments concerning weighting and links them to the potential need to exclude some unimportant variables.

Other aspects of suitability

One troublesome feature of the data is its split between 'individual accounts' and 'group accounts', following the format of the country descriptions in OKPMG. However, nearly all the 'individual' topics (e.g. the valuation of inventories and the treatment of foreign currency balances) are equally relevant for consolidated statements. Consequently, the data does not pick up cases where different rules can (or must) be used for individual and consolidated statements. For example, France is scored in O&S as not allowing LIFO or the capitalisation of leases, but this is incorrect for consolidated statements (see OKPMG, pp. 1308, 1324–1326). Consequently, the data set for France is not a good description of individual statements (because it includes 58 consolidation topics) and it is not a good description of consolidated statements (because it does not correctly record the rules for several non-consolidation topics in the context of consolidated statements).

A final aspect of suitability concerns the inclusion in O&S (and as 5 of the 129 variables used by d'Arcy) of a topic that might be better excluded from 'accounting': that is, the distributability of income. Just as rules relating to the calculation of taxable income have been properly omitted, it is suggested that rules relating to the calculation of distributable income should also have been omitted. The latter issue is not relevant in consolidated statements,[4] and it is not considered an 'accounting' issue in the US nor is it relevant in IASC rules.

Errors or contestable interpretations

Another type of problem with the data is errors or doubtful interpretations. The issue of whether there are errors in OKPMG is not investigated here, although some problems with that publication are noted elsewhere.[5] However, it is suggested below that some errors or doubtful interpretations were made in preparing O&S from OKPMG. Some of these were adjusted for as a result of the careful methods used in d'Arcy (1999), but others flow through to the codes used there. Some further errors or doubtful interpretations were added in cases where the scores were not clear. This is not surprising because, as explained below, a great deal of judgement was needed in interpreting the rules for 15 countries on 88 topics.

Appendices A–C to this paper list scores that seem to be in error for Australia, the UK and the US, using the page numbers from O&S, and referring to the topic numbers in d'Arcy (1999). Justifications for the proposed corrections are also given in the Appendices. This work would not have been possible without unstinting help from Anne d'Arcy, who explained the exact topics being coded for d'Arcy (1999, 2001), which were not always clear from O&S, and who also assisted in the elimination of my mistakes in previous drafts of the Appendices. Further checking of the Appendices was carried out by a number of experts mentioned in the acknowledgements.

It is admitted here that concentrating on only 3 countries might affect one's view of the correct coding for the variables. However, frequent reference was made to the O&S scores and the d'Arcy codes for other countries, as occasionally noted in the explanations following the Appendices.

Some of the errors as suggested in the Appendices are simple: e.g. for the UK, O&S incorrectly score[6] that it is 'required' instead of 'forbidden' to include certain subsidiaries in consolidation (the

---

[4] In the sense that groups cannot distribute profit, only companies can. Since groups are allowed to use different rules from the parent in many countries where distributable profit is seen as an accounting issue (e.g. Germany, but see details in O&S, pp. 44/47), there is no reason why distributability need constrain group accounting practices.

[5] Nobes (2001) identifies some errors in the second edition of OKPMG, and these can also be found in the first edition.

[6] See Appendix B to this paper, topics 13 and 14.

192   *C. Nobes / Accounting, Organizations and Society 29 (2004) 189–200*

error caused by concentrating on the fact that it was 'required' to *exclude*). Sometimes there are wholesale misunderstandings by the OKPMG contributors of the intentions of its editors. For example, for the section on 'Liabilities and provisions', most country authors took 'provisions' to refer to items shown on the liabilities side of the balance sheet. However, the Australian contributor discusses only a quite different meaning of provision: allowances against assets (OKPMG, p. 130). The confusion is partly caused by the common mistranslation of the German word *Verbindlichkeiten* as 'liabilities', instead of 'creditors' which are one type of liability.[7] The OKPMG heading should have been 'Creditors and provisions'. In O&S (p. 14), the statements about provisions in OKPMG are picked up as though Australian companies are required to show depreciation provisions as liabilities on balance sheets, and several other errors follow (see Appendix A, topics 3–6).

Another cause of problems is the assumption[8] for some purposes in O&S that a practice is forbidden unless there is a specific option allowing it. This assumption is culture-specific: it might apply in Germany but not generally in Australia, the UK or the US. As examples, this affects topics 4, 9 and 10 in Appendix B.

Similar difficulties arise because of the need to distinguish between what the rules say and what they mean. By this, I do not intend to say that a *de jure* study should measure company practices. I mean that a rule needs to be interpreted in the national regulatory context and in terms of its operational meaning. As to national context, UK examples would be the banning of LIFO[9] and of the exclusion of subsidiaries from consolidation

on the grounds of dissimilarity.[10] Strictly speaking, there are no such bans in UK rules, but listed companies and their auditors interpret the rules to mean that there are bans. O&S (p.29) and d'Arcy (1999, variable 53) interpret the UK rule on LIFO as a ban, but O&S (p. 43) and d'Arcy (1999, variables 80/81) take the opposite view[11] on dissimilarity.

As an example of the operational effects, I refer to Australian topics 8 and 9 in Appendix A: whether enterprises have to be consolidated and whether subsidiaries have to be consolidated even if this is expensive. The O&S scores are Ø (no specific rules) for these topics and this is interpreted as 'no requirement' in d'Arcy (1999). However, the *meaning* of the Australian rule[12] is that the former case would clearly fall within the requirements to be consolidated, and that there is no exemption on the grounds of expense. So, both variables should have been coded as a requirement to consolidate.

No attempt has been made here to assess the degree of error for the other 11 countries. However, there seems no reason to believe that the Australia/UK/US scores are more likely to have been recorded erroneously than others. Furthermore, since the main operating languages of the project were German and English, there would have been more scope for confusion during the interpretation of contributors who were not native speakers of one of those languages. Alexander, Archer, Delvaille, and Taupin (1996) explain some

---

[7] There are three main elements on the *passiv* side of a German balance sheet: *Rücklagen* (reserves), *Rückstellungen* (provisions) and *Verbindlichkeiten* (creditors). The last of these is often mistranslated as 'liabilities', even in the semi-official translation (Brooks and Mertin, 1993, p. E60). In English, liabilities include creditors and provisions.

[8] Confirmed by Anne d'Arcy in letter of 6 May 2002.

[9] The Companies Act 1985 (Schedule 4, para. 27) specifically allows LIFO. The body of SSAP 9 does not mention LIFO. However, in Appendix A (which is specifically said not to be part of the Standard), paragraph 12 suggests that LIFO is 'not usually appropriate'.

[10] The Companies Act 1985 (S.229 (4)) requires subsidiaries to be excluded if they are so different that inclusion would not allow a true and fair view. This is said not to apply merely because some are industrial and others commercial. FRS 2 (para. 25) says that exclusion is 'exceptional'. Paragraph 78 (a) says: 'Cases of this sort are so exceptional that it would be misleading to link them in general to any particular contrast of activities'. Banking/non-banking or profit/not-for-profit are said to be insufficiently different to qualify. The publication *GAAP 2001* (IFAD, 2001), which was signed off by the largest seven audit firms in the UK, does not record this topic as a UK difference from IAS 27, which does not allow exclusion.

[11] O&S records a score of 'F (in practice R. . .)' but this is coded as F (i.e. consolidation forbidden, which means no ban on exclusion).

[12] AASB 1024, para. 13.

C. Nobes / Accounting, Organizations and Society 29 (2004) 189–200   193

Table 1
Number of codes that are the same for country pairs

	D'Arcy (129 variables)	Revised (124 variables)
Australia/UK	67 (51.9%)	89 (71.8%)
Australia/US	72 (55.8%)	81 (65.3%)
UK/US	60 (46.5%)	81 (65.3%)
Germany/Australia	57 (44.2%)	62 (50.0%)
Germany/UK	83 (64.3%)	78 (62.9%)
Germany/US	51 (39.5%)	52 (41.9%)

major language difficulties between English and French on the subject of provisions.

Effects of amendments

Appendix D shows the effects of amendments for the problems that are discussed in the previous section and detailed in Appendices A–C. It lists the affected variables of the 129 used by d'Arcy (2001). For comparison, the codes for Germany are also included; these are unamended, as it is assumed that they are correct, given the German authorage of OKPMG, O&S and d'Arcy (1999, 2001).

Let us begin with the effects on Australia, which d'Arcy (2001) suggests has 'a clear outsider position' (p. 342). D'Arcy (2001) explains that, for Australia: 'The differences consist mainly of definitions of certain types of provisions and the rules according to the full consolidation set' (p. 344). However, as noted in the previous section, the Australian codes are wrong for all four provision topics (topics 3–6 of Appendix A, amounting to seven variables: Nos. 21–27 in Appendix D). Furthermore, topics 8 and 9 of Appendix A show amendments for the consolidation set. This removes two more alleged Australia/US differences (variables 86 and 88 in Appendix D). In sum, the two areas of apparent Australian eccentricity are caused by errors, and so the 'clear outsider position' is a figment.

Appendix E shows, for each variable, if the amendments affect whether each pair of the four countries (Australia, Germany, the UK and the

US) is the same. These data were used to prepare Table 1, which shows the degrees of similarities of the country pairs in the original data used in d'Arcy (2001) and then in the data as revised here. The five variables related to distributability have been excluded (see "Other aspects of suitability").

Turning to the UK and the US, Appendix D shows the proposed amendments, and Appendix E shows that these mostly remove alleged UK/US differences, as may be seen by the increases in the number of variables with the same code. The resulting degrees of similarity for the three pairs Australia/UK/US are greatly enhanced as a percentage of the variables, as shown in Table 1. For example, the proportion of the variables coded the same for the UK and the US rises from 46.5 to 65.3%. As the above example of Australia shows, the results of clustering/scaling can depend upon differences on a few topics. There are so many suggested amendments to the data, that d'Arcy's major finding of no Anglo-American cluster is not soundly based.

Let us now add a comparison with Germany. D'Arcy suggests that 'the British system belongs to the European cluster and separates clearly from the North-American group' (p. 342). The original codings do suggest that the UK and Germany are the most similar of any of the six pairs (see the 64.3% in Table 1). However, when the data is amended, Germany/UK has less in common than any Australia/UK/US pair. Of course, Table 1 should be interpreted in the context of the general lack of suitability of the data, as explained in previous sections.

Conclusions

D'Arcy (2001) provides a more up-to-date classification than many in the literature. She finds that there is no Anglo-American cluster and that Australia is an outlier. D'Arcy addresses these important matters with a well-written introduction and a careful conclusion. However, the core of the paper rests on deficient data, so that the classification and the major conclusions based on it cannot be relied upon.

194   *C. Nobes / Accounting, Organizations and Society 29 (2004) 189–200*

The problems with the data are of two types: suitability and accuracy. When corrections are made for some of these issues, the two specific reasons (as identified by d'Arcy) for Australia being an outlier are removed. In the case of UK/US differences in the data, 36% of them are removed.[13] Consequently, the finding that the UK can be grouped with Germany but not with the US is unreliable. Incidentally, d'Arcy points out that,[14] using the same data but a different analysis, she did find an Anglo-American cluster.

In sum, either the suitability or the accuracy problems, that have been examined here, might render the conclusions in d'Arcy (2001) unreliable. Taken together, they seem fatal. One specific caution for the future emerges: researchers might be tempted to use the more recent data of Ordelheide and KPMG (2001) for classification studies, but should do so only after considering the above problems.

Acknowledgements

The author is PricewaterhouseCoopers Professor of Accounting at the University of Reading. He is particularly grateful to Anne d'Arcy for providing a copy of her thesis (d'Arcy, 1999), for answering a number of questions about her work and for suggesting improvements on earlier drafts. He is also grateful for comments on earlier drafts from David Alexander (University of Birmingham), Terry Cooke and Bob Parker (University of Exeter), Paul Pacter (Deloitte & Touche, Hong Kong) and Alan Roberts (University of Canterbury, NZ). He acknowledges technical advice on the issues in Appendices 1–3 from Peter Holgate (Technical Partner, PricewaterhouseCoopers, UK), Jan McCahey (Technical Partner, PricewaterhouseCoopers, Australia), Malcolm Miller (University of New South Wales) and Wayne Upton (formerly of the staff of the Financial Accounting Standards Board, from 2001 of the staff of the IASB).

Appendix A. Amendments to the data relating to Australia

Topic	O&S page	Issue	O&S score	Amended score	D'Arcy (1999) variables
1	10	Capitalisation of purchased non-consolidation goodwill	A	R	14
2	14	Capitalisation of discount on loans	R	A	17/18
3	14	Provisions from legal requirements	F	R	21/22
4	14	Provisions for losses on uncompleted transactions	F	R	23
5	14	Provisions for expenditure	F	A	24/25
6	14	Provisions for depreciation	R	F	26/27
7	22	Inclusion of costs of administration	R	F	35/36
8	40	Consolidation when contractual right of control	Ø	R	78
9	40	Consolidation of subsidiary when high cost	Ø	R	86
10	44	Group can choose different policies from parent	N	Y	94

---

[13] That is, as derived from reciprocals from Table 1, 53.5% differences reduces to 34.7% differences.

[14] Letter of 9 August 2002, referring to d'Arcy (2000).

C. Nobes / Accounting, Organizations and Society 29 (2004) 189–200 195

Explanations of the amendments:

1. It is clear from OKPMG (p. 122) that goodwill cannot be written off against reserves; it must be capitalised.
2. AAG 10 of 1988 implies that discount should be deducted from debt. So, "R" is not correct. Given the limited authority of this document, "A" may be a better score than "F".
3–4. The Australian contributor to OKPMG took a different meaning of "provisions" from other country contributors, i.e. he interpreted them as "allowances" not as a type of liability. Consequently, the Australian reference in O&S (i.e. to OKPMG, VI·6·2) makes no mention of the latter. All these scores should not be "F" but "R" (as for the UK and the US).
5. Similar to topics 3 and 4 except that only some expected expenses have related obligations which should therefore be provided for.
6. The reverse problem to points (3–5) occurs here. The question relates to whether depreciation provisions are shown on the liabilities side. Clearly the answer should be "F" not "R".
7. The reference in O&S (p. 22) is to OKPMG, VI·3·3. This does not discuss administration overheads, but this issue is covered by Curran (1996, p.43) who confirms exclusion. There seems to be no reason why, in d'Arcy (1999), Australia, the UK and the US should be coded in three different ways on the resulting variables.
8. If there is a contractual right of control, this would obviously satisfy the Australian definition (AASB 1024).
9. Given that there is no specific mention of exclusions for cost, then consolidation is required.
10. AASB 1024 requires uniformity (para. 16) but does not require the parent's policies.

Appendix B. Amendments to the data relating to the UK

Topic	O&S page	Issue	O&S score	Amended score	D'Arcy (1999) variables
1	13	Capitalisation of costs of reorganisation or extension of productive capacity	F	A	5
2	13	Capitalisation of self-generated patents, etc.	R	A	12
3	17	Capitalisation of discount on loans	A	F	17/18
4	17	Provisions from legal requirements	F	R	21/22
5	17	Provisions for expenditure	R	A	24/25
6	21	Depreciation of reorganisation costs over 5 years or less	R	A	29
7	25	Inclusion of appropriate proportion of manufacturing overheads	A	R	34
8	25	Inclusion of social costs, pensions, etc.	F	R	37/38
9	33	Lump sum adjustment of debtors	F	A	64
10	33	Discounting of long-term liabilities	F	A	66
11	43	Small groups exempted	Y	N	73
12	43	Consolidation when dissimilar	R	F	80/81
13	43	Consolidation when long-term restrictions	R	F	82/83
14	43	Consolidation when held for sale	R	F	84/85
15	43	Proportional consolidation forbidden	N	Y	88
16	47	Group must follow rules that apply to parent	N	Y	94
17	53	Recognition of goodwill	A	R	109

C. Nobes / Accounting, Organizations and Society 29 (2004) 189–200

Explanations of the amendments:

1. There was no law nor accounting standard directly on this at the time. O&S refer to OKPMG VI·1·1·1, but this has no mention of these issues. However, where these costs extend the life or improve the recoverable amount, they should be capitalised. At least, this must have been 'allowed'. This fits the Australian note in O&S (p. 10): "R if material...and expected to contribute to the earning of future revenue which can reasonably be expected to absorb the expenses".

2. Just as there was no rule on brands, so there was no rule on other identifiable self-generated intangibles. They were sometimes capitalised.

3. Not allowed by FRS 4, para. 27 (issued December 1993). FRS 4 has an implementation date of periods ending on or after 22 June 1994. It is clear from O&S that even standards subsequent to FRS 4 are included. D'Arcy suggests[15] that a cut-off date in the second half of 1995 was used, with some account taken in d'Arcy (1999) of later changes.

4. There was no accounting standard, but there is no reason to believe that provisions should not be made resulting from legal requirements [Companies Act 1985, Schedule 4, para. 12(b)].

5. There was no rule in the UK at the time, nor even a Statement of Principles (except in draft). These provisions would depend on a series of other factors.

6. The "R" results from the answer to (1) above.

7–8. For most other countries, the reference for these items in O&S is to the cost of inventories. Using the same for the UK (i.e. OKPMG VI·4), the scores are both "R" for "appropriate" costs. See SSAP 9, paragraphs 19, 20.

9. For five other countries, an "A" is recorded in O&S for percentage provisions. The same applies in the UK, which should therefore also be an "A".

10. No specific rule is mentioned in OKPMG. I can find none elsewhere. By analogy with provisions, discounting would now be appropriate (FRS 12, para. 45). This suggests that it must have been legally allowed, since the law has not changed.

11 D'Arcy (p.332) says that she only considers the rules related to listed companies. The exemption, for small groups, from the preparation of consolidated statements does not apply to any group containing a public company (Companies Act 1985, s.248).

12. O&S record "F (in practice R because divergence is defined very stringently)". Because it is the *definition* that is stringent, this suggests a code of "R" for the rule, certainly compared to the wide meaning of the rule on exclusions in several other countries.

13–14. Inclusion is forbidden by FRS 2, para. 25. O&S coded "exclusion required" rather than "inclusion forbidden".

15. The topics in O&S relating to joint ventures (JVs) only make sense in the context of JV legal entities. That is, JV operations are accounted for on the basis of whose assets they are. For incorporated JV entities, proportional consolidation is forbidden by the Companies Act 1985, Schedule 4A, para. 19(1). This fits with the interpretation for the US.

16. This topic relates to whether the group must follow the rules that apply to (not the choices made by) the parent. This is the case in the UK. There is a different topic relating to uniformity.

17. To be consistent with Germany and the Netherlands (where goodwill could be written off against equity), the score should be "R". The goodwill is recognised before being written off. Alternatively, the scores for Germany and the Netherlands should be changed. However, another topic already deals with the write off against equity, so that would be scoring the same point twice.

---

[15] Letter of 19 February 2002.

C. Nobes / Accounting, Organizations and Society 29 (2004) 189–200   197

Appendix C. Amendments to the data relating to the US

Topic	O&S page	Issue	O&S score	Amended score	D'Arcy (1999) variables
1	13	Capitalisation of formation expenses and costs of capital	R	F	1/2
2	25	Inclusion of general administration costs	R	F	35/36
3	25	Inclusion of social costs, pensions, etc.	F	R	37/38
4	25	Equity method required in investor statements	R	A	42
5	47	Group must follow rules that apply to parent	N	Y	94
6	67	Netting of deferred tax assets and liabilities forbidden except if relating to the same tax-paying entity	Y	N	129

Explanations of the above amendments:

1. Until the AICPA's SOP 98-5 of 1998 (which prohibits capitalisation), there was no promulgated GAAP concerning formation expenses, which are generally immaterial. The SEC would not generally allow the capitalisation of start-up and pre-operating costs (OKPMG, p.3060). The costs of raising capital are set off against the proceeds. Consequently for one issue (generally immaterial), the score should have been (in 1995) "A", and for the other issue "F". The fact that an IRS guideline allows the deductibility if the costs are amortised is not relevant to the financial reporting requirements of listed groups.
2. Specifically excluded (OKPMG, VI·5·2·1).
3. Social/pension/etc. costs would be treated like wages (OKPMG, VI·5·2·2).
4. It is presumed that the issue here is the unconsolidated statements of an investor/parent. The equity method was required for these by APB 18 but this was repealed by SFAS 94 (see OKPMG, p.3149). The OKPMG reference (VI·6·5) appears to be dealing with the special case where an investor has no subsidiaries.
5. The topic relates to whether the group must follow the rules that apply to (not the choices made by) the parent. In the US, there is only one GAAP. Therefore, the answer is Y.
6. Anne d'Arcy notes[16] that this question relates to whether netting is allowed beyond the individual tax-paying entity. OKPMG (p.3157) confirms that it is not.

---

[16] Letter of 6 May 2002.

Appendix D. Revisions to Australia, UK and US codes

D'Arcy (1999) Variable	Australia	UK	US	Germany
1	0	0	1→0	0
2	0	1	0→1	1
3 (Delete)[a]	0	1	0	1
5	0	1→0	0	0
6 (Delete)[a]	1	0	1	0
7 (Delete)[a]	0	1	0	1
10 (Delete)[a]	0	0	0	0
11 (Delete)[a]	0	1	1	1
12	0	1→0	0	0
14	0→1	0	1	0
17	1→0	0	0	0
18	0	0→1	1	0
21	0→1	0→1	1	1
22	1→0	1→0	0	0
23	0→1	1	1	1
24	0	1→0	0	0
25	1→0	0	1	0
26	1→0	0	0	0
27	0→1	1	1	1
29	0	1→0	0	1
34	1	0→1	1	0
35	1→0	0	1→0	0
36	0→1	1	0→1	0
37	1	0→1	0→1	0
38	0	1→0	1→0	0
42	0	0	1→0	0
64	0	1→0	0	0
66	0	1→0	0	1
73	1	0→1	1	0
78	0→1	1	0	1
80	1	0→1	1	0
81	0	1→0	0	1
82	0	1→0	0	0
83	1	0→1	1	0
84	1	1→0	0	0
85	0	0→1	1	0
86	0→1	1	1	0
88	1	0→1	1	0
94	1	0→1	0→1	1
95	1→0	0	0	0
109	1	0→1	1	1
129	1	0	0→1	0

[a] The variables concern distribuability of income.

C. Nobes / Accounting, Organizations and Society 29 (2004) 189–200

Appendix E. Effects of Appendix D on the number of variables with the same code for each pair of countries

D'Arcy Variable	Aus/UK	Aus/US	UK/US	Germany/Aus	Germany/UK	Germany/US
1	–	+1	+1	–	–	+1
2	–	−1	+1	–	–	+1
3	–	−1	–	–	−1	–
5	+1	–	+1	–	+1	–
6	–	−1	–	–	−1	–
7	–	−1	–	–	−1	–
10	−1	−1	−1	−1	−1	−1
11	–	–	−1	–	−1	−1
12	+1	–	+1	–	+1	–
14	−1	+1	–	−1	–	–
17	+1	+1	–	+1	–	–
18	−1	–	+1	–	−1	–
21	–	+1	+1	+1	+1	–
22	–	+1	+1	+1	+1	–
23	+1	+1	–	+1	–	–
24	+1	–	+1	–	+1	–
25	+1	−1	–	+1	–	–
26	+1	+1	–	+1	–	–
27	+1	+1	–	+1	–	–
29	+1	–	+1	–	−1	–
34	+1	–	+1	–	−1	–
35	+1	–	+1	+1	–	+1
36	+1	–	+1	−1	–	−1
37	+1	+1	–	–	−1	−1
38	+1	+1	–	–	+1	+1
42	–	+1	+1	–	–	+1
64	+1	–	+1	–	+1	–
66	+1	–	+1	–	−1	–
73	+1	–	+1	–	−1	–
78	+1	−1	–	+1	–	–
80	+1	–	+1	–	−1	–
81	+1	–	+1	–	−1	–
82	+1	–	+1	–	+1	–
83	+1	–	+1	–	−1	–
84	−1	–	+1	–	+1	–
85	−1	–	+1	–	−1	–
86	+1	+1	–	−1	–	–
88	+1	+1	+1	–	−1	–
94	+1	+1	–	−1	+1	+1
95	+1	+1	–	+1	–	–
109	+1	–	+1	–	+1	–
129	–	+1	−1	–	–	−1
Total	+22	+9	+21	+5	−5	+1

References

Alexander, A., Archer, S., Delvaille, P., & Taupin, V. (1996). Provisions and contingencies: an Anglo-French investigation. *European Accounting Review, 5*, 271–298.

Brooks, J. P., & Mertin, D. (1993). *Deutsches Bilanzrecht.* Düsseldorf: IdW.

Curran, B. (1996). *A comparative study of Australian and international accounting standards.* Sydney: Coopers & Lybrand.

Da Costa, R. C., Bourgeois, J. C., & Lawson, W. M. (1978). A classification of international financial accounting practices. *International Journal of Accounting, Spring*, 73–85.

d'Arcy, A. (1999). *Gibt es eine anglo-amerikanische oder eine kontinentaleuropäische Rechnungslegung?* Frankfurt am Main: Peter Lang.

d'Arcy, A. (2000). The degree of determination of national accounting systems: an empirical investigation. *Schmalenbach Business Review, January*, 45–67.

d'Arcy, A. (2001). Accounting classification and the international harmonisation debate—an empirical investigation. *Accounting, Organizations and Society, 26*, 327–349.

Goodrich, P. S. (1982). A typology of international accounting principles and policies. *AUTA Review, 14*, 37–61.

Gordon, I., & Morris, R. D. (1999). The equity accounting saga in Australia: cyclical standard setting. *Abacus, September*, 153–177.

IFAD. (2001). *GAAP 2001: a survey of national accounting rules benchmarked against international accounting standards.* London: Andersen, and other firms (also at http://www.ifad.net).

Nobes, C. W. (1982). A typology of international accounting principles and policies. *AUTA Review, 14*, 62–65.

Nobes, C. W. (1983). A judgmental international classification of financial reporting practices. *Journal of Business Finance and Accounting, 10*(1), 1–19.

Nobes, C. W. (1992). *International classification of financial reporting (2nd ed).* London: Routledge.

Nobes, C. W. (1998). Towards a general model of the reasons for international differences in financial reporting. *Abacus, 34*(2), 162–187.

Nobes, C. W. (2001). Transnational Accounting. *Accountancy, April*, 144.

Nobes, C. W. (2003). On the myth of 'Anglo-Saxon' financial accounting: a comment. *International Journal of Accounting, 38*(1), 95–104.

Nobes, C. W., & Matatko, J. (1980). Classification of national systems of financial accounting. *AUTA Review, 12*, 57–78.

Ordelheide, D., & KPMG (Eds.). (1995). *Transnational accounting.* London: Macmillan.

Ordelheide, D., & KPMG (Eds.). (2001). *Transnational accounting.* Basingstoke: Palgrave.

Ordelheide, D. & Semler, A. (1995). A reference matrix. In D. Ordelheide and KPMG (Eds.) *Transnational accounting* (1–67).

Roberts, A. D. (1995). The very idea of classification in international accounting. *Accounting, Organizations and Society, 20*, 639–664.

[8]

Christopher Nobes

Accounting Classification in the IFRS Era

This paper investigates international differences in the way in which countries and companies have responded to IFRS. At the country level, some (for example, Cyprus) have adopted IFRS for all financial reporting, some have made a special national version for all reporting (for example, Australia), some have required IFRS for consolidated reporting by listed companies and allowed it for other reporting (for example, the UK), some have required it for certain purposes but not allowed it for others (for example, France), while some have not yet allowed it for any purpose (for example, the US, except for foreign companies). Where domestic accounting survives for at least one purpose, some countries are converging domestic accounting with IFRS (for example, the UK and the US), while others have made few such changes (for example, Germany and Italy in 2007). Several countries have converged national accounting with IFRS, but only for some reporting entities (for example, China for listed companies). At the company level, there are many differences of practice within IFRS, and specific national versions of IFRS practice are emerging.

As a result of all this, global comparability (especially for listed companies) has been improved by the arrival of IFRS, but there is still a long way to go. This paper uses the technique of classification of accounting systems to investigate the different national approaches to IFRS, and the reasons for them. The topic is relevant for companies, auditors and investors who operate internationally. It also comprises an extension and updating of the academic literature on classification.

Accounting classifications are the focus of some of the earliest writings on international accounting (for example, Hatfield 1911, published 1966; Seidler 1967; Mueller 1967, 1968; Buckley and Buckley 1974; AAA 1977; da Costa et al. 1978; Frank 1979). Classification was also, and still is, a natural introductory topic in textbooks on international accounting (for example, Choi and Mueller 1992: chapter 2; Roberts, Weetman and Gordon 2005: chapter 6; Walton, Haller and Raffournier 2003: chapter 1; Choi and Meek 2005: chapter 2; Radebaugh, Gray and Black 2006: chapter 2; Nobes and Parker 2008: chapter 3).

Classification, if done well, can help to organise a mass of data. It can sharpen description and analysis,

The degree to which, and the purposes for which, International Financial Reporting Standards (IFRS) have been adopted vary internationally. This paper uses classification techniques in order to investigate the reaction of countries, or companies within them, to IFRS. In addition, this paper investigates five aspects of this; for example, whether European countries mandate IFRS for unconsolidated financial reports. Previous classifications in accounting are used to help to predict and explain this.

Correspondence
Chris Nobes, School of Management, Royal Holloway, Egham TW20 0EX, United Kingdom. email: chris.nobes@rhul.ac.uk

doi: 10.1111/j.1835-2561.2008.0024.x

and reveal underlying structures. Sometimes it might explain, or enable prediction of, behaviour because members of a class can be expected to behave more similarly to each other than to members of other classes.

However, as explained later, criticisms have been made of the data used for classifications, of the results obtained, of the notion of 'Anglo-Saxon accounting', and even of 'the very idea of classification' (Roberts 1995). Furthermore, most listed companies are now using either IFRS or the generally accepted accounting principles of the United States (US GAAP), or rules based closely on them, at least for their consolidated statements. So, what is there to classify? In 2007, the Securities and Exchange Commission (SEC) announced the acceptance of IFRS for its foreign registrants, and began consultation on allowing IFRS for US companies (for example, SEC 2007). So the day when there may be one system rather than two for listed companies can now be foreseen more clearly. In this present or that future world, how can classification still be useful? This paper addresses that question.

Literature

Lack of clarity in what is being classified (see explanation in Roberts 1995) will reduce the quality of a classification. It is proposed here that, ideally, the objects to be classified in international accounting are financial reporting practices. An 'accounting system' is a set of reporting practices. If a set of reporting *rules* is detailed and well enforced on a particular category of companies, then they will exhibit a particular system. An example is that US-listed companies use US GAAP.

Several researchers have examined variables that might *affect* financial reporting practices (Seidler 1967; Mueller 1967, 1968; Buckley and Buckley 1974: 139–40; AAA 1977; Puxty et al. 1987; Gray 1988; Doupnik and Salter 1995; Nobes 1998a). These variables are at one or two removes from accounting practices.

Other researchers have, at first sight, made classifications based on financial reporting itself. However, those that use Price Waterhouse data (for example, da Costa et al. 1978; Frank 1979; Nair and Frank 1980) suffer from two problems: (a) the data mix practices and rules; and (b) the data contain errors (Nobes 1981). Classifications based on KPMG data (d'Arcy 2001) also have problems: (a) the data concern rules only; and (b) even the careful interpretation of the data generates errors (Nobes 2004). Nobes (1983) uses mostly (but not entirely) impressions of reporting practices, and Doupnik and Salter (1993) use reporting practices.

A two-group classification comprising 'Anglo-Saxon' and other has been a feature of some of the literature (for example, Nobes 1983 and 1998a), although a

concentration on the *differences* between the UK and the US is clear in Hatfield (1911), da Costa et al. (1978) and Frank (1979). Cairns (1997), Alexander and Archer (2000), and d'Arcy (2001) specifically question the two-group classification. Feige (1997) criticises some aspects of the labelling of the two groups, but not really the existence or contents of the groups. Nobes (1981; 1998b; 2003; 2004) suggests that criticisms of the two-group classifications are based on the use of incorrect data, or concentration on a few very large companies that are not following the normal rules for their country, or concentration on peripheral non-reporting features.

If a two-group classification can be justified, it might prove a valuable descriptor, explainer and predictor. Despite all the criticism, the two-group classification is, in practice, frequently adopted in the literature (for example, Guenther and Young 2000; Hung 2000; Ali and Hwang 2000; Benston et al. 2006: chapter 9; Ball et al. 2000; La Porta et al. 1997, 1998; Choi and Meek 2005: 56–9; Radebaugh et al. 2006: 55, 62; Walton et al. 2003: 6, 8). This paper will specify a two-group classification including a large number of countries, and then see if it can be used for explanation and prediction.

A Detailed Two-group Classification

I classify the member states of the European Union (EU) in 2006 plus two substantial countries outside the EU: Norway and Switzerland, which both have close ties with the EU. This 27-nation bloc is clearly defined economically and geographically, and there is useful accounting data on it, as will be seen below.

I will use my own previous writings to prepare the classification, so that readers can confirm that the classification has not been contrived *ex post* in order to prove the hypotheses raised. I apologise to readers for the amount of self-citation that this will imply.

The Nobes (1983) classification contains only nine of the above 27 European countries (see the Appendix), partly because another eight of the countries had communist regimes at the time and therefore no 'financial reporting', and partly because some of the other countries are very small. However, Nobes (1992a: 127–9) includes 14 of the countries (see Appendix). Using the same techniques and some more recent writings, the Appendix classifies the remaining 13 countries. The result is shown as Table 1, with IFRS added, in accordance with Nobes (1998a). It is intended that the objects being classified in Table 1 are not countries but accounting systems (that is, the set of financial reporting practices) as under national laws and standards. It is admitted that, in several cases, the previous writings used proxies to assess accounting practices.

Table 1 A two-group accounting classification

Class A (strong equity, commercially driven)	Class B (weak equity, government driven, tax-dominated)
Cyprus	Austria
Denmark	Belgium
Ireland	Czech Republic
Malta	Estonia
Netherlands	Finland
Norway	France
UK	Germany
IFRS	Greece
	Hungary
	Italy
	Latvia
	Lithuania
	Luxembourg
	Poland
	Portugal
	Slovakia
	Slovenia
	Spain
	Sweden
	Switzerland

Source: see Appendix.

Table 2 Whether European countries mandate national rules for unconsolidated accounting

Not required	Required
Cyprus	Austria
Denmark	Belgium
Estonia	Czech Republic[1]
Ireland	France
Italy	Germany[2]
Luxembourg	Hungary
Malta	Latvia
Netherlands	Lithuania
Norway	Poland[1]
Slovenia	Portugal
UK	Slovakia[3]
	Spain
	Sweden
	Switzerland

[1] Except for listed companies.
[2] Required for tax and distribution accounting, but for large companies, not for publication.
[3] Except for 'public interest' companies.
Source: <http://ec.europa.eu/internal_market/accounting/docs/ias/ias-use-of-options_en.pdf> accessed on 5 May 2007.

How Accounting Classification Might Still Be Useful

This section explains five ways in which classification might still be helpful in the IFRS era. First, the degree to which national regulators allow or require IFRS for various purposes differs. This can be presented as a classification; one that could have been predicted by previous classifications. Second, in many countries that have adopted IFRS for consolidated reporting by listed companies, the great bulk of accounting nevertheless continues under national rules. These national systems continue to differ and can be classified as before. Third, the degree to which those individual national systems are converging with IFRS differs, in a way that classification can predict. Fourth, whether foreign countries' accounting systems are acceptable on particular exchanges, because they are IFRS or converging to IFRS, can be explained by classification. Last, different national versions of IFRS practice are emerging, and these can perhaps be classified.

These proposed ways in which classification might still be useful are now examined.

National reactions to IFRS

In some jurisdictions (for example, Australia), IFRS or a version of it is required for all corporate financial reporting: consolidated and unconsolidated, for listed companies and unlisted. By contrast, in other jurisdictions where IFRS is required for the consolidated

reporting of listed companies, unconsolidated reporting is still *allowed* to use national rules (for example, in Denmark, the Netherlands or the UK) or is *required* to do so (for example, in Belgium, France and Spain).

Let us take the example of the 27 countries included in Table 1. For these, Table 2 shows whether or not companies are *required* to continue to use national accounting rules for unconsolidated accounting. Finland and Greece are excluded because different companies are treated differently: large companies with certain types of auditors are not required to use national rules, although the bulk of companies are.

The simple classification of Table 2 illustrates the 'sharpens description' use of a classification. It tells a story simply and clearly. However, as usual, the truth is more complicated than can easily be captured in a classification, as the footnotes to Table 2 explain. For example, some larger German companies are allowed to publish IFRS unconsolidated statements, but only if they also prepare statements under national rules for the purposes of the calculation of taxable and distributable profits (Haller and Eierle 2004).

Would previous accounting classifications have enabled a prediction of Table 2, and do they help to explain it? A prediction from the literature would be that countries in the right-hand column of Table 1 would not allow IFRS for unconsolidated accounting, as now explained. First, the use of IFRS would change profit figures, so in countries where tax and accounting are closely linked, the rules for the calculation of taxable income would in effect be put in the hands of the IASB, which is specifically uninterested in tax (IASB *Framework*, para. 6). This would obviously be politically and economically unacceptable. In principle, tax and financial reporting could be de-coupled in such countries, but that would be a major philosophical and practical problem. The same reasoning applies to the calculation of prudently distributable income, which again rests directly on accounting numbers in, for example, Germany but is de-coupled in various ways in the UK.[1] So, Germany could not easily allow the use of IFRS for the calculation of distributable income. Another issue is that, in some right-hand column countries, some of the requirements of IFRS are seen as unsatisfactory for legal reasons related to unconsolidated reporting. For example, in France, the capitalisation of finance leases as required by IFRS is regarded as showing fictitious assets on an entity's balance sheet, thus misleading creditors (for example, Standish 2000: 200).

Would the classification of Table 1 have successfully predicted Table 2? The relevant hypothesis can be stated as:

H_1 A country with a national accounting system on the right in Table 1 will not allow IFRS for unconsolidated accounting (that is, the country will also be on the right in Table 2).

The null hypothesis is:

H_{01} The classification of countries in Table 2 is only associated by chance with the classification in Table 1.

A chi-square test enables one to reject the null hypothesis at more than 99% significance. So, H_1 can be accepted. Indeed, the only countries that are not correctly classified by using Table 1 are Estonia, Italy and Luxembourg. Estonia has presumably taken the view that it wishes to move as fast as possible from its communist past to modern, international practice. Luxembourg has a long history of extending to companies any choices that are available within EU rules (Clark 1994: 107). One explanation for Italy granting permission to use IFRS is that Italy also likes to be seen as modern and international, and that in practice companies will not volunteer to use IFRS for their unconsolidated statements because they would then have to produce a different set for tax purposes. Nevertheless, in principle, tax and financial reporting can now be separate in Italy, which is a major change to law.[2]

The analysis of this section can be extended to other countries. For example, because Australia, New Zealand and South Africa would be on the left of Table 1 (for example, see Nobes 1992a: 127), they would be on the left of Table 2. In China, by contrast, which would have been put on the right of Table 1 (see Nobes 1998a), IFRS was only used in 2006 in the consolidated statements of some listed companies.[3]

Continuing national rules

The previous sub-section explains that, in many countries, IFRS is not allowed for unconsolidated accounting. Consequently, in Europe, IFRS is concentrated on the consolidated statements of listed companies. There are about 8000 listed companies among the millions of companies in Europe. Therefore, the great bulk of accounting in Europe and in other continents (for example, South America) continues under national accounting systems.

For multinational groups, for international audit firms and for tax authorities dealing with such entities, an appropriate classification of the accounting systems can remain a preliminary part of understanding the international differences. For example, Table 1 coupled with a list of typical accounting features to be found in the two groups (for example, Nobes 1998a: 168) would be a start for understanding European accounting differences.

Different degrees of convergence with IFRS

Given that national accounting systems have survived in many jurisdictions, at least for some purposes, a further issue is their convergence with IFRS. This process is the main explanation of change in accounting rules since 2000. The word 'convergence' is accurate when applied to the joint program of the IASB and the US's Financial Accounting Standards Board (FASB) because both have changed particular standards towards each other's[4] and have run many joint projects (for example, on performance reporting, deferred tax and revenue recognition). However, in the case of other countries, 'convergence with IFRS' is a euphemism for piecemeal adoption of IFRS.

The degree to which a jurisdiction's national accounting system is being changed towards IFRS varies. For example, in the UK, eight recent accounting standards (FRSs 20 to 26 and 29) were copies of international standards. By contrast, German rules related to unconsolidated statements (the *Handelsgesetzbuch*) had not changed at all by 2007.[5]

A hypothesis for explaining this difference between countries is similar to the first hypothesis, relating to national reactions to IFRS. That is, some aspects of IFRS can be regarded as imprudent for the calculation of distributable income and for the protection of creditors. Other aspects can be regarded as unsuitable for a tax base; for example, greater use of fair values or of estimations (such as IAS 11's percentage-of-completion method for contract accounting). Therefore, it is proposed that:

H_2 A country with a national accounting system on the right of Table 1 will be slower (than those on the left) to converge with IFRS.

It is more difficult, than for H_1, to measure this with precision. However, examples are easy to find, as in the convergence comparison of Germany and the UK above. Other systems on the left (for example, Cyprus, Malta and Australia) have been abandoned or converged out of existence. By contrast, there is no detectable movement in Belgium. This time, even Italy fits the hypothesis. It is on the right of Table 1, and its national system for unconsolidated statements has changed little since 2000.[6] It seems likely that the hypothesis could be confirmed by further research.

Acceptable accounting by foreign issuers

At the time of writing, the SEC directly accepted only US GAAP reporting from its registrants, requiring any other reporting to be reconciled to US GAAP. However, again at the time of writing, EU exchanges accept reporting in a number of GAAPs, under certain conditions related to their convergence with IFRS (CESR 2007). From 2009, it is proposed that only IFRS or accounting 'equivalent to IFRS' will be accepted.

The Committee of European Securities Regulators (CESR) has analysed whether the GAAPs used by over 90% of the issuers on European exchanges satisfy the pre-2009 conditions for acceptance by those exchanges. Table 3 summarises its conclusions, which are a combination of two issues: (a) the non-EU countries that are home jurisdictions for EU listers, and (b) whether the GAAP of those countries is converged or converging with IFRS or similar. Could the content of Table 3 have been predicted and can it be explained? The hypothesis would be that foreign-listed companies tend to come from 'strong equity' countries (in terms of Table 1), and that such countries would have accounting similar to IFRS or have adopted IFRS. So:

Table 3 Home jurisdictions of EU foreign issuers

Issuers from these countries should be able to include in the notes to the financial statements a statement of compliance with IFRS, as these countries have adopted IFRS.	• Australia • Hong Kong • New Zealand • South Africa • Singapore
These countries do not have 'national GAAP' as such and their issuers apparently apply US GAAP, IFRS or Canadian GAAP.	• Cayman Islands • Bermuda • Netherlands • Antilles • Isle of Man • Jersey • Guernsey • British Virgin Islands
The countries on the right could qualify ... as CESR found that there is a public statement of a convergence programme	• Taiwan • China • Brazil

Source: CESR (2007), p. 2.

H_3 Foreign countries whose companies list on EU exchanges and whose GAAP is, according to CESR, acceptably close to IFRS are Class A countries.

Inspection of Table 3 reveals that of the 12 jurisdictions in its top two categories of clear acceptance, 11 are present or former dependencies of the UK and one of the Netherlands. According to Nobes (1998a), all these countries would therefore be classified on the left of Table 1. We do not in this case need statistics to accept Hypothesis H_3, as there are no exceptions.

Different national versions of IFRS practice

Nobes (2006) set out the theory for the motives and opportunity for the emergence of different national versions of IFRS practice. It was suggested that variables such as financing systems, legal systems and tax systems that have been connected in the literature to the existence of international differences in accounting might still provide some motivation for different IFRS practice.

Opportunities for different IFRS practice come from, *inter alia*, the many overt options, covert options and measurement estimates in IFRS. It was suggested, for example, that Australian groups would not use proportional consolidation for joint ventures (because AASB 131 did not allow it), but that French groups might do so because of previous national practice; that UK companies are more likely than German companies to take actuarial gains and losses to 'other comprehensive income'; and that UK banks are less likely to use macro hedge accounting than French banks. If research now underway confirms, for example, that there is a typical set of UK IFRS practices that is different from a typical set of German IFRS practices, then it might be useful to classify such systems. This would be for the normal purpose of organising data and sharpening description.

Conclusions

Some countries have entirely abandoned national accounting rules in favour of IFRS; some others have almost done so by turning a version of IFRS into national standards. Other countries use IFRS for some purposes, either compulsorily or voluntarily. Where national accounting systems survive, some are converging with IFRS and some are not. Even where IFRS is used, different companies can still retain different practices. The differences are associated with previous national accounting traditions and the previous reasons for international differences.

This paper uses classification to illustrate how countries fall into groups with respect to the above issues. This should help practitioners who operate at the international level to make sense of the variety of national responses to IFRS. It reminds accountants and analysts that full international comparability has not yet been achieved, and it provides a technique for assessing where convergence has happened and where it has not.

Classifications have been a staple of the international accounting literature for nearly a century, and particularly for the last 40 years. If done well, they can be useful in organising data, which helps to sharpen description, and they can assist in predictions. Doing them well requires, *inter alia*, using correct data and being clear about what is being classified.

It has been suggested here that, even in the IFRS era, classifications can still be useful. First, previous classifications could have predicted and can explain national reactions to IFRS. This paper statistically proves a hypothesis that a requirement to continue using national rules for unconsolidated accounting is associated, in Europe, with a group of countries previously classified as 'weak equity, government-driven, tax-dominated'.

Second, previous classifications of national accounting systems are still relevant because national accounting continues in many countries even if IFRS is required for the consolidated statements of listed companies.

Third, some evidence is provided for the hypothesis that 'weak equity' countries are slower to converge their national systems with IFRS. More work is needed here.

Fourth, it would have been possible to predict, and to explain, which non-EU countries are the home to companies that list on EU exchanges and have accounting systems acceptable to the regulators of those exchanges. It has been shown that a hypothesis can be accepted that these are the 'strong equity, commercially driven' countries in previous classifications.

Finally, for further research, different national 'systems' of IFRS practice are emerging and will be classifiable.

Looking ahead, we can expect further progress in the area where comparability really matters: consolidated financial reporting by those listed companies reporting to users in more than one country. There are several reasons for this. First, much of the variety in national responses to IFRS relates to unconsolidated statements, for reasons connected to company law and tax law. This variety is likely to continue but need not hamper progress on the main issue of comparability of consolidated reporting. Second, the trend of convergence that began decades ago is likely to continue. Third, the IASB is committed to removing options and the scope for different interpretations within IFRS. Nevertheless, some of the variety investigated in this paper is likely to remain for many years, because of its deep-seated causes.

Christopher Nobes is Professor of Accounting at Royal Holloway, University of London. He is grateful to Greg

Clinch, R.H. Parker and Ann Tarca for comments on an earlier draft and to PricewaterhouseCoopers for research support.

Notes

1 For example, extra depreciation caused by revaluing assets is not deemed to affect distributable income. This and many other issues are, in effect, controlled by the accountancy bodies (for example, ICAEW 2004).

2 Legislative Decree of 28 February 2005, no. 38.

3 For 2007, new standards (ASBEs), based closely on IFRS, are in force for Chinese-listed companies, and available for others.

4 Convergence is the main explanation for the issuance of IFRS 5, IFRS 8 and IAS 23 (as revised in 2007); and of SFASs 150, 153, 154, 159.

5 Confirmation by Cornelia Flury of the *Institut der Wirtschaftsprüfer*, 26.6.2007.

6 Confirmation by Johannes Guigard, PricewaterhouseCoopers, Milan, 26.6.2007.

References

AAA 1977, *Accounting Review, Supplement to Vol. 52*, American Accounting Association: 65–132.

Alexander, A. and S. Archer 2000, 'On the myth of Anglo-Saxon financial accounting', *International Journal of Accounting*, 35, 4: 539–57.

Ali, A. and L.-S. Hwang 2000, 'Country-specific factors related to financial reporting and the value relevance of accounting data', *Journal of Accounting Research*, 38, 1: 1–22.

Ball, R., S.P. Kothari and A. Robin 2000, 'The effect of international institutional factors on properties of accounting earnings', *Journal of Accounting and Economics*, 29, 1: 1–51.

Benston, G.J., M. Bromwich, R.E. Litan and A. Wagenhofer 2006, *Worldwide Financial Reporting*, Oxford University Press, Oxford.

Buckley, J.W. and M.H. Buckley 1974, *The Accounting Profession*, Melville, Los Angeles.

Cairns, D. 1997, 'The future shape of harmonization: A reply', *European Accounting Review*, 6, 2: 305–48.

CESR 2007, 'CESR work to date in relation to the European Commission's measures on the use of third countries' GAAP in the EU,' ref. 07-022b, *Committee of European Securities Regulators*, Paris, April.

Choi, F. and G. Meek 2005, *International Accounting*, Prentice Hall, Upper Saddle River, New Jersey.

Choi, F. and G. Mueller 1992, *International Accounting*, Prentice Hall, Englewood Cliffs, New Jersey.

Clark, P. 1994, *European Financial Reporting: Luxembourg*, Routledge, London.

d'Arcy, A. 2001, 'Accounting classification and the international harmonisation debate – An empirical investigation', *Accounting, Organizations and Society*, 26: 327–49.

da Costa, R.C., J.C. Bourgeois and W.M. Lawson 1978, 'A classification of international financial accounting practices', *International Journal of Accounting*, 13, 2: 73–85.

Doupnik, T.S. and S.B. Salter 1993, 'An empirical test of a judgemental international classification of financial reporting practices', *Journal of International Business Studies*, 24, 1: 41–60.

Doupnik, T.S. and S.B. Salter 1995, 'External environment, culture, and accounting practice: A preliminary test of a general model of international accounting development', *International Journal of Accounting*, 30, 3: 189–207.

Feige, P. 1997, 'How "uniform" is financial reporting in Germany? The example of foreign currency translation', *European Accounting Review*, 6, 1: 109–22.

Frank, W.G. 1979, 'An empirical analysis of international accounting principles', *Journal of Accounting Research*, 17: 593–605.

Gray, S.J. 1988, 'Towards a theory of cultural influence on the development of accounting systems internationally', *Abacus*, 24, 1: 1–15.

Guenther, D.A. and D. Young 2000, 'The association between financial accounting measures and real economic activity: A multinational study', *Journal of Accounting and Economics*, 29, 1: 53–72.

Haller, A. and B. Eierle 2004, 'The adaptation of German accounting rules to IFRS: A legislative balancing act', *Accounting in Europe*, 1: 27–50.

Hatfield, A. 1911, published 1966, 'Some variations in accounting practices in England, France, Germany and the US', *Journal of Accounting Research*, 4, 2: 169–182.

Hung, M. 2000, 'Accounting standards and value relevance of financial statements: An international analysis', *Journal of Accounting and Economics*, 30, 3: 401–20.

ICAEW 2004, *Guidance on the Effect on Realised and Distributable Profits of Accounting for Employee Share Schemes . . .*, Technical Release 64/04, Institute of Chartered Accountants in England and Wales, London.

La Porta, R., F. Lopez-de-Silanes, A. Shleifer and R.W. Vishny 1997, 'Legal determinants of external finance', *Journal of Finance*, 52, 3: 1131–50.

La Porta, R., F. Lopez-de-Silanes, A. Shleifer and R.W. Vishny 1998, 'Law and finance', *Journal of Political Economy*, 106, 6: 1113–54.

Mueller, G.G. 1967, *International Accounting*, Part I, Macmillan, New York.

Mueller, G.G. 1968, 'Accounting principles generally accepted in the United States versus those generally accepted elsewhere', *International Journal of Accounting*, 3, 1: 91–103.

Nair, R.D. and W.G. Frank 1980, 'The impact of disclosure and measurement practices on international accounting classifications', *Accounting Review*, 55, 3: 426–50.

Nobes, C.W. 1981, 'An empirical analysis of international accounting principles: A comment', *Journal of Accounting Research*, 19, 1: 268–70.

Nobes, C.W. 1983, 'A judgmental international classification of financial reporting practices', *Journal of Business Finance and Accounting*, 10, 1: 1–19.

Nobes, C.W. 1992a, *International Classification of Financial Reporting* (2nd edition), Routledge, London.

Nobes, C.W. 1992b, *Accounting Comparisons: UK/Europe*, Vol. III, Gee & Co., London.

Nobes, C.W. 1992c, *Accounting Comparisons: UK/Europe*, Vol. IV, Gee & Co., London.

Nobes, C.W. 1992d, *Accounting Comparisons: UK/Europe*, Vol. V, Gee & Co., London.

Nobes, C.W. 1998a, 'Towards a general model of the reasons for international differences in financial reporting', *Abacus*, 34, 2: 162–87.

Nobes, C.W. 1998b, 'The future shape of harmonization: Some responses', *European Accounting Review*, 7, 2: 323–33.

Nobes, C.W. 2003, 'On the myth of "Anglo-Saxon" accounting: A comment', *International Journal of Accounting*, 38, 1: 95–104.

Nobes, C.W. 2004, 'On accounting classification and the international harmonisation debate', *Accounting, Organizations and Society*, 29, 2: 189–200.

Nobes, C.W. 2006, 'The survival of international differences under IFRS: Towards a research agenda', *Accounting and Business Research*, 36, 3: 233–45.

Nobes, C.W. and R.H. Parker 2004, *Comparative International Accounting*, Prentice Hall, Harlow.

Nobes, C.W. and R.H. Parker 2008, *Comparative International Accounting*, Prentice Hall, Harlow.

Nobes, C.W. and H.R. Schwencke 2006, 'Modelling the links between tax and financial reporting: A longitudinal examination of Norway over 30 years up to IFRS adoption', *European Accounting Review*, 15, 1: 63–87.

Puxty, A.G., H.C. Willmott, D.J. Cooper and T. Lowe 1987, 'Modes of regulation in advanced capitalism: Locating accountancy in four countries', *Accounting, Organizations and Society*, 12, 3: 273–91.

Radebaugh, L., S. Gray and E. Black 2006, *International Accounting and Multinational Enterprises*, Wiley, Hoboken, New Jersey.

Roberts, A.D. 1995, 'The very idea of classification in international accounting', *Accounting, Organizations and Society*, 20, 7/8: 639–64.

Roberts, C., P. Weetman and P. Gordon 2005, *International Financial Reporting*, Prentice Hall, Harlow.

SEC 2007, 'SEC announces next steps relating to international financial reporting standards', *Securities and Exchange Commission*, 24 April, Washington DC.

Seidler, L.J. 1967, 'International accounting – The ultimate theory course', *Accounting Review*, 42, 4: 775–81.

Standish, P.E.M. 2000, 'Financial reporting in France', in C.W. Nobes and R.H. Parker (eds), *Comparative International Accounting*, Prentice Hall, Harlow.

Walton, P., A. Haller and B. Raffournier 2003, *International Accounting*, Thomson, London.

Appendix: Table 1 Explanation

Nobes (1983) classifies 14 countries, including nine European ones. These are shown with single asterisks in Table A1. Nobes (1992a: 127–9) contains these nine plus a further five countries shown with two asterisks in Table A1. The remaining 13 countries in the table are classified as follows. Slovenia and the three small Baltic states were not included in the above literature, but are classified like the other former communist states of the EU. Cyprus and Malta were again too small to be included. They are former British colonies and therefore classified on the left in accordance with Nobes (1998a). Austria, Denmark, Finland, Greece, Luxembourg, Norway and Portugal are classified using various of the author's publications that comment on

them (Nobes 1992b: 3; Nobes 1992c: 3; Nobes 1992d: 2–3; Nobes and Parker 2004: 317; Nobes and Schwencke 2006).

Table A1 A two-group accounting classification

Class A (strong equity, commercially driven)	Class B (weak equity, government driven, tax-dominated)
Ireland*	Belgium*
Netherlands*	France*
UK*	Germany*
Cyprus	Italy*
Denmark	Spain*
Malta	Sweden*
Norway	Czech Republic**
	Hungary**
	Poland**
	Slovakia**
	Switzerland**
	Austria
	Estonia
	Finland
	Greece
	Latvia
	Lithuania
	Luxembourg
	Portugal
	Slovenia

* = in Nobes (1983).
** = added in Nobes (1992a).

PART III

INTERNATIONAL FINANCIAL REPORTING STANDARDS

[9]

Accounting Horizons
Vol. 19, No. 1
March 2005
pp. 25–34

Rules-Based Standards and the Lack of Principles in Accounting

Christopher W. Nobes

INTRODUCTION

In September 2002, the Financial Accounting Standards Board (FASB) of the United States published a discussion paper seeking views on whether U.S. standard setting should move from a "rules-based" approach toward a "principles-based" approach as sometimes associated with the International Accounting Standards Board (IASB). That paper was partly in response to the Sarbanes-Oxley Act, which was itself a response to such accounting scandals as Enron and WorldCom.

Schipper (2003) points out that the U.S. rules are often based on principles. That is, the standard setters use principles in order to produce the rules for the preparers of financial statements. Nelson (2003, 91) agrees, and suggests that a particular standard should rather be seen as more or less rules-based. He suggests that rules can increase the accuracy with which standard setters communicate their requirements and can reduce the sort of imprecision that leads to aggressive reporting choices by management. However, he notes that rules can also lead to excessive complexity and to the structuring of transactions.

One of the reasons why standards on several topics need to contain rules is that the standards are inconsistent with the conceptual frameworks of the standard setters. For several topics, the use of the appropriate principle could lead to clearer communication and to more precision without the need for the current rules. That is, before asking how rules-based a particular standard should be, we should ask whether the standard is based on the most appropriate principle.

I identify six topics on which the accounting standards have detailed technical rules. In each case, I suggest that part of the need for rules is caused by a lack of principle or by the use of an inappropriate principle (i.e., one that does not fit with higher-level principles). The lack of clear and appropriate principles can also lead to optional accounting methods in standards because no one policy is obviously the correct one; this leads to lack of comparability. I do not suggest that the use of appropriate principles would lead inexorably to standards with no optional methods but that, on some topics, optional methods could be eliminated.

The six topics are examined one by one. In each case, I attempt to locate the principles being used, to assess the appropriateness of the principles, and then to identify any arbitrary rules or optional methods that result from the absence of appropriate principles. I start with the IASB's standards (hereafter, IFRSs), with frequent comparison with U.S. GAAP. One reason for examining

Christopher W. Nobes is a Professor at the University of Reading, England.

Professor Nobes is grateful for comments on earlier drafts from David Alexander, Erlend Kvaal, R. H. Parker, Alan Roberts, and from the editor and two reviewers of this journal.

Submitted: February 2004
Accepted: October 2004
Corresponding author: Christopher W. Nobes
Email: c.w.nobes@reading.ac.uk

IFRSs in particular is that they are required for the financial reporting of listed companies throughout much of the world in 2005 onward,[1] and the FASB has announced plans for convergence of its standards with IFRSs.[2] The final section of the paper draws conclusions about how accounting might be improved by substituting principles (or better principles) for the existing requirements.

PRIOR LITERATURE AND PURPOSE OF THIS PAPER

Alexander (1999) investigates the nature of principles and rules in an accounting context. Below, I use the word "principles" to include Alexander's type A overall criteria (e.g., fair presentation, the definitions of elements of accounting and, in particular, the primacy of the asset and liability definitions) and his type B conventions (e.g., prudence). Such principles are contained in the standard setters' conceptual frameworks. I contrast this to "rules" which are Alexander's type C rules (e.g., the requirement to measure inventories at the lower of cost and market). My definition of "rules" includes Nelson's (2003, 91) "specific criteria, 'bright line' thresholds, examples, scope restrictions, exceptions, subsequent precedents, implementation guidance, etc." The use of the terms "principles" and "rules" seems broadly consistent among Alexander (1999), Nelson (2003), Schipper (2003), and me.

My purpose is not to investigate why the U.S. system tends toward the writing of rules (whether based on principles or not). Identifying the roles played by the existence since the 1930s of the Securities and Exchange Commission (SEC) as an enforcement agency and the perceived need of auditors to protect themselves from litigation by encouraging the setting of clear and detailed rules is left to Benston (1976), Zeff (1995), and future research. As discussed below, the IASB also frequently writes rules. Thus, my purpose is to evaluate how the failure to use the appropriate principles can lead any standard setter to rely too much on rules.

As noted earlier, the imposition of rules has some potential advantages. Those identified by Schipper (2003) and Nelson (2003) include:
- increased comparability;
- increased verifiability for auditors and regulators (and a related reduction in litigation);
- reduced opportunities for earnings management through judgments (but increased opportunities through transaction structuring); and
- improved communication of standard setters' intentions.

Nelson (2003) and the American Accounting Association's Financial Accounting Standards Committee (FASC) (2003) review the literature related to these issues. FASC concludes:

> Concepts-based standards, *if applied properly*, better support the FASB's stated mission of "improving the usefulness of financial reporting by focusing on the primary characteristics of relevance and reliability." (AAA FASC 2003, 74) (emphasis added)

In addition to balancing the advantages and disadvantages of more detailed rules, the standard setters sometimes face competing principles. An obvious example is the difficulty of trading off relevance and reliability: for instance, estimates of current values or future cash flows might be potentially relevant data, but some such estimates have low reliability. Departure from one principle might be justified by the need to follow another one.

Standard setters are also subject to political pressure, especially from the management of large companies (e.g., Hope and Gray 1982; Solomons 1978; Watts and Zimmerman 1978; Nobes 1992; Zeff 1997). Giving way to political pressure might be an explanation for departing from principles. However, a bad standard cannot be re-classified as a good one because issuing it enabled the standard setter to survive.

---

[1] For example, this is a requirement for consolidated statements in the 25 countries of the European Union, and in Australia, Norway, and Russia.

[2] The "Norwalk Agreement" of September 2002 between FASB and IASB.

As noted earlier, my purpose is to identify several accounting topics for which the accounting standard could be improved by being based more closely on a principle from the conceptual frameworks. In some cases, merely removing a rogue "principle" that is not contained in the conceptual frameworks is sufficient. The improvements come in the form of increased clarity, decreased complexity, and decreased motivation for the structuring of transactions. That is, in some cases, increased clarity can be associated with a *reduction* in rules.

This is not to say that principles-based standards are always clearer than rules-based standards. For example, development costs can represent an asset that meets reasonable recognition criteria; IAS No. 38 (para. 57) is based on this argument. In this context, the U.S. requirement (in SFAS No. 2) to expense development costs could be seen as an un-principled rule. However, in this case, the U.S. "rule" leads to a clearer instruction and to several resulting advantages (see above), although not necessarily to a better balance sheet.

Because some accounting topics are not susceptible to solution by use of appropriate principles without rules, standard setters are then forced to choose, for example, between an unclear principle and a clear rule. However, I and most other authors quoted above do not welcome rules for their own sake. They should be kept to the minimum necessary to achieve the various advantages claimed for them, such as clarity. This warrants an examination of each accounting topic to see if a more appropriate principle could achieve the advantages of rules and yet reduce the amount of rules at the same time.

As mentioned earlier, the use of appropriate principles can reduce optional accounting treatments, with a consequent increase in comparability. I am not talking here of judgments by preparers, but of overt optional methods in accounting standards. Optional methods are not prevalent in U.S. accounting standards, although some exist.[3] However, several options continue to exist in IFRS even after the removal of many in December 2003. The options were needed to achieve a three-quarters majority on the IASC Board, but arguing for the options was easier in the absence of clear principles. Using appropriate principles does not guarantee a reduction in options, but the discussion below finds several instances where a focus on principles can reduce options.

EXAMPLES
Lease Accounting

I begin with the well-known case of the capitalization of leases. The IFRS requires[4] that a lease should be capitalized as an asset and a liability when it "transfers substantially all the risks and rewards" to the lessee. The IFRS contains no numerical or other technical rules surrounding that vague principle, which is itself based on the principle of substance over form. In order to make the same principle practicable and auditable in the U.S., SFAS No. 13 requires[5] capitalization when any one of four technical tests is satisfied, including cases where the length of the lease equals or exceeds 75 percent of the useful life of the asset or where the present value of the lease payments equals or exceeds 90 percent of the fair value of the asset. These rules bring several of the advantages mentioned above (e.g., clarity and verifiability) although, as AAA FASC (2003) points out, the bright lines lead to the structuring of leases so that the lease liabilities can be kept off the balance sheet.

This is an example of the FASB making a rule that is based on a principle: substance over form. However, I contend that the IFRS's vagueness and the SFAS's arbitrary detail are caused by using the wrong principle. The more appropriate principles are the definitions of assets and liabilities. For reference, the IASB's definitions are shown in Exhibit 1. McGregor (1996) and Nailor and Lennard

---

[3] For example, the choices for the presentation of comprehensive income in SFAS No. 130; and the choice not to use the "corridor" in SFAS No. 87 (see later).

[4] IAS No. 17, paras. 4 and 20.

[5] SFAS No. 13, para. 7; SFAS No. 29, paras. 10 and 11.

EXHIBIT 1
IASB's Definitions of Asset and Liability

An asset is a resource controlled by the entity as a result of past events and from which future economic benefits are expected to flow to the entity.

A liability is a present obligation of the entity arising from past events, the settlement of which is expected to result in an outflow from the entity of resources embodying economic benefits.

Source: Extract from para. 49 of IASB's *Framework*.

(1999) propose that obligations under all noncancelable leases meet the definition of "liability" and should therefore be recognized. Similarly, the lessee has control over resources for a period, and therefore has an asset. Once we adopt the appropriate principle, rounding out the vague "substantially all the risks and rewards" with the arbitrary 75 percent and 90 percent is unnecessary. An alternative view of this principle is given below.

Incidentally, the principle of substance over form in leasing is a distraction; it is the exact legal form of the lease contract that gives rise to the lessee's obligation and to control over the leased asset. That is, the legal form and the economic substance are not at odds, assuming that one concentrates on the relevant principle of control rather than on ownership.

In the case of this accounting topic, basing a standard on the appropriate principle (the definitions of assets and liabilities) does not lead to the alleged disadvantages of principles as opposed to rules. That is, the principles approach would not lead to imprecision, lack of verifiability, or lack of comparability. All noncancelable leases would be treated in the same way. This reduces the point of transaction structuring to avoid the thresholds. Also, the intentions of the standard setter would be accurately communicated.

An alternative view of applying the asset/liability definitions to leasing is that a lease is an executory contract, i.e., a contract that is equally unperformed by the lessee and the lessor for the remaining period of the lease. To be consistent with other executory contracts (e.g., see IAS No. 37, para. 3), leases would not be recognized as assets or liabilities. Disclosure of the lease commitments would then be the suitable alternative. Whichever of the two views is taken, capitalizing leases on the basis of whether they exceed a 75 percent/90 percent threshold makes no sense.

What explains the lack of use of the definitions by the standard setters? The explanation seems to be that the leasing standards pre-date clear definitions of asset and liability.[6] The standard setters have moved only slowly[7] toward sorting this out because they are aware that any extension of the scope of lease capitalization would be politically unpopular.[8]

Employee Benefits

Unlike the leasing standards, the standards on post-employment benefits are consistent with the definition of a liability. However, this time there are problems with measurement rules.

Measurement rules are necessary in the standards on this topic because the definition of liability does not solve all issues; for example, it is unclear whether to restrict the size of the liability to the benefits already vested. However, some of the measurement rules are complex and not based on

---

[6] For example, SFAS No. 13 of 1976 pre-dates SFAC No. 3 of 1980; and IAS No. 17 of 1982 pre-dates the IASC's *Framework* of 1989. The APB's Statement No. 4 of 1970 has a much less clear definition of a liability (para. 132).

[7] The point was acknowledged by IASC when revising IAS No. 17 in 1997 and again in 2003 (see paragraph IN.4 of IAS No. 17).

[8] For example, see the extensive lobbying by the leasing industry against capitalization in the comment letters relating to IAS No. 17.

principles. In particular, IAS No. 19 and SFAS No. 87 contain devices to protect the income statement from the truth of the effects of actuarial gains and losses on the net pension obligation. The first device is that "small" actuarial gains and losses (those within a "corridor") can be ignored (IAS No. 19, para. 92; SFAS No. 87, para. 32). The size of the corridor is set, by an arbitrary rule, at 10 percent of the larger of the obligation and the fund's assets. The second device is that the remaining actuarial gains and losses can be smoothed over a period related to the service lives of the employees (IAS No. 19, paras. 93/96; SFAS No. 87, paras. 32–33).

These devices were inserted at the demand of preparers in order to reduce volatility in the balance sheet and the income statement. However, the result is a deliberately wrong figure in the balance sheet (because management's best estimate of the liability is not recorded there) and an expense with no economic meaning (because only a small proportion of the change in the liability is recognized). This seems unlikely to serve the needs of investors. AAA FASC (2003, 82) agree that these devices are "not appropriate."

Because the rules are so clearly unprincipled, the standards allow[9] entities to choose not to use the corridor and to choose to recognize actuarial gains and losses immediately in full. This results in lack of comparability. In 2004, the IASB proposed[10] to add yet a further option: full recognition of the liability with actuarial gains and losses taken to the statement of changes in equity.

The application of the principles that liabilities should be measured reliably, neutrally, and show a faithful representation[11] would remove the need for these rules and options. The gain or loss in the income statement would not be smoothed but would be the change in the liability, which is what the frameworks suggest.[12]

Financial Assets

IAS No. 39 was a distillation of the voluminous[13] promulgated U.S. GAAP on the subject of financial instruments. The key feature of both IASB and U.S. requirements is that they contain a mixed measurement model: cost-based for some assets and fair value[14] for others. The only underlying principle that I can discern is that the measurement of assets should be based on the intentions of management. For example, held-to-maturity investments (measured on a cost basis) are those "that an enterprise has the positive intent and ability to hold to maturity," whereas trading assets (fair valued) are those "principally for the purpose of selling ... in the near term" (IAS No. 39, para. 9, with similar definitions in SFAS No. 115, paras. 7 and 12).

The "intentions of the directors" is not a principle to be found in the frameworks. It is a poor principle because intentions can change, cannot directly be audited, and are sometimes unclear even to the directors. This poor principle brings with it numerous rules about intermediate categories, changes of intentions, and the audit of intentions. This is partly what made the U.S. GAAP voluminous and led the IASB to publish 351 pages of rules as "Implementation Guidance."

The unsatisfactory nature of the principle led, in the case of IFRS, to the inclusion of optional methods in the standard. IAS No. 39 (former para. 103) originally allowed the gains and losses on available-for-sale securities to be taken either to income or to equity. The revisions of 2003 to IAS No. 39 insert[15] other choices by allowing any financial asset to be designated as "fair value through profit or loss" and therefore treated like a trading asset.

---

[9] IAS No. 19, para. 93; SFAS No. 87, para. 32.
[10] Exposure Draft of April 2004.
[11] For example, see paras. 31–36 of the IASB's *Framework*.
[12] For example, IASB's *Framework*, para. 70.
[13] The IAS No. 39 file at the IASB records that the project director, Paul Pacter, considered 12 FASB Statements, 9 FASB Technical Bulletins, 7 APB Opinions, 19 AICPA Statements of Position, and 109 EITF consensuses.
[14] In this paper, "fair value" is used with its standard IASB meaning of a current market exchange price (e.g., IAS No. 16, para. 6).
[15] As part of the definitions in para. 9.

An alternative approach would be that all financial assets should be measured at fair value. This would remove the need for much of the complexity, documentation of intentions, and audit judgments involved in the present standards. It would also increase comparability because identical assets would be valued identically, irrespective of what management states that it thinks about the assets. If the "principle" of intentions is discarded, a standard with far fewer rules results, as shown in the Draft Standard[16] issued by the FASB, the IASC, and others in December 2000. Political pressure explains, rather than excuses, the lack of movement toward this solution.

A further use of the "principle" of directors' intentions in U.S. GAAP[17] and in IAS No. 39 (para. 71) is that hedge accounting can be used when an enterprise documents its intentions for signing various financial contracts. This leads to very complex rules (e.g., paragraphs 72 to 84 of IAS No. 39) that could be avoided if these contracts were all treated in the same way, irrespective of the alleged intentions of directors. The latest twist to the story is that IFRS No. 1 has to make rules (paras. 29 and 30) about the retrospective documentation of intentions.

A caveat relates to the term "these contracts" in the previous paragraph. Unless all contracts were required to be marked to market, a principle or a rule would be necessary to establish a clear distinction between financial contracts (that should be marked to market) and nonfinancial contracts (that should not be).

A further caveat is that hedge accounting relates to the measurement of performance rather than to the measurement of assets and liabilities. The lack of clear principles for performance measurement is the concern of a current project of the FASB and the IASB. Several of the suggestions in this paper raise issues that might lead to controversial outcomes in reporting performance.

Government Grants

U.S. GAAP contains limited guidance on government grants. IFRS deals with this subject in IAS No. 20, para. 12), which is based on the principle of matching:

> Government grants should be recognized in income over the periods necessary to match them with the related costs, which they are intended to compensate.

The inappropriateness of IAS No. 20's principle becomes clear when applied to grants for the purchase of fixed assets. The grant is treated as income over the life of the asset. This leaves unanswered (and unanswerable) the question of what to do with a grant for the purchase of land, which has no depreciable life. It also raises the problem of what to do with the credit balance until it is fully taken to income. In the absence of a proper principle, a choice is given in IAS No. 20 (para. 24): net off against the asset or show as "deferred income." The first treatment leads to no clear measurement basis for the asset, and the second leads to an item shown like a liability[18] that does not meet the definition.

IAS 20 is at odds with the *Framework*, which states that: "Income is increases ... of assets or decreases of liabilities" (para. 70) and that "the application of the matching concept ... does not allow the recognition of items in the balance sheet which do not meet the definition of ... liabilities" (para. 95). Following the *Framework* would lead to the treatment of unconditional grants as immediate income, because the recipient has an asset (cash) and no liability. Westwood and Mackenzie (1999) champion this treatment, and it is already adopted by IAS No. 41 (para. 34) in the context of biological assets.

---

[16] *Draft Standard on Financial Instruments and Similar Items*, Joint Working Group of Standard Setters, 2000 (published by FASB, IASC, and others).

[17] SFAS No. 133, para. 18.

[18] IAS No. 20 (para. 12) states that the amount should not be taken to equity.

Subsidiaries

An Enron-related example of a "rule" is the U.S. definition[19] of a subsidiary, which is primarily based on ownership of more than one half of the voting shares of another entity.[20] The IASB's principle[21] in this area is that a subsidiary is an entity that another entity has the *power* to control. It is not necessary actually to exercise control because the first entity's management would be unlikely to go against the wishes of the other entity. This principle follows directly from the definition of an asset. For something to be an asset, it must be controlled,[22] so for a subsidiary's assets to be included in the consolidated balance sheet, the subsidiary must be controlled.

Either type of definition might need elaboration. For example, in order to counter off-balance-sheet finance, a U.S. group was required[23] to show that outsiders had financed at least 3 percent of the total assets of a special purpose vehicle before it could be excluded from consolidation. This added a rule on top of a rule. By contrast, the IASB points out[24] that potential shares should be considered when assessing power to control. This clarifies the IASB principle.

In this case, the trade-off faced by the standard setters is clear. The U.S. system has chosen a complex set of rules whereas IFRS has chosen a somewhat vague principle. The resulting structuring of transactions in the U.S., as evidenced by the creation of Enron's special purpose vehicles, was one of the results of the rules-based approach.

Equity Accounting

As noted above in the context of financial assets, difficulties can arise when the standard setters invent "principles" that are not found in any conceptual framework and do not fit with other principles. An example relates to one of the most egregiously arbitrary rules in accounting: the use of a threshold interest of 20 percent of voting shares in the context of equity accounting. The alleged underlying principle of "significant influence" is sufficiently vague that it has to be supported by a rebuttable presumption (in APB Opinion No. 18, para. 17 and IAS No. 28, para. 6) that refers to the numerical threshold.

Nobes (2002) shows how the 20 percent threshold arose, without good arguments, in the U.K. and then slowly spread worldwide. Mulford and Comiskey (1986) show that the arbitrary threshold leads to manipulations of the size of holdings around the threshold.

The "principle" of significant influence is not found in the FASB or IASB conceptual frameworks, and it cannot be clearly related to other principles or to the definitions of asset and liability. Equity accounting involves the group (or the investor)[25] taking credit for income that has not been received in cash and could not be successfully demanded. It also involves a curious rule[26] that requires a group (or an investor) to eliminate some profit on sales to an associate even though the control of goods has fully passed to (and cash has been fully received from) that entity, which is outside the group.

Rather than being derived from a principle, the equity method as used for associates can be seen as an *ad hoc* valuation method. The arbitrary threshold (and the rule on profit elimination) could be dispensed with if investments were instead treated as available-for-sale financial assets (at fair

---

[19] APB Opinion No. 18, para. 3.
[20] FIN No. 46 now requires the consolidation of certain variable interest entities despite this general rule.
[21] IAS No. 27, para. 4.
[22] e.g., IASB's *Framework*, para. 49(a).
[23] EITF 90-15.
[24] IAS No. 27, para. 14 (formerly SIC No. 33).
[25] The method has been used in some countries (e.g., Denmark, The Netherlands, and Norway) in an investor's unconsolidated statements.
[26] IAS No. 28, para. 22 (formerly SIC No. 3).

value), assuming that the investments do not involve the control of the underlying assets.

The lack of sound principle led, once again, to optional accounting methods. Before the revision of 2003, IAS No. 28 (former para. 12) allowed an investor to account for an associate using the equity method, the cost basis, or as an available-for-sale investment.

In this case, accounting would be improved by abandoning the rogue "principle" and the rules that are needed to operationalize it. Instead, the associate would need no special principles or rules. It would be accounted for like other investments in noncontrolled entities. This would improve comparability and remove the opportunities for structuring. This idea has already been proposed by some standard setters (Milburn and Chant 1999).

CONCLUSIONS

I follow Schipper (2003) by starting with the assumption that comparability/consistency in financial reporting is a good thing. I further agree with Schipper (2003) and with Nelson (2003) that rules can help with clarity/comparability. However, this paper argues that some of the rules in existing standards occur because a standard is based on a poor principle or because it lacks principle. Use of a more appropriate principle would reduce the need for arbitrary and detailed rules. That is, the removal of rules can sometimes be associated with *increased* clarity and comparability. For some topics, use of a better principle would also help in the reduction of optional accounting methods.

I do not mean to imply that a principles-based standard is always better than a rules-based standard, or that concentration on principles will always lead to less complex rules. However, the standards on some topics contain extensive rules and optional accounting methods because of a lack of principle or because of the use of an inappropriate principle not found in the frameworks. In these cases, the standards could be clearer and could lead to greater comparability at the same time as reducing the rules. My analysis concentrates on six examples from IASB standards because listed companies throughout much of the world will adopt IASB standards from 2005 onward and because the FASB has agreed to converge its standards with IASB's. In some cases, standard setters have already examined similar proposals in discussion papers.

Table 1 summarizes the findings of the paper for the six topics. The existing and proposed principles are noted. For three of the topics, the proposed improvement is the use of the frameworks' definitions of asset and liability. In two other cases, the proposal is that the standard should drop a "principle" that is not in the frameworks.

I conclude that complexity of the rules could be reduced by adopting a more appropriate principle in all six cases. This reduction in complexity is in itself a good thing, although it could be outweighed by deterioration in other qualities. For example, in the case of the definition of subsidiaries, verifying control is more difficult than verifying ownership; for associates, verifying fair value is more difficult than verifying equity accounting. Nevertheless, for these two topics, reduced incentives for management to structure transactions would weigh in favor of the proposed improvements.

For topics, 1 through 4 (see Table 1), decreased complexity could be achieved at the same time as improvements in some aspects of verifiability or reduced structuring or both. Further, for most topics, optional methods could be reduced.

A major issue that is difficult to summarize is the degree to which the proposed improvements would lead to better information for investors. In the end, this is an empirical matter, but Table 2 summarizes some of the relevant points.

TABLE 1
Synopsis of Six Topics

Topic	Existing Principle	Proposed Improvement	Complexity?	Structuring?	Verifiability	Reduce Options?
1. Leasing	Transfer of substantially all risks and rewards	Definitions of asset and liability	Decrease	Decrease	Increase[a]	No
2. Employee benefits	Protect financial statements from volatility	Faithful representation	Decrease	—	Increase	Yes (U.S./IFRS)
3. Financial assets	Documented intentions of directors	Removal of rogue principle	Decrease	Decrease	Increase[b]	Yes (IFRS)
4. Government grants (IFRS)	Matching	Definition of liability	Decrease	—	Increase	Yes (IFRS)
5. Subsidiaries (U.S.)	Ownership	Definition of asset; control	Decrease	Decrease	Decrease	No
6. Equity accounting	Significant influence	Removal of rogue principle	Decrease	Decrease	Decrease	Yes (IFRS)

[a] An increase in the sense that policing the capital/operating boundary would cease. However, the measurement of the lease would involve estimations.
[b] An increase in the sense that the intent would no longer be audited. However, fair values would be used more extensively, and some of those are difficult to verify.

TABLE 2
The Quality of Information

Topic	Improvements in the Quality of Information
1. Leasing	All leases would be treated in the same way. All liabilities would be recognized.
2. Employee benefits	The size of liabilities could no longer be hidden. Meaningless expenses would be removed from the income statement. An option would be removed, thereby improving comparability.
3. Financial assets	Assets of a similar nature would be measured similarly. Options could be removed from IFRS, thereby improving comparability.
4. Government grants (IFRS)	The item "deferred income" that is difficult to interpret would be removed from balance sheets. Income that has been received would no longer be spread over an irrelevant period. An option could be removed, thereby improving comparability.
5. Subsidiaries (U.S.)	The group's assets and liabilities would be revealed.
6. Equity accounting	Investments of a similar nature (e.g., those of 18 percent interests and 22 percent interests) would be measured in the same way.

REFERENCES

Alexander, A. 1999. A benchmark for the adequacy of published financial statements. *Accounting and Business Research* 29 (Summer): 239–253.

American Accounting Association Financial Accounting Standards Committee. 2003. Evaluating concepts-based vs. rules-based approaches to standard setting. *Accounting Horizons* 17 (1): 73–89.

Benston, G. J. 1976. Public (U.S.) compared to private (U.K.) regulation of corporate financial disclosure. *The Accounting Review* 51 (July): 483–498.

Hope, T., and R. Gray. 1982. Power and policy making: The development of an R & D standard. *Journal of Business Finance and Accounting* 9 (4): 531–558.

McGregor, W. 1996. *Accounting for Leases: A New Approach.* Norwalk, CT: Financial Accounting Standards Board for the G4 + 1.

Milburn, J. A., and P. D. Chant. 1999. *Reporting Interests in Joint Ventures and Similar Arrangements.* Norwalk, CT: Financial Accounting Standards Board for the G4 + 1.

Mulford, C. W., and E. Comiskey. 1988. Investment decisions and the equity accounting standard. *The Accounting Review* 61 (July): 519–525.

Nailor, H., and A. Lennard 1999. *Leases: Implementation of a New Approach.* Norwalk, CT: Financial Accounting Standards Board for the G4 + 1.

Nelson, M. W. 2003. Behavioral evidence on the effects of principles- and rules-based standards. *Accounting Horizons* 17 (1): 91–104.

Nobes, C. W. 1992. A political history of goodwill in the U.K.: An illustration of cyclical standard setting. *Abacus* 28 (2): 142–161.

———. 2002. An analysis of the international development of the equity method. *Abacus* 38 (1): 16–45.

Schipper, K. 2003. Principles-based accounting standards. *Accounting Horizons* 17 (1): 61–72.

Solomons, D. 1978. The politicization of accounting. *Journal of Accountancy* 146 (November): 65–72.

Watts, R. L., and J. L. Zimmerman. 1978. Toward a positive theory of the determination of accounting standards. *The Accounting Review* 53 (January): 1128–1133.

Westwood, M., and A. Mackenzie. 1999. *Accounting for Recipients for Non-reciprocal Transfers, Excluding Contributions by Owners.* Norwalk, CT: Financial Accounting Standards Board for the G4 + 1.

Zeff, S. A. 1995. A perspective on the U.S. public/private sector approach to the regulation of financial reporting. *Accounting Horizons* 9 (1): 52–70.

———. 1997. Playing the congressional card on employee stock options: A fearful escalation in the impact of economic consequences lobbying on standard setting. In *The Development of Accounting in an International Context,* edited by T. E. Cooke, and C. W. Nobes, 177–192. Oxford, U.K.: Routledge.

[10]

Christopher Nobes

'57 Varieties of Serious Defect in IFRS?'

Haswell and Langfield-Smith (2008, hereafter HLS) record 57 'serious defects' (p. 46) in the Australian versions of International Financial Reporting Standards (AIFRS). They suggest that only 17 of these defects existed in former Australian standards; and they conclude that IFRS are not yet acceptable as a world-class framework of standards (p. 60).

HLS write clearly and they cite several convincing examples of defects. However, I suggest below that they have exaggerated the defectiveness of IFRS and the comparison with previous Australian standards. Further, to show that IFRS has defects does not show that Australia or the rest of the world should not adopt IFRS.

Given that this journal has an international audience, and that HLS's conclusion refers to IFRS and not AIFRS, I will refer to the individual standards within IFRS not within AIFRS, but the two have the same paragraph numbers.

Moving Target

Australia has chosen not to 'adopt' IFRS, but to converge its standards with IFRS. This leads to at least two problems. First, foreign readers of Australian reports might be confused about whether or not IFRS is being complied with. This has been partially addressed[1] by new audit requirements requiring reference to IFRS as well as to AIFRS. Second, there is a time lag in turning IFRS into AIFRS, although the dates for mandatory adoption are kept the same. This affects HLS's paper.

HLS use a date of 1 September 2007 for their study of AIFRS. They therefore include comments on IAS 14 (AASB 114), which was then the appropriate standard in Australia. HLS note (p. 55) that this is replaced in Australia by IFRS 8 (AASB 8) for periods beginning in 2009 or later. However, by September 2007, IFRS 8 had already replaced IAS 14 in the IASB's 2007 bound volume of standards[2]. IFRS 8 was allowed for years beginning 1 January 2006 (or even 1 December 2005). Although IAS 14 was still *available* for use as part of IFRS, I suggest that non-Australian readers might wish to disregard HLS's criticisms of it. Of course, HLS would have some criticisms of IFRS 8, instead (for example, p. 55).

In a previous issue of this journal, Haswell and Langfield-Smith (HLS) recorded 57 'serious defects' in IFRS. This commentary suggests that some of these are not defects and some others are not serious. Points are also made about the different implementation dates of standards in Australia compared to elsewhere, and about HLS's comparison of IFRS and previous Australian standards. HLS's conclusion that IFRS is not yet ready for world-wide adoption is challenged on the grounds that a world standard is already needed for listed companies and that no plausible alternative to IFRS would be better.

Correspondence
Chris Nobes, School of Management, Royal Holloway, Egham TW20 0EX, United Kingdom. email: chris.nobes@rhul.ac.uk

doi: 10.1111/j.1835-2561.2008.0033.x

C. Nobes   '57 Varieties of Serious Defect in IFRS?'

There is also an issue concerning different versions of IAS 1, as now explained. HLS note that the 'income statement' in IAS 1 does not lead to a total of 'income', whereas AASB 1018 'used consistent terminology' (p. 48). Indeed, the IAS income statement leads to 'profit or loss'. There is an irony here: older versions[3] of IAS 1 included the UK term 'profit and loss account', but this was replaced by the more modern and US 'income statement'. A further irony is that this term is no longer majority US practice, being gradually supplanted by 'statement of operations' (AICPA 2006, p. 295). Incidentally, the old Australian standard (AASB 1018) required a 'statement of performance' that did not end in something called 'performance'. So, HLS should not imply[4] that this is more consistent than IAS 1's 'income statement' that does not end in something called 'income'.

As noted above, HLS use a date of 1 September 2007 for their version of the standards as in force in Australia. A few days later, a new version of IAS 1 was issued (though not in Australia) that addresses the above problem by requiring a 'statement of comprehensive income' that leads to 'total comprehensive income' (IAS 1.82), via 'profit and loss'. Admittedly, the words 'total comprehensive' are somewhat tautologous. Also, entities are, for the moment, allowed to show the amounts leading to 'profit and loss' separately as an 'income statement' (IAS 1.81).

HLS also note that the old IAS 1 has no consistent criteria for putting items 'directly in equity', and that this is a feature shared by AASB 1018. Again, this is true, but the problem is partly addressed by the new IAS 1 that does not allow any gains or losses to go directly to equity. Nevertheless, the IASB are still working on the problem of establishing criteria for whether or not items go into 'profit or loss'.

This 'moving target' point is not a criticism of HLS. It does mean, though, that some of the IFRS defects that they list are less relevant outside Australia because entities might have moved to new standards earlier than is allowed in Australia. The old defects might, of course, have been replaced by new ones.

Some Disagreement on Defects

Revenue, earnings

HLS say (Table 1) that IAS 16 'illogically' states that a gain on disposal of a non-current asset is not revenue. However, this is not illogical. The *Framework* (paras 74–6) divides 'income' into 'revenue' and 'gains'. So, this item is a gain, not a revenue. Perhaps there is confusion here because 'revenue' in former Australian standards (for example, AASB 1018) is the equivalent of 'income' in IFRS.

Then, HLS object to the term 'earnings' in both IFRS and Australian standards. HLS say that 'earnings' is the same thing as 'profit and loss' (p. 58). However, 'earnings' is adjusted for various issues connected to preference shares (IAS 33.12), so it is useful to have a different term. The standard setters are here sensibly using the term of the users, especially analysts.

Provisions

HLS say (Table 1) that IAS 16's rules for recognition of a liability are inconsistent with IAS 37's rules. However, they later correctly say (p. 55) that IAS 16 'limits the recognition of a liability to those recognised' under IAS 37. So, the alleged defect should be deleted from Table 1. The context is the costs of obligations to dismantle, clean up and so on.

HLS then find the process of dealing with these costs 'extremely peculiar' (p. 55) because IAS 2 (Inventories) is said to apply. They wonder whether one should subsequently use impairment (IAS 16/36) or 'lower of cost and net realisable value' (IAS 2). However, this is not peculiar. IAS 2 only applies to those costs 'incurred . . . as a consequence of having used the item to produce inventories' (IAS 16.18). Consequently, those amounts are included in the cost of inventories, so other parts of IAS 2 apply. For the parts of cost added to non-current assets, IASs 16/36 subsequently apply.

HLS also say (p. 59) that IAS 37 is unclear about measuring the best estimate of an obligation. Should account be taken of any impossibility or prohibitive expense in settling or transferring an obligation at the balance sheet date? I believe that IAS 36.37 advises not, because the sentence immediately following the discussion of impossibility/prohibitive begins 'However, . . . '. That is, an entity should estimate the maximum that it would pay to dispose of the obligation, irrespective of whether there is a counter-party willing to transact. I admit, though, that it might not only be HLS who find this unclear.

HLS then complain (p. 59) that an increase in a provision due to the unwinding of a discount is called 'borrowing costs', whereas a provision is not a borrowing. However, it is quite normal to include this unwinding as a sort of interest expense (for example, in pension accounting under IAS 19). Furthermore, HLS are disingenuous about saying (in Table 1) that the old Australian standard did not take this approach. AASB 1044 agreed with IAS 37 that the amount 'conceptually, ought to be classified as interest' (para 8.3.2), but that the cost of separating it out exceeds the benefit.

Group accounting

HLS say that 'It can be argued that a consistent adherence to the entity concept means that there is no need to distinguish ... parent share and minority interest' (p. 57). That is true. However, there is no suggestion in IAS 27 that it is attempting a pure entity concept. The IASB has concluded that:

> Adopting the entity perspective does not preclude the inclusion in financial reports of additional information that is primarily directed to the needs of an entity's equity investors or to another group of capital providers. (IAS 2008a, p. 15)

Indeed, equity analysts concentrate on returns to parent company (ordinary) shareholders, so it seems that the separation of parent from minority interest *is* useful, and that to suppress the information *would* lead to a serious defect.

HLS then criticise IAS 28 because it does not lead to a number showing distributable profit resulting from holdings in associates (p. 57). However, since equity accounting is only allowed in consolidated statements not in unconsolidated statements,[5] the issue does not arise. There is no such thing as the distributable profit of a group, so we should not expect to see information on distributability in consolidated statements.

HLS also say (p. 57) that it is inconsistent to use the equity method for associates in consolidated statements, but not in parent statements. There is, indeed, a case to be made for using the equity method in both sets of statements or, better still, for not using it at all (Milburn and Chant 1999; Nobes 2002). However, if there is any point[6] in having unconsolidated statements (for example, to help in calculating distributable profit, see above), it must rest on their being different from the consolidated statements. It is therefore not obvious that inconsistency is a defect in this case.

IAS 39

It pains me to have to disagree with any of HLS's criticisms of IAS 39. I voted[7] against the standard. However, Table 1 incorrectly accuses IAS 39 of including transaction costs in something called 'fair value'. IAS 39.43 requires fair value to be adjusted by costs, except for items held at fair value through profit or loss. It does not say that the adjusted amount is still called fair value.

Serious?

The title of HLS's paper refers to 'serious defects'. It is not clear to me that all 57 of them are 'serious'. HLS do not define the word. My suggestion is that a defect is serious if it would lead to preparers or users being misled. For example, is it 'serious' that IAS 16 uses an outmoded term 'depreciation charge', rather than HLS's preferred 'depreciation expense' (p. 55) or that IAS 36 refers to 'impairment loss' rather than 'impairment

expense' (p. 58)? In my view, the IFRS terms are unlikely to mislead users. Again, is it 'serious' that IAS 33 discusses the treatment of partly paid shares for EPS calculations in its application guidance rather than in the body of the standard (p. 58)? Taking details on unusual matters into application guidance is designed to make a standard easier to understand. This might outweigh any chance that preparers would be misled by having to look there.

Australian Comparison

In Table 1 and in their Conclusion, HLS make a comparison with former Australian standards to see if the 57 defects existed in them. They say that, of the 57:

> ... only 17 were present in the pre-2005 set of Australian-manufactured standards. We therefore ask if the present set of IFRS can be a serious candidate for the role of a world-class financial reporting framework. Our view is that IFRS are surely not yet acceptable for such a role. (p. 60)

Let us examine this comparison. For the several reasons explained above, I would reduce the list of 57 'serious defects' in IFRS. Also, it is important to note, as HLS do in other paragraphs, that IFRS is a more complete set of standards than previous Australian standards were. So, for this comparison purpose, it is unfair to include those defects in areas on which there was no Australian standard (the six[8] defects in IAS 39). This is not to deny the defects in IAS 39, but to try to make a more even-handed comparison.

Also, I would add to the 17 Australian defects, as explained above.[9] Further, as HLS say (p. 60), AIFRS remedy some problems that were found in Australian standards and not covered in Table 1. So, something should be added to the Australian total.

As a result, for the purpose of comparison, the 57 should be reduced and the 17 increased. Having adjusted for that, the excess of IFRS defects is more than halved.

World-class Framework?

HLS have shown that there are many defects in IFRS. One can agree with them that it is important for these to be addressed by the IASB; and in some cases that would be easy. However, does this mean that IFRS is not yet a 'world-class framework' of standards (p. 60, as quoted above)? Indeed, what is a 'world-class framework'? I take it as a set of standards suitable for adoption across the world.

To show that IFRS has defects is not a strong argument against adopting IFRS as the world standard. A good argument would be that a plausible alternative for such a purpose (that is, US Generally Accepted Accounting Principles, GAAP?) was 'better' than IFRS. However, it seems (p. 50) that HLS would find even more defects in US GAAP.

HLS say (p. 60, as quoted above) that the comparative lack of Australian defects 'therefore' calls into question whether IFRS is suitable as a world standard. However, given that it is not plausible that the world will adopt Australian standards, their comparative lack of defects is not relevant for the choice. Assuming that it is now useful to have a world standard, at least for financial reporting by listed companies, the currently imperfect IFRS is arguably suitable because there is nothing more suitable. It *is* therefore 'a serious candidate' (perhaps the only candidate) for worldwide adoption. That is not to say that it could not be, or should not be, improved.

Conclusion

HLS record 57 'serious defect' in AIFRS. I agree with many of their findings. However, I disagree with some of the 57 (see the nine cases[10] in 'Some disagreement', above). Second, I believe that some of the defects are not 'serious'. For non-Australians, there would also be the issue of which standards to examine, given that new standards are allowed to be used earlier outside Australia. However, this would not necessarily reduce the total of 57, as a new standard might contain new defects.

For comparisons with previous Australian standards, which were said to have had only 17 of the serious defects, adjustments are needed to reduce the 57 for the above, to adjust for issues not covered in Australian standards and to increase the 17 for defects in Australian standards that are solved by IFRS.

Despite the defects in IFRS (and even if they are more numerous than those in some other sets of standards), IFRS is perhaps the only serious candidate for the role of world standard. None of this is to deny HLS's main point that IFRS needs to be improved.

Christopher Nobes is Professor of Accounting, Royal Holloway, University of London. The author is grateful for comments on an earlier draft from Gary Doree and Jan McCahey (PricewaterhouseCoopers, Sydney and Melbourne), Stephen Haswell (Macquarie University),

Ian Langfield-Smith (formerly Monash University), R.H. Parker (University of Exeter) and Christian Stadler (Royal Holloway). The author remains solely responsible for the content.

Notes

1   Revised ASA 700 from the Australian Auditing and Assurance Standards Board, June 2007.
2   IFRS 8 was issued in November 2006 and it allowed (para 35) immediate application. Like AASB 8, it is compulsory from 2009.
3   For example, the 1993 version of IAS 1 (para 3) refers to 'income statements or profit and loss accounts'.
4   Lack of asterisk for item 1 of Table 1.
5   See IAS 28.35.
6   The recent discussion paper on the reporting entity (IASB 2008b, section 3) notes that there are several arguments on both sides of this.
7   As a member of the two-man UK delegation on the Board of the IASC.
8   Although I already count one of those in my questioned cases above.
9   For example, for the point about 'statement of performance' not leading to 'performance'.
10 In HLS's Table 1, items 18, 24, 33, 36, 37, 40, 46, 47 and 52.

References

AICPA 2006, *Accounting Trends and Techniques*, American Institute of Certified Public Accountants, New York.

Haswell, S. and Langfield-Smith, I. 2008, 'Fifty-seven serious defects in "Australian" IFRS', *Australian Accounting Review*, 18, 1: 46–62.

IASB 2008a, *Exposure Draft of an Improved Conceptual Framework for Financial Reporting*, International Accounting Standards Board, London.

IASB 2008b, *Preliminary Views on an Improved Conceptual Framework for Financial Reporting: The Reporting Entity*, International Accounting Standards Board, London.

Milburn, J.A. and Chant, P.D. 1999, *Reporting Interests in Joint Ventures and Similar Arrangements*, Financial Accounting Standards Board for the G4 + 1.

Nobes, C.W. 2002, 'An Analysis of the International Development of the Equity Method', *Abacus*, 38, 1: 16–45.

[11]

Accounting and Business Research, Vol. 36. No. 3. pp. 233-245. 2006

The survival of international differences under IFRS: towards a research agenda

Christopher Nobes*

Abstract—The compulsory use of IFRS for the consolidated statements of listed companies in the EU and elsewhere, and the convergence of IFRS with US GAAP, might imply the end of 'international accounting' as an important field of study. However, there are motives and opportunities for international differences of practice to exist within IFRS usage. Some of the original motives for international accounting differences may still be effective in an IFRS context, though in different ways. The opportunities for different IFRS practices are divided into eight types. Hypotheses relating to each of these are proposed, and some ways of testing them are suggested. Some implications of the existence of different national versions of IFRS are noted.

1. The end of the field of 'international accounting'?

The fall of the Berlin Wall led some commentators to ask whether history had ended (e.g. Fukuyama, 1989). The subsequent re-unification of Germany affected accounting, as now explained. Economic difficulties hit the German economy[1] in the early 1990s and the cost of re-unification caused tax rates to rise. These developments restricted funds for investment at exactly the time that opportunities had opened up for expansion by German companies into East Germany and other parts of Eastern Europe. Large German companies needed to access foreign capital for the first time. Partly[2] for this reason, they succumbed to the commercial imperative of publishing financial statements using 'internationally accepted accounting principles',[3] starting with Daimler-Benz in 1993.

The inconvenience of preparing two sets of consolidated financial statements led, in 1998, to permission to use the internationally accepted principles instead of the conventional rules of the *Handelsgesetzbuch* (HGB). This was one of the precursors to the EU's requirement to use International Financial Reporting Standards (IFRS) for the consolidated statements of listed companies that was announced in 2000 and came into effect in 2005 for most EU listed companies.

This compulsory use of IFRS in the EU (and beyond, e.g. Australia) has major implications for accounting research. For example, empirical research on 'German accounting' can no longer be done using current accounting data from listed German groups. Similarly, there is limited interest from academics or students in the causes and nature of differences between German and UK (or even German and IFRS) accounting rules. This gradual disappearance of traditional 'international accounting' will continue as IFRS and US rules converge.[4]

Although the fall of the Wall did not[5] signify the end of history, did it signify the end of the academic field of 'international accounting'? That is, have differences between jurisdictions disappeared for listed companies under IFRS? This paper suggests ways in which international differences have survived and can be the objects of research. The focus is mostly the consolidated statements of EU listed companies from 2005.

This paper aims to identify both the motive and the opportunity for international differences to continue. The motive is investigated in Section 2 by examining the reasons why international differ-

*The author is PricewaterhouseCoopers Professor of Accounting at the University of Reading. He is grateful for comments on an earlier draft from Julie Cooper (University of Reading), Maria Gee (University of Reading), Axel Haller (University of Regensburg), Anja Hjelström (Stockholm School of Economics), Erlend Kvaal (Norwegian School of Management), Andrew Lennard (Accounting Standards Board), Alan Roberts (Groupe ESC, Rennes), Stephen Zeff (Rice University), and from two referees and the editor of this journal. Correspondence address: Professor C.W. Nobes, School of Business, University of Reading, RG6 6AA. E-mail: C.W.Nobes@reading.ac.uk

The final version of this paper was accepted in May 2006.

[1] For example, Germany's largest industrial company, Daimler-Benz, declared losses under US GAAP of DM1,839m in 1993 and DM5,729m in 1995.

[2] Another reason was to increase the familiarity of German companies for customers or group employees.

[3] The phrase used in the 1998 *Kapitalaufnahmeerleichterungsgesetz* (KapAEG).

[4] As agreed by the FASB and the IASB in the Norwalk Agreement of 2002, and as confirmed and made more detailed in a *Memorandum of Understanding* of February 2006. This has led, for example, to IFRS 5 which converges to US GAAP on the subject of held-for-sale assets and discontinued operations, and to SFAS 154 which converges to IFRS on the subject of accounting policy changes.

[5] As, for example, the events of 11 September 2001 showed.

ences existed in the past, and asking whether any of these reasons survive the arrival of IFRS. The opportunity for international differences in IFRS practice to exist is split in Section 3 into eight sources: different versions of IFRS; different translations of IFRS; gaps in IFRS; overt options in IFRS; covert options, vague criteria and interpretations in IFRS; measurement estimations in IFRS; transitional or first-time issues in IFRS; and imperfect enforcement of IFRS. Section 4 summarises the resulting research agenda and notes some policy implications relating to the continuation of national differences within IFRS. A relevant piece of context here is that the Securities and Exchange Commission (SEC) is monitoring[6] whether to accept IFRS from EU companies without the need for reconciliation to US GAAP.

2. Motives for the survival of international differences

As noted above, Section 3 will examine whether there is opportunity within IFRS for international differences in practice to survive. A prior question is whether there is motivation. That is, are corporate managers of listed groups driven by different objectives in different countries when preparing consolidated financial statements under IFRS? This question is investigated in this section.

As already suggested, this paper will focus on the EU. For some illustrations, it will be useful to narrow down further to the EU's two largest economies and capital markets: Germany and the UK. In this context, by 'international differences', I mean systematic differences in the IFRS practices of German groups compared to those of UK groups. A starting point is to examine the literature on German/UK differences to see whether the suggested drivers of difference could survive into an IFRS context.

From the earliest classifications (Hatfield, 1911; Mueller, 1967; Seidler, 1967; AAA, 1977; Nair and Frank, 1980), Germany and the UK are put into different groups, even in classifications with only three or four groups. Nobes (1983) goes further and puts them on opposite sides of a two-group classification. This has some later theoretical and empirical support (e.g. Perera, 1989; Doupnik and Salter, 1993). However, it has also created controversy, especially when the US has been put with the UK (e.g. Cairns, 1997; Nobes, 1998a; Feige, 1997; Nobes and Mueller, 1997; Alexander and Archer, 2000; Nobes, 2003; d'Arcy, 2001; Nobes, 2004).

The suggested reasons for the differences between the German and UK national 'accounting systems' include differences in financing systems, legal systems and tax systems. Zysman (1983) proposes three types of financing system: capital market (e.g. UK, US), credit-based governmental

(e.g. France and Japan), and credit-based financial institutional (e.g. Germany). Nobes (1988) proposes two types: shareholder 'outsiders' (e.g. UK, US) and bank/state/family 'insiders' (e.g. Germany, France). More recent research (e.g. Franks and Meyer, 2001) is consistent with a continued but less pronounced dichotomy. Nobes (1998b) suggests that, unless a country is culturally dominated by another, its financing system is the main driver of its financial reporting system. Some evidence now supports this (Xiao et al., 2004; Tarca et al., 2005; Sellhorn and Gornik-Tomaszewski, 2005).

The largest of German listed companies were already adapting to a shareholder/outsider financial culture by voluntarily using IFRS or US GAAP from the middle 1990s (Weissenberger et al., 2004). However, many German listed companies waited to use IFRS until driven by compulsion from the Deutsche Börse and then the EU Regulation. Such German companies might still be dominated by 'insider' finance and might still feel no commercial need for the creative accounting and extensive disclosures seen in UK or US markets. They might therefore have motivations towards a particular style of IFRS reporting, assuming that opportunities for different styles exist (see Section 3).

The literature also divides the *legal* systems of the developed world into two main types: Roman (code) law and common law (e.g. David and Brierley, 1985). This affects the regulation of financial reporting. For example, the preparation of financial statements under German national rules is largely specified by the HGB and tax law, whereas the detail in UK national rules is found in accounting standards written in the private sector.

La Porta et al. (1997 and 1998) find a statistical connection between strong equity markets and common law countries, noting a tendency for stronger legal protection of investors in such countries. Empirical research also suggests a relationship between legal systems and financial reporting practice. Jaggi and Low (2000) find that companies in code law countries make fewer disclosures. Ball et al. (2000) find that accounting income in code law countries is less timely, particularly in incorporating economic losses. Bushman and Piotroski (2006) also show that bad news is reported faster in countries with higher quality legal systems (which they connect, in this context, to common law). For each of these last three papers, a relationship is suggested between better financial reporting and common law countries. However, a relationship between stronger equity markets and better reporting would presumably also have been found, which would have been a more parsimonious hypothesis.

---

[6] For example, see Nicolaisen article at www.sec.gov/news/speech/spch040605dtn.htm.

For IFRS reporting in Germany and the UK, the content of the standards is now the same. However, monitoring and enforcement remain national. This includes the nature and regulation of audit, the stock exchange rules, the activities of the stock exchange regulator and of any other monitoring or review bodies. International differences in these areas continue. So, the Roman/common dichotomy could still affect financial reporting practice. Section 3 suggests examples.

Turning now to the third issue, the dominance of tax over German financial reporting has been well documented (e.g. Haller, 1992). Lamb et al. (1998) compare Germany and the UK in some detail and suggest that the operational linkage between tax and financial reporting is much stronger in Germany. Nobes (1998b) suggests a connection with financing systems. That is, unless there is a strong competing purpose for accounting, taxation will dominate it. The existence of an 'outsider' financing system creates the strong competing purpose for accounting of giving useful information to investors. Consequently, under UK national requirements but not German, two sets of rules are needed on several accounting issues: one for taxation and one for financial reporting.

However, does this difference remain relevant in the context of the use of IFRS for consolidated statements? At first sight, it does not, because IFRS consolidated accounting is, even in Germany, separated from tax calculations which begin with the pre-tax accounting profit of unconsolidated individual entities. However, as explained below, there are two reasons why tax practice may influence IFRS consolidated statements: convenience (in Germany) and tax conformity (in the UK).

In Germany, companies are required to continue to prepare unconsolidated financial statements under the conventional rules of the HGB for calculations of taxable income and distributable income. This is irrespective of any use of IFRS for consolidated or unconsolidated statements (Haller and Eierle, 2004). In some areas, the tax-driven accounting choices of the unconsolidated statements might flow through to consolidated IFRS statements. For example, asset impairments are tax deductible in Germany (but not in the UK), so there is a bias in favour of them. They might survive into IFRS consolidations in Germany, given the room for judgment in IFRS impairment procedures (see Section 3).

In the UK, IFRS is allowed for individual company financial statements and therefore as a starting point for calculations of taxable income. The tax authorities generally expect the statements of a parent and other UK group members to use the same accounting policies as group statements.[7] To take an example, the recognition and measurement of intangible assets has tax implications.[8]

Consequently, given that IFRS requires considerable judgment in this area, individual companies using IFRS will have an incentive to make interpretations of IAS 38 (Intangible Assets) in order to minimise capitalisation and therefore tax, and then these will flow through to consolidated statements.

A way of summarising this section is to say that national accounting traditions are likely to continue into consolidated reporting where scope for this exists within IFRS rules. This is not to suggest that this continuation of practices results merely from inertia, but that the reasons for the different traditions will in some cases remain relevant. However, inertia might be a further explanation in itself, as might a company's conscious desire to disrupt its accounting as little as possible for the better understanding of internal and external users.

A further aspect of this concerns not companies but the regulators of companies. Regulators might be one of the causes of the existence of national versions of IFRS, as explained further in Section 3. The mix of political pressures on regulators varies from country to country, caused partly by the above factors: financing system, legal system and tax system. For example, some countries have well-organised lobby groups of finance directors. Some countries have experienced a major use of leasing because of particular features of their tax systems. A regulator in a country with an important leasing industry and an assertive lobby group might be more likely to issue a pro-industry[9] interpretation on lease accounting.

Another way of approaching this is to suggest that culture affects accounting (e.g. Gray, 1988; Doupnik and Salter, 1995). This may be true, but Nobes (1998b) suggests that it might be better to see national culture as affecting or including the above factors (e.g. the legal system or the financing system) that then affect accounting. Therefore, it might not be necessary to consider culture separately, especially as there are difficulties in measuring it (Gernon and Wallace, 1995; Baydoun and Willett, 1995).

3. Opportunities for the survival of international differences

The purpose of this paper is to identify potential systematic and sustained international differences in practice among IFRS companies. Section 1 proposed eight sources of opportunity for the survival

---

[7] I am grateful to Joan Brown (then of the Inland Revenue's Large Business Office) for this point (meeting of 23.7.2003). It related to parents and groups both using UK GAAP, particularly to the FRS 18 (para. 17) requirement to use the most appropriate accounting policy. A similar conclusion might be arrived at under IAS 8 (para. 10).

[8] Finance Act 2002, Schedule 29.

[9] That is, an interpretation that makes leases more popular by restricting the recognition of liabilities by lessees.

of international differences of practice despite the adoption of IFRS. These are now examined in turn. It is assumed in this section that some motive (including inertia) exists for the differences, as discussed in Section 2. It is not intended always to link particular motives to particular types of practice difference, although in some cases references are made to this for illustration. In many cases several motives may contribute.

Following from Section 2, several of the illustrations in the section compare Germany and the UK, but examples are taken from elsewhere when they are more relevant.

Different versions of IFRS

Despite adoption or alleged adoption of IFRS, international differences in the IFRS rules in force at a particular date can occur. Three cases are examined here. First, there are differences between IFRS and EU-endorsed IFRS. In the first half of 2005, three such differences existed, two of which were resolved by the second half of 2005. Given that more such differences are likely to arise in the future (McCreevy, 2005), it is worth looking at these three as examples.

Two of the differences of early 2005 between IFRS and EU-endorsed IFRS related to IAS 39. The IASB's version of IAS 39 (para. 9) (that was permitted for 2004 and 2005 reports) allowed an entity to designate any financial asset or liability as 'at fair value though profit or loss'(marked to market). This was regarded as unacceptable by, among others, the European Central Bank, and this led to the removal of this option from the EU-endorsed version (Van Hulle, 2005; Zeff, 2006). Consequently, a non-EU company following IFRS could have marked to market its held-to-maturity investments but an EU company following IFRS could not have. This particular issue was resolved by IASB issuing, in June 2005, an amendment[10] to IAS 39 that restricted the option, and this was endorsed by the EU.[11]

The other difference relating to IAS 39 concerned the restrictions on the permission for hedge accounting. This time, political pressure in the EU had led to *more* flexibility in the EU-endorsed IAS 39 than in the IASB's version (Whittington, 2005). This difference remains for 2006 reports. So, for example a French bank that exercises the full EU-endorsed permission will have a less volatile profit figure than a UK bank that denies itself the fuller permission or than an Australian bank that must follow AASB 139, a standard based on the restrictive non-EU version of IAS 39.

The above has outlined two types of endorsement issue: greater non-EU options and greater EU options. A third type is illustrated by the problem with IFRIC Interpretation 3, 'Emission Rights' of 2004. The EU objected to the solution required by IFRIC 3 and refused to endorse it. This led the

IASB, in June 2005, to withdraw IFRIC 3, although to confirm that IFRIC's interpretation of IAS 20 and IAS 38 was correct. In the brief period when IFRIC 3 was in force but unendorsed, an EU company (unlike non-EU companies) need not have complied with it. However, in this case, presumably the EU company should have come to the same conclusion as IFRIC 3. There may be future cases where non-endorsement could lead to different accounting results.

The next case of an area of difference within IFRS rules does not relate to the EU but to Australia. In that country, direct compliance with IFRS is not required but instead IFRS has been turned closely, *but not exactly*, into Australian standards that are then legally imposed on companies. To take an example of the differences, IAS 31 allows a group to choose between proportional consolidation and equity accounting for its holding in a joint venture entity. By contrast, AASB 131 (para. 38) requires equity accounting. This is an Australian 'carve out', although the Australian standard can correctly state that compliance with it ensures compliance with IFRS. However, it is possible to envisage a national standard that was 'converged with' IFRS but did not ensure full compliance. More generally, the precedent of carve outs will be noticed by regulators around the world as they respond to political pressure from companies, which will vary internationally (see Section 2).

The last case of difference within IFRS rules concerns implementation dates and year ends. New standards generally have an in force date of 'annual periods beginning on or after 1 January 200X'. However, early application is usually allowed, so two quite different versions of IFRS can be in force at the same time. Another aspect of this is that the EU endorsement process can take many months. So, some parts of IFRS might be in force but not endorsed at a particular company's year end. An EU company would be required not to obey such parts of IFRS unless they were consistent with endorsed IFRS (KPMG, 2005).

Furthermore, many companies in some countries (e.g. in Australia and the UK, but not in Germany) have accounting periods that do not begin on 1 January. So, researchers might find that a sample of companies with annual reports relating to years ending in 2006 are subject to different versions of IFRS. More subtly, some companies (e.g. UK retail groups) choose to have accounting years comprising exactly 52 or 53 weeks, so some have accounting years that begin on 28 December, thereby escaping a new standard.

In conclusion, this sub-section's hypothesis is:

---

[10] With effect from 1 January 2006.
[11] On 15 November 2005.

Vol. 36 No. 3. 2006

H$_1$:   International differences in practice exist among IFRS companies due to differences in the version of IFRS being used.

Examples of sub-hypotheses here are:

H$_{1(a)}$:   French banks exhibit less earnings volatility than British or Australian banks because of using less restrictive hedge accounting criteria.

H$_{1(b)}$:   Australian groups do not use proportional consolidation for joint ventures whereas some continental European groups do.

This latter sub-hypothesis includes the idea (of Section 2) that national accounting traditions are likely to continue under IFRS: proportional consolidation was compulsory in France (Richard, 2001) and common elsewhere in continental Europe (e.g. Ordelheide, 2001:1,389). Proportional consolidation, compared to equity accounting, increases the group's sales, cash and other important figures.

Different translations of IFRS

Under the EU Regulation 1606, the various translations of IFRS into European languages have legal status in their various countries. As in any field, there is a risk that the process of translation will change or lose meaning from the original version, in this case English. Two examples are given here.

Cash flow statements are required by IAS 7, reconciling to 'cash and cash equivalents'. The term 'cash equivalents' is defined in paragraphs 6 to 9, including:

An investment normally qualifies as a cash equivalent only when it has a short maturity of, say, three months ...

This is a risible attempt to avoid writing a rule, as opposed to a principle. It is not clear why it was necessary to include 'normally' in a sentence that continues with 'say'. The Portuguese translation[12] of the standard omits the word 'say'. This improves the standard but does not translate it accurately. As a result, it would be more difficult in Portugal than in Ireland to argue successfully that an investment with a maturity of just over three months is a cash equivalent.

As a further example, IAS 41 (para. 34) requires an unconditional government grant related to a bi-

ological asset to be recognised as income when the grant becomes 'receivable'. The Norwegian[13] version (DnR, 2006. 543) translates this as '*mottas*', which means 'received'. This is an important difference.

This all leads to:

H$_2$:   For some topics, different translations of IFRS lead to different practices.

Gaps in IFRS

In a sense, there are no gaps in IFRS because IAS 8 (para. 10) tells an entity how to choose accounting policies when no other part of IFRS applies. In such a case, resort is made to the general criteria of the IASB's *Framework*, to parts of IFRS related to the gap, and to standards of other bodies that use a similar *Framework* (most obviously,[14] US GAAP). This leaves entities with considerable room for manoeuvre, and allows the continuation of differences in practice.

An example of such a gap in 2005 and 2006 is accounting for insurance contracts. The general topic is addressed by IFRS 4 but a number of areas are left unresolved. Furthermore, entities were specifically exempted (IFRS 4, para. 13) from the requirements of IAS 8 for some aspects of policy choice. A second example of a gap in 2005 was oil and gas exploration, because IFRS 6 did not apply until 2006 (and, anyway, allows many choices).

From Section 2, the hypothesis here is that national traditions will continue as a way of filling any gaps in IFRS. This will include different ways of interpreting the Framework as part of applying IAS 8. That is,

H$_3$:   For topics on which there are no specific rules in IFRS, German practice is different from UK practice.

A particular sub-hypothesis would currently relate to accounting for insurance contracts.

Overt options in IFRS

In the early 1990s, there were large numbers of options in international standards. This was caused partly because many standards had been written before the *Framework* was published in 1989. Also, the IASC operated on the basis of the need for a 75% majority of votes of its Board members. The members (mainly accountancy bodies) and their representatives at the Board (mainly partners in large audit firms or employees of large companies) came from diverse backgrounds and were subject to political pressure (e.g. see Zeff, 2002). One way of passing a standard in this context was to insert options.

These options have been gradually removed, particularly in 1993 and in 2003 as a result of two 'improvement' exercises. In the first of these, many options were highlighted by the IASC with the labels 'benchmark treatment' and 'allowed alternative'. The IASB has not continued this

---

[12] Discussions with José Gonçalves Roberto of the Ordem dos Revisores Oficiais de Contas, 15.11.2002. For the Portuguese text, see the Annexes to Regulation 1725/2003.

[13] Norway, although not an EU country, has implemented the Regulation as a member of the European Economic Area.

[14] I refer to the US rather than the UK here not because the US Framework is necessarily closer but because fewer UK standards than US standards cover more ground than IFRS or are more detailed than IFRS.

Table 1
Examples of overt options in IFRS*

IAS 1	Choice of content of statement of changes in equity (paras. 8, 96).
IAS 1	No format requirements for balance sheets or income statements (paras. 76, 81).
IAS 2	FIFO or weighted average for the determination of the cost of inventories (para. 25).
IAS 2	Marking to market allowed for inventories of commodity broker-traders (para. 3).
IAS 7	Net basis allowed for cash flow statements (para. 21).
IAS 7	Choice of classification for interest and dividend flows (para. 31).
IAS 16	Cost or fair value measurement basis for classes of property, plant and equipment (para. 29).
IAS 19	Actuarial gains and losses can be taken (a) immediately in full to the SORIE, (b) immediately in full to the income statement, (c) in full to income over the remaining useful lives of employees in the plan, (d) in part to income over that period, (e) in full or in part to income over a shorter period (paras. 92 – 93A).
IAS 20	Asset grants can be shown as a deduction from the asset or as deferred income (para. 24).
IAS 23	Choice of capitalisation or expensing for interest costs on constructed assets (paras. 7 and 10).
IAS 27	In parent statements, subsidiaries can be shown at cost or as available-for-sale investments (para. 37).
IAS 28	In investor statements, associates can be shown at cost or as available-for-sale investments (para. 38).
IAS 31	In group statements, a choice of proportional consolidation, or equity accounting for joint venture entities (para. 30).
IAS 31	In venturer statements, joint ventures can be shown at cost or as available-for-sale investments (para. 46).
IAS 38	Cost or fair value measurement for some types of intangible asset (para. 72).
IAS 39	Choice of cost basis or marking to market for some financial assets and liabilities (para. 9). (Other choices are also available within para. 9.)
IAS 40	Permission to classify a property held under an operating lease as an investment property (para. 6).
IAS 40	Entity-wide choice of cost or fair value as measurement basis for investment property (para. 30).

* Paragraph numbers as at 30 April 2006.

---

practice for any new or revised standards, but the terminology still remains in some un-revised standards (e.g. IAS 23).

Table 1 shows examples of overt options in IFRS. These do not include the large number of options in IFRS 1 (first-time adoption), but these are discussed later. The issue for this paper is whether options are exercised systematically differently from one jurisdiction to another, so that 'international accounting differences' survive. I suggest that this is likely to be the case, as now explained.

Let us again take the example of the UK and Germany, restricting ourselves as usual to the consolidated statements of listed companies. I suggest that tradition will be a major influence on the choices. Overall, the hypothesis is:

H₄: The choice of IFRS options by UK and German groups is different.

In more detail, taking five examples from Table 1, I suggest that:

(a) (IAS 1) UK groups will generally continue to

use the financial position format of the balance sheet (format 1 of Schedule 4A of the Companies Act 1985). For example, this is used in the model IFRS formats suggested by the UK firm of PricewaterhouseCoopers (2005). However, German groups will mostly continue to use the report format, as found in the HGB §266 and then adopted by German groups that moved to IFRS from the mid-1990s.

(b) (IAS 1) UK groups will present a Statement of Recognised Income and Expense (SORIE) which is similar to the UK Statement of Total Recognised Gains and Losses, whereas German groups will present the broader Statement of Changes in Equity.[15]

(c) (IAS 2) UK groups will mainly continue to use FIFO whereas many German groups will use weighted average because it is common under HGB practice, given that FIFO is restricted by tax law (Kesti, 2005). LIFO is also found in unconsolidated statements in Germany, but not allowed by IAS 2.

(d) (IAS 19) UK groups will take actuarial gains and losses immediately in full to the SORIE

---

[15] The choice will be removed if a standard based on the IASB's exposure draft of March 2006 is issued.

Table 2
Examples of covert options or vague criteria in IFRS

IAS 1	Determination of whether a liability is current on the basis of expected date of settlement or purpose of holding (para. 60).
IAS 8	The determination of materiality for various purposes (para. 5).
IAS 11	Use of percentage of completion method only if the outcome of a contract can be estimated reliably (para. 22).
IAS 12	Recognition of deferred tax asset for a loss carryforward only if future taxable profit is probable (para. 34).
IAS 12	Recognition of deferred tax liability on unremitted profits from subsidiaries only if dividends are probable in the foreseeable future (para. 39).
IAS 14	The determination of reportable segments based on a mixture of factors (para. 9).
IAS 17	Lease classification based on 'substantially all the risks and rewards' with no numerical criteria (para. 8).
IAS 21	Determination of functional currency based on a mixture of criteria (paras. 9–12).
IAS 27	The identification of a subsidiary on the basis of 'power to control' (para. 4).
IAS 28	The identification of an associate on the basis of 'significant influence' (para. 2).
IAS 31	The identification of a joint venture on the basis of joint control of 'strategic financial and operating decisions' (para. 3).
IAS 36	Identification of an indication of impairment based on a mixture of criteria (paras. 12–14).
IAS 37	Recognition of a provision based on probability of outflow of resources (para. 14).
IAS 38	Capitalisation of development costs when all of various criteria are met (para. 57).
IAS 38	Amortisation of intangible assets only if useful life is assessed as finite (para. 88).
IAS 39	Use of cost basis where equity instruments cannot be measured reliably (para. 46).
IAS 39	Estimation of hedge effectiveness as a condition for use of hedge accounting (para. 88).
IAS 40	Use of cost basis, despite entity-wide choice of fair value, for an investment property whose fair value cannot be measured reliably (para. 53).
IAS 41	Use of cost basis for a biological asset whose fair value cannot be measured reliably (para. 30).
IFRS 3	Identifying the acquirer in a business combination presented as a merger of equals (para. 20).
IFRS 5	Treatment of assets as held-for-sale if expected to be sold within one year (para. 8).

whereas German groups will continue to take them to income using the corridor (smoothing approach).

(e) (IAS 40) some UK groups will continue to use fair value for investment properties but German groups will continue to use cost.

Further predictions such as these could be made, and expressed as testable sub-hypotheses.

Covert options, vague criteria and interpretations in IFRS

There is further scope for internationally different practice because of different interpretations, covert options or vague criteria in IFRS. I separate this from different practice caused by the inevitable estimations involved in operationalising the standards (see below). Examples of covert options or vague criteria are shown in Table 2. As may be seen, some of these depend upon what is 'probable'. Doupnik and Richter (2004) suggest that German accountants interpret the word 'probable' (which occurs in many places in IFRS) more conservatively than US accountants. I now examine four of the items in Table 2: the definition of a subsidiary, identifying the functional currency, capitalisation of development costs, and indications of impairment.

Under IAS 27, a subsidiary is an entity over which another has 'the power to govern the financial and operating policies' (para. 4). This power can exist *de facto* for a minority shareholder if the other shareholders are widely dispersed and in practice do not exercise their voting rights. However, IAS 27 does not address this exact issue, and the IASB notes that some preparers of financial statements have misunderstood this, perhaps being influenced by pre-IFRS national practices (IASB, 2005: 2).

As a second example, under IAS 21, a group must identify the functional currencies of its subsidiaries, branches, joint ventures and associates. Such companies are seen as coming in two types, as in Table 3.

One might expect that an entity's functional currency would generally be that of its country of operation. If so, IAS 21 gives the same result as using

Table 3
Two types of foreign entity

	Distant entity	*Highly integrated entity*
Functional currency	Foreign	Parent's
Translation rates	Closing/average (i.e. current rate method)	Historical for historical cost items (i.e. temporal method)
Gains and losses	To equity	To income

the current rate method. This has been virtually universal practice in the UK under SSAP 20 (e.g. ICAEW, 1992; ACCA, 1992). However, under IAS 21, subsidiaries are sometimes seen as on the right of Table 3, leading to quite different results. For example, the German chemical company, Bayer, notes in its 2005 Report (p.93) that: 'Where the operations of a company outside the euro zone are integral to those of Bayer AG, the functional currency is the euro'. Bayer states that this is rare, meaning that the current rate method is generally used. However, a similar German company, BASF, states (pp.96/7) that the functional currency throughout Europe is the euro, and this would include UK subsidiaries. That is, for them, the temporal method is used. So, if the pound falls against the euro, a UK's subsidiary's buildings fall in Bayer's consolidated balance sheet but not in BASF's. It seems unlikely that these differences reflect different economic realities. They result from the need to assess a company's functional currency based on potentially conflicting indications from a series of criteria in IAS 21.

The third example is the requirement to capitalise certain development costs under IAS 38 (para. 57). Under EU national requirements, capitalisation is sometimes banned (e.g. the German HGB, §248) and sometimes allowed but not required (e.g. the UK's SSAP 13, para. 25). EU national requirements do not generally[16] contain a *requirement*, like IAS 38's, to capitalise when certain criteria are met. A famous example of the effect of this is Volkswagen's voluntary transition to IFRS from German accounting in 2001: the increase in shareholders' equity caused by capitalisation of development costs was 41%. A similar large effect occurred for BMW.

It is somewhat difficult to compare these large German motor car companies with an equivalent British company. However, the point is that capitalisation depends on demonstrating that all of a list of vague criteria are met, such as feasibility of completion, intention to complete, and availability of adequate resources to complete. Therefore, there is scope for deliberate or unconscious systematic international difference, driven by the factors discussed in Section 2. For example, as explained there, it is clear that German capitalisa-

tion for IFRS consolidation purposes has no tax implications. However, the position for the UK is different. On the other hand, capitalisation runs far more against the German tradition of conservatism than it does against the British tradition.

A fourth example of covert options relates to impairment of assets. The issue of *measurement* of impairments is dealt with below under 'estimations'. However, the prior issue is whether there is an impairment at all. This may depend upon several factors, including the degree of prudence in the valuation of assets before any impairment (more prudence means less need for impairments) and how IAS 36's criteria for identifying indications of impairment are used. Kvaal (2005) finds that the occurrence of impairments of non-goodwill intangibles was associated with changes in top executives in Germany but not in the UK, under very similar impairment standards and before annual impairment of goodwill became standard practice.

In conclusion, a general hypothesis is as follows:

H_5:   Covert options in IFRS are exercised differently by UK groups than by German groups.

For many covert options of Table 2, such as the four examined above, there should be sufficient published information to test several sub-hypotheses of H_5. For example:

$H_{5(a)}$:   UK groups use the current rate method for foreign subsidiaries more extensively than German groups do.

Another way of looking at this is that the existence of the IASB's International Financial Reporting Interpretations Committee (IFRIC) and its predecessor[17] is evidence of the potential for different interpretations of standards. The IASB's preference for principles-based rather than rules-based standards (Schipper, 2003; Nobes, 2005) means that it tries to avoid detailed prescription. IFRIC publishes lists of topics that have been raised with it but that it has decided not to deal

---

[16] The author is not aware of any that do in the 25 member states, although plans for convergence with IFRS might lead to this in some cases.

[17] The Standing Interpretations Committee (SIC).

Table 4
Examples of estimations in IFRS

IAS 2   Net realisable value of inventories (paras. 30, 31).

IAS 11   Costs attributable to a contract (para. 16).

IAS 12   Tax rate for deferred tax calculations based on the expected manner of settlement or recovery (para. 51).

IAS 16   (and IASs 17, 38, 40) Depreciation (or amortisation) based on estimates of useful life, residual value, and pattern of consumption (paras. 50, 51 and 60).

IAS 16   (and IASs 38, 40) Fair value when selected as a measurement basis (paras. 31 – 34).

IAS 19   Pension obligations based on estimates of mortality, final salary, etc. (para. 64).

IAS 36   Discounted cash flows or net realisable values for impairments (para. 18, etc.)

IAS 37   Best estimate of provisions based on percentage likelihoods of outflows (para. 40).

IAS 39   Fair values for certain financial assets and liabilities (para. 48).

IAS 41   Fair values for biological assets (para. 12).

IFRS 2   Fair value of equity instruments (e.g. share options or shares in an unlisted company) granted to employees (para. 11).

IFRS 3   Allocation of cost of a business combination to assets and liabilities of acquiree based on fair values (para. 36).

---

with (e.g. IFRIC, 2005). At least two answers were thought plausible by those who raised these topics. A research approach would be to examine practice in areas considered but not acted on by IFRIC or to examine practice in areas where an IFRIC Interpretation or draft has been issued, but before it comes into force. A difficulty may be that the issue is not sufficiently major for accounting policies to be disclosed by companies, so that data cannot be collected.

Schipper (2005) warns that pressure on the IASB to write interpretations will increase. If the IASB does not respond, one source of interpretations will be the SEC's prescriptions on the IFRS financial statements of the several hundred EU companies that are registered with it. These interpretations will only apply directly to SEC-registered companies but may have influence more widely. There will also be pressure for interpretations from individual national regulators or from regional bodies, such as the Committee of European Securities Regulators or the European Financial Reporting Advisory Group (e.g. see EFRAG, 2005). Although the regulators will attempt to co-ordinate their activities (IOSCO, 2005), different national interpretations may arise formally as well as informally.

Estimations in IFRS

As IAS 8 (para. 23) reminds us: 'The use of reasonable estimates is an essential part of the preparation of financial statements …'. The use of management judgment in estimates is seen as one aspect of earnings management by Healy and Wahlen (1999), who examine the scope for it in a US context. Over time, the need to use estimates to operationalise IFRS has increased. I distinguish these estimations related to measurement from es-

timations related to recognition or classification as in the sub-section above. Table 4 gives some examples of measurement estimations, two of which are examined below.

Depreciation (or amortisation) is required for assets with limited useful lives that are measured on a cost basis under IASs 16 (property, plant and equipment), 17 (finance leases), 38 (intangibles) and IAS 40 (investment property). It is also required for assets held at fair value under IASs 16 and 38 but not, curiously, under IAS 40 (see Nobes, 2001). Where depreciation *is* required, it is necessary to estimate useful life and residual value, the latter now at current prices.[18] The depreciation method (e.g. straight line or reducing balance) is also an estimate not a policy choice, because it depends on how the asset wears out.

I suggest that tradition, convenience and tax will play roles here. UK tradition (FEE, 1991) is that a convenient method is used (typically for plant: straight line, zero residual value and 10-year life). This is done in the knowledge that an entirely separate scheme of capital allowances operates for tax purposes. German tradition was (Haller, 1992), and for unconsolidated statements remains, to accelerate expenses by using the minimum lives allowed by tax law and the reducing balance method (but changing to straight line near the end of an asset's life).

It is clear that the tax-based useful lives and other estimates should be abandoned by German groups for IFRS purposes. For example, Volkswagen's transition showed an increase in

---

[18] IAS 16 (para. 6) of 2003, whereas IAS 16 (para 46) of 1993 required the continued use of the original price level.

shareholders' funds of 36% as a result. Related to this, reducing balance has largely[19] been abandoned for IFRS statements, partly perhaps because an amendment to the HGB[20] had already required the removal of tax-based policies from consolidated statements prepared under German domestic rules. However, in some other EU countries, reducing balance might continue under IFRS.

The general hypothesis is that:

H$_6$:   Estimations under IFRS are biased differently in German groups than in UK groups.

Sub-hypotheses based on the contents of Table 4 could be created.

Transitional or first-time adoption issues
One transitional issue has already been dealt with under 'different versions of IFRS': sometimes a new standard allows a period during which its requirements are merely encouraged. This subsection focuses on transitional issues that can lead to long-run effects on IFRS financial statements.

An example concerns business combinations. The original version of IAS 22 (of 1983) had allowed goodwill to be written off immediately against reserves; formerly a common German and UK practice. The 1993 version of IAS 22 required capitalisation followed by amortisation over a life limited to 20 years, but it allowed companies to retain the old write-off practice with respect to old goodwill. Then the 1998 version of IAS 22 allowed an amortisation life in excess of 20 years but only with annual impairment calculations. IFRS 3 does not allow any of these practices but once more 'grand-fathered'[21] them (para. 79). Consequently, German IFRS statements might have old goodwill amounts at zero, but might not, depending on their previous German practice. The potential amounts of missing goodwill are larger for later dates of transition to IFRS.

For adoption of IFRS in 2005 (the normal case for UK listed groups), IFRS 1 applies. Paragraph 15 of IFRS 1 also permits previous goodwill practice to continue for old goodwill. For a UK company this usually means to treat pre-1998 goodwill at zero[22] and to amortise subsequent goodwill over 20 years. The resulting incoherent goodwill figure from a UK balance sheet[23] is allowed to be brought into the opening IFRS balance sheet. Consequently, under IFRS, German and UK groups are likely to have smaller amounts of goodwill from otherwise similar French groups (which never wrote off goodwill against reserves). This difference will last for many years, and will also affect goodwill impairments.

Another example of an IFRS 1 transition option concerns the measurement of land and buildings. Before IFRS, German groups were required to measure land and buildings at historical cost, depreciated and impaired, perhaps excessively as noted earlier. UK groups were required (by SSAP 19, para. 11) to measure investment properties at current values, and allowed (by FRS 15, para. 42) to do this for other properties. However, FRS 15 (which applied from 2000) allowed previous non-current revaluations to be retained. IFRS 1 (para. 17) allows these old values (or current fair values) to be brought into the opening IFRS balance sheet as though they were costs. However, these values can be much higher than depreciated costs, particularly than German depreciated 'costs'. There is evidence[24] that these traditions will affect the starting point for IFRS. If so, the international difference in balance sheet values, depreciation charges and impairment losses will last as long as the fixed assets are held.

There are several further options in IFRS 1 (para. 13) which might have systematically different effects in different countries. The general hypothesis is:

H$_7$:   Pre-IFRS differences between national practices have a significant effect on IFRS financial statements.

Examples of sub-hypotheses, from above, are:

H$_{7(a)}$:   German and UK groups have more goodwill written off against reserves than French groups do.

H$_{7(b)}$:   The ratio of IFRS book value to market value of land and buildings is lower for German groups than for UK groups.

Imperfect enforcement of IFRS
The last of the suggested sources of opportunity for international differences despite a requirement to use IFRS is that the degree of enforcement of rules (and therefore compliance with them) varies internationally. To illustrate this, I will retain the EU as a context, and particularly the contrast of Germany and the UK.

As noted earlier, enforcement (including monitoring) of compliance with IFRS remains a nation-

---

[19] A survey by the author of the 2002 IFRS statements of 28 German listed companies (names starting with K-N) shows only two companies still using reducing balance, and three providing no information.

[20] §298, as amended in 1998.

[21] That is, allowed previous practices to be left in place for previous transactions.

[22] The UK standard, FRS 10, also contained grand-fathering clauses allowing old goodwill to remain written off as had been common practice under SSAP 22.

[23] For example, that of 31 December 2003, for a date of transition to IFRS of 1 January 2004 (i.e. for first IFRS statements for 2005).

[24] Values in excess of cost are not allowed under HGB rules, and the option to bring assets in at a fair value deemed to be cost did not exist when most large German companies adopted IFRS. By contrast, some UK companies (e.g. Marks & Spencer) have used the option for first-time adoption.

Table 5
Summary of main hypotheses

H_1: International differences in practice exist among IFRS companies due to differences in the version of IFRS being used.

H_2: For some topics, different translations of IFRS lead to different practices.

H_3: For topics on which there are no specific rules in IFRS, German practice is different from UK practice.

H_4: The choice of IFRS options by UK and German groups is different.

H_5: Covert options in IFRS are exercised differently by UK groups than by German groups.

H_6: Estimations under IFRS are biased differently in German groups than in UK groups.

H_7: Pre-IFRS differences between national practices have a significant effect on IFRS financial statements.

H_8: Compliance with IFRS by German groups is lower than that by UK groups.

---

al matter within the EU. It has been suggested (La Porta et al., 1997) that enforcement of accounting rules is stronger in the UK than in Germany. Hope (2003) constructed an index of compliance and registered Germany substantially lower than the UK. Furthermore, a great deal of evidence has been amassed that compliance by German groups with international standards was lax despite an audited statement of compliance by directors (e.g. Street and Bryant, 2000; Street and Gray, 2001). By contrast, compliance with standards in the UK since the creation of the Financial Reporting Review Panel (FRRP) in 1990 is generally regarded as having been high (Brown and Tarca, 2005).

In 2005, a body loosely based on the model of the FRRP was established in Germany (Brown and Tarca, 2005). It remains to be seen whether this will dramatically improve compliance with IFRS. Unless it does, the following hypothesis might be confirmed:

H_8: Compliance with IFRS by German groups is lower than that by UK groups.

Much of the historical evidence for this relates to missing disclosures in the case of German groups. If this continues, analysts will be less able to interpret German financial statements than UK ones. If German compliance improves, researchers could choose another EU country, and it is likely that one could be found where compliance remains poor.

4. Conclusion: a research agenda and some policy implications

International differences in financial reporting have been the subject of a large field of research and teaching, especially from the 1980s onwards. The compulsory use of IFRS for consolidated statements from 2005 in several major capital markets, and the convergence of IFRS and US GAAP, have had a major impact on this. This paper investigates whether international differences are likely to continue to exist for such consolidated statements.

The *motives* for differences in national accounting systems were examined in Section 2. It was suggested that, although some aspects of these no longer apply for the consolidated statements of listed companies, other aspects of the systems of financing, law and tax could still drive international differences in practice under IFRS where scope for it exists. Inertia and the desire to minimise change for preparers and users would contribute to the desire to maintain pre-IFRS practices.

The *opportunity* for systematic international differences in IFRS practice was examined in Section 3 under eight headings. This led to eight main hypotheses, with some proposals for sub-hypotheses, many expressed in terms of differences between German and UK IFRS reporting. The main hypotheses are summarised in Table 5. Suggestions were made about how some of the hypotheses could be tested. The hypotheses could be rephrased for other pairs of countries or more widely.

In addition to addressing whether international differences have survived, the hypotheses are important taken together because of their implications for the international comparability of financial statements, such as whether there are international differences in the quality of earnings. Some of the hypotheses are more important than others and some are more easily testable than others. However, this will depend on the countries chosen for investigation, so no ranking by importance is suggested here.

Some types of difference investigated by the hypotheses may reduce over time while others continue or increase. Those that may reduce include the gaps in IFRS (H_3), overt options (H_4) and transitional issues (H_7). Those that may increase include special EU versions or other versions of IFRS (H_1).

In conclusion, it is suggested that, like rumours of the death of history, those of the death of 'international accounting' have been greatly exaggerated. Researchers are encouraged to critique the hypotheses and, if they seem plausible, to test them. Major changes to accounting rules and practices, such as the arrival of IFRS, will also have created other new opportunities for research.

The implications for users of IFRS financial statements are that international comparability may have increased but that large differences are likely to remain. For the IASB and other regulators, this paper identifies areas that might be addressed if international differences are to be removed. A further policy implication relates to the SEC's assessment of whether IFRS statements should be accepted without reconciliation to US GAAP. At first sight, the analysis here might provide excuses for further delay by the SEC. However, some of the opportunities for international differences within IFRS were already apparent to the SEC (e.g. overt options) and some others are inherent in any set of standards (e.g. covert options and measurement estimations). There are arguments here for assessment of IFRS practice on a country-by-country basis rather than EU-wide.

References

AAA (1977). *Accounting Review*, Supplement to Vol. 52.
ACCA (1992). *The Operation of SSAP 20*. London: Association of Chartered Certified Accountants.
Alexander, A. and Archer, S. (2000). 'On the myth of Anglo-Saxon financial accounting'. *International Journal of Accounting*, 35(4): 539–557.
Ball, R., Kothari, S.P. and Robin, A. (2000). 'The effect of international institutional factors on properties of accounting earnings'. *Journal of Accounting and Economics*, 29(1): 1–51.
Baydoun, N. and Willett, R. (1995). 'Cultural relevance of Western accounting systems to developing countries'. *Abacus* (March): 67–92.
Brown, P. and Tarca, A. (2005). 'A commentary on issues relating to the enforcement of international financial reporting standards in the EU'. *European Accounting Review*, 14(1): 181–212.
Bushman, R. and Piotroski, J. (2006). 'Financial reporting incentives for conservative accounting'. *Journal of Accounting and Economics*. Forthcoming.
Cairns, D. (1997). 'The future shape of harmonization: a reply'. *European Accounting Review*, 6(2): 305–48.
d'Arcy, A. (2001). 'Accounting classification and the international harmonisation debate – an empirical investigation'. *Accounting, Organizations and Society*, 26: 327–349.
David, R. and Brierley, J.E.C. (1985). *Major Legal Systems in the World Today*. London: Stevens.
DnR (2006). *IFRS på Norsk*, DnR Forlaget.
Doupnik, T.S. and Richter, M. (2004). 'The impact of culture on the interpretation of "in context" probability expressions'. *Journal of International Accounting Research*, 3(1): 1–20.
Doupnik, T.S. and Salter, S.B. (1993). 'An empirical test of a judgemental international classification of financial reporting practices'. *Journal of International Business Studies*, 24 (1): 41–60.
Doupnik, T. and Salter, S. (1995). 'External environment, culture, and accounting practice: a preliminary test of a general model of international accounting development'. *International Journal of Accounting*, 30(3): 189–207.
EFRAG (2005). *Achieving Consistent Application of IFRS in the EU: A Discussion Paper*, Brussels: European

Financial Reporting Advisory Group.
FEE (1991). *European Survey of Published Accounts*. London: Routledge.
Feige, P. (1997). 'How 'uniform' is financial reporting in Germany? The example of foreign currency translation'. *European Accounting Review*, 6(1): 109–122.
Franks, J. and Meyer, C. (2001). *Ownership and Control of German Corporations*, London: Centre for Economic Policy Research, discussion paper 2898.
Fukuyama, F. (1989). 'The end of history?' *The National Interest*, 16 (Summer).
Gernon, H. and Wallace, R.S.O. (1995). 'International accounting research: a review of its ecology, contending theories and methodology'. *Journal of Accounting Literature*, 14: 54–106.
Gray, S.J. (1988). 'Towards a theory of cultural influence on the development of accounting systems internationally'. *Abacus*, 24 (1): 1–15.
Haller, A. (1992). 'The relationship of financial and tax accounting in Germany: a major reason for accounting disharmony in Europe'. *International Journal of Accounting*, 27: 310–23.
Haller, A. and Eierle, B. (2004). 'The adaptation of German accounting rules to IFRS: A legislative balancing act'. *Accounting in Europe*, 1: 27–50.
Hatfield, H.R. (1911). 'Some variations in accounting practices in England, France, Germany and the US'. Published in *Journal of Accounting Research*, (2) 1966: 169–82.
Healy, P.M. and Wahlen, J.M. (1999). 'A review of the earnings management literature and its implications for standard setting'. *Accounting Horizons*, 13 (4): 365–383.
Hope, O.-K. (2003). 'Disclosure practices, enforcement of accounting standards, and analysts' forecast accuracy: An international study'. *Journal of Accounting Research*, 41 (2): 235–73.
IASB (2005). *Update*, London: International Accounting Standards Board, October.
ICAEW (1992). *Financial Reporting*, London: Institute of Chartered Accountants in England and Wales.
IFRIC (2005). *IFRIC Update*, London: International Accounting Standards Board, August: 7.
IOSCO (2005). 'Regulators to share information on International Financial Reporting Standards'. Media release from the International Organization of Securities Commissions, 4.10.2005.
Jaggi, B. and Low, P.Y. (2000). 'Impact of culture, market forces, and legal system on financial disclosures'. *International Journal of Accounting*, 35 (4): 495–519.
Kesti, J. (2005). 'Germany' in *European Tax Handbook*. Amsterdam: International Bureau of Fiscal Documentation, part A.1.3.4.
KPMG (2005). 'IFRSs and the EU endorsement process: a status report', *IFRS Briefing*, Issue 37 (November); also see Issue 41 (December): 2.
Kvaal, E. (2005). *Topics in Accounting for Impairment of Fixed Assets*. Oslo: BI Norwegian School of Management, ch. 3.
Lamb, M., Nobes, C.W. and Roberts, A.D. (1998). 'International variations in the connections between tax and financial reporting', *Accounting and Business Research* (Summer): 173–188.
La Porta, R., Lopez-de-Silanes, F., Shleifer, A. and Vishny, R.W. (1997). 'Legal determinants of external finance'. *Journal of Finance*, 52(3): 1,131–50.
La Porta, R., Lopez-de-Silanes, F., Shleifer, A. and Vishny, R.W. (1998). 'Law and finance'. *Journal of Political Economy*, 106(6): 1113–54.
McCreevy, C. (2005). 'Governance and accountability in financial services', speech on 1.2.2005 (Speech/05/64),

Vol. 36 No. 3. 2006   245

European Commission, Directorate of Internal Market and Services, p.3. Also see *Accountancy Age*, 10.11.2005, p.10; and *IAS Plus*, Deloitte (November) 2005: 17.

Mueller, G.G. (1967). *International Accounting*, Part I, New York: Macmillan.

Nair, R.D. and Frank, W.G. (1980). 'The impact of disclosure and measurement practices on international accounting classifications'. *Accounting Review* (July): 426–450.

Nobes, C.W. (1983). 'A judgmental international classification of financial reporting practices'. *Journal of Business Finance and Accounting*, 10(1):1–19.

Nobes, C.W. (1988). 'The causes of financial reporting differences', ch. 2 in C.W. Nobes and R.H. Parker, *Issues in Multinational Accounting*. Oxford: Philip Allan.

Nobes, C.W. (1998a). 'The future shape of harmonization: some responses'. *European Accounting Review*, 7(2): 323–30.

Nobes, C.W. (1998b). 'Towards a general model of the reasons for international differences in financial reporting'. *Abacus*, 34(2): 162–187.

Nobes, C.W. (2001). *Asset Measurement Bases in UK and IASC Standards*. London: Association of Chartered Certified Accountants, ch. 4.

Nobes, C.W. (2003). 'On the myth of "Anglo-Saxon" Accounting: A comment'. *International Journal of Accounting*, 38(1): 95–104.

Nobes, C.W. (2004). 'On accounting classification and the international harmonisation debate'. *Accounting, Organizations and Society*, 29(2): 189–200.

Nobes, C.W. (2005). 'Rules-based standards and the lack of principles in accounting'. *Accounting Horizons* (March): 25–34.

Nobes, C.W. and Mueller, G.G. (1997). 'How uniform is financial reporting in Germany: some replies'. *European Accounting Review*, 6(1): 123–9.

Ordelheide, D. (2001). 'Germany – Group Accounts' in Ordelheide and KPMG, *Transnational Accounting*, Vol. 2. Oxford: Palgrave.

Perera, M.H.B. (1989). 'Towards a framework to analyse the impact of culture on accounting'. *International Journal of Accounting*, 24: 42–56.

PricewaterhouseCoopers (2005). *IFRS/UK Illustrative Financial Statements for 2005*. London: PricewaterhouseCoopers.

Richard, J. (2001). 'France – Group Accounts' in D. Ordelheide and KPMG, *Transnational Accounting*, Vol. 2. Oxford: Palgrave.

Schipper, K. (2003). 'Principles-based accounting standards'. *Accounting Horizons*, 17(1): 61–72.

Schipper, K. (2005). 'The introduction of international accounting standards in Europe: implications for international convergence'. *European Accounting Review*, 14(1): 101–26.

Seidler, L.J. (1967). 'International accounting – the ultimate theory course'. *Accounting Review* (October): 775–81.

Sellhorn, T. and Gornik-Tomaszewski (2005). 'Implications of the 'IAS Regulation' for research into the international differences in accounting systems'. Paper presented at the University of Regensburg, September.

Street, D.L. and Bryant, S.M. (2000). 'Disclosure level and compliance with IASs. A comparison of companies with and without US listings and filings'. *International Journal of Accounting*, 35(3): 305–29.

Street, D.L. and Gray, S.J. (2001). *Observance of International Accounting Standards: Factors Explaining Non-compliance*. London: Association of Chartered Certified Accountants.

Tarca, A., Moy, M. and Morris, R.D. (2005). 'An investigation of the relationship between use of international accounting standards and source of company finance in Germany'. Paper presented at the University of Sydney, March 31 (under journal review).

Van Hulle, E. (2005). 'From accounting directives to international accounting standards'. Ch. 6.1 in C. Leuz, D. Pfaff and A. Hopwood, *The Economics and Politics of Accounting*. Oxford: University Press.

Weissenberger, B.E., Stahl, A.B. and Vorstius, S. (2004). 'Changing from German GAAP to IFRS or US GAAP: A survey of German companies'. *Accounting in Europe*, 1: 169–89.

Whittington, G. (2005). 'The adoption of international accounting standards in the European Union'. *European Accounting Review*, 14(1): 127–53.

Xiao, J., Weetman, P. and Sun, M. (2004). 'Political influence and co-existence of a uniform accounting system and accounting standards: recent developments in China'. *Abacus*, 40(2): 193–218.

Zeff, S.A. (2002). '"Political" lobbying on proposed standards: a challenge to the IASC'. *Accounting Horizons* (March): 46–48.

Zeff, S.A. (2006). 'Political lobbying on accounting standards – national and international experience'. Ch. 9 in C.W. Nobes and R.H. Parker, *Comparative International Accounting*. Hemel Hempstead: Prentice Hall.

Zysman, J. (1983). *Government, Markets and Growth: Financial Systems and the Politics of Industrial Change*. Ithaca: Cornell University Press and Oxford: Martin Robertson.

[12]

Accounting and Business Research, Vol. 40. No. 2, pp. 173–187, 2010

International differences in IFRS policy choice: a research note

Erlend Kvaal and Christopher Nobes*

Abstract — Building on literature that suggests motives and opportunities for national versions of IFRS practice, we examine whether there are systematic differences in IFRS accounting policies between countries. Using information from the annual reports of companies in the blue chip indices of the largest five stock markets that use IFRS, we reject a null hypothesis that IFRS practice is the same across countries. For 16 accounting policy issues, we find instead significant evidence that pre-IFRS national practice continues where this is allowed within IFRS. By this, we document the existence of national patterns of accounting within IFRS. We also point out some policy implications that arise from our findings.
Keywords: international standards; international differences; policy choice

1. Introduction

It has been suggested that there are motives and opportunities for the survival of international differences under International Financial Reporting Standards (IFRS) (Ball, 2006; Nobes, 2006; Zeff, 2007). This paper seeks to answer two questions relating to this. First, are there systematic differences between countries with respect to the accounting policies that companies use within IFRS, so that one can identify national IFRS patterns? Second, if there are, can we explain how policies were chosen on transition to IFRS?

We investigate these questions using the 2005–06 IFRS annual reports of companies based in five countries: Australia, France, Germany, Spain and the UK. In all these countries, IFRS is compulsory,[1] at least for the consolidated statements of listed companies. Strictly speaking, it is EU-endorsed IFRS[2] that is compulsory for the EU companies, and IFRS-based Australian standards that are compulsory in Australia. This point presents one of the drivers of different practices. Other opportunities for variety arise from options clearly available within IFRS, and we concentrate on

these. Given the motives and opportunities for national versions of IFRS, we expect to find such differences in practice.

This paper contributes to the literature in a number of ways. First, we document formally that there are different national versions of IFRS practice. Related to this, we show that companies not only have an opportunity to pursue pre-IFRS practices originating in their national GAAP,[3] but also extensively use this opportunity.

These findings are important for several reasons. For financial statement users, they imply that full international comparability has not yet arrived. Therefore, it has been suggested, investors might be misled by an apparent uniformity (Ball, 2006: 15). As long as accounting standards contain options and require use of judgment, some variation in accounting practice is inevitable. However, the existence of systematic differences in practice related to national borderlines is clearly in conflict with the objective of international harmonisation and may mislead financial statement users who do not pay attention to them. Some differences are observable and can be adjusted for by alert analysts (e.g. the location of dividends in a cash flow statement); other differences are easily observable but cannot be adjusted for without a large degree of estimation (e.g. the effects of the

*Erlend Kvaal is at the Norwegian School of Management, BI and Christopher Nobes is at Royal Holloway, University of London.
The authors are grateful for comments on previous drafts from Steinar Kvifte (Ernst & Young), John Christian Langli (BI), R.H. Parker (University of Exeter) and Christian Stadler (Royal Holloway), from participants in workshops at the UK's Financial Reporting Council, BI and the 2008 European Financial Reporting Conference in Lund, and from two reviewers and the editor of this journal. Christopher Nobes acknowledges research support from ACCA.
Correspondence should be addressed to: Prof. C.W. Nobes, School of Management, Royal Holloway, Egham TW20 0EX, UK. E-mail: chris.nobes@rhul.ac.uk.
This research note was accepted for publication in August 2009.

[1] In some countries, e.g. Germany, certain companies were allowed to wait until 2007. However, no companies that took advantage of this have been included in our study.
[2] The main difference between IFRS and EU-endorsed IFRS is greater permission to use hedge accounting in the latter. There are also lags in endorsement. However, none of these differences affects our study.
[3] We use this acronym to mean 'generally accepted accounting practices', i.e. those practices that result from national requirements or from predominant choices.

inventory flow method on profit, or the absence of a gross profit figure in a by-nature income statement); yet others are not observable (e.g. the application of criteria for making impairments or for capitalising development costs). Some users of financial statements might be misled by even the first type of differences, but many might be misled by the third type. The second and third types create difficulties for international comparative analysis.

There are also policy implications. First, the IASB aims not just to issue standards but to facilitate comparable information (IASCF, 2005). This paper illustrates topics on which more work would be needed to achieve this objective. Second, the Securities and Exchange Commission (SEC) is monitoring the use of IFRS for foreign registrants on US exchanges (SEC, 2008, II, D). Part of this consideration includes an assessment of IFRS practice from 2005, but we show that there are several national versions of IFRS practice.

The paper proceeds as follows: Section 2 summarises relevant literature; Section 3 draws on this to state our main hypothesis and outline our research design; Section 4 explains our selection of countries, companies and accounting topics for this; Sections 5 and 6 present detailed hypotheses and results; and Section 7 draws interpretations and conclusions.

2. Literature

One strand of literature that is relevant to what follows is research on the motives and opportunities for international differences in accounting before the adoption of IFRS. This is examined in many papers and textbooks. The objective of our paper is not to try to explain pre-IFRS accounting differences. We ask, instead, whether there is evidence that country-specific variables affect choices within IFRS. To our knowledge there is no scientific literature that addresses this issue.

Nobes (2006) summarises the literature on the reasons for pre-IFRS accounting differences, asking whether these reasons might continue to operate in the context of transition to IFRS. A large number of factors has been proposed as pre-IFRS influences. The most proximate to accounting itself are legal systems, taxation systems and financing systems. These could still be relevant to IFRS practice. As examples of the three influences in turn: monitoring and enforcement of IFRS still depends on national regulatory institutions; tax motivations can still affect practice in unconsolidated statements, and some of this might flow through to consolidated statements; and companies in equity-finance coun-

tries might be the more interested in voluntary disclosures.

The national literature on IFRS is also likely to perpetuate national practices (e.g. PwC (2005) on formats).[4] Ball (2006: 15) suggests about IFRS that:

'The fundamental reason for being sceptical about uniformity of implementation in practice is that the incentives of preparers (managers) and enforcers (auditors, courts, regulators, boards, block shareholders, politicians, analysts, rating agencies, the press) remain primarily local.'

Commentators sometimes even argue in favour of attempting to preserve a national flavour of IFRS (Küting, 2007: 2557).

The international differences in accounting policies that we study mostly result from companies' policy choices, and research on this subject is potentially relevant to our work. Much of it is directed at revealing the incentives and motivations of such choices, e.g. in the context of earnings management (for comprehensive literature reviews, see Healy and Wahlen, 1999; Fields et al., 2001). These perspectives are not so important for the policy choices studied in this paper, because only a few of our issues (pension accounting, fair value option) affect the inter-period allocation of net income. Closer to our study is the research that explores the causes and effects of companies' adopting high-quality GAAP. It is often argued that companies accept the costs of such adoption in order to reduce their cost of capital (Leuz and Verrecchia, 2000; Ashbaugh and Pincus, 2001; Cuijpers and Buijink, 2005). Although there is ample evidence that voluntary adoption of IFRS has enhanced accounting quality (Barth et al., 2006; Gassen and Sellhorn, 2006), the benefits of mandatory adoption are more doubtful (Daske et al., 2007; Christensen et al., 2008). The importance of an adequate institutional framework for reporting incentives has also been emphasised (Ball, 2001; Ball et al., 2000; Bushman and Piotroski, 2006). Although this paper does not address the extent to which companies reap the rewards of IFRS reporting, the tendency to preserve national practice that we document may be one of the phenomena that limit the benefits of common reporting requirements.

There is some professional literature on IFRS practices from 2005 onwards. KPMG and von Keitz (2006) focus on 199 IFRS reports of the largest

---

[4] This publication shows a financial position form of balance sheet (like Format 1 in the UK Companies Act) as an example of IFRS practice.

Vol. 40, No. 2. 2010

companies of ten countries (seven of them in the EU), using year-ends of 2005 or before. The use of those year-ends excludes the first implementation by many UK companies,[5] and also means that countries such as Australia[6] were excluded. The KPMG study reports on the choice of options, in some cases including a breakdown by country. However, that study is not designed to produce a formal comparison of practices between countries. ICAEW (2007) reports on a survey of 200 listed companies of all sizes across 24 EU countries for 2005–06. A similar report for 2006–2007 has also been published (European Commission, 2008). In general, the data in these reports on the choice of options are aggregated rather than shown by country, although there are some exceptions to that.

There is also some literature that records pre-IFRS national practices (rather than investigating motives for international differences in them) and the differences between national GAAP and IFRS. To explore this, we have consulted national laws and standards, and analyses of them, such as TRANSACC (2001). We have also looked at surveys of practice, such as FEE (1991). Differences between national rules and IFRS were analysed by Nobes (2001), whose data form the basis of a study of factors influencing the scale of these differences by Ding et al. (2007).

3. General hypothesis and research design

The differences in IFRS practice that we study relate to policy choices. We base our hypotheses on the literature (of the previous section) that suggests that companies tend to continue with their previous national practices where this is possible under IFRS. However, we note that there are four distinguishable reasons for this. First, as explained above, the underlying causes of previous differences between national accounting practices (such as enforcement systems) may still have scope to affect IFRS practice. Essentially, many drivers of policy choice remain national. Second, and relatedly, IFRS consolidated statements are drawn up from unconsolidated statements. So, for example, the practices required or chosen in the unconsolidated financial statements of a German parent or a German subsidiary under German law might flow through to the consolidated IFRS financial statements where the practices are permitted under IFRS. A third reason is that directors of a group might try to maintain consistent accounting policies over time,

despite the transition to IFRS, so as to create as much continuity as possible for the users of the financial statements. Fourth, and relatedly, the directors might wish to minimise the number of changes to their accounting systems, thereby reducing the company's costs of transition to IFRS, by retaining pre-IFRS practices where possible.

A potential explanation for a particular predominant pre-IFRS policy in a country might be the importance of certain sectors in that country. For example, perhaps a particular sector mostly uses first in, first out (FIFO) inventory valuation whichever country it is in, and this sector is especially strong in one country, making FIFO more than averagely common there. Our prediction is that FIFO would continue to be common in that country under IFRS. However, this might mean that the option was not being chosen in a way that reduced international comparability among similar companies. Nevertheless, as will be shown, many of the international differences are so strong that sectoral imbalances cannot explain them. For example, no German company in our sample uses only FIFO in its IFRS statements whereas half of the UK companies do.

In order to discover whether internationally different versions of IFRS practice exist, we selected large companies from five major stock markets and examined their IFRS policies for 16 issues. We propose the following null hypothesis: IFRS practice is the same across all countries. We test the null hypothesis against an alternative of non-homogeneity by chi-square tests for each topic. We further test the validity of the null hypothesis against a number of alternative hypotheses that predict national practice relating to each issue. The predictions implied in the alternative hypotheses are based on our presumption that companies, in the absence of strong incentives to do otherwise, will pursue a policy previously adopted if it is still allowed. We by no means exclude a company-specific motivation for any choices previously made under the national GAAP (see Section 2), but our focus is only on the company's behaviour on transition to IFRS.

4. Selection of countries, companies and policy issues

Nobes (2006) suggests a series of hypotheses about international differences under IFRS, mainly expressed by using Germany and the UK as exemplars of previously different accounting 'systems'. We study companies from these two countries, but add Australia, France and Spain. The rationale for this list of five is that, of the countries

---

[5] Many UK companies do not have 31 December year-ends, so their first IFRS reports related to years ending in 2006.

[6] Australian usage of IFRS began, for most companies, on 1 July 2005.

Table 1
Country and sector* distribution

	Australia	UK	France	Spain	Germany
0 Oil and gas	3	4	1	1	0
1 Basic materials	6	10	1	2	3
2 Industrials	5	6	7	8	3
3 Consumer goods	1	12	7	1	5
4 Health care	2	5	2	0	1
5 Consumer services	8	22	6	6	3
6 Telecommunications	1	3	1	1	1
7 Utilities	1	9	4	5	1
8 Financials	17	26	4	7	6
9 Technology	0	1	2	1	0
Total	44	98	35	32	23

* Sectors according to Industry Classification Benchmark.

where IFRS are compulsory for listed companies, they had the five largest stock markets.[7]

Australia is different from the other four countries in not being a member of the EU. We do not expect that, by itself, to cause differences in IFRS practice.[8] However, one particular feature of Australian IFRS is relevant here: for two of the 16 accounting issues that we study, there was no option in Australian IFRS in 2005–2006. So, Australian policies on these issues in that period were not choices. Nevertheless, the requirements in Australian IFRS continued previous national requirements, so this is consistent with our general hypothesis that IFRS practice will preserve national practice. Further, the IFRS options were re-inserted in Australia for 2007–2008 reports onwards, so we investigate whether Australian companies continue with the 'Australian' policies on these two issues even when they are not required to.

From each of the five countries, we select the largest listed companies by examining the members of the 'blue chip' indices, respectively the ASX 50, CAC 40, DAX 30, IBEX 35 and FTSE 100. To some extent, the different number of companies in the indices adjusts for differences in the size of stock markets. We exclude foreign[9] companies and those that do not use IFRS. The only country for

which the last point was a significant issue was Germany where seven of the DAX 30 used US GAAP. After these exclusions, we have a sample of 232 IFRS reports. This is a much larger set of companies for our five countries than used by KPMG and von Keitz (2006) or by ICAEW (2007). Also, our sample is a complete set of domestic IFRS reporters in the indices, whereas the samples in the professional studies are likely to suffer from some selection bias, as already noted. Table 1 shows the sectoral distribution of the sample companies, analysed by country.

The selection of large companies is justified for both conceptual and practical reasons. Large companies are probably more attentive than smaller companies to the requirements and expectations of the global investor community (e.g. Chaplinsky and Ramchand, 2000; Wu and Kwok, 2002). Therefore, international notions about 'best practice' under IFRS will spread more rapidly among the large companies. For that reason, whenever we observe national differences in practice among the largest companies, we expect that similar differences exist among smaller firms, which are less likely to feel international influences. For the topics discussed in this paper, we can make inferences from the samples of large companies to the whole IFRS-reporting population that we could not make as easily the other way round.

As noted earlier, sectoral issues affect some accounting policies. For example, in the EU there are three different versions[10] of the Fourth Directive (for banks, insurance companies and others) which

---

[7] For example, see data from the World Federation of Exchanges, as at June 2005.

[8] As explained earlier, the difference between EU-IFRS and IFRS on the subject of IAS 39 is not relevant in our study.

[9] We define 'foreign' as meaning not legally registered in the country. That is, for example, we exclude from the French sample Belgian-registered companies that prepare IFRS statements in the context of Belgian law. We exclude Rio Tinto from the Australian sample because it is also in the FTSE 100 and prepares IFRS statements in the context of UK law. We also exclude AXA Asia Pacific from the Australian sample because it is a subsidiary of AXA (France).

[10] The Directives for banks (1986) and insurance companies (1991) are derived from the fourth company law Directive 'on the annual accounts of certain types of companies' of 1978.

Table 2
IFRS policy choices

1	(a)	income statement by function
	(b)	by nature
	(c)	neither
2	(a)	inclusion of a line for EBIT or operating profit
	(b)	no such line
3	(a)	equity accounting results included in 'operating'
	(b)	immediately after
	(c)	after finance
4	(a)	balance sheet shows assets = credits
	(b)	showing net assets
5	(a)	liquidity decreasing in balance sheet (cash at top)
	(b)	liquidity increasing
6	(a)	Statement of Changes in Equity, including dividends and share issues
	(b)	SORIE, not including them
7	(a)	direct operating cash flows
	(b)	indirect
8	(a)	dividends received shown as operating cash flow
	(b)	as investing
9	(a)	interest paid shown as operating cash flow
	(b)	as financing
10	(a)	only cost for PPE
	(b)	some fair value
11	(a)	investment property at cost
	(b)	at fair value
12	(a)	some designation of financial assets at fair value
	(b)	none
13	(a)	capitalisation of interest on construction
	(b)	expensing
14	(a)	FIFO for inventory cost
	(b)	weighted average
15	(a)	actuarial gains and losses to SORIE
	(b)	to income in full
	(c)	corridor
16	(a)	proportional consolidation of some joint ventures
	(b)	only equity method

contain pre-IFRS requirements on many presentation and policy issues. For such (and other) reasons, many empirical studies exclude banks and other financial institutions. As a result, these companies are under-researched. We include them. However, for several of the policy issues that we study, it is obviously appropriate to treat the banks or financial institutions separately.

We examine the annual reports for 2005–2006, that is those relating to accounting years starting in

2005. Many of these years begin on 1 January, but some UK companies have chosen other dates (especially 1 April), and many Australian companies use 1 July. The 2005–2006 reports were the first for which IFRS was compulsory[11] in our five countries, and they were also the last full set available[12] when we collected our data. All the companies were subject to the same requirements, as there were no changes to IFRS in this period.

Nobes (2006) identifies eight types of opportunity for international variations in IFRS practice: different versions of IFRS; different translations of IFRS; gaps in IFRS; overt options; covert options; measurement estimations; transitional issues; and imperfect enforcement. For several of these, detailed lists are provided: e.g. 18 overt options, 21 covert options. From these lists, we identified all the issues[13] for which data are observable in published annual reports. The resulting 16 issues of accounting policy are shown as Table 2. Nine of these relate to presentation and seven to measurement. Of the presentation issues, some are cosmetic (such as issues 4, 5 and 6), whereas others (such as issues 2, 3, 8 and 9) directly affect the content of key items within the income and cash flow statements. For our purpose, it is important to collect all the available information on international differences in IFRS policies. This is because on some other major issues, e.g. the criteria for assessing impairments (Ball, 2006: 17), it is not possible to detect and measure differences. The more that we can demonstrate systematic international differences for issues that can be observed (however important or otherwise), the more we can be confident that there will be differences for important issues that cannot be observed.

Our policy issues are not, of course, a random selection. They are deliberately chosen as those for which IFRS offers a choice and for which the chosen policy is observable. We are not claiming that the adoption of IFRS has led to no standardisation of practice. We are investigating whether there remain substantial systematic international differences in practice even under IFRS.

The data relating to the 16 accounting policy issues of Table 2 are not available on any database and were hand-picked from the annual reports[14] for the 232 companies in our sample. For many of the issues, a full set of data was obtained. For a few issues no data were available for some companies,[15] because the issue did not apply or because of poor disclosure.

5. Hypotheses

As explained in Section 3 we have a general null hypothesis of similar IFRS practice across countries that we analyse by a chi-square test. In addition, we make pair-wise comparisons between countries on all of the 16 issues covered by our study. The hypotheses underlying these comparisons are explained below. Our expectation is that pre-IFRS national practices will continue. We briefly review these practices and then set out our predictions for the 16 issues of Table 2. In nearly all of our hypotheses below, the pre-IFRS practices that we refer to result from national requirements. We assume that practices conformed with requirements (especially for these easily visible practices of listed companies, which were all audited by Big Four audit firms). In three cases (issue 13 for Spain, and issues 4 and 14 for the UK), we refer to predominant pre-IFRS practice. Strictly speaking, we should refer, company by company, to the actual pre-IFRS practices. So, in Section 6, we do ask whether particular companies continued with their pre-IFRS policies, but that detailed approach is not necessary for the general prediction of the IFRS practices of companies.

1. *Presentation of income statements (non-financials).* The Spanish law of 1989 sets out a by-nature format for the income statement. By contrast, the pre-IFRS rules in all the other countries allowed by-nature or by-function. We therefore predict for IFRS practice that:

H1: Spanish companies are more inclined than

---

[11] Of our five countries, only Germany contained companies voluntarily using IFRS immediately prior to 2005. A majority of our sample of German companies used IFRS before 2005. However, we do not anticipate that this would affect policy choices except where new options were introduced in 2005 or shortly before. In our list of policy areas, the only new option was to take actuarial gains and losses to the SORIE, introduced in 2005. It is therefore possible that this recent option was more likely to be ignored by German companies. However, this is still a country-specific factor.

[12] For example, reports for years ending in November 2007 were not available until well into 2008. We collected data during the second half of 2007.

[13] The 16 issues are all 'overt options'. We excluded six issues from Table 1 of Nobes (2006) because they related to unconsolidated statements (the options in IASs 27, 28 and 31 concerning investor statements) or to rare issues on which little or no data was available (commodity broker traders (IAS 2), government grants (IAS 20) and revaluation of intangibles (IAS 38)). Similarly, it is not possible to gauge the use of 'covert options' by using published annual reports. However, a few of the overt options in Nobes (2006) cover several issues (e.g. the treatments of interest and dividends in cash flow statements). So we have separated them.

---

[14] We used the English language reports in all cases, but we do not expect that this would affect our data.

[15] See the 'N' numbers in Table 3.

others to use the by-nature format of the income statement.

This is an important issue for analysis because it is not possible for users to obtain the same information[16] from the two different formats.

2. Operating profit shown (non-financials). Pre-IFRS national regulations on formats differ on whether a sub-total for 'operating profit' should be shown. There is such a line in the French *plan comptable général* (section I.III.III) and in the Spanish plan derived from it. Similarly, the formats found in the German *Handelsgesetzbuch* (HGB § 275) and the UK Companies Act[17] show operating items (specifically thus labelled) separately from others, although without specifically showing the subtotal. By contrast, there were no such headings or subtotals in Australia in ASRB 1018 (para. 4.1). We therefore predict:

H2: Australian companies are less likely than other companies to show a line for operating profit.

3. Treatment of equity-accounted profits (non-financials). IAS 1 has few format requirements for the income statement. However, its non-mandatory implementation guidance shows equity-accounted profit after finance costs and therefore outside of operating profit. The same applies to the French *plan comptable général* (Appendix to Chapter IV) and the related Spanish requirements. By contrast, the German HGB (§ 275) and the UK standard (FRS 9) show such profits after operating but before finance items. There has been no clear tradition in Australia. Many Australian companies do not show an 'operating' heading (see 2 above). Pre-IFRS guidance from AASB 1018 (para. 4.1) showed equity-accounted profits after finance costs, as do IFRS illustrations[18] from Australian audit firms.

Given that the French and Spanish national requirements show equity-accounted profits lower down the income statement than in the other countries which have a concept of 'operating', and given that only in those countries are the requirements mandatory (for non-IFRS reporting), we predict:

H3: French and Spanish companies are more inclined than others to show equity-accounted profits after finance items.

4. Presentation of balance sheets (non-financials). The pre-IFRS requirement in Australia was in the Corporations Law (and AASB 1034) which specified a format that showed 'net assets' but no total of credit balances such as total shareholders' funds and liabilities. The same applied in Format 1 of the UK *Companies Act 1985* (CA 1985), which also showed 'net current assets' and did not show total assets. This was the predominant format used in practice (Gordon and Gray, 1994: 76; and our own survey of pre-IFRS policies of our companies, discussed later). These can be called 'financial position' formats, although the UK's was a purer form.

By contrast, the accounting plans of France and Spain showed a two-sided T-account format, and the German *Handelsgesetzbuch* (HGB § 266) had a vertical version of this. In all three continental cases, there is no heading for 'net assets' but there is a heading for the total of the credit balances.

We therefore predict:

H4: Australian and UK companies are more inclined than others to use a version of a financial position format.

5. Liquidity order (non-financials). The pre-IFRS regulations for balance sheets (referred to above) show items in order of decreasing liquidity in Australia but (except for banks) increasing liquidity in the other four countries. Therefore, we predict:

H5: Australian companies are more inclined than others to present liquidity-decreasing balance sheets.

6. Statement of changes in equity. Only in the UK did pre-IFRS rules (FRS 3) require a performance statement in addition to the income statement. This UK statement was the model for IAS 1's statement of recognised income and expense (SORIE) – equivalent to the 'other comprehensive income' of a later version of IAS 1 – as opposed to the alternative statement of changes in equity of IAS 1 (para. 97).[19] So, we predict:

H6: UK companies are more inclined than others to present a SORIE.

7. Method of calculation of operating cash flow. Pre-IFRS rules on cash flow statements were

---

[16] For example, gross profit cannot be calculated from the by-nature format.

[17] Schedule 4 to CA 1985, now replaced by 'Company Regulations' in Statutory Instruments.

[18] For example, KPMG's *Reporting Under Australian Accounting Standards*, Example Public Company Limited (for 2007), p. 21; and PwC's *Value AIFRS Holdings*, p. 63.

[19] We refer to the version of IAS 1 in force in 2005 and 2006.

lacking in detail in Germany and were noticeably different from IAS 7 in France, Spain and the UK. However, only in Australia was the direct method required (AASB 1026) and this found its way into the Australian version[20] of IAS 7 that was in force in 2005–2006. However, IAS 7's choice of the indirect method was re-inserted into the version in force in 2007–2008, so we used data for that period for the Australian companies (typically periods ending on 30 June 2008). Given that the direct method is more onerous for preparers, we predict a continued[21] avoidance of it elsewhere:

H7: Australian companies are more inclined than others to use the direct method to calculate operating cash flows.

8/9. Presentation of dividends received and interest paid in cash flow statements (non-financials). IAS 7 (para. 33) suggests that dividends received might be either operating or investing flows and that interest paid might be either operating or financing, except that financial companies 'usually' treat them both as operating. In the UK, FRS 1 (para. 14) requires both dividends received[22] and interest paid to be shown as 'returns on investments and servicing of finance'. In Australia, AASB 1026 (para. 7.1) required both cash flows to be shown as operating. The French requirement[23] for consolidated statements is also to show both dividends received and interest paid as operating. There is no requirement for a cash flow statement in Spain; rather the law[24] requires a statement of sources and applications of funds. In Germany, cash flow statements are required for listed companies (from 1999 onwards) but the pre-IFRS rules lack detail.

There is therefore no clear national practice for Germany or Spain, but we can predict:

H8: UK companies are less likely than Australian or French ones to show dividends received as operating.
H9: UK companies are less likely than Australian or French ones to show interest paid as operating.

10. Use of fair value to measure property, plant and equipment (PPE). Pre-IFRS requirements in France, Germany and Spain were to base measurement on

historical cost except for occasional revaluations in France and Spain according to government regulations (TRANSACC, 2001: 1162, 2263). Only in Australia (AASB 1041) and the UK (FRS 15) was revaluation freely allowed. We predict:

H10: Australian and UK companies are more inclined than others to measure PPE at fair value.

11. Use of fair value to measure investment property. As for other PPE (above), pre-IFRS requirements in France, Germany and Spain were generally to measure investment property on a cost basis. However, as for other PPE, there was an option to use fair value in Australia. By contrast, continuous valuation[25] is required under UK GAAP by SSAP 19. We therefore predict:

H11: The tendency to measure investment property at fair value will be found in decreasing order in the UK, Australia and continental Europe.

12. Designation of financial assets to fair value (non-financials). Pre-IFRS requirements concerning the measurement of financial assets by non-financial companies differed by country. German law required measurement at cost or lower for all assets (HGB § 253). French and Spanish accounting laws were less resolutely opposed to measurement above cost,[26] so we use Germany in the hypothesis below. UK law allowed various versions of market value (CA 1985, Sch. 4, para. 31). UK standards and Australian law and standards had no requirements in this area. We therefore predict for non-financial companies:

H12: Australian and UK companies are more inclined than German companies to designate financial assets to fair value.

Financial institutions had different laws (for example, different Directives; see Section 4 and Hypothesis 5) allowing marking to market. We do not test hypotheses for financial institutions because of the small number of such companies in our sample of continental countries.

13. Interest capitalisation. The pre-IFRS requirement in Australia was to capitalise interest (AASB 1036). In Spain, the ICAC Resolution of 30 July 1991 deals with the issue in some detail, and it was

---

[20] That ruling in 2005–2006.
[21] For example, all our UK companies used the indirect method under UK GAAP in 2004–2005; see discussion later.
[22] Except that dividends received from associates and joint ventures are shown separately, also outside of operating.
[23] Second Methodology, § 426.
[24] Law 19/1989.

[25] SSAP 19 (para. 11) requires measurement at 'open market value' which is similar to fair value.
[26] For example, revaluations of various assets were required for listed companies in France in 1978 and in Spain in 1996.

almost universal pre-IFRS practice of our com-panies.[27] By contrast, in the other three countries, capitalisation of interest was allowed[28] but was not covered in detail in the regulations and was less common.[29] We predict:

H13: Australian and Spanish companies are more inclined than others to capitalise borrowing costs on construction.

14. *Inventory flow assumptions (non-financials).* Excluding consideration of last in, first out (LIFO) (which is not allowed in IAS 2), the UK and Germany stand out as having predominant flow assumptions in pre-IFRS national practice. In the UK, FIFO was the normal practice (FEE, 1991: 164; as also confirmed in our own survey of pre-IFRS policies). In Germany, weighted average was generally required by tax law (TRANSACC, 2001: 1293). In Spain, although there was no legal favouring of weighted average, there was also evidence of a clear pre-IFRS preference for it (FEE, 1991: 167; Gonzalo and Gallizo, 1992: 114). In the other two countries, no predominant basis was clear. We therefore predict:

H14A: German companies are more inclined than others (except Spanish) to use weighted average only.

H14B: UK companies are more inclined than others to use FIFO only.

15. *Actuarial gains and losses.* Most German DAX companies were already using IFRS before 2005 when an extra option was added to IAS 19 (para. 93A) to allow actuarial gains and losses to be taken in full to the SORIE. Therefore, they were already using the corridor approach (IAS 19.92/93). By contrast, the pre-IFRS requirement in the UK (under FRS 17) was the same as the SORIE option. Neither of these options was available in the laws of the other three countries. So, we predict:

H15A: German companies are more inclined than others to use the corridor approach.

H15B: UK companies are more inclined than others to use the SORIE approach.

---

[27] We surveyed the 2004 annual reports for the companies that specified their practice in 2005. Of the 17 companies, 16 capitalised interest, and one company capitalised some interest.
[28] For example, by AktG § 255(3) in Germany, or CA 1985, Sch. 4, para. 26(3)(b) in the UK.
[29] For example, our survey of UK reports of 2004–2005 showed that 35% of companies disclosed a policy of capital-isation. Only 13% disclosed a policy of non-capitalisation, but our expectation is that this would have been the policy of the non-disclosers.

16. *Proportional consolidation.* Pre-IFRS rules in Australia (AASB 1006) and the UK (FRS 9) did not allow proportional consolidation of interests in joint venture entities. By contrast, pre-IFRS French regulations required proportional consolidation (*Loi sur les Sociétés Commerciales*, Art. 357-3). In Spain, the method was required[30] in some industries and common in others (Gonzalo and Gallizo, 1992: 168). In Germany, proportional consolidation was allowed and used by some groups (TRANSACC, 2001: 1389). However, it was not typical practice, as it had been banned in Germany until 1987. We, therefore, predict:

H16: The tendency to use proportional consolida-tion is found in the following countries in decreasing order: France, Spain, Germany, UK and Australia.

As in policy issue 7 above, there is a complica-tion with the data for Australia. In the Australian 2005–2006 version of IFRS (i.e. AASB 131 in this case), the proportional option in IAS 31.30 was deleted. So we cannot measure policy *choice* for 2005–2006. However, the option was re-inserted for 2007–2008, so we use data for that period.

6. Results

6.1. Tests of hypotheses
Table 3 shows the results of testing the above hypotheses. First, it summarises the data collected for the five countries relating to all the issues of Table 2. For each country and issue, the table shows the policies used, as percentages of the companies for which the policy was observable (see the 'N'). In most cases, the data can be reduced to the percent-ages using one policy out of two available in IFRS, although in a few cases (e.g. issue 3) we record the scores for three possibilities.

As explained earlier, we conduct two sorts of statistical tests on these data. The chi-square test measures the overall independence between policy choice and country for each of the 16 issues. The null hypothesis of similar practice is rejected at the 1% level for 14 issues and at the 5% level for two of them.

Table 3 also shows the results of the binomial tests. The testing of issues that have two choices is carried out with conventional methods of approxi-mations to the normal distribution. In practice we do the same tests for the issues that have more than two choices, by formulating the hypothesis with respect

---

[30] At least, information on a proportional basis had to be included in the balance sheet for joint ventures in the construction industry (TRANSACC, 2001: 2314).

Table 3
Policy choices (percentages of companies by country) and hypothesis testing

	Policy choices by country; %					χ² tests[a]		Alt. hypothesis	Binomial tests[b] Hypothesis testing (pair-wise)	H0 reject. (level)
	Australia	UK	France	Spain	Germany	P-value	Cramer conting. coeff			
1a) income statement by function	59.3	47.2	54.8	4.0	76.5	.000	.242	H1	Sp vs. Au, UK, Fr and Ge	.01
1b) by nature	29.6	13.9	45.2	96.0	23.5					
1c) neither	11.1	38.9	0.0	0.0	0.0					
N (= non-financials)	27	72	31	25	17					
2a) inclusion of a line for EBIT or op profit	51.9	97.2	100.0	96.0	100.0	.000	.335	H2	Au vs. UK, Fr, Sp and Ge	.01
N (= non-financials)	27	72	31	25	17					
3a) equity acc included in operating	63.2	24.5	6.9	0.0	18.8	.000	.230	H3	Fr vs Au, UK and Ge	.01
3b) immediately below	15.8	32.1	3.4	8.3	62.5				Sp vs Au, UK and Ge	.01
3c) below finance	21.1	43.4	89.7	91.7	18.8					
N (= non-financials with equity accounting)	19	53	29	24	16					
4b) showing net assets	100.0	84.7	0.0	0.0	0.0	.000	.783	H4	Au vs. Fr, Sp and Ge	.01
N (= non-financials)	27	72	31	25	17				UK vs. Fr, Sp and Ge	.01
5b) liquidity increasing	0.0	100.0	100.0	96.3	85.0	.000	.893	H5	Au vs. UK, Fr, Sp and Ge	.01
N (= non-banks)	37	90	32	27	20					
6b) SORIE only	65.9	83.7	5.7	25.0	21.7	.000	.391	H6	UK vs. Au, Fr, Sp and Ge	.01
N (= all)	44	98	35	32	23					
7b) indirect cash flows	0.0	98.0	100.0	87.5	100.0	.000	.785	H7	Au vs. UK, Fr, Sp and Ge	.01
N (= all)	44	98	35	32	23					
8a) dividends received as operating	87.5	36.7	92.9	50.0	66.7	.000	.265	H8	UK vs Au and Fr	.01
N (= companies showing dividends)	40	60	28	18	6					
9a) interest paid as operating	90.9	68.4	88.6	38.7	61.9	.000	.134	H9	UK vs Au and Fr	.01
N (= companies showing interest paid)	44	98	35	31	21					
10b) some PPE at fair value	13.6	12.2	0.0	0.0	0.0	.014	.054	H10	Au vs. Fr, Sp and Ge	.05
N (= all)	44	98	35	32	23				UK vs. Fr, Sp and Ge	.05
11b) some investment property at fair value	42.9	73.1	0.0	0.0	0.0	.000	.411	H11	UK vs. Au	.05
N (= companies with investment properties)	28	26	7	14	15				UK vs. Fr, Sp and Ge	.01
									Au vs.Sp and Ge	.01
12a) some fair value designation	29.6	12.5	32.3	12.0	5.9	.033	.061	H12	Au vs. Fr	.05
N (= non-financials)	27	72	31	25	17				Au vs. Ge	.05
									UK vs. Ge	NR

Vol. 40, No. 2. 2010

Table 3
Policy choices (percentages of companies by country) and hypothesis testing (*continued*)

	Policy choices by country, %					χ^2 tests[a]		Binomial tests[b]		
	Australia	UK	France	Spain	Germany	P-value	Cramer conting. coeff	Alt. hypothesis	Hypothesis testing (pair-wise)	H0 reject. (level)
13a) interest capitalisation	75.8	47.5	40.0	94.4	22.2	.000	.186	H13	Au vs. UK, Fr and Ge	.01
N (= companies specifying borrow. costs)	33	59	25	18	18				Sp vs. UK, Fr and Ge	.01
14a) FIFO only	27.3	50.0	11.5	5.9	0.0	.000	.129	H14A	Ge vs. UK	.01
									Ge vs. Au and Fr	NR
14b) weighted average only	59.1	29.2	57.7	88.2	71.4			H14B	UK vs. Fr, Sp and Ge	.01
N (= companies with inventory)	22	49	26	17	14				UK vs. Au	.05
15a) actuarial gains/losses to SORIE	72.7	84.4	20.0	12.5	47.6	.000	.235	H15A	Ge vs. Au and UK	.01
15b) to income in full	18.2	3.3	5.7	37.5	0.0				Ge vs. Fr and Sp	NR
15c) corridor	9.1	12.2	74.3	50.0	52.4			H15B	UK vs. Au	NR
N (= companies with defined benefit plans)	33	90	35	16	21				UK vs. Fr, Sp and Ge	.01
16a) some proportional consolidation	5.3	22.4	81.3	84.6	31.3	.000	.381	H16	Fr vs. Au, UK and Ge	.01
N (= companies with joint venture entities)	19	67	32	26	16				Fr vs. Sp	NR
									Sp vs. Au, UK and Ge	.01
									Ge vs. Au	.05
									Ge vs. UK	NR
									UK vs. Au	.05

[a] The χ^2-test measures the independence of the cells of a contingency table with accounting choice cross-tabulated with country. The Cramer's contingency coefficient defined as $\chi^2/N(q-1)$, where q is the number of alternative choices, measures the strength of the association (cf. Bhattacharyya and Johnson, 1977: 434).
[b] The rejection level of the binomial tests refers to all the pair-wise tests included in that row. NR means no rejection.

Table 4
Deviations per company from pre-IFRS national requirements

	Australia	*UK*	*France*	*Spain*	*Germany*
N (= non-financials)	27	72	31	25	17
1. Average number of deviations	1.04	1.72	0.48	0.20	0.35
2. Maximum possible deviations	8	9	9	7	7
3. Average as percentage of maximum	13.0	19.0	5.4	2.9	5.0

to one specific alternative. It follows from the idea underlying the alternative hypotheses that, for testing purposes, the sample of companies from each country should be treated as separate populations. When, for example, it is claimed that Spanish companies are more inclined than others to present an income statement by nature, the related testing consists of pair-wise comparisons between the scores of the Spanish sample and the scores of each of the other samples, i.e. a total of four tests. If we had been certain that the null hypothesis were true for all companies except Spanish ones, we might, of course, have pooled the scores of the latter four for the purpose of the testing. However, whether the statistical distributions are identical or not is precisely the question we seek to answer, and the consequence is that all samples are treated separately. As we have designed the statistical analysis, each of the four tests should result in a non-rejection of the null hypothesis if it is true.

One problem that we encounter by this pair-wise approach is that some of the samples compared are under the threshold recommended for approximations to the normal distribution (typically 25, see for example, Bhattacharyya and Johnson, 1977: 295). In this study each single test is not essential for the conclusion, so we report all results, being aware that some of them may be based on insufficient sample sizes.

Thus, hypothesis H1, which proposes that Spanish companies have a greater tendency than others to use an income statement by nature, was tested pair-wise for each of the other four countries. In all four cases, the null hypothesis that Spanish choices are the same as others is rejected at the 1% level.

We ran 82 binomial tests. Of these, 62 led to the rejection of the null hypotheses at the 1% level, and a further 12 tests did so at the 5% level. The remaining eight tests did not enable rejection of the null hypotheses but in six of these cases the data were consistent with our alternative hypotheses.

In sum, there is a large amount of highly significant evidence that policy choice under IFRS varies internationally and is not random.

Furthermore, we have shown that the national profile of IFRS practice is explained by national pre-IFRS requirements (or predominant practice).

6.2. Comparisons with pre-IFRS practices

The above hypotheses largely concern the continuation of policies previously required by national GAAP. The only cases where we relied on predominant national choices for our hypotheses related to Spain (issue 13) and the UK (issues 4 and 14). A more precise hypothesis is that a particular company continued with its particular pre-IFRS policy choice. To test this, we looked at all the 2004–05 (pre-IFRS) reports of our Spanish and UK companies for these issues. For issue 13 (capitalisation of interest), 94% of Spanish companies[31] maintained their pre-IFRS practice of capitalisation. For issue 14 (FIFO, weighted average or a mixture), all 69[32] UK non-financial companies made exactly the same policy choice under IFRS as they had done pre-IFRS. For issue 4 (balance sheet format), 88% of the UK companies maintained their policies.[33]

On the assumption (defended earlier) that, pre-IFRS, our companies complied with national requirements, Table 4 shows the policy switches under IFRS. As can be seen, there are few such switches (e.g. less than 3% of policies were switched by Spanish companies). If we add in the other policy issues for which there was no national requirement, by studying the pre-IFRS practices of the particular companies, we find similar results.[34]

7. Conclusions

The central objective[35] of the IASB is to foster the provision of comparable financial information for participants in the world's capital markets. This

---

[31] Seventeen companies disclosed a policy for both years.
[32] There were 72 non-financial companies in our UK data, but three of them did not publish UK GAAP reports for 2004–2005.
[33] Of the 69 companies, seven changed from showing net assets to not doing so, and one changed the other way.
[34] For example, for the UK, we add six more issues, and find 18.8% switches for all 15 issues. We omit issue 12 because there was no pre-IFRS requirement or practice on designation.
[35] IASB's *Preface to International Financial Reporting Standards*, para. 6.

Vol. 40, No. 2. 2010

would be achieved if similar transactions were measured and presented similarly throughout the markets, i.e. uniform practice. The existence of systematic differences in accounting policies due to non-economic characteristics – such as country of incorporation – is clearly contrary to this ambition.

This paper highlights 16 accounting issues for which the literature identifies international differences in pre-IFRS reporting, and for which variation within IFRS is allowed and is observable if it occurs. An examination of the policies used by all the domestic IFRS reporters in the stock indices of five major capital markets for the first year of compulsory IFRS adoption allows us confidently to conclude that IFRS practice is subject to systematic differences across countries.

The continuation of national traditions seems to explain variations in IFRS policies between countries. However, that is merely a proxy for our more precise hypothesis that a particular company continued with its pre-IFRS policies on transition to IFRS. For each non-financial company of the five countries, we compare its practice under IFRS with pre-IFRS requirements and find that there were few deviations from those earlier requirements. When we extend this to look at policy switches even where there was no pre-IFRS requirement, we again confirm the preservation of previous practices.

Our research shows that systematic differences exist both in trivial matters (such as the liquidity order of the balance sheet) and in more complex matters (such as the composition of cash flows from operations or the treatment of actuarial losses). Whereas the former are hardly any obstacle to comparability, the latter most likely are. Some of our policy issues are not as important as others but they bolster the evidence for the existence of national versions of IFRS practice. This allows strong inferences to be made about variation in practices that cannot easily be measured, e.g. the tendency to make impairments.

We believe that our results are extensible in various ways. First, we examined very large listed companies. These are probably the least likely to evince national practices. We expect that test results would be at least as strong for other companies, but this can be examined. Second, our choice of blue chip companies limited the size of the sample, especially for Germany. We do not expect that a larger sample would change our results, except to make them even stronger, but it would enable an extended analysis of whether a company's sector affects its policy choices. This would add to our findings of some differences between financial and non-financial companies. Third, we examined 16

areas of policy choice. There are many others which are less observable. For example, there are several covert options and estimations in the issue of impairment, such as whether to recognise impairments, how to measure cash flows, and what discount rate to use. National traditions (and, specifically, previous practices of companies) are likely to continue in some of these areas. It is not clear how to examine these covert options, but other researchers might try. Fourth, we examined five countries, but would expect national versions of IFRS to be observable in smaller IFRS-using capital markets. Fifth, we concentrated[36] on one year's worth of annual reports; mostly[37] the first year of IFRS adoption. Later research could address whether companies gradually exploit options more fully, at least up to reports published in 2010 when some[38] IFRS options will no longer be available. To the extent that we look at data after 2005–2006 (for 2007–2008 for two Australian issues), we find national practice continuing.

The five points above are limitations of our research. A more general limitation is that, although we can largely explain why particular companies adopted particular IFRS policies in the context of the transition to IFRS, more work is needed to go deeper into why, over a long period, particular policies have been preferred in particular countries or by particular companies. For some issues (e.g. the German preference against measurement above cost), the literature is extensive. For others, 'accidents' are the apparent cause (such as the German use of the 'corridor' pensions method because German companies adopted IFRS before other countries did, when the 'SORIE' method was not available). For yet other issues (e.g. why the Spanish prefer to capitalise interest), there is no convincing theory. It might be necessary to theorise about each policy choice, one by one, such that no overall theoretical model would be explanatory.

We remind readers of other caveats. First, for most of our hypotheses, we assume that, pre-IFRS, national requirements were followed. We believe that this is highly likely to be a correct assumption for our large listed companies for our easily observable policy choices. However, there might be some exceptions. Second, for two of the policy issues for Australia, companies had no choice in

---

[36] Although, we examined 2008 reports for two Australian issues.

[37] Except for the German companies.

[38] Of our 16 issues, the presentation of the income statement, the capitalisation of interest, and perhaps the treatment of joint ventures will be affected, but not compulsorily until 2009 year-ends or later.

2005–2006. Although this does not alter our findings about the continuation of pre-IFRS practices, these are different cases from all the other countries and all the other issues. Nevertheless, by substituting data for 2007–2008 (when there was a choice), we can rectify that. This time, we need to assume that a company would have chosen in 2005–2006, what it chose in 2007–2008. We know of no reason to doubt that.

In addition to the possible extensions to our research resulting from the limitations mentioned above, another opportunity is to examine whether a two-class model (Anglo-Saxon versus Continental European) that was discussed[39] before the adoption of IFRS exists under IFRS. That is, for example, do Australian and UK companies tend to choose IFRS options in the same way (and perhaps in conformity with US GAAP), at least compared to continental European companies? A further possibility is to ask why certain companies deviate from pre-IFRS practices and national profiles, and why this is more common for UK companies than for Spanish ones (see Table 4).

Another issue to be investigated is whether market participants are able to see through the different policy choices. If it turns out that they can, then the differences are less important for users and regulators. However, investigations in this area are complex, and previous studies (e.g. on LIFO adoption) are both numerous and inconclusive.

There are policy implications from our findings. We believe that options in accounting standards are justified to the extent that they enable companies with different economic characteristics to produce a fair presentation of their activities. The systematic differences in practice between countries, that we document in this paper, are an unwanted corollary. In our view the disadvantages of systematic differences outweigh the advantages of having options, so we encourage the IASB to continue its efforts to remove options. Second, analysts of financial statements should be alert to the continuing international differences within ostensibly 'international' standards. Analysts might benefit from knowing the national profiles when trying to construct comparable figures. For example, it might be helpful to know that French IFRS companies tend to proportionally consolidate the cash of joint ventures, to show interest paid as an operating cash flow and to charge actuarial losses as expense, whereas UK IFRS companies tend not to do those things. It might also be helpful to know that

other, potentially more important, country-related differences (e.g. on impairment) exist beneath the surface of IFRS practice. Third, this variation in IFRS practice is likely to be of interest to regulators, especially to the SEC as it monitors IFRS practice of foreign registrants and perhaps, in future, of US companies. The SEC's acceptance of IFRS has been made on the assumption[40] of further progress in removing options.

References

Ashbaugh, H. and Pincus, M. (2001). 'Domestic accounting standards, international accounting standards, and the predictability of earnings'. *Journal of Accounting Research*, 39(3): 417–434.

Ball, R. (2001). 'Infrastructure requirements for an economically efficient system of public financial reporting and disclosure'. *Brookings-Wharton Papers on Financial Services*: 127–169.

Ball, R. (2006). 'International Financial Reporting Standards (IFRS): pros and cons for investors'. *Accounting and Business Research, International Accounting Forum*: 5–27.

Ball, R., Kothari, S. and Robin, A. (2000). 'The effect of international institutional factors on properties of accounting earnings'. *Journal of Accounting and Economics*, (29): 1–51.

Barth, M., Landsman, W., Lang, M. and Williams, C. (2006). 'Accounting quality: international accounting standards and US GAAP', SSRN.

Bhattacharyya, G. and Johnson, R. (1977). *Statistical Concepts and Methods*. Hoboken, New Jersey, NJ: John Wiley & Sons.

Bushman, R. and Piotroski, J. (2006). 'Financial reporting incentives for conservative accounting: the influence of legal and political institutions'. *Journal of Accounting and Economics*, 42: 107–148.

Chaplinsky, S. and Ramchand, L. (2000). 'The impact of global equity offerings'. *Journal of Finance*, 55(6): 2767–2789.

Christensen, H., Lee, E. and Walker, M. (2008). 'Incentives or standards: what determines accounting quality changes around IFRS adoption?', SSRN.

Coopers & Lybrand (1997). *Accounting Comparisons: UK, Belgium, Italy and Spain*. London: Accountancy Books.

Cuijpers, R. and Buijink, W. (2005). 'Voluntary adoption of non-local GAAP in the European Union: a study of determinants and consequences'. *European Accounting Review*, 14(3): 487–524.

Daske, H., Hail, L., Leuz, C. and Verdi, R. (2007). 'Mandatory IFRS reporting around the world: early evidence on the economic consequences', SSRN.

D'Arcy, A. (2001). 'Accounting classification and the international harmonisation debate – an empirical investigation'. *Accounting, Organizations and Society*, 26(4): 327–349.

Ding, Y., Hope, O-K., Jeanjean, T. and Stolowy, H. (2007). 'Differences between domestic accounting standards and IAS: measurement, determinants and implications'. *Journal of Accounting and Public Policy*, 26(1): 1–38.

European Commission (2008). *Evaluation of the*

---

[39] See, for example, the disagreement between d'Arcy (2001) and Nobes (2004).

[40] SEC, 2008, II, B.

Vol. 40, No. 2. 2010

Application of IFRS in the 2006 Financial Statements of EU Companies, at http://ec.europa.eu/internal_market/accounting/docs/studies/2009-report_en.pdf.

FEE (1991). *European Survey of Published Accounts 1991*. London: Routledge.

Fields, T., Lys, T. and Vincent, L. (2001). 'Empirical research on accounting choice'. *Journal of Accounting and Economics*, 31: 255–307.

Gassen, J. and Sellhorn, T. (2006). 'Applying IFRS in Germany – determinants and consequences'. *Betriebswirtschaftliche Forschung und Praxis*, 58(4).

Gonzalo, J.A. and Gallizo, J.L. (1992). *European Financial Reporting: Spain*. London: Routledge.

Gordon, P.D. and Gray, S.J. (1994). *European Financial Reporting: United Kingdom*. London: Routledge.

Healy, P. and Wahlen, J. (1999). 'A review of the earnings management literature and its implications for standard setting'. *Accounting Horizons*, 13(4): 365–383.

IASCF (2005). *Constitution*, London: International Accounting Standards Committee Foundation, para. 2 (a).

ICAEW (2007). *EU Implementation of IFRS and the Fair Value Directive*. London: Institute of Chartered Accountants in England and Wales.

KPMG and von Keitz, I. (2006). *The Application of IFRS: Choices in Practice*. London: KPMG.

Küting, K. (2007). 'Unterschiedliche Erfolgs- und Gewinngrössen in der internationalen Rechnungslegung: was sollen diese Kennzahlen aussagen?'. *Der Betrieb*, 47, 23 November: 2549–2557.

Leuz, C. and Verrecchia, R. (2000). 'The economic consequences of increased disclosure'. *Journal of Accounting Research*, 38 (Supplement): 91–124.

Nobes, C.W. (2001). *GAAP 2001: A Survey of National Accounting Rules Benchmarked against International Accounting Standards*. London: Arthur Andersen and other firms.

Nobes, C.W. (2004). 'On accounting classification and the international harmonisation debate'. *Accounting, Organizations and Society*, 29(2): 189–200.

Nobes, C.W. (2006). 'The survival of international differences under IFRS: towards a research agenda'. *Accounting and Business Research*, 36(3): 233–245.

PwC (2005). *IFRS/UK Illustrative Financial Statements for 2005*. London: PricewaterhouseCoopers.

SEC (2008). *Acceptance from Foreign Private Issuers of Financial Statements Prepared in Accordance with International Financial Reporting Standards without Reconciliation to U.S. GAAP*, RIN 3235-AJ90. Washington, DC: Securities and Exchange Commission.

TRANSACC (2001). *Transnational Accounting*, edited by D. Ordelheide and KPMG, New York, NY: Palgrave.

Wu, C. and Kwok, C. (2002). 'Why do US firms choose global equity offerings?'. *Financial Management*, Summer: 47–65.

Zeff, S. (2007). 'Some obstacles to global financial reporting comparability and convergence at a high level of quality'. *British Accounting Review*, 39(4): 290–302.

[13]

Auditors' Affirmations of Compliance with IFRS around the World: An Exploratory Study*

CHRISTOPHER W. NOBES, *University of London*

STEPHEN A. ZEFF, *Rice University*

ABSTRACT

It is widely believed that international financial reporting standards (IFRS) have been adopted in many countries, at least for the consolidated reporting of listed companies. However, in nearly all cases, what the rules require is some national or supranational version of IFRS. This might create problems for investor confidence and comparability. We examine what companies and auditors report concerning compliance with IFRS, focusing on the first full year of IFRS reporting by companies in the stock market indices of four major European countries and Australia. We find that, even when companies were complying with IFRS, they were generally not saying so, which seems to miss part of the point of the 35-year project on international harmonization. In a small number of cases, auditors provided dual reports: on full IFRS in addition to the mandated reference to national GAAP where the latter corresponds with full IFRS. These cases were found only in Germany and the United Kingdom, and mainly related to companies that filed with the Securities and Exchange Commission as foreign private issuers. We propose explanations for the general lack of dual reports and for the exceptions. We call for widespread adoption of dual reporting where a plain report on IFRS is not yet possible.

Keywords Audit; Compliance; IFRS; Reporting

AFFIRMATIONS DES AUDITEURS QUANT À LA CONFORMITÉ AUX IFRS DANS LE MONDE : UNE ÉTUDE EXPLORATOIRE

RÉSUMÉ

L'on tend à croire que les normes internationales d'information financière (IFRS) ont été adoptées dans de nombreux pays, tout au moins en ce qui a trait à l'information consolidée des sociétés cotées. Or, dans presque tous les cas, les règles n'exigent qu'une version

* The authors are grateful for comments on an earlier draft of this paper from Philip Brown (University of Western Australia), Kees Camfferman (Vrije Universiteit, Amsterdam), Paul Cherry (Accounting Standards Board, Canada), Geoffrey Everingham (University of Cape Town), Axel Haller (University of Regensburg), Liesel Knorr (German Accounting Standards Committee), Erlend Kvaal (Norwegian School of Management), Steinar Kvifte (Ernst & Young, Oslo), Christopher Napier (Royal Holloway), Paul Pacter (Deloitte, Hong Kong), R. H. Parker (University of Exeter), Christian Stadler (Royal Holloway), and Ann Tarca (University of Western Australia). They are also grateful for advice from J. Efrim Boritz (editor) and to Zhang Wei-Guo (International Accounting Standards Board).

AP Vol. 7 No. 4 — *PC* vol. 7, n° 4 (2008) pages 279–92 © CAAA/ACPC
doi:10.1506/ap.7.4.1

nationale ou supranationale des IFRS, ce qui pourrait soulever des problèmes au chapitre de la confiance des investisseurs et de la comparabilité. Les auteurs examinent l'information que communiquent les sociétés et les auditeurs en ce qui a trait à la conformité aux IFRS et s'intéressent plus particulièrement à la première année complète de publication d'information sous le régime des IFRS chez les sociétés que regroupent les indices boursiers de quatre importants pays européens ainsi que de l'Australie. Les auteurs constatent que, même dans les cas où les sociétés observent les IFRS, elles n'en font généralement pas mention, ce qui paraît contraire à l'objet même des 35 ans d'efforts du projet d'harmonisation internationale. Dans un petit nombre de cas, les auditeurs produisent un double rapport, l'un portant sur l'information intégralement conforme aux IFRS et l'autre contenant les références obligatoires aux PCGR nationaux lorsque ces derniers correspondent aux IFRS intégraux. Ces cas ont été relevés en Allemagne et au Royaume-Uni seulement et sont principalement ceux de sociétés qui rendent compte à la SEC à titre de sociétés émettrices étrangères fermées. Les auteurs tentent d'expliquer la rareté du double rapport de même que les exceptions. Ils préconisent l'adoption généralisée du double rapport jusqu'à ce que le rapport portant sur l'information intégralement conforme aux IFRS soit possible.

Mots clés : audit, conformité, IFRS, information

In 1976, Sir Henry Benson[1] said that he foresaw the "dominating importance" of international accounting standards "by about the year 2000" (Benson, 1976). Perhaps his listeners thought that this was a forgivable, but gross, exaggeration that was to be expected from the founding chairman of the International Accounting Standards Committee (IASC). However, the European Union's (EU's) regulation concerning the compulsory use of IFRS from 2005 (EU, 2002) was a major step toward the goal. With the announcements in 2007 from the Securities and Exchange Commission (SEC) accepting international standards (IFRS) for foreign registrants, and perhaps for all registrants, Benson's dream is coming true.

As part of assessing whether IFRS should be accepted without reconciliation to U.S. generally accepted accounting principles (GAAP), the SEC expected to be able to review several hundred sets of IFRS financial statements from 2005 onward. However, as Commissioner Campos of the SEC complained,[2] only about 40 filings that straightforwardly affirmed compliance with IFRS were received. Many said they complied with "IFRSs as adopted by the EU"; others said they complied with national rules, which, they said, corresponded with IFRS. Even in those cases where compliance with full IFRS[3] was almost certainly being achieved (e.g., in Australia), the audit report did not say so in 2005–6.

The central purpose of IFRS, as posited by the IASB and some commentators, is that users all around the world can better compare company financial statements, so that the cost of capital falls because information risks are reduced. Decades of effort have been

---

1. Later, Lord Benson. Henry Benson was the great nephew of the Cooper brothers, as in PricewaterhouseCoopers.
2. Roel C. Campos, "SEC Regulation Outside the United States," speech on March 8, 2007 in London (http://www.sec.gov/news/speech/2007/spch030807rcc.htm).
3. By this, we mean IFRS as issued by the International Accounting Standards Board (IASB).

made toward this end, which will not be achieved merely because statements *are* internationally comparable, but only when users understand and believe that they are comparable. It is startling that many companies have been complying with full IFRS but not feeling it necessary to say that they are, and therefore potentially not reaping the full rewards. We investigate possible reasons for this. The Canadian securities regulators and the International Organization of Securities Commissions (IOSCO) have both commented[4] on the expected incremental benefits to investors of clarity on this subject.

We have two main objectives in this paper. First, we survey major capital markets in order to identify where IFRS are required or where, instead, some local version of IFRS is required. We find that direct application of IFRS is required in only one major capital market. Given the rarity of direct application of IFRS, it becomes important for users to be alerted to the accounting rules being used. This leads us to our second objective. We examine audit reports with respect to IFRS for all the companies in the main stock indices of the world's five largest capital markets that require IFRS. We find little reporting directly on IFRS.

The paper proceeds as follows. First, we survey the degree to which IFRS have been adopted or adapted in major capital markets and distinguish between adoption of IFRS and convergence with them. The issue whether financial statements really have complied with IFRS is important but beyond this paper's scope. We then look at the rules relating to reporting on IFRS by management and auditors. Then we report on audit practice in five major countries, and try to explain it. Finally, we offer some conclusions and policy recommendations.

ADOPTION OR CONVERGENCE?

It is important to distinguish between adoption of IFRS and convergence with IFRS. Adoption (whether of process or of content) means that IFRS are used instead of domestic financial reporting rules. This might apply in certain countries for all companies or for some companies. It might apply compulsorily by law or de facto. An example of the former is that, in South Africa, domestic standards no longer apply to listed companies.[5] Instead, there is a requirement[6] to comply with IFRS and therefore for directors and auditors to report on that basis (de jure adoption). The situation is similar in Israel. An example of de facto adoption is the use of IFRS by many Swiss listed companies[7] for their consolidated statements.

In contrast to adoption, convergence with IFRS is a *process*, whereby domestic standards and IFRS are gradually brought into line. That is, part of the convergence could be

---

4. OSC (2008), section 3; IOSCO (2008) refers to the "risk of investors making investment decisions without a full understanding".

5. Unlisted companies use national standards based very closely on IFRS.

6. The listing requirements (para. 8.62) of the Johannesburg Stock Exchange require financial statements from 2005 onward to comply with national law and with IFRS.

7. The Swiss Exchange's directive on *Requirements for Financial Reporting* (as revised on November 1, 2006) allows several GAAPs, including IFRS and U.S. GAAP.

achieved by changes to IFRS. Indeed, various different countries might be able to contribute good answers to technical problems. However, extensive multilateral convergence is problematic, because converging with one country could mean diverging from another. Because of the economic importance of the U.S. capital markets and because of the importance of securing the acceptability of IFRS to them, convergence in the case of the United States has meant moving both IFRS and U.S. GAAP toward each other. However, convergence in the case of the Accounting Standards Board of Japan (ASBJ, 2006), for example, effectively means changing Japanese standards. In 2007, a new series of accounting standards came into force in China for listed companies (Deloitte, 2006). These remove many of the previous differences from IFRS; this was a further example of one-sided convergence.

The remarkable point that we now investigate is that nearly all the famous examples of alleged *adoption* of IFRS do not strictly satisfy our definition of de jure adoption. As noted earlier, this can be an important issue, especially for foreign users of financial statements. To our knowledge, the only consequential capital market that requires the use of IFRS as issued by the IASB is South Africa.

THE ADOPTION THAT NEVER WAS

As explained above, although the EU has brought virtually all of the content of IFRS into force for various purposes, it is not exactly IFRS as issued by the IASB that is required. For example, in France, what is used for consolidated reporting by listed companies is the French-language version of the IFRS as endorsed in the EU by a particular date. New or amended IFRS must be approved by a legal mechanism (Whittington, 2005). This always adds a delay between an IFRS being approved by the IASB and its being endorsed by the EU. Sometimes the delay can last a year.[8] In a few cases, standards or interpretations (or parts of them) have not been endorsed, the most conspicuous example relating to the hedge accounting rules in IAS 39 (Whittington, 2005; Zeff, 2008).

A quite separate point is that, in many countries outside of North America, companies are required to publish unconsolidated statements of each legal entity, so that there are hundreds of such sets of financial statements produced by large groups, whether the top company is listed or not, and by entities that are not part of a group. Such reporting is not allowed to use IFRS in France, although it is in the United Kingdom. This complexity is noted elsewhere (e.g., Haller and Eierle, 2004; Nobes, 2008: 286–8) but its discussion is outside the scope of this paper.

Another high-profile version of "adoption" is that of Australia, where the law still requires Australian standards to be followed by reporting entities.[9] The Australian Accounting Standards Board (AASB) initially took IFRS and turned them into Australian standards by making numerous amendments to IFRS, to delete options, to add disclosure requirements, and to include requirements for public sector entities. For example, IAS 31

---

8. IFRS 8 was issued by the IASB in November 2006, but was not endorsed until November 2007.
9. Listed companies and some others.

contains[10] an option to use proportionate consolidation, whereas AASB 131 did not. Nevertheless, it could therefore be claimed that compliance with Australian standards would also achieve compliance with IFRS. This approach was abandoned[11] in 2007, and Australian standards are now based exactly on IFRS, except for amendments relating to public-sector entities.

This was proposed by the Accounting Standards Board as the position for Canada when IFRS is brought into force in 2011 (OSC, 2008: Appendix). That is, IFRS would not exactly be "adopted" but incorporated into the *Handbook* of the Canadian Institute of Chartered Accountants, which is imposed on companies by the corporations and securities laws. However, such a process involves the need, as in Australia, constantly to turn IFRS into national standards, and it means that time lags occur, as noted earlier. It also reduces the clarity, for foreigners, of whether or not IFRS are being complied with. Partly for this reason, the securities regulators in Canada have begun consulting[12] on a more direct approach to IFRS adoption.

In some other jurisdictions that claim to put IFRS into national regulations (e.g., Singapore), there is not only a potential for lags but also a series of differences.[13] Similarly, in China, where the new standards of 2007 came close to IFRS, there are some differences and more might arise as the IASB changes its standards. Of course, in these and other countries, certain companies choose to publish an additional set of financial statements that comply with IFRS for various purposes, including foreign listings.

DE FACTO ADOPTION

Even where there is no direct adoption de jure of IFRS (i.e., in nearly all jurisdictions), it is in some cases possible or inevitable for a company to comply with IFRS. It is (and was) apparently inevitable in Australia, assuming compliance with the rules and no delays in turning new IFRS into Australian standards. It is also achieved in the EU, assuming that a company does not wish to take advantage of the more lax hedge accounting rules in the EU's version of IAS 39. A survey (ICAEW, 2007: 78) suggests that this issue affects only non-U.K. banks. The possibility of EU compliance also assumes that there are no relevant implementation lags. For example, for EU companies with September 30, 2007 year-ends, this would have meant complying with IAS 14 rather than with IFRS 8 for segment reporting. Only IAS 14 was EU-endorsed at the date, and it was still optional IFRS in 2007. However, unendorsed IFRS can be followed in the EU if they do not conflict with endorsed IFRS.

---

10. The IASB proposed to delete the option in an exposure draft of 2007.
11. By AASB 2007-4.
12. *CSA Concept Paper 52-402* of February 2008.
13. For example, in the case of Singapore, there are differences in effective dates for IAS 40, IFRS 2, and IFRS 7; and IFRIC 2 (effective 2005) has not been adopted as we write in April 2008. Malaysia and the Philippines also have a series of differences from IFRS. We are grateful to Paul Pacter for this information.

As mentioned earlier, where law is permissive, such as in Switzerland, de facto adoption of IFRS is also possible.

WHAT SHOULD THE REPORTS SAY?

So far, we have established that IFRS (as issued by the IASB) are directly required in only a very few jurisdictions, but that they might be complied with in many. We now ask what management and auditors should state in these many jurisdictions.

Where the requirement is for a national adaptation of IFRS or for national standards based on IFRS, management and auditors have to refer, inter alia, to whatever the legal requirement is. In the case of EU audit reports, the exact wording was discussed by the Fédération des Experts Comptables Européens (FEE),[14] which originally recommended the wording "in accordance with IFRSs as adopted for use in the EU". This was turned into a recommendation in the United Kingdom and Ireland by the Auditing Practices Board (APB, 2005). However, after discussion at the Accounting Regulatory Committee (ARC)[15] of the European Commission, the phrase "adopted for use in the EU" was replaced by "adopted by the EU", in order to suggest that such reports should be acceptable outside the EU (e.g., in the United States). This formulation (hereafter called "EU-IFRS") can be found in the final version from FEE (2005), which also contained translations into 20 European languages, and in APB (2006). The change of mind led to some variety in audit reports, as explained in the next section.

In Australia and various Asian jurisdictions, management and auditors must refer to compliance with national laws and standards, even if they are based closely or exactly on IFRS. Therefore, given the widespread de facto compliance with IFRS, can the management and auditors refer additionally to IFRS, and do they do so? We know of no reason why management and auditors cannot add to their statements by referring also to IFRS in the many cases where this de facto compliance is achieved, although in some countries there are disadvantages, as explained below. For ease of reference, we call this "dual IFRS reporting". We restrict this term to references to both full IFRS and another version of IFRS in the statutory financial statements. However, it can come in two forms: two separate opinions, or references both to IFRS and to a version of IFRS in one opinion (perhaps in the same sentence). We do not consider it to be dual reporting when companies or auditors refer to IFRS and to a legal framework — for example, "in accordance with IFRS, and in the manner required by the Companies Act" — in the case of South Africa. Another issue (see below) is whether there is another statement or report somewhere else (e.g., in a Form 20-F deposited with the SEC).

Under IAS 1 *Presentation of Financial Statements* (para. 16),[16] management cannot claim compliance with IFRS unless it complies with all requirements. More subtly, a pro-

---

14. FEE is a professional body representing European auditors.
15. See the "Draft Summary Record" of the meeting of ARC on November 30, 2005 at http://ec.europa.eu/internal_market/accounting/docs/arc/2005-11-30-agenda_en.pdf.
16. As revised in 2007.

posed amendment to IAS 1 of September 2007 adds a requirement concerning the case where a company "refers" to IFRS but does not fully comply. The amended IAS 1 would require such a company to describe the differences between its reporting and IFRS. Because, in this case, the company is *not* complying with IFRS, it is hard to see why it should necessarily comply with this new requirement.

In conclusion, there is no impediment to dual IFRS reporting by *management* if compliance with full IFRS is achieved. Under the International Standards on Auditing,[17] dual reporting by *auditors* is allowed where financial statements comply simultaneously with two frameworks. The SEC (2007: section III.A.2) confirms that it also sees no impediments.

Dual reporting is not a new idea. For example, some U.S. managements asserted compliance with U.S. GAAP and with "International Accounting Standards" in the 1980s and early 1990s (Camfferman and Zeff, 2007: 156-7, 249). In some cases (e.g., Salomon Inc.), the auditor also dual-reported. This was the case for Microsoft in 1996 and 1997. Especially from 1995,[18] international standards became less permissive, and simultaneous compliance was increasingly difficult to achieve.

WHAT DO THE REPORTS SAY?

In the countries where a version of IFRS is required, dual IFRS reporting by auditors has been rare. We have surveyed the audit reports[19] of all the companies in the main stock indices[20] in Australia, France, Germany, Spain, and the United Kingdom for 2005–6 (255 companies in all). These were the largest[21] stock markets for which IFRS[22] were required at that date. Our data relate to reports of 2005–6,[23] which was generally the first year of compulsory IFRS reporting, and was also the most recent year for which a full set of reports was available.[24] In some cases, we comment also on 2006–7 reports.[25] Because a few companies use foreign accounting (e.g., U.S. GAAP), the numbers of companies surveyed is slightly smaller than the numbers in the indices. The largest such reduction relates to Germany, where seven of the DAX 30 used U.S. GAAP, which was still allowed by the EU regulation, under various conditions, for 2005 and 2006.

We examined the audit reports of all 255 companies to see whether the opinion related to "local" IFRS only or to full IFRS as well. Of the five countries that we examined in detail, only Germany and the United Kingdom produced examples of dual IFRS reporting

---

17. *International Auditing Practice Statement 1014* of March 2003.
18. Several options were removed from international standards in 1993, with effect from 1995.
19. We examined the English-language reports in all cases where these were available. However, we looked at the original-language reports when necessary to resolve doubts.
20. Respectively, the ASX 50, CAC 40, DAX 30, IBEX 35, and FTSE 100 as in June 2007.
21. By market capitalization, according to the 2006 World Federation of Exchanges annual report: http://www.world-exchanges.org/reports/annual-report.
22. That is, IFRS with various provisos as explained above.
23. That is, we looked at the earliest reports for accounting years beginning on or after January 1, 2005.
24. For example, companies with November year-ends did not produce their second IFRS reports until 2008.
25. We used the same companies as for 2005–6 in each case.

by auditors. In the United Kingdom, 17 out of 99 companies dual-reported. In nearly all cases, the management reported in the same way as the auditors — that is, not referring to full IFRS except where the auditors did. However, in the case of BG, for example, management dual-reported but the auditors referred only to EU-IFRS.

In Germany, 5 companies[26] out of the 23 IFRS reporters (22 percent) had dual IFRS audit reports. Where there *was* a dual audit report, the reporting by the management in accounting policy notes was varied — for example, Hypo Real Estate's management referred to the two bases, Henkel's to IFRS only.

In France and Spain, the audit reports uniformly referred only to EU-IFRS, both in the annual reports and in the Forms 20-F of the companies listed on U.S. exchanges.[27]

A published survey of IFRS practice in Europe (Institute of Chartered Accountants in England and Wales [ICAEW], 2007: chap. 8) sheds further light on EU practices. However, it studies 200 listed companies of all sizes across the whole of the EU for 2005–6. So, our sample size for our four EU countries is larger and more homogeneous in terms of size. It is, therefore, difficult to compare results. The ICAEW finds examples of references to IFRS only, to EU-IFRS only, and to dual IFRS reporting. However, it concentrates on management rather than auditors, and does not note that the auditors sometimes dual-report when management does not, or vice versa. The ICAEW finds some dual reporting by *management* in countries other than the United Kingdom and Germany. In percentage terms, this is highest in the Netherlands (ICAEW, 2007: 76).

We noted earlier that the approved wording in the EU is "IFRSs as adopted by the EU". However, in the United Kingdom, all of the Deloitte reports and two PwC reports[28] refer to "IFRS as adopted for use in the European Union", which was the rejected draft wording. A KPMG report[29] refers to "adopted IFRS" without saying who has adopted them. Nearly all this wording is corrected for the 2006–7 reports, except for a few[30] Deloitte reports.

In Australia, for 2005–6 reports (mostly years ending June 30, 2006), the auditors uniformly reported on "Accounting Standards in Australia." This is also the case in the Forms 20-F of those few[31] Australian companies that were SEC-registered. Indeed, the auditors of SEC-registered companies of all the countries except Germany (see below) generally did not dual-report in Form 20-F unless they had done so in the annual report.

---

26. Henkel, Hypo Real Estate, Linde, Lufthansa, and ThyssenKrupp.
27. For example, Alcatel Lucent, AXA, and Total from France; and Banco Santander, Endesa, and Telefónica from Spain.
28. Kingfisher and Schroders.
29. Scottish and Southern Energy.
30. For example, the reports on Vodafone and Shire refer again to "use in". Not all audit reports on this second year were available at the time of writing.
31. The only Australian-index companies on the New York Stock Exchange (on December 14, 2007) that used Australian standards were Alumina and Westpac. BHP Billiton used EU-IFRS, and James Hardie used U.S. GAAP.

As noted earlier, the widespread failure to assert compliance with IFRS when compliance has probably been achieved seems to miss an important part of the point of 35 years' worth of effort on international harmonization. What explains this; what explains the few exceptions; and is the position changing?

SOME EXPLANATORY FACTORS

We suggest that the explanation for the lack of reference to full IFRS in 2005–6 is prosaic: companies and auditors increasingly do merely what they are required to do by regulation. Reporting and auditing are now largely seen as part of "compliance",[32] rather than being seen as a useful commercial or professional activity. The rules are now more detailed (2,600 pages of IFRS) and the enforcement more strict (e.g., CESR, 2007), so there is little incentive to think or act beyond the rules.

The examples of auditors' dual reporting are, in a sense, easy to explain. The 17 U.K. dual IFRS reporters are mostly (i.e., except for 3) "foreign private issuers" (FPIs) in the United States. Table 1 shows the figures. It is necessary here to distinguish between two types of FPIs in the context of the SEC: (a) those with only Level I American Depositary Receipts, and (b) those that are listed. The former can trade their securities over-the-counter only and have minimal reporting requirements. The latter must register with the SEC, including (until the changes of 2007) filing U.S. GAAP reports or reconciling to U.S. GAAP on Form 20-F.

The use of dual IFRS reporting by FPIs is an example of how greater clarity for foreign investors can be a motivation for wanting an audit opinion that refers to full IFRS. In two cases,[33] this explanation is particularly obvious, because the second opinion, on full IFRS, is headed "U.S. opinion" even in the U.K. annual report. The United Kingdom's Auditing Practices Board specifically notes the possibility of a dual report, and expresses a preference for two clearly separate opinions (APB, 2006: para. 8). This is generally the approach of U.K. auditors, whether or not the IFRS opinion is headed "U.S. opinion". Discussions[34] with the Big 4 audit firms in the United Kingdom confirm that a dual report would generally have been easy to provide. This is confirmed by more formal evidence to the SEC (2007: section III.A.2).

As Table 1 shows, 12 out of the 17 U.K. dual IFRS audit reports (71 percent) were written by Deloitte, which is disproportionately large for its share of FTSE 100 companies (which is 19 percent) or of FPIs.[35] None of the dual reports was by KPMG, although the firm was not opposed in principle to giving them.[36] We believe that the predominance of

32. With which we include avoidance of litigation.
33. Royal Bank of Scotland and Vodafone. In the case of Royal Bank of Scotland, there are three opinions: EU-IFRS, IFRS, and U.S. opinion on IFRS.
34. Correspondence with Mary Tokar of KPMG on August 24, 2007, and Andy Simmonds of Deloitte on August 28, 2007.
35. For example, 22 of the FTSE 100 companies were listed on the New York Stock Exchange (on December 17, 2007). Of these, only 4 were audited by Deloitte, 10 by PwC, 6 by KPMG, and 2 by Ernst & Young.
36. Correspondence with Mary Tokar (IFRS partner, KPMG) on August 24, 2007.

TABLE 1

U.K. dual audit reports in 2005–6

	Total	SEC-registered	Other FPI	Not FPI
Deloitte & Touche	12	5	5	2
		(2 with "U.S. Opinion")		
Ernst & Young	3	1	1	1
KPMG	0	0	0	0
PricewaterhouseCoopers	2	1	1	0
Total	17	7	7	3

Deloitte can be explained by the deliberate policies of the firms. Only Deloitte expressed[37] a clear view in favor of dual reporting.

However, we cannot explain[38] why the 3[39] companies of the 17 that are not FPIs had dual audit reports. Two different audit firms were involved. Furthermore, there are many other U.K. companies that are FPIs or even fully SEC-registered that did *not* dual-report.[40]

As an example of the confusion in this area, the journal of the ICAEW reports that only 11 of the FTSE 100 companies reported on full IFRS and that this shows how many companies would be affected by the SEC's proposal to accept only full IFRS (Accountancy, 2007). In addition to having a smaller count from us,[41] this is wrong because most of the remaining 89 companies are not SEC-registered and so would not be affected. Furthermore, nearly all the companies are probably already complying with full IFRS and merely need to ask their auditors to affirm that.

In the case of Germany, it was noted above that five DAX companies provided dual IFRS audit reports. More detail is given in Table 2. As may be seen, there were 24 FPIs in the DAX. Of these, seven were using U.S. GAAP, as then permitted by the German adaptation of the EU Regulation. Three others were dual reporters (Henkel, Hypo Real Estate, and Lufthansa). The remaining 14 FPIs (e.g., Adidas, Allianz, and Commerzbank) neither used U.S. GAAP nor had a dual audit report. Surprisingly, in addition to the above three FPI dual reporters, another two (Linde and ThyssenKrupp), which were not FPIs, did dual-report.

---

37. Martyn Jones (U.K. Audit Technical Partner) reports that they had been "pushing it strongly ... from the beginning" (correspondence of January 15, 2008).
38. We have written to the finance directors of the companies. We have received two replies. One does not explain the decision to seek a dual report except that it shows an awareness that IFRS and EU-IFRS were potentially different. The other reply suggests that the company's investors were aware of uncertainty in 2005 about endorsement but are less interested now, such that dual reporting has been dropped. The company also confirmed that the dual report had created no problems for its auditors.
39. Capita, Daily Mail, and Hammerson.
40. For example, the SEC lists 40 FTSE companies as registered at December 31, 2005 but only 7 of them had dual audit reports.
41. We find 14 dual reports for 2006–7.

TABLE 2

DAX companies: To which GAAP do auditors refer (2005)?

Audit reference	Type of company			Total
	SEC-registered	Other FPI	Not FPI	
U.S. GAAP	7	—	—	7
Dual IFRS	—	3	2	5
EU-IFRS	4	10	4	18
Total	11	13	6	30

The partial explanation for the majority usage of EU-IFRS in Germany, even for FPIs, is that most of the FPIs (including all the dual reporters) were Level 1 only and not required to use U.S. GAAP or to reconcile to it. The only DAX companies with full SEC registrations that neither used U.S. generally accepted auditing standards nor dual-reported were Allianz,[42] BASF, Bayer, and Deutsche Telekom. The first three of these[43] had EU-IFRS reports in their annual reports but IFRS reports in Form 20-F. Deutsche Telekom had EU-IFRS reports in both places.

In Germany and Austria, there is a particular legal reason for restricting an audit assignment in the annual report to EU-IFRS: the legally required audit opinion (reference to EU-IFRS) activates a cap on auditor liability. In Austria, for example, the *Unternehmensgesetzbuch* limits the liability of auditors when operating within its legal framework — that is, in the context of EU-endorsed IFRS. An audit report relating to anything else (e.g., full IFRS) would not enjoy a liability cap, except by separate negotiation.[44] This is also the position for Germany.[45] It means that a report on full IFRS would be riskier for auditors and, therefore, costlier for companies. A further complication is that the SEC requires auditors to use U.S. GAAP rather than international standards on auditing as used in the EU, so a separate opinion for SEC purposes is necessary anyway.

Another potential[46] explanation for avoiding a dual IFRS report in the EU is that EU-IFRS could, in the future, depart further from IFRS such that simultaneous compliance might become more difficult. To avoid the embarrassment of having later to drop the reference to full IFRS, it would be better never to make it.

---

42. Allianz is unusual in another way: it is an SE (a *societas Europaea*, a European public company), so in principle it is European, not German.
43. BASF had an EU-IFRS report in its German-language annual report but an IFRS report in its English-language document.
44. We are grateful to Gerhard Prachner (PricewaterhouseCoopers, Vienna) for this information.
45. We are grateful to Alfred Wagenhofer for this information (correspondence of December 5, 2007).
46. Our suggestion here received confirmation from Liesel Knorr of the German Accounting Standards Committee (correspondence of January 2, 2008).

IS THE POSITION CHANGING?

The remaining question from above is whether the position is changing. We found a slight decrease in the number of dual IFRS audit reports for 2006–7 compared with 2005–6.[47] The position has changed in another way for foreign registrants of the SEC for 2007 reports onward (SEC, 2007). At least for their SEC filings, their auditors will have to report on full IFRS if they wish to avoid reconciliation. Given that these auditors will specifically have to address the issue of full IFRS conformity in the audit reports designed for the SEC, it would then presumably be costless (except in Austria and Germany, as explained above) for them to opine on full IFRS in their domestic audit reports. This will presumably increase the number of domestic opinions on full IFRS — that is, it will increase dual reporting, given the continued legal need for opinions on national versions of IFRS.

Elsewhere, in June 2007, the Australian Auditing and Assurance Standards Board revised auditing standard ASA 700 to require an additional reference to IFRS (i.e., dual reporting). In New Zealand, the Professional Standards Board of the Institute of Chartered Accountants had done the same one month earlier with AGS-1012[48] (Fisher and Perry, 2007). We applaud these changes because they will make it clear to foreign users whether or not IFRS are being followed. These revisions seem to be the world's first requirements for dual IFRS reporting.

In Canada, it is intended (OSC, 2008) that IFRS will be the primary basis of reporting, although it remains unclear whether dual reporting will be necessary because of a continued need to comply with national laws and regulations and the phasing in of some IFRS, which may themselves be undergoing change at the time of adoption.

CONCLUSIONS AND POLICY IMPLICATIONS

Few jurisdictions have directly adopted IFRS, partly because of the widespread and long-standing reluctance of the state to allow a private-sector body to control accounting. South Africa has accepted the process of international standard setting by the IASB. The SEC and the Canadian regulators are considering doing so as well. However, this is not the position in the EU, nor is it likely to become the position.

Where, despite the lack of direct adoption of IFRS, they are nevertheless in practice fully complied with, it was not normal for auditors to be asked to affirm this in 2005 or 2006. The exceptions were some German and U.K. companies that were generally FPIs in the United States. However, some FPIs from those countries did not dual-report and some dual reporters were not FPIs.

---

47. The U.K. numbers fell from 17 to 14; the numbers per auditor falling to 11 (Deloitte), 1 (Ernst & Young) and 2 (PwC). The German numbers fell from 5 to 4 (Linde had only an EU-IFRS opinion).

48. *Audit Implications of the Transition to New Zealand Equivalents to International Financial Reporting Standards*, 2007.

For 2007 onward, Australia and New Zealand have moved to a requirement for dual audit reports. The SEC's requirement for full IFRS from foreign registrants that wish to avoid reconciliations might increase the frequency of dual reporting elsewhere.

Where it is not possible, for local reasons, to report simply on full IFRS, we believe that companies and auditors in the EU and elsewhere should consider the issuance of a dual report that includes opining on full IFRS, as now required in Australia and New Zealand. In most cases, it would be costless but would increase the clarity of reporting, which regulators suggest would entail an incremental benefit especially for companies with international investors. For those few companies unable to claim IFRS compliance, useful information would be forthcoming that is now hidden. If there are specific local reasons[49] why dual reporting has disadvantages, then we would encourage regulators to remove them.

IOSCO (2008) has urged listed companies to state that their financial statements comply with IFRS as issued by the IASB, if that is the case, and otherwise to explain the differences. At present, the International Auditing and Assurance Standards Board appears to be unable to encourage or require dual audit reporting because it is "framework neutral".[50] Nevertheless, we believe that the International Federation of Accountants, FEE, and other audit-related bodies should consider encouraging or requiring dual reporting so as to make it widely known that they are, or are not, adhering to full IFRS.

REFERENCES

Accountancy. 2007. Compliance with IFRS. *Accountancy*, September, 28.

Accounting Standards Board of Japan (ASBJ). 2006. *Statement on Japan's progress towards convergence*. Tokyo: ASBJ.

Auditing Practices Board (APB). 2006. *Auditor's reports on financial statements in the United Kingdom*, Bulletin 2006/6. London: APB.

Auditing Practices Board (APB). 2005. *Auditor's reports on financial statements in Great Britain and Ireland*, Bulletin 2005/4. London: APB.

Benson, H. 1976. The story of international accounting standards. *Accountancy*, July, 34.

Camfferman, K., and S. Zeff. 2007. *Financial reporting and global capital markets: A history of the International Accounting Standards Committee, 1973–2000*. Oxford: Oxford University Press.

Committee of European Securities Regulators (CESR). 2007. *CESR's review of the implementation and enforcement of IFRS in the EU*. Committee of European Securities Regulators, 07-352, November.

Deloitte. 2006. *China's new accounting standards*. Hong Kong: Deloitte.

European Union (EU). 2002. *Regulation 1606/2002 of the European Parliament and of the Council of 19 July 2002 on the application of international accounting standards*.

---

49. For example, as in the case of the liability cap in Austria and Germany,

50. This point was made to us by James M. Sylph, IFAC's executive director of professional standards, in correspondence of November 19, 2007.

Fédération des Experts Comptables Européens (FEE). 2005. *Reference to the financial reporting framework in the EU in accounting policies and in the audit report and applicability of endorsed IFRS.* Brussels: FEE.

Fisher, F., and Perry, J. 2007. Complying with IFRS: Guidance amended. *Chartered Accountants Journal* 86 (6): 28–9.

Haller, A., and Eierle, B. 2004. The adaptation of German accounting law to IFRS: A legislative balancing act. *Accounting in Europe* 1: 27–50.

Institute of Chartered Accountants in England and Wales (ICAEW). 2007. *EU implementation of IFRS and the fair value directive.* London: ICAEW.

International Organization of Securities Commissions (IOSCO). 2008. Statement on providing investors with appropriate and complete information on accounting frameworks used to prepare financial statements, IOSCO Technical Committee, February 6.

Nobes, C. W. 2008. The context of financial reporting by individual companies. In *Comparative International Accounting*, eds. C. W. Nobes and R. H. Parker, chap. 13. Harlow, Essex, U.K.: Prentice Hall.

Ontario Securities Commission (OSC). 2008. *CSA Concept Paper 52-402*, Canadian Securities Administrators, http://www.osc.gov.on.ca/Regulation/Rulemaking/Current, February 15.

Securities and Exchange Commission (SEC). 2007. *Acceptance from foreign private issuers of financial statements prepared in accordance with international financial reporting standards without reconciliation to U.S. GAAP*, RIN 3235-AJ 90, December 21. Washington, DC: SEC.

Whittington, G. 2005. The adoption of international accounting standards in the European Union. *European Accounting Review* 14 (1): 127–153.

Zeff, S. A. 2008. Political lobbying on accounting standards — US, UK and international experience. In *Comparative International Accounting*, eds. C. W. Nobes and R. H. Parker, chap. 10. Harlow, Essex, U.K.: Prentice Hall.

PART IV

ON TRUTH AND FAIRNESS

[14]

Accounting and Business Research, Vol 31. No. 2. pp. 83-90. 2001

The true and fair view requirement in recent national implementations

Sally Aisbitt and Christopher Nobes*

Abstract—This note examines the implementation of the true and fair view requirement into the laws of Austria, Finland, Norway and Sweden. It builds on an earlier analysis of the 12 EU member states that had previously implemented the requirement. It is found that three of the four countries depart from the wording of the appropriate language versions of the Fourth Directive. Also, two of the countries do not implement the 'override', and the other two implement it in a way not done before, by reserving to the member state the specification of the allowed departures.

1. Introduction

The implementation and impact of the EU Fourth and Seventh Directives' true and fair view (TFV) requirement (as reproduced in Appendix 1) was examined by Nobes (1993) for 12 countries. Since that time, three new member states (Austria, Finland and Sweden) have joined the EU, and the requirement to implement the Directives has been complied with in non-EU members of the European Economic Area[1] (the largest such country being Norway). This note marshals the facts for these four countries and puts them in the context of the earlier 12 countries. The paper looks first at the signifiers used in the Directives; then at the signifiers in national laws; then at the implementation of the 'override'.

Other researchers may wish to use these facts in order to explain the choices made or to try to assess the extent to which the implementation of the Directives is likely to contribute to the harmonisation of European financial reporting. The variations in interpretation and understanding of TFV within and between countries and over time (e.g. Nobes and Parker, 1991; Nobes, 1993) have demonstrated that this is an area where the process of harmonisation is far from complete.

* The authors are at the Open University and the University of Reading, respectively. They are grateful for advice from Kristina Artsberg (Lund University, Sweden), Harald Brandsås (Den norske Revisorforening), Sigvard Heurlin (Öhrlings PricewaterhouseCoopers, Stockholm), Pekka Pirinen (University of Jyväskylä, Finland), Gerhard Prachner (Coopers & Lybrand Inter-truehand, Vienna), and Alan Roberts (University of Reading). The authors are most grateful for the helpful suggestions on an earlier draft from the referees and the editor. Correspondence should be addressed to Professor Nobes at the Department of Economics, the University of Reading, P.O. Box 218, Whiteknights, Reading RG6 2AA. E-mail: c.wright@reading.ac.uk

The final version of this paper was accepted in November 2000.

2. Signifiers in the Directive

Nobes (1993) follows others in distinguishing between the signifier and the signified relating to the TFV, but also notes that the signifiers implemented in member state laws are not the same in all cases as those in the official versions of the Directives. For the four countries studied here, there are three new language versions of the Fourth and Seventh Directives, given that Austria is covered by the earlier German version. Table 1 shows the signifiers equivalent to 'a true and fair view' of Article 2 of the Fourth Directive for these languages. A full table for comparison of all the languages is shown as Appendix 2.

Figure 1 adds the three new language versions to the 10 others in terms of their approximate literal meanings in English. Two interesting points emerge. First, like all the earlier versions except the original[2] English, the Norwegian and Swedish versions use a unitary signifier. In the case of the Swedish version of the Directives,[3] Wennberg (1991) explained that the first drafts were produced by accountants in Sweden, under the guidance of the Justice Department for approval in Brussels. The English version of the Directive was the primary source, but the Danish version (and occasionally the German and French) was used where there were difficulties in interpretation. TFV, perhaps the most difficult requirement to interpret, seems to have been an area where recourse was made to the Danish Directive. On the other hand, the Finnish Directive, with no linguistic relative in previous versions of the Directive seems to have looked to the English and produced a dual signifier.

---

[1] Iceland, Liechtenstein and Norway.
[2] The evidence for this is strong and is reviewed in Nobes (1993).
[3] Wennberg gives particular emphasis to the Eighth Directive.

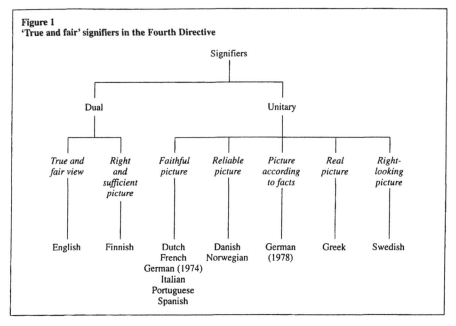

Figure 1
'True and fair' signifiers in the Fourth Directive

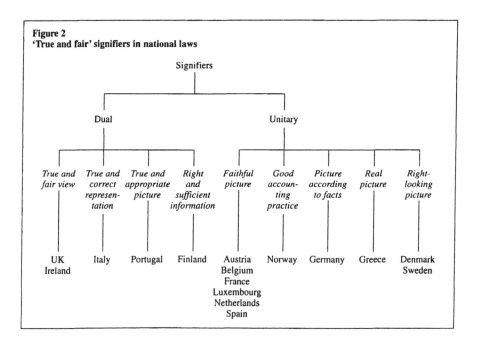

Figure 2
'True and fair' signifiers in national laws

Table 1
Signifiers for a true and fair view (for translations, see Appendix 3)

Country	Words in Directive	Implementation of Directive	Words in law if different from Directive
Austria	ein den tatsächlichen Verhältnissen entsprechendes Bild	1990[1]	ein möglichst getreues Bild
Finland	oikea ja riittävä kuva	1992[2]	oikeat ja riittävät tiedot … (oikea ja riittävä kuva)
	en rättvisande bild[3]		en riktig och tillräcklig bild …. (rättvisande bild)[4]
Norway	et pålitelig bilde	1998	god regnskapsskikk
Sweden	en rättvisande bild	1995	–

[1] Approximate implementation; full implementation was achieved by the *EU-Ges RÄG* of 28 June 1996, but the relevant section numbers of the ÖHGB did not change.
[2] The expression was incorporated in the Accounting Act 1992, although implementation of the Fourth Directive was not complete until the Accounting Act 1997 became effective. References in this paper are therefore to the 1997 Act.
[3] Swedish is also an official language in Finland, so Finland has two signifiers for the TFV.
[4] The paragraph heading is "Riktiga och tillräckliga uppgifter". In the Finnish version, the heading and the text use identical wording.

The second point is that the Swedish version of the Directive does not use 'faithful' as many versions of the Directive do or the similar 'reliable' as for the Danish[4] and Norwegian Directives, but uses 'right-looking', which is the same as in the Danish implementation as law (see Figure 2 and Appendix 3). Although this may not represent a significant difference, it seems to be further evidence of bureaucratic negotiation over translation as proposed in Nobes (1993), for example in the change of the German version from 1974 to 1978.

3. Signifiers in member state laws
This section deals with the words that have been used to implement the Directives' TFV requirement in national legislation. Nobes (1993) notes that several member states departed substantially or marginally from the words laid out in the Directive. This precedent is continued in three of the new implementations (i.e., except for the Swedish), as summarised on the right of Table 1. Austria departs from the Directive's '*ein den tatsächlichen Verhältnissen entsprechendes Bild*' and substitutes '*ein möglichst getreues Bild*' (ÖHGB § 195 and § 222 (2)), which is much closer to the '*einen getreuen Einblick*' of the German version of the 1974 draft of the Fourth Directive (and the 1976 draft of the Seventh Directive).

Unlike the German law (DHGB § 264 (2)), the Austrian law does not modify the requirement

by adding the words 'in compliance with accepted accounting principles' ('*unter Beachtung der Grundsätze ordnungsmässiger Buchführung*' (GoB)). There is, of course, a requirement to comply with GoB, but as an additional requirement to the TFV, not as a modification of it. However, the above modification *is* to be found in the Austrian instruction on the duties of the auditors (ÖHGB § 274), as it is in the analogous German instructions (DHGB § 322). Its absence from the instructions for Austrian *preparers* may, in practice, not represent a significant difference from German law.

The Nordic countries have a long tradition of the concept of 'good accounting practice' (GAP) (Flower, 1994, p.241–2) which has some similarities to the German GoB. In the same way that the German implementation of the Fourth Directive retained this principle, the Swedish version states, in addition to the TFV requirement:

> Årsredovisningen skall upprättas på ett överskådligt sätt och i enlighet med god redovisningssed. [Annual accounts should be prepared clearly and in accordance with good accounting practice.] (*Årsredovisningslag*, SFS 1995: 1554, ch. 2, para. 2)

Other countries had also continued their former words (e.g. '*régularité et sincérité*' in France, and

---

[4] The Danish and Norwegian words can be literally translated as 'reliable', but this may convey the same meaning as the 'faithful' used by Nobes (1993) for Denmark.

'*inzicht*' in the Netherlands) in combination with TFV.

The Norwegian law goes further and implements the TFV concept by using the expression GAP. In complete contrast, Finland has broken away from its previous legislation by omitting references to GAP in the chapter on annual financial statements. Nevertheless, GAP is a requirement in Chapter 1 of the Act, which deals with the obligation to keep accounting records. This is not dissimilar to the Danish approach: GAP was not included in *Årsregnskabsloven* 1981 but persists in *Bogføringsloven* (see Erhvervs– og Selskabsstyrelsen, 1990) and the Stock Exchange's information requirements. The Finnish law paraphrases the wording of the Directive, but the exact phrase from the Directive is included in the law in parentheses:

> Tilinpäätöksen tulee antaa oikeat ja riittävät tiedot kirjanpitovelvollisen toiminnan tuloksesta ja taloudellisesta asemasta (*oikea ja riittävä kuva*). [The accounts shall give right and sufficient information on the reporting entity's result and on its financial position (*right and sufficient picture*).] (*Kirjanpitolaki*, 1336/1997, ch. 3, para. 2, emphasis original)

The explanation accompanying the proposal to the government for the law (RP, 1997, p.15) states that the use of the two expressions is a technical legal device to bring a number of pieces of legislation in line and to demonstrate that the two expressions are synonymous. The expression *oikeat ja riitävät tiedot* was considered to be a translation of the English term, true and fair view, from Article 2(3) of the Fourth Directive. However, the alternative phrase, *oikea ja riittävä kuva*, had already been used in previous legislation (769/1990 and 39/1889).

There may be a danger of making too much of the differences in literal wordings of signifiers. In this context, one notes that, since there are two official languages in Finland, there is an official Swedish language version of the Finnish law. In it, the above sentence uses wording that is closer to the Swedish language version of the Directive:

> Bokslutet skall ge en riktig och tillräcklig bild av resultatet av den bokföringsskyldiges verksamhet och om dennes ekonomiska ställning (*rättvisande bild*). [The accounts shall give a right and sufficient picture of the reporting entity's result and of its economic position (*right-looking picture*)]

Another detail of the wording is that the language versions examined here, except the Finnish, refer to "a" rather than "the" TFV. As noted in Nobes (1993), there are also some exceptions in other languages. However, in the Finnish language, there are no definite or indefinite articles, such concepts being conveyed by word order. This is of little consequence for the Finnish language version of the law because of the reference to "informa-

tion" rather than "picture". The bracketed reference to "right-looking picture" (see in italics above) uses no article even in the Swedish language version of the Finnish law. The decisive clue is that the Swedish language version refers to "*a* right and sufficient picture" in the unbracketed text.

4. The override

As is well known (e.g. Ordelheide, 1990; Otte, 1990), the German implementation of the Fourth Directive does not comply with Article 2(5) which requires departure from the provisions of the Directive 'in exceptional cases' (see text in Appendix 1). The Austrian and Swedish implementations follow this precedent, with no mention of departure or exceptional cases, although departure in exceptional cases had been included in the first draft of the Swedish law (SOU, 1994, ch. 2, para. 2). One could argue that these implementations are examples of member states taking the option of the last sentence of Article 2 (5) (whereby the legislators may prescribe the cases of departure) but specifying no departures. This could be seen as implicit implementation of Article 2 (5).

By the time of the Swedish implementation, no national law had specified any cases of departure and few individual companies had departed from the law (e.g. Van Hulle, 1997; Jönsson Lundmark, 1996). Thorell (1995) argues, in a Swedish context, that a strong interpretation of the override would allow member states to specify departures from a provision of the Directive, which would clearly be unreasonable and would be in contravention of pronouncements from the EC Contact Committee. That Committee (EC, 1990) and Van Hulle (1993) had already supported this interpretation of the Directive. However, Alexander (1993) and Nobes (1993) argue in favour of an interpretation found in the UK whereby the standard-setters have used the override, for example in the context of investment properties and goodwill.[5] The EC Commission (EC, 1997, p.3) has subsequently confirmed that it believes that member states (and presumably standard-setters) are not allowed to promulgate general rules in contradiction of the Directive, but the authority of this statement is ambiguous, and clearly less than that of a Directive.

Contrary to this, the Finnish and Norwegian Acts implement the override using the disputed last sentence of Article 2(5). The Finnish Act specifies that the Ministry of Trade and Industry will decide when and how an entity must depart from the Act in order to give a TFV (*Kirjanpitolaki*,

---

[5] SSAP 19 does this by requiring investment properties (which are fixed assets with limited useful lives) not to be depreciated, in contradiction to Article 35(1)(b). Similarly, FRS 10 allows the lack of depreciation of capitalised goodwill.

1336/1997, ch. 3, para. 2). This may amount to a subtle way of arriving at a German, Austrian or Swedish result (i.e., no override) without breaking the letter of the Directive. The Finnish proposal (RP, 1997, p.15) explains that limiting the occasions when the override is permitted is essential to the system of enforcing the law. However, the Finns do not seem to have entirely ruled out the possibility of using the override. There are no examples within the Act, although the proposal (RP, 1997, pp.15–6) included an example about limiting the use of LIFO to certain companies. The override has already been the basis for a ministerial decision (Handels- och industriministeriet, 1998) allowing the use of International Accounting Standards by certain companies in their consolidated financial statements. The preamble to the decision is that:

> Handels- och industriministeriet har *med stöd av 3 kap. 2§2 mom. bokföringslagen den 30 december 1997* (1336/1997) beslutat: …

> [The Ministry of Trade and Industry has decided with *the support of Chapter 3, paragraph 2§2 of the Accounting Act of 30 December 1997* (1336/1997): …] (emphasis added)

The Norwegian law is the most interesting. The legislators have interpreted the last sentence of Article 2(5) as meaning that the law itself can specify when companies must depart from the Directives. The closest precedent for this is the UK use of standards to specify departures (see above). Early drafts of the Norwegian law included a number of 'exceptions' from the valuation rules, but the final law includes only one clear departure from the Directives:[6] the requirement that marketable investments held as part of a liquid trading portfolio should be marked to market (i.e., held at market value, with gains and losses recognised in the profit and loss account). This requirement is included in the law under the heading of '*spesielle vurderingsregler*' (special[7] valuation rules). The European Commission was already proposing to amend the Directive to allow it (EC, 1998), partly in order to be consistent with requirements of International Accounting Standards (see E 62 of 1998 leading to IAS 39). Norway was merely ahead of developments here and could take comfort from implicit approval of the change by the Commission.

The other issues included under 'special valuation rules' are of a different type in that the Norwegian law interprets or extends the Directives in particular directions, without directly overriding it. These issues are research and development, goodwill,[8] pension costs, leasing, long-term work-in-progress and currency translation. They were also unlikely to be controversial with the Commission, which had issued (EC, 1997) several imaginative[9] interpretations of the Directives

which might be interpreted as suggesting that the Norwegian legislators need not have expressed their rules as departures from the Directive's provisions. For example, the Norwegian law requires the use of the closing rate of exchange for translation of foreign currency monetary balances, which is an issue not explicitly dealt with in the Directive. Most member states[10] accept or require translation at the closing rate, and the Commission (EC, 1997, p.9) regards it as acceptable under the Directives.

The objective of the Norwegian legislation (Ot. Prp., 1988–89) was said to be to move away from the legal formulations of the 1970s and towards internationally accepted practices of the 1990s. Interestingly, the EC Commission now has sympathy for this general approach, as part of supporting the work of the International Accounting Standards Committee (EC, 1995).

A related point is that the Swedish Act allows for work-in-progress to be shown at higher than cost. One could argue that this, too, is supported by the Commission's interpretation, because of its acceptance of the percentage of completion method (EC, 1997, p.8).

5. Summary

The application of the Fourth and Seventh Directives to Austria, Finland, Norway and Sweden involved three new language versions of

---

[6] In addition there are instances where the Norwegian Act is more prescriptive than the Directive. For example, Article 35 (3) and (4) of the Directive indicates that indirect costs and interest may be added to production cost, whereas Chapter 5, paragraph 4, amplified by Ot. Prp. (1997–8) implies that these costs must be included for enterprises other than small enterprises. The committee drafting the proposals saw any such narrowing of choice or implementation of Member State options, as well as true derogations, as departures from the Directive, i.e. as a regulated override (NOU, 1995, 2.3.4 Regulert overstyring).

[7] In the proposal from the Accounting Act Committee and the Ministry of Finance, "special valuation rules" were distinguished from "exceptions from valuation rules". The latter comprised the use of market value for financial instruments and the closing rate of exchange. It is unclear why the Parliament merged the two types.

[8] Goodwill on consolidation is not distinguished from other types of goodwill.

[9] For example, the Commission (EC, 1997, p.9) believes that gains on unsettled long-term foreign currency monetary items could be treated as 'made' (Fourth Directive, Article 31(1)(c)). The British law implemented this word as 'realised' (Companies Act 1985, Schedule 4, para. 12 (a)), and SSAP 20 (para. 65) believes that an 'override' is necessary to take such profit into the profit and loss account. Some other member states have an even more restrictive understanding of this provision.

[10] This is required in the UK and Ireland (see footnote 10). It is also the practice in Denmark, France, Greece, the Netherlands, Portugal, Spain and Sweden. (Alexander and Archer, 1995, pp. 133–4, 189, 332–3, 588–9, 685, 853–4 and 1199–2000).

the Directives. The Norwegian and Swedish versions have a unitary signifier; the Finnish a dual signifier. The Norwegian version follows the Danish Directive; the Swedish version follows the Danish law.

Three of the implementations in law depart from the appropriate language versions of the Directive. The Norwegian law retains 'good accounting practice' instead of TFV. The Finnish language version of the Finnish law has 'right and sufficient information', but the Swedish version of the Finnish law is closer to the Directive. The Austrian law departs from the German language Directive but not in order to follow the German law. All the laws refer to "a" rather than "the" TFV.

None of the laws allows directors to use judgment to depart from legal provisions in order to give a TFV. However, the Finnish law allows the government to specify departures, which it has not yet done; and the Norwegian law contains specified departures from the Fourth Directive.

References

Alexander, D. (1993). 'A European true and fair view?'. *European Accounting Review*, 2 (1).

Alexander, D. and Archer, S. (1995). *European Accounting Guide*. Harcourt Brace, 2nd edition.

EC (1990). *Accounting Harmonisation in the EC. Problems of Applying the Fourth Directive*. EC Commission.

EC (1995). *Accounting Harmonisation: A New Strategy vis-à-vis International Harmonisation*. EC Commission, COM 95 (908).

EC (1997). *Interpretative Communication Concerning Certain Articles of the Fourth and Seventh Council Directives on Accounting*. EC Commission, XV/7009/97 EN.

EC (1998). *Fair Value Accounting for Financial Instruments: A Proposal for the Amendment of the 4th Directive*. EC Commission, XV/7002/98 EN.

Erhvervs- og Selskabsstyrelsen (1990). *Bekendtgørelse om erhvervsdrivende virksomheders bogføring, årsregnskaber og opbevaring af regnskabsmateriale*, Erhvervs- og Selskabsstyrelsens bekendtgørelse nr. 598 af 21. august 1990.

Flower, J. (1994). *The Regulation of Financial Reporting in the Nordic Countries*. Publica.

Handels- och industriministeriet (1998). *Handels- och industriministeriets beslut om upprättandet av koncernbokslut i enlighet med det regelverk som används allmänt på den internationella kapitalmarknaden*, 766.

Jönsson Lundmark, B. (1996). 'Nya årsredovisningslagen inte så dålig som det påstås'. *Balans*, 4: 16–24.

Nobes, C.W. (1993). 'The true and fair view requirement: impact on and of the fourth directive'. *Accounting and Business Research*, Winter: 35–48.

Nobes, C.W. and Parker, R.H. (1991). 'True and fair: a survey of UK financial directors'. *Journal of Business Finance and Accounting*, 18 (3).

NOU (1995). *Ny Regnskapslov*. Norges Offentlige Utredninger: 30.

Ordelheide, D. (1990). 'Soft transformations of accounting rules in the 4th Directive in Germany'. *Les Cahiers Internationaux de la Comptabilité*, Editions Comptables Malesherbes, 3: 1–15.

Ot. Prp. (1988–89). Nr. 35.

Ot. Prp. (1997–98). *Om lov om årsregnskap m.v.* (regnskapsloven). Odeltings proposisjon, Nr. 42.

Otte, H-H. (1990). 'Harmonisierte Europäische Rechnungslegung'. *Zeitschrift für Betriebswirtschaft*, 42.

RP (1997). *Regeringens proposition till Riksdagen med förslag till bokföringslag samt till lagar om ändring av 11 och 12 kap. lagen om aktiebolag och 79 c § lagen om andelslag*, 173 rd.

SOU (1994). *Års- och Koncernredovisning enligt EG-direktivet*. Statens Offentlilga Utredningar: 17.

Thorell, P. (1995). 'Perspektiv på den nya årsredovisningslagen'. *Balans*, 11: 31–9.

Van Hulle, K. (1993). 'Truth and untruth about true and fair'. *European Accounting Review*, May.

Van Hulle, K. (1997). 'The true and fair override in the European Accounting Directives'. *European Accounting Review*, 6 (4): 711–20.

Wennberg, I. (1991). 'Jättejobb översätta EG-regler till svenska'. *Balans*, 5: 14–16.

Appendix 1
English language version of Article 2 of the Fourth Directive

1. The annual accounts shall comprise the balance sheet, the profit and loss account and the notes on the accounts. These documents shall constitute a composite whole.

2. They shall be drawn up clearly and in conformity with the provisions of this Directive.

3. The annual accounts shall give a true and fair view of the company's assets, liabilities, financial position and profit or loss.

4. Where the application of the provisions of this Directive would not be sufficient to give a true and fair view within the meaning of para. 3, additional information must be given.

5. Where in exceptional cases the application of a provision of this Directive is incompatible with the obligation laid down in para. 3, that provision must be departed from in order to give a true and fair view within the meaning of para. 3. Any such departure must be disclosed in the notes on the accounts together with an explanation of the reasons for it and a statement of its effect on the assets, liabilities, financial position and profit or loss. The Member States may define the exceptional cases in question and lay down the relevant special rules.

Appendix 2
Signifiers for a true and fair view

Country	Words in law before Fourth Directive (first appearance)	Words in Directive	Implementation of Directive	Words in law if different from Directive
UK	a true and fair view (1947)	a true and fair view	1981	–
Ireland	a true and fair view (1963)	a true and fair view	1986	–
Netherlands	1. geeft een zodanig inzicht dat een verantwoord oordeel kan worden gevormd ... 2. geeft getrouw en stelselmatig (1970)	een getrouw beeld	1983	1. (as in 1970) 2. geeft getrouw, duidelijk en stelselmatig
Denmark	–	et pålideligt billede	1981	et retvisende billede
France }	–	{une image fidèle,	1983	–
Luxembourg }		{een getrouw beeld	1984	–
Belgium }		{(in Flemish)	1985	–
Germany	–	ein den tatsächlichen Verhältnissen entsprechendes Bild	1985	Unter Beachtung der Grundsätze ordnungs- mässiger Buchführung (then, as Directive)
Greece	–	tin pragmatiki ikona	1986	
Spain	–	una imagen fiel	1989	la imagen fiel ... de conformidad con las disposiciones legales[1]
Portugal	–	uma imagem fiel	1989	uma imagem verdadeira e apropriada (1989 plan)
Italy	–	un quadro fedele	1991	rappresentare in modo veritiero e corretto
Austria	–	ein den tatsächlichen Verhältnissen entsprechendes Bild	1990[2]	ein möglichst getreues Bild
Finland	–	oikea ja riittävä kuva	1992[3]	oikeat ja riittävät tiedot
Norway	–	et pålitelig bilde	1998	god regnskapsskikk
Sweden	–	en rättvisande bild	1995	en rättvisande bild

[1] The words as found in the *Código de Commercio* (Art. 34).
[2] Approximate implementation.
[3] The expression was incorporated in the Accounting Act 1992, although implementation of the Fourth Directive was not complete until the Accounting Act 1997 became effective. References in this paper are therefore to the 1997 Act.

Appendix 3
Literal translations of words in Table 1 and elsewhere

Netherlands	– geeft een zodanig inzicht dat een verantwoord oordeel kan worden gevormd	presents an insight such that a well-founded opinion can be formed
	– geeft getrouw, duidelijk en stelselmatig	presents faithfully, clearly and consistently (over time)
Denmark	– et pålideligt billede	a reliable picture
	– et retvisende billede	a right-looking (or fair-looking) picture
Germany, Austria	– (unter Beachtung der Grundsätze ordnungsmässiger Buchführung) ein den tatsächlichen Verhältnissen entsprechendes Bild	(in compliance with accepted accounting principles) a picture in accordance with the facts
	– ein möglichst getreues Bild	a picture as faithful as possible
France	– une image fidèle	a faithful picture
Greece	– tin pragmatiki ikona	the real picture
Spain	– una (la) imagen fiel ... (de conformidad con las disposiciones legales)	a (the) faithful picture ... (in conformity with the legal provisions)
Portugal	– uma imagem fiel	a loyal view
	– uma imagem verdadeira e apropriada	a true and appropriate view
Italy	– un quadro fedele	a faithful picture
	– rappresentare in modo veritiero e corretto	represent in a true and correct way
Finland	– oikea ja riittävä kuva	[a?] right (or true) and sufficient picture
	– oikeat ja riittävät tiedot	right (or true) and sufficient information
	– en riktig och tillräcklig bild	a right (or true) and sufficient picture
	– riktiga och tillräckliga uppgifter	right (or true) and sufficient information
Norway	– et pålitelig bilde	a reliable picture
	– god regnskapsskikk	good accounting practice
Sweden	– en rättvisande bild	a right-looking (or fair-looking) picture

15

Accounting and Business Research, Vol. 30. No. 4. pp. 307–312. 2000

Is true and fair of over-riding importance?: a comment on Alexander's benchmark

Christopher Nobes*

'He dared well to despise vain things', Alexander as described by Livy (*History*, book ix, section 17).

1. Introduction

In the context of establishing criteria against which to judge the adequacy of published financial statements, Alexander (1999) distinguishes between a general over-riding requirement (Type A), an integrated framework (Type B) and detailed regulation (Type C). Alexander adds clarity to the analysis of the hierarchy of principles and policies. Much of his analysis seems correct and useful, but the major conclusion concerning the desirability of an over-ride in standards does not.

Part of Alexander's argument is that:

> unequivocal agreement is necessary that either the Type A criterion is superior to the Type C criterion, or the reverse. (p. 252)

This seems right both for those who make the rules (regulators) and for those who use them (preparers and auditors), although Alexander does not distinguish between these parties. He continues:

> supremacy of Type C specification...is inadequate in a dynamic economy, as choice or change in such regulation is inevitably without reference to a more broadly based objective. (p.252)

Alexander therefore approves (p.251) of IAS 1, which gives supremacy to 'fair presentation' in the preparation of financial statements. It will be argued here that, when considering an over-ride, the analysis would be improved by distinguishing between law and standards, between choice by preparers and choice/change by regulators, and be-

tween national and international regulation. It will further be argued that choice by preparers to disobey a regulation is probably a bad thing, even in a dynamic economy, so that Type C regulation should prevail for them; and that choice or change of Type C regulation (by standard setters or other regulators) can nevertheless make reference to a broadly-based objective. That is, Type C should prevail for preparers (and auditors) but Type A for regulators. Consequently, it will be suggested that Alexander is wrong about the need for supremacy of Type A in the *application* of standards, and so is IAS 1.

The argument below begins by examining the purpose and effect of the TFV over-ride in law, and then the differences for national and international standards. Then some examples are given of the dangers of allowing an overriding Type A criterion in international standards. The concluding section suggests that IAS 1 is unusual in the context of Anglo-Saxon standards.

2. True and fair in the UK context

2.1. The purpose of the TFV over-ride in law

The TFV (including the over-ride) in UK law provides a Type A criterion which might be used for several purposes:

i. to help preparers and auditors to choose between the available Type C rules in law or standards;

ii. to help preparers and auditors to interpret Type C rules in law or standards;

iii. to help preparers and auditors where there are no Type C rules;

iv. to force preparers and auditors to assess the need for extra disclosures beyond those in Type C rules;

v. to guide standard setters when developing Type C rules that do not involve breaking Type C rules in law but that are more restrictive than the law (e.g. eliminating LIFO);[1]

*The author is PricewaterhouseCoopers Professor of Accounting at the University of Reading; and has been one of the two UK representatives on the Board of the International Accounting Standards Committee since 1993. He is grateful for comments on earlier drafts from David Alexander, Malcolm Miller, Bob Parker, Alan Roberts, two referees and the editor of this journal. Professor Nobes can be contacted at the Department of Economics, the University of Reading. P.O. Box 218. Whiteknights, Reading RG6 2AA. The final version of this paper was accepted in April 2000.

---

[1]SSAP 9 suggests that LIFO will normally not give a true and fair view, which therefore normally over-rides the permission to use LIFO in the Companies Act 1985. Schedule 4, para 27 (2).

vi. to force or to enable preparers and auditors to depart from Type C rules in standards in undefined circumstances;

vii. to guide standard setters when developing Type C rules in cases where they conflict with Type C rules in law; and then to force or to enable preparers and auditors to follow the standard (e.g. lack of depreciation of investment properties);[2] and

viii. to force or to enable preparers and auditors to depart from Type C rules in law in undefined circumstances, even beyond point (vii).

Points (vi) to (viii) are expressed as 'to force or to enable' because there is judgement involved and because preparers may *wish* to make the departures.

The TFV over-ride in law is not necessary for points (i) to (v) and is not strictly necessary[3] for point (vi). However, the legal over-ride is the essence of points (vii) and (viii), which is probably why the British were so keen on it as part of the Fourth Directive (Hopwood, 1990; Nobes, 1993). It would enable British standards and other practices to over-ride 'foreign' rules in Directives made by lawyers, civil servants and politicians; and it would enable continual British developments despite the fact that the Directives were unlikely to change for decades.

2.2. The legal TFV over-ride of standards

Alexander (p.243) takes us carefully through the relationship between law and standards. In principle, of course, the law over-rides standards. However, as Alexander points out, the ASB obtained and published counsel's opinion to the effect that there is 'a likelihood that the court will hold that compliance with the standard is necessary to meet the true and fair requirement'. In other words, although the ASB actively uses the legal Type A over-ride so that its own Type C rules can outrank legal Type C rules (points (v) and (vii) above), it has been keen to establish that there should in practice be no Type A over-ride of its own Type C rules by preparers (unlike point (vi) above).

When considering whether domestic *standards* need to be capable of being over-ridden, the main practical purpose of the over-ride as in the Directive does not apply. That is, the standards are not 'foreign'; they are not made by lawyers, civil servants and politicians; and they are not immutable

or impervious to developments in practice. Assuming that Type C rules in standards are more detailed than Type C rules in law, the issue boils down to whether Type A criteria in law should outrank Type C rules in standards *for preparers*. English-speaking regulators have reached the opinion (explicitly or otherwise) that this should not be the case. For example, in the US the SEC requires compliance with standards, and in Australia the law does. As noted above, this is approximately the UK position in practice.

This dislike of the over-ride of standards is due to the fear that preparers would use vague Type A criteria to over-ride Type C rules in order to improve the look of their financial statements. In Australia, the legal over-ride was removed at the suggestion of the standard-setter (McGregor, 1992). In the UK, doubts about the advisability of leaving a lot of discretion with preparers and auditors stem partly from the observation that the TFV was not in practice used to prevent 'creative compliance' in the days before the Financial Reporting Review Panel (Griffiths, 1986; Tweedie and Whittington, 1990; Shah, 1996).

2.3. An over-ride written into standards

Another issue is whether there should be an over-ride written into domestic standards. Again, the main practical purpose of the Directive's over-ride does not seem to apply, because the domestic standard setters are in charge of the rules and can change or interpret them. In the US and Australia, the standards themselves do not contain an over-ride. In the UK, no such over-ride is to be found in SSAP 2 of 1971, although in 1999 the ASB proposed to introduce one (FRED 21, para. 13). This over-ride would be unlikely to be of practical use because of counsel's opinion that compliance would probably be held to be necessary in general in order to give a TFV.

2.4. Conclusion on Type A over-ride

Alexander has two main arguments in favour of making a Type A criterion over-riding. First, he notes that there is '...an almost infinitely wide range of users...enterprises...situations...decisions' (p.250), so that detailed prescription will not work in forcing financial statements to provide useful information. There seem to be flaws here. It is unclear how the use of an over-riding Type A criterion could help a single set of financial statements to satisfy more of the infinity of needs than the use of over-riding Type C rules would (given that Type A would still be present, requiring disclosures and so forth). Also, as noted above (see sub-section 2.2), any over-riding Type A criterion may be used by some preparers to mislead rather than to inform.

Alexander's second main argument is that:

---

[2]In order to give a true and fair view, SSAP 19 requires the annual revaluation of investment properties, with no depreciation. The latter point over-rides the requirement to depreciate all fixed assets with limited useful lives in the Companies Act 1985, Schedule 4, para 18.

[3]It is not necessary to have a specific legal over-ride in order for the legal requirement to give a TFV to over-ride extra-legal standards.

if regulation is going to be changed...then some *over-riding* criterion greater than that enshrined in regulation itself must, as a matter of logical necessity, be employed to decide on the changes (p.250, emphasis in original)

Taken literally, Alexander scores an own goal here. He appears to be saying that the Type A criterion should not be enshrined in regulation but should be employed by the regulator. I would agree. However, he meant[4] that a Type A criterion greater than the Type C rules should be enshrined in legislation. This, of course, is not a 'logical necessity' because the regulators could use a Type A criterion when making Type C rules whether or not it was enshrined in regulation as over-riding for preparers and auditors.

3. IAS 1

I now turn to international standards. I do not wish to defend the detail of E 53 any more than Alexander does (p. 250). However, this does not mean that IAS 1 is right.

Alexander quotes Karel Van Hulle (1997) and Sir David Tweedie[5] as reporting that the US, Canada, Australia and Germany were against an over-ride in IAS 1, whereas the UK and most other Europeans were in favour. The reports are slightly inaccurate. The Scottish representative on the IASC Board (Sir David) did indeed speak passionately in favour of an over-ride, but the English representative[6] spoke passionately against.

The arguments against an over-riding Type A (e.g. TFV) criterion relating to a domestic standard (purpose (vi) in Section 2) have been made above. First, TFV can still be used by preparers for purposes (i) to (iv). Second, TFV can still be the over-riding criterion for standard setters (purpose (v)). Third, one can still have an over-riding TFV for Type C legal rules in law (purposes (vii) and (viii)). Fourth, the experience of standard setters in the English-speaking world (including the UK) suggests that it is a bad idea to allow preparers a means to break standards. One should not lightly dismiss the views of experienced standard setters in the US, Canada and Australia; and one should judge the ASB by its domestic actions (i.e. obtaining and publishing counsel's opinion, as examined above) rather than by its international words. These standard setters have observed that, particularly in the absence of a strong oversight and enforcement mechanism, for every case where a TFV over-ride of a standard would force a preparer to depart from a 'wrong' Type C rule, there

would be dozens where a preparer would contrive to depart from a 'right' Type C rule. So, this form of the over-ride would make finanical reporting worse.

An alternative approach to allowing the rare necessity of an over-ride of Type C rules is for preparers to disclose the problem and its effects, even to the extent of pro forma financial statements. If the issue is substantial and not extremely rare, then the standard setters can change the Type C rule or issue an interpretation of it.

The case against a TFV over-ride becomes even stronger in an international standard than in a domestic standard. Alexander reports (p. 245) that he and I have separately argued that there are many European meanings to TFV; but that other writers have argued that there is one 'European TFV' which might be different from a British TFV. Either way, there is agreement that the interpretation of TFV differs internationally. It seems clear, too, that there is greater scope for international variation in the interpretation of a Type A criterion than of a Type C rule. Consequently, a Type A over-ride in IAS 1 will be interpreted with even more variance internationally than nationally, so that Type C rules will be over-ridden to different degrees and in different ways in different places even in similar circumstances. Users of sets of financial statements prepared in different countries but all under IAS rules would presumably prefer to reduce such differences.

A second international issue concerns oversight and enforcement. The cost of a Type A over-ride in standards (i.e. abuse of it) is likely to be minimised if there is an effective oversight and enforcement mechanism. To the extent that there is an over-ride of the Type C rules of standards in the US or the UK (see above, and Alexander, Sections 3 and 6), it is now little abused (or even used) because of legally backed oversight and enforcement in the respective countries by the Securities and Exchange Commission and the Financial Reporting Review Panel. There is presently no such body on an international basis to oversee and enforce the IASC's package of standards and interpretations (called IAS GAAP, below), as has been lamented by the World Bank and others.[7] This increases the likelihood of abuse.

Incidentally, although IAS GAAP lacks a specific legal context for a Type A over-ride to be written into, this does not mean that an over-ride has therefore to be put into IAS GAAP itself. As noted above, four of the uses of the Type A criterion for preparers (see points (i) to (iv) of Section 2) do not rely on an over-ride, and two other uses (points (vii) and (viii)) are not relevant in the absence of a specific legal context. The remaining use

---

[4]Confirmed by David Alexander in correspondence of 19 October 1999.
[5]'SEC miffed at UK Victory'. *Accountancy*, August: 17.
[6]That is, the present author.

[7]'Big five on board—just'. *Accountancy International*, July: 7.

for preparers (i.e. for the over-ride of Type C rules in standards) is the one that I believe is inappropriate anyway. For standard setters with no specific legal context, insertion of an over-ride into standards is also not appropriate, given that standards are addressed to preparers and auditors, not to standard setters. For the latter, the Type A criterion can be made paramount in other ways, such as being written into a conceptual framework.

In addition to the above arguments against an over-ride in IAS 1, there was the political point that inserting an over-ride would be used by those opposed to IOSCO[8] endorsement of IAS GAAP to suggest that the standards were so loose that they contained an in-built non-compliance device (e.g. FASB, 1999, p.47). There is no reason to criticise Alexander for not including this in his logic, but it is relevant in the wider scheme of things for those who believe that the spread of IAS GAAP would be likely to improve accounting around the world.

Fortunately, the problem with IAS 1 was mitigated in the final drafting discussions by adding a requirement to disclose the reasons for departure and details of the financial effect (IAS 1, para. 13 (c) and (d)). It might be concluded that there is little difference between (i) breaking a Type C rule with a full financial explanation of why this is necessary to comply with a Type A criterion, and (ii) complying with a Type C rule with a full financial explanation of how different things would have looked if one had complied with the Type A criterion. In a world of universally honest preparers, fully independent auditors and fully effective overseers, one might be comfortable with indulging a philosophical preference for the former. However, for practical and political reasons, the latter might have been better.

4. Examples of Type A/Type C conflict

Some examples may be useful to illustrate the dangers of Type A over-ride in standards. IASs are chosen as the context.

IAS 12 (paras. 15 and 53) imposes Type C rules whereby an enterprise must account for deferred tax on a temporary difference arising on the revaluation of an asset; and the amount should not be discounted. Some British preparers and auditors (and standard setters) claim[9] that this is 'wrong', particularly in the normal case where there is no intention to sell the asset and where

anyway roll-over relief could be claimed to postpone any tax on a capital gain. It is 'wrong' because the resulting credit balance would not meet the definition of a liability, [10] in that there is no obligation to a third party at the balance sheet date. Furthermore, for such a long-dated 'liability', it is badly misleading not to discount it, particularly given the requirement to discount pension liabilities (IAS 19, para. 54) and other types of provisions (IAS 37, para. 45). One could argue that zero would be a better estimate of any liability rather than the full nominal amount. Presumably, the consciences (or inclinations) of British preparers or auditors might therefore require them to use the Type A over-ride in IAS 1 in order to disobey the Type C rules of IAS 12.

As a second example, IAS 19 (para. 83) contains a Type C requirement to take account of estimated future pay rises when calculating defined benefit pension liabilities. Some German preparers and auditors claimed[11] that this is 'wrong' because there is no obligation to make the pay rises. This seems to be a mistaken[12] argument, but that is not the issue here.

If preparers or auditors honestly believe (or can plausibly claim to believe) that a Type C rule leads to 'wrong' accounting, then Alexander and IAS 1 would require them (or, in the bracketed case, allow them) to break the Type C rule in order to comply with the Type A criterion. If this hierarchy were taken literally and seriously, chaos would result. British companies could break IAS 12 and German companies could break IAS 19 while still claiming compliance with IAS GAAP. It would be difficult for auditors to qualify their opinions, even if they wanted to; and there would be no oversight/enforcement mechanism beyond that.

5. Conclusion

While agreeing with many of Alexander's arguments and conclusions, I challenge Alexander's conclusions that Type A criteria should over-ride Type C rules in standards, and that IAS 1 is therefore a good standard in this respect. The problem arises because of the lack of sufficient distinction in the following cases:

i. between a Type A over-ride in law and one in standards;

ii. between a Type A supremacy for regulators and a Type A over-ride for preparers;

---

[8]International Organization of Securities Commissions, whose members include the Securities and Exchange Commission of the US.

[9]The following were arguments used by the UK representatives on the Board of the IASC during the debate leading up to IAS 12 (revised). Such arguments can also be seen in British and the other submissions to the IASC on E 49, which are on public record.

[10]IASC, *Framework*, paras. 49, 60, 91.

[11]See, for example, FEE (1999), p.40.

[12]This is mistaken because the existence of an obligation is necessary to establish that there is a liability (*Framework*, para 49) rather than to measure the size of the liability. There is no doubt that there is a pension liability in this case (irrespective of future pay rises); the issue is how to arrive at the best estimate of it. There is a probability that there will be future pay rises, so they need to be taken into account in the estimations.

and

iii. between a national setting and an international setting.

Consequently, Alexander's two main arguments (inflexibility/stultification and change to regulation) do not work. First, Type C rules in law may be stultified but this is not necessary for standards. The latter can be changed reasonably quickly or an interpretation can be issued. In the meantime, supposing that the standard setters had already been using a Type A criterion to make the Type C rules, flexibility in terms of a Type A over-ride for preparers would be likely to entail higher costs in terms of abuse than benefits in terms of a rare case of better accounting. Secondly, although supremacy of a Type A criterion is necessary for coherent change to Type C rules, it is necessary in the minds of the regulators not as an over-ride for preparers.

The arguments in this comment paper suggest the following:

a) A Type A criterion is useful in law or standards or both, so that preparers and auditors can interpret Type C rules, choose between options in them and fill gaps.

b) A Type A criterion should be used by legislators or standard setters when making Type C rules. (Obviously this means that Type A overrides Type C.)

c) Within a law, a Type A over-ride of the law's Type C rules is useful, assuming that there are reasonably detailed Type C rules in standards.

d) The law should not contain a Type A over-ride of Type C rules in standards, or at least there should be a strong legal presumption in favour of standards and an effective oversight or enforcement mechanism.

e) Standards should not contain a Type A over-ride of Type C rules in standards.

f) Conclusion (e) applies particularly if there is no effective oversight or enforcement mechanism.

g) Conclusion (e) applies particularly in an international setting where the Type A criterion would be interpreted variously.

In the US, (a), (b)[13] and (e)[14] are complied with, and the rest are not relevant.[15] In Australia, (a), (b), (d) and (e) are complied with, and the rest are not relevant (including (c) because there are a few Type C rules in law). In Canada, standards are inserted into law and there is an over-ride which is at least as restricted and overseen as that in the

UK. Consequently, (a) to (e) are in effect complied with. Furthermore, in Australia and Canada, standards are specifically mandatory by law, which is effectively the US position because of the SEC's requirements. In the UK, (a), (b), (c) and (d, second option) are complied with. At the time of writing, so is (e), and in effect this will continue, as noted in Section 2.3. As in the other countries, (f) and (g) are not relevant. Consequently, all these countries satisfy my desiderata. IAS 1 is the odd one out. There is compliance with (a) and (b), and (c) and (d) are not relevant. However, (e) is broken, which is particularly serious given that (f) and (g) are relevant. Fortunately, the problem with IAS 1 is mitigated by the compulsory disclosures.

None of the above arguments should be construed as implying that the TFV is a bad idea. Clearly, the ultimate objective must be for financial statements to give useful information (presumably implied by giving a TFV) rather than to obey a set of rules. The argument here is that, on balance, the former is more likely to be achieved by specifically demanding the latter with no exceptions. This is particularly the case in the present international setting.

Also, it is not intended to imply that standard setters are perfect. For example, the above suggestion that the English-speaking standard setters comply with my desideratum (b) by *using* a Type A criterion does not mean that they always publish the 'right' Type C rules. Sometimes the standard setters are overcome by practical or political considerations. However, it *is* implied here that standard setters are more likely to make (and amend where necessary) Type C rules that contribute to a TFV than are parliaments or lawyers, and that across-the-board compliance is more likely to maximise the output of useful and comparable information than leaving the interpretation of TFV (and any resulting departure from rules) to individual preparers and auditors.

References

Alexander, D. (1999). 'A benchmark for the adequacy of published financial statements'. *Accounting and Business Research*, 29 (3): 239–253.

FASB (1999). *The IASC-US Comparison Project*, Financial Accounting Standards Board.

FEE (1999). *Comparison of the EC Accounting Directives and IASs*, FEE.

Griffiths, I. (1986). *Creative Accounting: How to Make Your Profits What You Want Them to be*, Sidgwick and Jackson.

Hopwood, A. (1990). 'Ambiguity, knowledge and territorial claims: Some observations on the doctrine of substance over form: a review essay'. *British Accounting Review*, March: 79–87.

McGregor, W. J. (1992). 'True and fair—an accounting anachronism'. *Australian Accountant*, February: 68–71.

Nobes, C. W. (1993). 'The true and fair view requirement: impact on and of the fourth directive'. *Accountant and Business Research*, Winter: 35–48.

---

[13]Although Alexander notes (p.248) that 'fair presentation' need not be used by the FASB, there are other statements of purpose (i.e. Type A criteria) in the FASB's Framework.

[14]To the extent that (e) is not complied with because of AICPA rule 203 (Alexander, p. 248) then this is sorted out by SAS 69 and because (f) does not apply.

[15]Because of the lack of Companies Acts (points (c) and (d)), because of the SEC (point (f)) and the domestic context (point (g)).

Shah, A. (1996). 'Creative compliance in financial reporting'. *Accounting Organizations and Society*, 21 (1): 23–39.

Tweedie, D. and Whittington, G. (1990). 'Financial reporting: current problems and their implications for systematic reform'. *Accounting and Business Research*, Winter: 87–102.

Van Hulle, K. (1997). 'The true and fair over-ride in European Accounting directives'. *European Accounting Review*, 6 (4): 711–720.

16

Accounting in Europe, Vol. 3, 2006

Revenue Recognition and EU Endorsement of IFRS

CHRISTOPHER W. NOBES

University of Reading Business School, UK and Norwegian School of Management

ABSTRACT   This paper comments on a previous paper in this journal concerning EU endorsement of IFRS. It is suggested here that the previous authors should consider whether there can be more than one true and fair view even in one country and especially across European countries. It is further suggested that the previous analysis of five accounting standards does not support the claim that the European Commission wrongly endorsed them. It is also argued here that the previous analysis of the nature of most gains under IFRS is faulty.

1. Introduction

Wüstemann and Kierzek (2005; hereafter WK) provide a clear and stimulating analysis of current and proposed International Financial Reporting Standards (IFRS) on the subject of revenue recognition. On the way, they make important points about European endorsement of IFRS. Some parts of their analysis are convincing, as mentioned later. However, in the author's opinion, other parts of the analysis are faulty. This is explained below under three headings, followed by a conclusion.

2. European True and Fair View

Context

WK note that the EU Regulation 1606/2002 (Art. 3) requires an endorsed IFRS to be not contrary to the principle that financial statements should give a true and fair view. They suggest that this should be interpreted in the light of such

---

Correspondence Address: Christopher W. Nobes, PricewaterhouseCoopers Professor of Accounting, University of Reading Business School, PO Box 218, Whiteknights, Reading RG6 6AA, UK. E-mail: c.w.nobes@reading.ac.uk

0963-8180 Print/06/030081–9 © 2006 European Accounting Association
Published by Routledge Journals, Taylor & Francis, on behalf of the EAA

principles as prudence, realisation and accrual (p. 72), but not necessarily compliance with all the provisions of the Directive (Regulation, preamble, para. 9).
WK claim (p. 72) that there is such a thing as 'the European true and fair
view'. They repeatedly use this phrase in their Sub-section 2.2, and clearly
they believe that this is a singular concept. This was indeed the opinion of one
respected German commentator (Ordelheide, 1993), but it was countered by
Alexander (1993) and Arden (1997), and even by van Hulle (1993, p. 100)
who was the European Commission's Head of Accounting. Furthermore, the
1996 European Court of Justice case referred to by WK seems itself to accept
that there can be different national meanings, as explained later in this section
under 'IAS 18'. So the weight of opinion seems to be against WK, and they
would need to prove their point rather than to assert it.

WK make the major claim (p. 72) that the Commission has endorsed 'a number
of IFRS' that do not comply with 'the European notion' of a true and fair view.
They illustrate this by looking at IAS 11, IAS 18, IAS 41, IAS 39 and IFRS 2. To
the extent that the arguments might affect future endorsements of IFRS, this is a
vital issue that needs to be examined further.

Another key introductory point is that the Directive requires *a* true and fair
view not *the* true and fair view. Therefore, endorsement of an IFRS can be
quite proper even if a non-IFRS treatment could also give a true and fair view.

IAS 11 (Construction Contracts)

WK analyse revenue recognition at length later in their paper (see, also, Section 4
below). The present issue is whether IAS 11's requirement to use the percentage-
of-completion method should have prevented endorsement. WK appear to conclude so (p. 72), on the grounds that the method does not comply with the
realisation principle. However, they do not define this principle (see further
below) or explain why it is contravened. Nor do they explain what happens if
the accrual principle contradicts it. Incidentally, Evans and Nobes (1996) point
out that prudence overrides accrual in the German language version of the
Fourth Directive (and therefore in the resulting German law) but not in the
English language version (and the British law). Evans (2004) discusses how
the Commission seems to accept that different EU states have different interpretations of prudence. What does all that do for '*the* European true and fair view'?

To the author's knowledge, no European legislation defines 'realised' as
requiring the receipt of cash. It then becomes impossible to define 'realised'
clearly. In the case of a sale on credit, revenue is recognised before the receipt
of cash because there is a contract (written or not) that requires the customer
to pay later. IAS 18.8 concurs by defining revenue as including inflows that
are 'received *and receivable*' (italics added). In the case of a construction contract, the constructor also has a contract signed by the client and has done
work. Of course, completion decreases uncertainty but, since both cases
involve a contract but no cash, it is not self-evident why revenue on a credit

sale is realised but revenue resulting from work done under a construction contract is not,

Applying the Fourth Directive's accrual principle, it remains unclear why it is wrong under the Directive to take profit as production is carried out. Let us take the example of a five-year contract that is within one month of completion at a balance sheet date. The contract contains no stages, so no work has been signed off by the customer. However, the customer has accepted and paid for similar contracts in the past. By implication, WK claim that the *only* possible true and fair treatment here is to take no profit until the last day of the contract when the customer accepts the completed product. Any other treatment is alleged to be not 'European'.

Incidentally, even before the EU Regulation on IFRS, the percentage-of-completion method was allowed or required[1] in at least the following EU countries (out of 15): Belgium, Denmark, Finland, France, Ireland, Italy, the Netherlands, Portugal, Spain, Sweden and the UK. WK imply that these countries were not being 'European'. Since there seem[2] to have been no specific rules on this topic in Greece and Luxembourg, that just leaves only two (German-speaking) countries in which the method was not allowed.

IAS 18 (Revenue)

WK refer (p. 72) to a European Court of Justice judgement (Court, 1996) concerning whether dividends are sometimes revenue for an investor before approval by the paying company's general assembly. If they are, this would contradict the requirement in IAS 18.30(c) for the right to dividends to be established before revenue can be recognised, so WK question whether IAS 18 leads to a true and fair view and therefore whether it should have been endorsed by the Commission.

However, two points need to be made. First, the Court pointed out (para. 15) that:

It should be emphasized at the outset that ... the question arises in the context of a highly specific set of circumstances ...

WK would need to show that endorsement of an IFRS should be withheld just because it does not deal with a particular highly specific set of circumstances.

In this case, though, another point is more important. The Court did *not* conclude that the unapproved dividends should be treated as revenue, even in the highly specific circumstances. It concluded (para. 25) that:

... it is not contrary to [a true and fair view] for the national court to consider that the profits in question must be entered in the parent company's balance sheet ...

84   *C. W. Nobes*

That is, far from the Court believing that accrual was necessary in order to give a true and fair view, the Court merely held that it might be possible for some national courts to hold so.

Not only does this remove WK's objection to endorsement of IAS 18, it also shows that the European Court of Justice believes that one EU country can take a different view of what is necessary from another EU country. This seems to undermine WK's claim (see above) that there is one European true and fair view.

IAS 41 (Agriculture)

WK then look at 'marking to market' for biological assets under IAS 41. WK note that, in 2001, the Contact Committee held that marking to market was contrary to the Directive whereas, in 2003, the Commission endorsed IAS 41 that requires it. In between, the Fourth Directive had changed to allow marking to market. WK suggest (pp. 72–73) that this proves that the meaning of 'true and fair' is closely tied to the contents of the Directive. However, unlike the Commission, the Contact Committee was not considering 'true and fair', it was considering the specific requirements of the Directive. So this case does not illustrate the point that WK were trying to make about the narrowness of the true and fair view requirement.

Incidentally, WK state (p. 73) that the EU Contact Committee believed that IAS 41's 'fair value approach' was 'contradictory to central valuation principles of the Accounting Directives such as ... historical cost measurement'. However, a reading of the EU document (European Commission, 2001, pp. 5, 47) shows that this is not the case. IAS 41 *was* found to be contrary to the realisation principle but no mention was made of historical cost because Article 33 of the Directive (although not the German implementation of it) has always allowed all sorts of departures from historical cost, even before the amendments of 2001 and 2003.

IAS 39 (Financial Instruments) and IFRS 2 (Share-Based Payments)

WK complete their discussion of how the Commission did not satisfy the true and fair view requirement by noting (p. 73) that it used other arguments when explaining the endorsement decisions on IAS 39 and IFRS 2. However, this tells us nothing about whether or not those standards were consistent with a true and fair view, or whether the Commission thought that they were. Perhaps the Commission believed that the true and fair view requirement is so vague that other arguments would be more pertinent.

Conclusion on True and Fair View

WK suggest that the Commission flouted the requirement for 'the European true and fair view' when making several of their endorsement decisions. However, WK's examples of doubtful endorsement are unconvincing: on IAS 11, they choose one European interpretation rather than the majority interpretation; on IAS 18, they present the European Court's flexibility to allow a non-IFRS view in special circumstances as though it were a barrier to endorsement; on IAS 41, they make a false contrast of the Contact Committee's consideration of the specific requirements of the Directive and the Commission's consideration of the true and fair view requirement, and they mis-state the Contact Committee's reasons for opposing IAS 41; on IAS 39 and IFRS 2, they offer no direct evidence.

WK do not address the issues of whether there might be more than one European concept or, indeed, more than one acceptable view in any one European country. Another important point that could be discussed is the potential relevance of the opinion of English lawyers that the true and fair view requirement is a 'dynamic concept' (Arden, 1993, para. 14). Just as national legislators can implement the true and fair view requirement differently (e.g. see next section, and Aisbitt and Nobes, 2001), so the legislators or standard setters can affect its meaning by constraining practice, as can companies by making policy choices. That is, true and fair needs to be interpreted in the light of accounting practice, which changes over time, partly as a result of new standards. So, for example, if users of financial statements expect to see contract profit calculated according to the percentage-of-completion method (e.g. because IAS 11 requires it), then that is good evidence of what is needed in order to give a true and fair view. That is, the meaning of 'true and fair' depends on the requirements of standards as much as vice versa.

To the extent that EU companies are now using IFRS for some purposes, their financial statements are required, by IAS 1, to give a fair presentation rather than a true and fair view (ICAEW, 2005). Whether these two concepts are the same has been discussed elsewhere (e.g. Zeff, 1990; Evans, 2003).

3. Principles-Based Standards

WK contrast (p. 74) a German principles-based system that 'leaves little room for professional judgement' with the International Accounting Standard Board's (IASB) principles-based system that attaches importance to judgement. This seems to misunderstand the contrast in the literature (e.g. Nelson, 2003) between principles-based standards and rules-based standards. Standards that are full of rules can be written with principles in mind (Schipper, 2003), but such standards are nevertheless characterised as rules-based. So, if WK are right about the lack of room for judgement, the German system should be called rules-based. It is true that the debate would be better phrased as a contrast between standards that require compliance with principles as opposed to those that require compliance with rules. However, WK do not explore that. Nelson (2003) and Nobes (2005) examine some of the arguments for and against detailed prescription.

WK express opposition to the exercise of judgement. For example, they examine the 'interpretation guidelines in IAS 8.10 to 12 relying on management's professional judgement in the selection of accounting policies'. WK suggest that 'it is not evident that [these] ... are applicable in the European Union' (p. 75). This is despite the fact that all of IAS 8 was endorsed by the EU and is now part of the Regulation, and despite the fact that the whole of paragraphs 10–12 are 'black letter standards' and *not* just 'interpretation guidelines'.

There is a link between the previous section (true and fair view) and this section. The true and fair view requirement is the top principle in the Fourth Directive. In order to make a principles-based system work, judgement is required. WK's opposition to the exercise of judgement is reminiscent of the German opposition to the true and fair view requirement of the Fourth Directive. The 1971 draft of the Directive contained no reference to the true and fair view as it was based closely on the 1965 *Aktiengesetz*. This was before Denmark, Ireland and the UK joined the EU. The final (1978) version of the Directive gave prominence to the true and fair view requirement, but the German implementation reduced its importance by four means: (i) a questionable translation;[3] (ii) restriction of the true and fair view requirement, in the 1985 *Bilanzrichtliniengesetz*, with the words 'in compliance with orderly principles of bookkeeping/accounting';[4] (iii) failure to enact the overriding aspect of the true and fair view requirement as required by Art. 2 (5) (van Hulle, 1993, p. 102); and (iv) insisting on a Council minute that specifies that complying with the rest of the Directive will generally achieve a true and fair view (Council, 1978; Ordelheide, 1990).

4. Revenue

One can agree with WK that revenue recognition under IFRS is not at present fully based on either an asset/liability view or on a revenue/expense view (pp. 78 and 84). However, WK can be questioned on some issues, and some extra points should be made. No comment is made here on WK's proposals for contract revenue, because this topic is investigated in great detail by a current Financial Accounting Standards Board (FASB)/IASB project.

WK quote (p. 79) IAS 18's definition of revenue: 'the gross inflow ... arising in the course of the ordinary activities ... when those inflows result in increases in equity ...'. WK say (p. 80) that the IASB's *Framework* (para. 75) does not clearly distinguish between revenue and gains. However, paragraphs 74–76 of the *Framework* do a better job than IAS 18. They make it clear that revenue includes sales, whereas gains include the results of disposing of fixed assets. WK's suggestion that, under IFRS, 'gains predominantly arise from value changes of assets and liabilities' (p. 80) seems in error. It is clear from WK's next two sentences that they are referring to unrealised value changes. However, gains can also arise from the sale of assets that had been measured at cost or at depreciated cost, including such items as: (i) tangible assets under

IAS 16 or IAS 40; (ii) intangible assets under IAS 38; (iii) held-to-maturity investments under IAS 39, and (in an investor's statement) investments in subsidiaries, associates and joint ventures under IAS 27, 28 and 31. These are surely the preponderance of gains for most[5] enterprises, and they rely on sale transactions not on fair value changes.

A related problem is that WK claim (p. 83) that, under IFRS, 'most increases in the fair value of financial assets or decreases of the fair value of financial liabilities are recognised as gains in the income statement'. However, this would only be true if 'most' financial assets and liabilities were treated as trading.[6] Observation[7] of IFRS financial statements, other than those of financial institutions, suggests that this is not the case because non-derivative financial assets are generally treated as available-for-sale or held-to-maturity (IAS 39.55b and 56), and most financial liabilities are not trading liabilities and therefore are held at amortised proceeds (confusingly[8] called 'amortised cost' by IAS 39.47). WK offer no evidence for their 'most'.

These misunderstandings lead to the statement in WK's conclusion (p. 102) that the *Framework's* recognition criteria (i.e. probable inflows and reliable measurement) are 'virtually irrelevant for the recognition of gains'. However, the analysis above suggests that generally gains under IFRS are not recognised until sale, whereupon the probability of inflows and the reliability of their measurement are assured.

Incidentally, WK do not point out that IAS 18's definition of revenue (which refers to ordinary activities and to increases in equity; see second paragraph of this section) makes little sense, because no activities are now extraordinary (see IAS 1.85), and very little was extraordinary even before (see the 1993 version of IAS 8.12). Consequently, the sale of a fixed asset at above its book value is 'ordinary' and would fit the definition of revenue. By contrast, the sale of inventory at below its book value would appear not to fit the definition because there is no increase in equity.[9] Clearly, the International Accounting Standards Committee (IASC) was not paying proper attention when it approved IAS 18 in 1993 (incidentally, the author was there[10]). Since then, IAS 18 has been up-dated to state (para. 5(f)) that it does not cover 'revenue in the form of ... changes in the fair value of biological assets related to agricultural activity (see IAS 41 *Agriculture*) ...'. However, changes in fair value are not revenue because they are not a gross inflow of economic benefits. So, this does not make sense either.

5. Conclusion

WK take it for granted that there is one European true and fair view, but they do not examine the contrary arguments. They do not discuss the fact that the EU Regulation makes it necessary for an IFRS merely to be not contrary to the requirement for *a* (as opposed to *the*) true and fair view (whether or not a specifically European one), or that the meaning of this might change over time, in the light of changes to standards.

None of WK's suggestions of contentious endorsement decisions are convincing. For example, on IAS 11, they promote the German (minority EU) view as *the* European view. On IAS 18, they misrepresent the European Court's finding, which did not require a non-IFRS treatment. Connected to this, WK argue unconvincingly against the EU-endorsed requirements of IAS 8 for judgement in the choice of accounting policies.

On revenue recognition, WK exaggerate the need for judgement in IFRS by claiming, with no evidence, that under IFRS: (i) gains are predominantly based on fair value changes; (ii) most gains on financial instruments go through income; and (iii) therefore the recognition criteria are virtually irrelevant.

Acknowledgements

The author is grateful for comments on an earlier draft from David Alexander (University of Birmingham), Lisa Evans (University of Stirling), Axel Haller (University of Regensburg), Sigvard Heurlin (EFRAG), Erlend Kvaal (Norwegian School of Management), Andrew Lennard (Accounting Standards Board), Bob Parker (University of Exeter), Alan Roberts (University of Rennes), and from a reviewer and the editor of this journal.

Notes

[1] I rely here on FEE (1991, ch. 7) and Ordelheide and Semler (1995).

[2] Papas (1993, p. 122) and Clark (1994, p. 154).

[3] Van Hulle (1993, p. 100) confirms that the English was the original. Nobes (1993) explains that the Commission had translated the true and fair view as '*einen getreuen Einblick*' (in the 1974 draft of the Directive) but Germany regarded this as too vague, so '*ein den tatsächlichen Verhältnissen entsprechendes Bild*' was substituted. At the least, the components of the German signifier are different from the English, stressing 'true' rather than 'fair'.

[4] '*unter Beachtung der Grundsätze ordungsmässiger Büchfuhrung*'.

[5] The obvious exception being financial institutions.

[6] Or as derivatives or designated as at fair value through profit or loss (IAS 39.9).

[7] For example, this is the case for the first three German companies' 2005 reports that I looked at: Bayer, p. 98; Volkswagen, p. 128; and Lufthansa, p. 87. I have never seen anything different in my previous studies of German use of IFRS or in recent UK use of IFRS or in US use of the similar standard, SFAS 115.

[8] This is confusing because liabilities (unlike assets) do not have a cost; they have the opposite of a cost.

[9] I say 'appear' because it could be argued that the gross inflow is an increase in equity, and the loss of the inventory is a decrease. This would be an obscure use of words and would render the words 'when those inflows result in increases in equity' redundant.

[10] The author was a UK representative on the Board of the IASC from January 1993 to March 2001. The November 1993 vote was on a whole package of standards. IAS 18 had been provisionally approved in 1992.

References

Aisbitt, S. and Nobes, C. W. (2001) The true and fair view requirement in recent national implement-ations, *Accounting and Business Research*, 31(2), pp. 83–90.

Alexander, D. (1993) A European true and fair view?, *European Accounting Review*, 2(1), pp. 59–80.

Arden, M. (1993) The true and fair requirement, Counsel's opinion, published as part of the Foreword to *Accounting Standards* (London: Accounting Standards Board).

Arden, M. (1997) True and fair view: a European perspective, *European Accounting Review*, 6(4), pp. 675–679.

Clark, P. (1994) *European Financial Reporting: Luxembourg* (London: Routledge).

Council (1978) Council R 1961/78 [ES93] 18.7.1978, No. 2.

Court (1996) Waltraud Tomberger v Gebrüder von der Wettern GmbH, Case C-234/94. Available at: curia.eu.int

European Commission (2001) *Examination of the Conformity between IAS 1 to IAS 41 and the European Accounting Directives*, Directorate-General Markt, April 2001.

Evans, L. (2003) The true and fair view and the 'fair presentation' override of IAS 1, *Accounting and Business Research*, 33(4), pp. 311–325.

Evans, L. (2004) Language, translation and the problem of international accounting communication, *Accounting, Auditing and Accountability Journal*, 17(2), pp. 210–248.

Evans, L. and Nobes, C. W. (1996) Some mysteries relating to the prudence principle in the Fourth Directive and in German and British Law, *European Accounting Review*, 5(2), pp. 361–373.

FEE (1991) *European Survey of Published Accounts 1991* (London: Routledge).

ICAEW (2005) True and fair under IAS. Available at: www.icaew.co.uk/index.cfm?route=103896 (accessed 23 May 2006).

Nelson, M. W. (2003) Behavioural evidence on the effects of principles- and rules-based standards, *Accounting Horizons*, 17(1), pp. 91–104.

Nobes, C. W. (1993) The true and fair view requirement: impact on and of the fourth Directive, *Accounting and Business Research*, Winter, pp. 35–48.

Nobes, C. W. (2005) Rules-based standards and the lack of principles in accounting, *Accounting Horizons*, 19(1), pp. 25–34.

Ordelheide, D. (1990) Soft transformations of accounting rules in the 4th Directive in Germany, *Les Cahiers Internationaux de la Comptabilité*, Vol. 3, pp. 1–15 (Paris: Editions Comptables Malesherbes).

Ordelheide, D. (1993) True and fair view: a European and a German perspective, *European Accounting Review*, 2(1), pp. 81–90.

Ordelheide, D. and Semler, A. (1995) A reference matrix, appendix to D. Ordelheide and KPMG, *Transnational Accounting* (London: Macmillan).

Papas, A. A. (1993) *European Financial Reporting: Greece* (London: Routledge).

Schipper, K. (2003) Principles-based accounting standards, *Accounting Horizons*, 17(1), pp. 61–72.

Van Hulle, K. (1993) Truth and untruth about true and fair, *European Accounting Review*, May, pp. 99–104.

Wüstemann, J. and Kierzek, S. (2005) Revenue recognition under IFRS revisited: conceptual models, current proposals and practical consequences, *Accounting in Europe*, 2, pp. 69–106.

Zeff, S. A. (1990) The English language equivalent of 'Geeft een Getrouw Beeld', *De Accountant*, No. 2(October), p. 83.

17

Accounting and Business Research, Vol. 39. No. 4, pp. 415–427, 2009

The importance of being fair: an analysis of IFRS regulation and practice – a Comment

Christopher Nobes[*]

Editorial note: This paper is published as a Comment to encourage researchers to incorporate the nuances of the requirement for fair presentation in their research design and to consider the implications of jurisdictional differences when interpreting accounting practices.

Abstract — This paper examines the 'present fairly' (PF) requirement in IFRS. There were eight relevant developments from 2005 to 2008, and these are mostly not yet considered in the academic literature. The paper synthesises the resulting regulatory position, especially for UK companies. Contrary to official guidance, it is suggested here that the PF requirement and the conditions for using it as an override in IFRS are not the same as for a true and fair view. Examples of the use of the PF override in practice are critically examined, as is a recent Opinion on PF by legal Counsel. Developments in US regulation make US opposition to a PF override clearer. The implications for financial reporting and for research into it are examined.
Keywords: fair presentation; IFRS

Introduction

The purpose of this paper is to investigate the implications of various requirements in law and accounting standards for financial reporting to be fair, in the light of several recent developments in regulations and practice. In order to make the focus clear, I concentrate on reporting under International Financial Reporting Standards (IFRS) by UK companies. However, many of the issues raised here are relevant to companies reporting under UK standards or to IFRS reporters in countries other than the UK.

For UK-based IFRS reporters, the following eight[1] developments from 2005 to 2008 are of relevance. The revised IAS 1 ('Presentation of Financial Statements') that came into force in 2005 introduced a new version of the 'present fairly' (PF) requirement that apparently can work differently in different countries; and this is retained in the further revision of IAS 1 of 2007. The IASB (2008) has also issued an exposure draft of the chapter on

qualitative characteristics to be included in a revised *Conceptual Framework*, and unlike the current *Framework*[2] it does not include PF or 'give a true and fair view' (GTFV) at all.

In the UK, there has also been guidance from the FRC (2005) on whether PF is the same as GTFV. The UK's *Companies Act 2006* (CA 2006) did not merely retain the GTFV requirements of the 1985 Act but added to them. The Financial Reporting Review Panel had taken legal advice on GTFV in the context of international standards (Freshfields, 2005) but this has been overtaken by events, so the Financial Reporting Council (FRC) has obtained and published a new Counsel's Opinion on the TFV that updates the 'almost iconic' (Moore, 2008: para. 7) Opinions of Hoffman and Arden. The UK adopted International Standards on Auditing, which affects the wording of the audit opinion on GTFV. In the field of practice, there have been both UK (National Express) and French (*Société Générale*) examples of the use of IAS 1's override.

In the US, the Financial Accounting Standards Board (FASB) has issued a new hierarchy of the components of GAAP (FASB, 2008). This makes no mention of PF and, for the first time, specifically excludes any override of standards. As explained later, American voices on the IASB have suggested that the override should be removed from IAS 1. Given IASB/FASB convergence, these factors are potentially relevant beyond the US.

The topic of this paper is clearly important, as demonstrated by: the FRC's decision to seek and

[*] The author is Professor of Accounting at Royal Holloway, University of London. He is grateful for comments on an earlier draft from David Alexander (University of Birmingham), Jane Davison (Royal Holloway), Lisa Evans (University of Stirling), R.H. Parker (University of Exeter), Christian Stadler (Royal Holloway), Stephen Zeff (Rice University), and to the editor and two referees of this journal. He thanks the following for technical advice on use of the fair presentation override: Peter Holgate (PricewaterhouseCoopers), Robert Overend (Ernst & Young) and Andy Simmonds (Deloitte). He is also grateful for support for research from PricewaterhouseCoopers.

Correspondence should be addressed to: Professor Christopher Nobes, Professor of Accounting, Royal Holloway, University of London, Egham, Surrey, TW20 0EX. E-mail: Chris.Nobes@rhul.ac.uk.

This paper was accepted for publication in March 2009.

---

[1] These are listed in the next eight sentences, respectively.
[2] See the section below on 'True, fair, presentation and view'.

publish guidance on PF; the controversy surrounding whether to include an override in IAS 1 (see below); the publicity given to the use of the override by *Société Générale*; and the mass of academic literature (see below). The contribution of this paper is to analyse in a critical manner the eight recent developments.

After a note on literature, the paper proceeds as follows. First, there is a synthesis of the current regulatory position for UK-based IFRS reporters. Then, I ask whether 'present fairly' is the same thing as 'give a true and fair view'. This leads to a consideration of the current status of the 'override', followed by examination of the use of the override in IFRS practice. Next, I critique the recent Counsel's Opinion. This is followed by a note on US developments related to PF, and whether they are relevant outside the US. Then, there are conclusions and a note on implications. Finally, the relevance of all this for research in financial reporting is examined.

The academic literature on GTFV/PF is so extensive that it would be cumbersome to make reference to it all. As well as a large number of papers, the literature includes monographs (e.g. Chastney, 1975; Walton, 1991) and compendia of papers (e.g. Parker and Nobes, 1994; Parker et al., 1996). In each section that follows, the relevant literature is reviewed. None of it takes account of developments from 2005 onwards.

Current regulatory position

This section outlines the current position (e.g. for annual reports of 2009) for UK companies reporting under IFRS, which is compulsory for the consolidated statements of listed companies and optional for other purposes (CA 2006, s. 395). Strictly speaking, the IAS Regulation 1606/2002 requires (or allows) IFRS 'as adopted by the EU' (hereafter, EU-endorsed IFRS) rather than IFRS as issued by the IASB (ARC, 2005; FEE, 2005). However, the requirements relating to PF are the same despite non-endorsement of parts of IAS 39 and lags caused by endorsement for all IASB output, including IAS 1.[3]

IFRS reporting by UK companies is carried out in the context of the Companies Act. However, IFRS statements are not covered by the traditional requirements (CA 1985, s. 226; now CA 2006, s. 396), derived from the Fourth and Seventh Directives, that they must give a TFV and that the detailed provisions of the Act must be set aside if that would be necessary for a TFV to be given. This is because the IAS Regulation relieves companies

from most of the law derived from the Directives (e.g. what was formerly Schedule 4 to the 1985 Act).

However, a new clause was inserted into the Companies Bill in 2005, and is now s. 393 of the 2006 Act. It applies to companies reporting under either IFRS or UK GAAP, and provides that:

'The directors of a company must not approve accounts for the purposes of this Chapter unless they are satisfied that they give a true and fair view of the assets, liabilities, financial position and profit or loss ... '

As Counsel notes (Moore, 2008: para. 55), this is expressed as a negative obligation. Presumably, it will serve to continue the traditional approach to TFV in British law, despite the lack of an overt mention in law of the override for IFRS reporting (see below).

A question arises here about the legal position of IFRS reporting in the UK before CA 2006 came into force,[4] such as annual reports for calendar years 2005–2008. In that period, there was no requirement (either positive or negative) for directors to ensure that financial statements gave a TFV when reporting under IFRS. So, directors were required to ensure a fair presentation (because the IAS Regulation imposed IAS 1), whereas auditors were required to give an opinion on TFV (under the Act). The ministerial statement[5] relating to the insertion of s. 393 in the 2006 Act notes the potential confusion and seeks to avoid this and to give directors and auditors a common objective. The profession had wanted[6] to avoid any possibility that a court might hold that the decision to implement[7] the IAS Regulation in 2004 without a GTFV requirement implied that there had been a change of substance.

The requirement for *auditors* to give an opinion on TFV remains unchanged from the 1985 Act, as s. 495 of the 2006 Act. However, UK auditing standards have been replaced by 'International Standards on Auditing (UK and Ireland)',[8] and this involves a move from a two-part opinion (on TFV *and* on compliance with rules) to a one-part opinion (on TFV *in accordance with* rules).

---

[3] I use here the version of IAS 1 issued by the IASB in 2007, which was endorsed by the EU in December 2008.

[4] The Act came into force at various dates, but the relevant sections came into force for accounting periods beginning on or after 6 April 2008.
[5] See Moore (2008: para. 55).
[6] Interview on 8 February 2009 with Kathryn Cearns, chairperson of the Financial Reporting Committee of the ICAEW. See also a press release from the ICAEW of 19 May 2008: 'Institute welcomes revised opinion on true and fair'.
[7] By SI 2004/2947.
[8] This oxymoronic title fits well with an oxymoronic set of 'EU-International Financial Reporting Standards'.

Vol. 39, No. 4. 2009

The TFV is particularly relevant when interpreting or applying an accounting standard, when choosing between permitted accounting policies,[9] when selecting policies on issues not covered by standards, and when considering whether extra disclosures are necessary. The need to give a TFV may also lead to a departure from the detail of a regulation.

Obviously, the use of the TFV override to depart from details of the *law* in order to comply with the requirements of UK standards (e.g. SSAP 19 on accounting for investment properties; see *Company Reporting*, 1997) is not relevant for IFRS reporters. First, as noted above, the IAS Regulation removes the relevance of most of the detailed accounting rules of the Act. Second, UK standards are not relevant for IFRS reporters.

However, the new negatively-written GTFV obligation in law applies to IFRS reporters. In addition, they must comply with IAS 1, which has an analogous requirement (paras. 15 and 19) to that in FRS 18 (paras. 14 and 15) concerning both the need for PF/GTFV and the occasional resulting necessity to depart from the detailed requirements of the standards.

In summary, UK companies that comply with IFRS (compulsorily or voluntarily) do so in the context of the *Companies Act 2006*. This requires annual accounts to be prepared, to give a TFV, to be audited (including an opinion on TFV) and to be filed. However, most of the accounting requirements of the law and all of the UK standards are replaced by EU-endorsed IFRS, which includes a PF requirement. As a result, UK audit reports on IFRS statements refer to: International Standards on Auditing, the TFV, EU-endorsed IFRS, the Companies Act and the IAS Regulation. In some cases, they also refer to plain IFRS, where a company has requested this, perhaps because the company is listed on a US exchange (see Nobes and Zeff, 2008). Many of these issues are discussed further below.

True, fair, presentation and view

As noted above, IFRS statements must both GTFV and PF, because they must comply with both the Act and IAS 1. Similarly, auditors of such statements must form an opinion on both requirements because, under the Act, they opine on TFV in the context of EU-endorsed IFRS.

This raises the practical question of whether GTFV is identical to PF. This question needs to be asked jurisdiction by jurisdiction, because the legal

and linguistic context will affect the answer. That is, for example, it is probably necessary to distinguish a British TFV from other types (Alexander, 1993). The academic literature on the contrast between GTFV and PF mostly concerns PF in its US context because PF only arrived in IFRS in 1997. Cowan (1965) suggested that GTFV (in New Zealand or the UK) and PF (in the US) were much the same but that both expressions were unsatisfactory because of the lack of a clear definition of the objectives of reporting. By contrast, Zeff (1990) argued that there was an important transatlantic difference in audit practice. In particular, PF was dependent on its context of generally accepted accounting principles (GAAP), whereas GTFV was a separate requirement. Elsewhere, Zeff (1992) commented on the development of the one-part opinion in the US, noting however that one audit firm used to give a two-part opinion. Zeff (2007) provides more analysis of the historical developments and argues in favour of a two-part opinion. McEnroe and Martens (1998) found that both UK and US investors perceived GTFV to preclude misleading statements and bias more than PF did. Kirk (2006) found that preparers, auditors and users in New Zealand all perceived TFV differently from PF.

However, for the UK, these conclusions might now have to be modified because, as noted above, auditors have moved to a one-part opinion ('give a true and fair view in accordance with IFRS as adopted by the EU') with the adoption of International Standards on Auditing (APB, 2004). The FRC (2005: 3) concludes that TFV and PF are now 'similar'. Counsel's Opinion is also that the GTFV and PF 'do not describe two different concepts' (Moore, 2008, para. 28). However, Counsel principally relies for this conclusion on a sentence in the IASB's *Framework* which says, concerning GTFV and PF, that:

'Although this Framework does not deal directly with such concepts, the application of the principal qualitative characteristics and of appropriate accounting standards normally results in financial statements that convey what is generally understood as a true and fair view of, or as presenting fairly such information.' (para. 46, as quoted directly from the *Framework*, not from Counsel's Opinion which contains errors).[10]

This tangential statement, which is not in a

---

[10] Paragraph 28 of the Opinion has 'this' not 'the' Framework in line 3, and there is an 'a' missing before 'true and fair view' in line 6. Incidentally, para. 25 should not say that the IASB 'prepared' the *Framework*, because its predecessor, the IASC, did.

Standard and has not been endorsed by the EU seems a thin basis for concluding that the concepts are the same. Further, the *Framework* pre-dates the Opinion by 19 years, during which time the meanings of words might have changed (Hoffman and Arden, 1983: para. 13; Arden, 1993: para. 14).

Counsel also reasons (para. 29) that 'present fairly' is 'very similar to' *quadro fedele* or *image fidèle* which are, respectively, the Italian and French translations of TFV in the Directives. If both 'true' and 'fair' are covered in French by '*fidèle*', can Counsel be right that '*fidèle*' can also mean only one of them (i.e. only fair)? The Italian legislators saw the problem (Nobes, 1993: 41), and used two adjectives: '*rappresentare in modo veritiero e corretto*' (*Decreto Legislativo* n.127/1991). Evans (2004) notes that translating technical terms is fraught with difficulty, and uses the translation of TFV as an example (pp. 231–232).

Part of the answer to whether '*fidèle*' can mean both 'fair' and 'true and fair' might lie in whether 'true and fair' is a portmanteau term (a hendiadys) or whether the words should be taken separately. If 'true and fair' is a hendiadys, then it could mean the same as 'fair', and 'true' would be redundant. Parker and Nobes (1991: 353) find that UK auditors discern separate meanings to the two words, but Nobes and Parker (1991: 366) do not find much evidence for this among UK directors. The same applies to Australian auditors (Deegan et al., 1994). The Opinions of Hoffman and Arden also largely dealt with 'true and fair' as a portmanteau term, but Arden (1993: para. 14) says that:

> 'the Court will not in my view seek to find synonyms for the words "true" and "fair" but will seek to apply the concepts which those words imply.'

So, there is no clear conclusion on this issue: 'fair' could mean the same as 'true and fair', particularly if the words are placed in different situations.

Given that the 2008 Opinion calls in aid the Italian and French translations of TFV in the Directives, it might be useful to see where this path leads by investigating translations of GTFV and PF in IFRS literature. A caveat is that each language has different 'registers' within it for various professional activities (Evans, 2008). A word may signify different things in different registers. The discussion below needs to be interpreted in this light.

The IASB's *Framework* exists in several official IASB translations, although the *Framework* is not part of EU-endorsed IFRS. The Italian and French

versions of para. 46 (reproduced in the original English as an indented quotation above) say, for TFV and fair presentation:

> '*una rappresentazione veritiera e corretta o una presentazione attendibile*'; and

> '*une image fidèle ou une présentation fidèle*'.

It is noticeable that '*fedele*' does not appear in either of the two Italian formulations, although strangely it does appear in the heading above para. 46, suggesting that the translators had changed their minds and forgotten to alter the heading. Instead, there is '*attendibile*' which means[11] reliable or trustworthy. As before, in French, the word '*fidèle*' can apparently mean both 'true and fair' and 'fair'. The Italian translators discerned some difference between the signifiers but the French translators did not.

The Italian and French translations of IAS 1's PF requirement (which *are* EU-endorsed) both use the same adjectives as in the *Framework's* translation of PF (i.e. *attendible* and *fidèle*). In both those cases and others,[12] the GTFV expression is translated for the *Framework* as it is in national laws not as in the Directives themselves. It seems that an effort has been made to ensure that the laws' GTFV requirements can be equated to IAS 1's PF requirement. Table 1 records the translations.

As may be seen in Table 1, the German translators have taken this to its logical conclusion. Although the 1974 draft of the Fourth Directive contained '*einen getreuen Einblick*' (a faithful insight), the Directives contain '*ein den tatsächlichen Verhältnissen entsprechendes Bild*' (a factual picture). This latter term is used in German law. The German translation of the *Framework* avoids the 'faithful equals faithful' problem seen in the French translation (above and Table 1) by abbreviating para. 46 and presenting only one phrase: the one in German law. This is repeated in the German translation of IAS 1. Thus, the issue of whether PF and GTFV are the same disappears in German.

In conclusion, on unconvincing grounds, all the recent authorities state that PF is the same thing as GTFV. The argument largely proceeds by assertion, and the citing of previous assertions.[13] The assumption that the phrases are the same is convenient since both are required for IFRS reporters. Also, it must

---

[11] *Collins Sansoni Italian Dictionary*, third edn, 1991.
[12] I have looked at the German and the Spanish.
[13] There is an assertion in the IASB's *Framework*, which is used as authority by Counsel (Moore, 2008). An assertion of similarity can also be found in FRC (2005).

Vol. 39, No. 4. 2009

Table 1
Translations in official documents

	Directive	Law	Framework	IAS 1
English	true and fair	true and fair	true and fair = fair	fair
Italian	*fedele*	*veritiero e corretto*	*veritiera e corretta = attendibile*	*attendibile*
French	*fidèle*	*fidèle*	*fidèle = fidèle*	*fidèle*
German	*getreuen* (1974) *ein den tatsächlichen Verhältnissen entsprechendes Bild* (1978)	*ein den tatsächlichen Verhältnissen entsprechendes Bild*	*ein den tatsächlichen Verhältnissen entsprechendes Bild*	*ein den tatsächlichen Verhältnissen entsprechendes Bild*

be admitted that this author is not aware of any suggestions of how PF and GTFV could or should be different in practice, except for the use of the 'override' (see below), which depends not on the words PF or GTFV but on other words surrounding them.

Other aspects of the terminology should be mentioned in order to be clear about the full context. The British Companies Acts have used the formulation 'accounts must *give* a true and fair *view*', whereas IAS 1 requires that 'financial statements shall *present* fairly' (emphases added). Incidentally, the recent Counsel's Opinion generally[14] refers to 'show' a TFV, but that does not seem different from 'give'. All the terms imply that the directors are required to ensure that the financial statements are engaged in a process of doing something. There seems to be no important distinction between them, but they are clearly less onerous requirements than that the users of the statements should *receive* a sound insight as, for example, in previous Dutch law (Zeff et al., 1992: 365) or in the German version of the 1974 draft of the Fourth Directive (see above).

Also, IAS 1[15] and recent Counsel's Opinion[16] use the terms 'present fairly' (IAS 1's prime instruction) and 'achieve a fair presentation' interchangeably. It might be possible to discern a distinction here, where the former implies 'equitable' and the latter 'clear'.

The IASB's exposure draft of a revised *Framework* (IASB, 2008, ch. 2) does not include GTFV or PF. It says (para. BC 2.41) that these are not included because they are the same as 'faithful representation', which *is* included as a qualitative characteristic. So, according to the IASB, true and

fair equals fair equals faithful. This would suggest much redundancy in the English language.

The 'override' for IFRS reporters

As noted earlier, the Directives and laws also contain a feature in addition to the GTFV requirement: an 'override', that is a requirement to depart from the detailed rules of the laws when this would be necessary to achieve a TFV. In this section, it will be important to distinguish between the override in law and the override in standards, and to distinguish between the override *of* law and the override *of* standards.

One conclusion from the Opinions of Hoffman and Arden was that, since a court would be likely to hold that compliance with a standard is necessary in order to give a TFV, there was some room to depart from the details of law, especially to comply with UK standards, but there was little room to depart from the standards. That is, an override *in* law was expected to lead to overrides *of* law but not to overrides *of* standards.

An override (in standards of a standard) is required in the *Foreword* to UK accounting standards (para. 19) in 'exceptional circumstances', and this was inserted into FRS 18 (para. 15) in 2000. Such an override was introduced into IAS 1 (para. 13; now para. 19) in 1997 for 'extremely rare circumstances'. Evans (2003) provides a useful outline of the development of the override in IAS 1.

Alexander (1999) approved of the override in IAS 1, on the grounds that the objective of financial statements must surely be for PF rather than to obey rules. Nobes (2000) disapproved on the grounds that: (i) the override was more appropriate for law than for standards; (ii) different countries understood PF differently; and (iii) many countries had no monitoring/enforcement agency to check the proper use of the override. Incidentally, just as an override in law of standards might be an empty category (at

---

[14] For example, paras. 4(C), 4(G), 8(A), 8(G), 9, 18.
[15] For example, both are found in para. 15.
[16] For example, paras. 28 and 29 contrasted with paras. 42, 44, 46.

least in the UK), so an override in standards of law might be empty (because standards do not require compliance with law). For example, the use of the law's override to avoid depreciation of investment properties is an override in law of law, although the reason was to obey SSAP 19.

A difference between the override in law and that in standards concerns whether or not it is a last resort. In the Directives and in the Companies Act (as it applies to UK GAAP, i.e. s. 396), the departure is a last resort after exhausting the possibilities of giving a TFV through extra disclosures. However, this is not so clearly the case in IAS 1 (or in FRS 18).[17] IAS 1 does require extra disclosures where this is necessary in order to PF, but says that disclosures cannot rectify inappropriate accounting (paras. 17 (c) and 18). This last point can be interpreted as a rejection of the view in some continental European countries that, for example, tax-driven items in the financial statements were 'fair' once explained in the notes (Ordelheide and Pfaff, 1994: 107–108). The sort of extra disclosures intended by IAS 1 might include explanations of large disasters or surprising triumphs after the balance sheet date, which need to be explained in order to PF. Of course, these particular disclosures are already required by IAS 10.

The exact criteria for departures under IAS 1 include the existence of the extremely rare circumstances but also that compliance would be 'so misleading that it would conflict with the objective of financial statements set out in the *Framework*' (IAS 1, para. 19), which is:

'to provide information about the financial position, performance and changes in financial position of an entity that is useful to a wide range of users in making economic decisions.' (*Framework*, para. 12)

In other words, IAS 1's override is not a 'PF override'. The above objective is sufficiently vague that it would be difficult for a treatment to be so misleading as to conflict with it. However, IAS 1 then states that the departing entity shall disclose that it has complied with IFRS 'except that it has departed from a particular requirement to achieve a fair presentation' (IAS 1, para. 20 (b)). So, perhaps an inability to achieve a fair presentation is what is really meant; and that might be more likely to occur. By contrast, the overrides in law and UK standards are clearly TFV overrides.

The revised versions of IAS 1 (both the 2003

---

[17] See paras. 16 and 18 of FRS 18.

version and the 2007 version) raise a more complex issue because the PF override only applies:

'... if the relevant regulatory framework requires, or otherwise does not prohibit, such a departure.' (para. 19 of the 2007 version)

It would appear that the EU or UK regulatory frameworks do not directly require such departures *from IFRS standards*, but neither do they prohibit them, so the override applies in the EU.

The legal Opinions of Hoffman and Arden dealt hardly at all with the 'override', but Moore's (2008) Opinion considers several points related to it. First, he asks (paras. 36–40) whether IAS 1's 'extremely rare circumstances' are the same as FRS 18's 'exceptional circumstances'. He concludes that they *are* the same and 'very limited indeed'. Moore does not further consider whether they are the same as the Directive's 'exceptional circumstances' and the Act's 'special circumstances'. Presumably, the convenient answer would be that they are all the same.

In the literature, there is debate about whether the Directives' 'exceptional circumstances' that require departures from law can occur across the board (e.g. non-depreciation of investment properties) or whether they must be unique to a particular company. Alexander (1993, 1996) and Nobes (1993) argue for the wider interpretation. Ordelheide (1993) and Van Hulle (1993 and 1997) argue against. In UK corporate practice, the former view held without legal challenge. For example, many companies did depart from the law in order to obey SSAP 19, as noted earlier.

An across-the-board departure from the Act's requirement to depreciate investment property buildings might be said to be an 'exceptional' or a 'special' circumstance, even though it was not 'extremely rare'. That is, departures by dozens of companies every year could still be exceptional/special if all the departures relate to the same issue, but it would be less easy to argue that these departures were extremely rare. In my view, IAS 1's criterion for departures should therefore be seen as more restrictive than those in the other documents. Evans (2003: 321) comes to a similar conclusion because IAS 1's requirement is 'far less clearly or explicitly stated'.

Moore (2008: Appendix) also refers to a decision of the European Court of Justice (ECJ), concerning a German company (the *ES Bauunternehmung* case of 2000). The ECJ held, referring to the Fourth Directive, that:

'The exceptional cases referred to in art 31(2) are therefore those in which separate valuation would not give the truest and fairest possible view of the actual financial position of the company concerned.'[18]

Moore, with remarkable restraint, calls this 'rather opaque' and 'puzzling' (Appendix: paras. 16 and 17). To put it another way, this is a complete misunderstanding by non-British lawyers of a form of words invented by British accountants.[19] First, it is not 'the' view but 'a' view that is required; second it is not 'truest and fairest' that is required. The 'the' for 'a' error had been made before, for example, in the Spanish implementation of the Fourth Directive (Nobes, 1993: 42). This apparent[20] double error by the ECJ, if followed by other courts, would set an impracticably high standard for directors and auditors and would open up a wide scope for litigation by users of financial statements who subsequently suffer loss.

A final point is that the requirement that the circumstances for departure should be 'extremely rare' is not a practicable criterion for the directors of a particular reporting entity. Whether the circumstances will be rare or not depends on the other criteria for when they should occur. Since there are no clear criteria, the requirement for rarity amounts to the standard-setters imploring the preparers not to use the override.

The IFRS override in practice

ICAEW (2007) surveyed 200 annual reports of EU listed companies relating to 2005. They found no examples of the use of IAS 1's override (p. 11). CESR (2007) do not report any examples; and technical partners[21] of audit firms cannot name any more than the two below. Nobes and Zeff (2008) looked at the audit reports of all the companies included in the main stock market indices of Australia and four EU countries, and again find no examples, although audit reports might not disclose use of the override, as explained below.

---

[18] As quoted by Moore (2008, Appendix: para. 16).
[19] Rutherford (1985) records that the *words* 'true and fair view' were suggested to the Cohen Committee on company law reform (that led to the 1947 Act) by the Institute of Chartered Accountants in England and Wales. There is some detail on this in Parker and Nobes (1994: 1–2). The *concept* that there should be some goal beyond accuracy, correctness or compliance with rules can also be said to be a British invention rather than a continental one, given that it is not generally found in the laws of EU member states until the 1980s or later (see Nobes, 1993).
[20] As noted earlier, one must allow for different professional registers and different degrees of flexibility in different languages. However, from the perspective of English law and an English court dealing with such a case, this conclusion is erroneous, as English Counsel suggests.
[21] Interviews with Andy Simmonds of Deloitte on 10 July 2008, Peter Holgate of PricewaterhouseCoopers on 25 June 2008 and Robert Overend of Ernst & Young, 21 August 2008.

It seems that there is certainly no 'routine' use of the override in IFRS accounting, as seen for example under UK GAAP as a mechanism for departing from law in order to obey standards. However, there are two one-off examples, which are examined here: National Express Group PLC of the UK, and *Société Générale SA* of France. Incidentally, these examples are both expressed as overrides of IFRS through the mechanism of IAS 1 rather than through the mechanism of law. That is, technically, the context is PF rather than GTFV, although this would not be evident in French, as noted earlier.

In the case of National Express (NE), an IAS 1 override was used for the 2005, 2006 and 2007 statements. In each case, the auditors, Ernst & Young, gave an unqualified audit opinion on TFV in accordance with EU-endorsed IFRS, and on compliance with the Companies Act and the IAS Regulation. Indeed, assuming that use of the IAS 1 override is appropriate, a clean audit opinion can also be appropriate.

The override concerns the group's pension obligation. The directors explain[22] that NE owns train operating franchises. As such, it has defined benefit pension obligations for the related employees. Industry practice is for owners to fund plans while they own a franchise, and then to transfer any pension deficit to a new owner. NE calls the obligation 'that arises under the terms of each franchise agreement' a 'constructive obligation'. It contrasts this to the 'legal obligation' to fund a deficit that might potentially[23] arise (but never has before) under certain conditions at the end of a franchise. NE says that it accounts for the con-structive but not the legal obligation, and that this involves a departure from IAS 19 in order to PF.

Incidentally, obligations arising under the terms of an agreement are not 'constructive' as NE calls them but 'legal' (IAS 19, para. 52). Whether legal or constructive, an obligation should be recorded at its present value (IAS 19, para. 54), which involves estimating future cash outflows and discounting them. This requires estimations of such data as future salary increases, mortality rates and employee turnover (IAS 19, paras. 69, 73, 88). For example, if a company expected all the employees in its defined benefit plan to leave before

---

[22] See, for example, notes 2 and 35(b) of the 2007 Annual Report.
[23] NE (note 35(b) of the 2007 Annual Report) refer to an opinion from legal advisers about a liability that could theoretically arise if subsequent franchisees did not take over the deficit. However, this would break contracts, and has not been experienced in practice.

their benefits had vested or to die on their retirement days, then the pension obligation might[24] be measured at zero. In conclusion, if particular obligations are not expected to lead to any payments, they should be measured at zero. So, NE is right to focus on what it calls the constructive obligation. However, I suggest that this does not require a departure from IAS 19, and therefore does not need the use of the override in IAS 1. The 'legal' obligation should indeed be taken account of, but measured at zero.

In support of this conclusion, one can look at the treatment of similar[25] defined benefit obligations of train operating companies in other groups. For example, FirstGroup plc (audited by Deloitte) and Stagecoach plc (audited by Pricewaterhouse-Coopers) each state[26] that the company recognises the obligation that it 'expects to fund'. NE and FirstGroup, but not Stagecoach, provide disclosures of what the financial statements would have looked like if the obligations that they do not expect to pay for had been fully accounted for. So, all three companies account in the same way, but NE thinks that it needs to depart from IAS 19 to do so, and FirstGroup thinks that it needs to give an extra disclosure to PF.

The other case involving a PF override concerns the unauthorised trading at *Société Générale* that dominated the financial news in early 2008. The directors of the company explain in the 2007 Annual Report (note 40) that, in accordance with IAS 1, they are departing from IAS 10 ('Events after the balance sheet date') and from IAS 37 ('Provisions, contingent liabilities and contingent assets') in order to PF. They say that, if they had known of the unauthorised trading, they should (according to the standards) have recorded a gain of €1,471m in 2007. On 19 January 2008 onwards, the unauthorised trading (some of which had been conducted in that month) was uncovered. It was unwound in a falling market, creating a loss of €6,382m.

Société Générale explain that, in contravention of IAS 10 (para. 3), this unwinding was treated as an 'adjusting event';[27] and in contravention of IAS 37

(para. 14), a provision was shown in the 2007 balance sheet even though there was no liability to anyone at that date. As a result, *Société Générale* charged a net loss of €4,911m in 2007.

It is clear why the directors might have wanted to do this. First, it got the bad news out of the way rather than repeating it when the 2008 results were announced in early 2009. Second, it bolstered the evidence that led to the result that: 'The loss thus recognized has been considered tax deductible.' (Note 40).

We can now ask whether this complies with IAS 1. First, were there 'extremely rare circumstances'? The company refers to trading activities 'of an exceptional scale', and must hope that the loss will indeed prove to be 'extremely rare'. The second condition is that compliance would be 'so misleading that it would conflict with the objectives of financial statements set out in the *Framework*' (para. 19). As explained earlier, this is taken to mean that the statements would not have presented fairly.

The company is required (IAS 1, para. 20(c)) to explain why compliance would be 'so misleading'. The nearest it came to doing this was to say: 'In order to provide more relevant information for understanding the financial performance of the Group in 2007 ...'. Of course, non-compliance does not do that in this case. The loss occurred (in both the unrealised/unsettled sense and in the realised/settled sense) in 2008.

Fearnley (2009) writes in favour of *Société Générale*'s treatment and asks: 'How can a sensible person believe it is right to treat unrealised gains on securities held for trading as distributable profits ...?' However, this question contains two misunderstandings. First, there is no clear definition of 'unrealised'. It has different meanings in different countries. For example, in the UK, we have for decades been taking gains on unsettled monetary balances to the profit and loss account (under SSAP 21 or now FRS 23). We have been treating them as realised for legal purposes. Approximately speaking, if accountants say that gains are realised, then they are (CA 1985, s. 262(3); CA 2006, s. 853(4)). The ICAEW (2008: 9) regards fair value increases on trading instruments as realised. So, sensible accountants can believe it is right. Second, the financial statements in question were consolidated, so they can tell us nothing about distributable profit. There is no such thing as a distributable profit of a group. *Société Générale*'s distributable profit is

---

[24] Assuming, for example, that no lump sums were due to an estate and that pensions did not transfer to spouses.

[25] The technical partners of the three audit firms mentioned in this section (see footnote 21) believe that, as all the obligations arise under rail franchise agreements, the facts of the cases are likely to be similar.

[26] Stagecoach, 2008 *Annual Report*, p. 51; FirstGroup, 2008 *Annual Report*, p. 88.

[27] One that provides 'evidence of conditions that existed at the end of the reporting period ...'. It could perhaps be argued that the 'conditions' were the unauthorised trading. However, if this

had been discovered (and closed down) by the end of 2007, a gain would have been recorded in 2007 whereas SG charged a loss.

Vol. 39, No. 4. 2009

calculated under French law relating to the parent company financial statements. Anyway, IFRS is not designed to show distributable profits any more than it is designed to show taxable profits or regulatory capital for banks. It would be wise to have different rules for all these different purposes.

Before turning to the reaction of the auditors, it is relevant to note that the company had pre-cleared the use of the override with both the banking supervisor and the stock market regulator in Paris (Annual Report, note 1), both of which organisations would have reasons for trying to 'draw a line under' the affair.

Large French listed companies are required[28] to appoint two auditors. Some, like *Société Générale*, choose two Big Four firms; in this case, Deloitte and Ernst & Young. Faced with the management of one of the largest and (previously) most respectable companies in France and compliant governmental regulators, the auditors would have been in a difficult position. Once one of the firms had accepted the need for an override, the other would have presumably found it especially difficult to disagree. The joint audit report (pp. 266–267) mentions the override twice but states that this is 'Without qualifying the opinion' on 'true and fair view ... in accordance with IFRS as adopted by the European Union'.

In summary, *Société Générale* broke several accounting standards, but it does not explain why it was impossible to PF by waiting until 2008 to record losses that did not exist by the end of 2007 (in some cases relating to contracts that did not exist by the end of 2007). Some might wish to argue, under a quite different accounting system, that the part of the loss that related to contracts of 2007 should be recorded in 2007, even though the contracts were in profit at the end of 2007. However, PF and GTFV exist in a context (Hoffman and Arden, 1983: paras. 8–11; Arden, 1993: para. 4; Alexander, 1993: 297), and the context was IFRS. This is not to say that complying with IFRS will automatically cause statements to PF. It is to say that a departing company would need to make a strong case that it is impossible to PF (in the general context of IFRS) by complying with the rules of IFRS. No case was made. Incidentally, the rules (IAS 10) require disclosures in the 2007 statements concerning the events of January 2008, but not in an attempt to correct the financial statements of 2007, rather to give useful information for interpreting those statements by decision-making investors.

---

[28] *Lois sur les Sociétés Commerciales*, art. 223.

The conclusion from this section is that use of the PF override is very rare in IFRS practice. In my opinion, in the first case above (National Express), the presentation was fair, but this could have been achieved without using the override. In the second case (*Société Générale*), fairness could have been achieved by complying with the standards, so the override should not have been used. This supports the case against the override made by Nobes (2000) and the decision of the FASB (2008) to exclude the override, i.e. on the rare occasions that the IAS 1 override is used, it is used wrongly.

A critique of Counsel's Opinion

The original Opinion of Hoffman and Arden (1983) dealt primarily with the extent to which an accounting standard could restrict usage of the options allowed within the law. The context was the attempt by the standard-setters to impose current cost accounting. The conclusion was that standards would be persuasive in a court that was seeking to establish the practices necessary for a TFV to be given. Arden (1993) focussed especially on the effects of the *Companies Act 1989* and the new standard-setting machinery from 1990. She concluded that standards had been strengthened. Neither Opinion dwelt at any length on the 'override'.

As noted above, the FRC obtained and published an up-dated Opinion on the TFV from Michael Moore QC (hereafter, 'Counsel'). Some aspects of this have been referred to above where relevant. This section draws these references together and then adds further comment.

Counsel concludes (Moore, 2008: para. 4B) that the requirement to GTFV remains supreme. It has been supported in UK and EU courts (see below) and by the new s. 393 of the Companies Act. Counsel believes (para. 4C) that GTFV is not different from PF, although that has been questioned above.

Counsel notes (para. 4E) that the override has been preserved. Incidentally, Counsel repeatedly refers to a company's 'ability' to depart from standards (paras. 4E and 37) and states that IFRS 'permits' departures (para. 36). The relevant section of the Opinion (paras. 36–40) is headed '... when departures ... are permitted'. However, this is misleading: no discretion is allowed in law (CA 2006, s. 396) or by FRS 18 (para. 15) or by IAS 1 (para. 19). If an accounting treatment would enable financial statements to GTFV/PF, a departure is forbidden; if it would not, a departure is *required*. Counsel then goes on to say that, where compliance would not enable PF, departure 'may be necessary' (para. 38) and 'is appropriate' (para. 40) but still avoids the clearer 'is necessary'.

Counsel concludes that departures should be 'very limited' (para. 4F) or 'very limited indeed' (para. 40), which presumably are intended to mean the same thing. However, there is no discussion of the difference between overrides of law and overrides of standards. As noted above, Counsel's conclusion that the UK's 'exceptional' is the same as IFRS's 'extremely rare' is not convincing.

Counsel also says that:

'... as accounting standards have become more detailed ... the scope for persuading a Court that financial statements which do not comply with relevant accounting standards give a true and fair view, or achieve a fair presentation has become very limited ...' (para. 44)

At first sight, this seems counter-intuitive. If standards were still broad-brush and lacking in detail, there would be fewer requirements that could potentially need to be departed from. On the other hand, a broad-brush requirement might generate the need for departures because it did not allow for specific exceptions regarded as necessary for a TFV. However, Counsel is not commenting on the trend in the quantity of potential *causes* for departures but rather on the trend in the scope for persuading a court that departures are necessary. It is certainly plausible that the instructions of the standard-setters will be taken more seriously by the courts if the standard-setters show that they have already considered special/exceptional circumstances, either by allowing exceptions or by discussing in a *Basis for Conclusions* why they are not allowed.

The court cases considered by Counsel (paras. 11–17) include five British ones that were decided after the Opinions of Hoffman and Arden. Counsel believes that these confirm that the courts 'rely very heavily upon the ordinary practices of professional accountants', and confirm 'the likelihood that a Court would hold that compliance with a standard is necessary to meet the true and fair requirement' (para. 8).

Counsel also considers two cases concerning German companies that had come before the ECJ. One of these ('*ES Bauunternehmung*') is referred to above. The other ('*Tomberger*' of 1996) also confirms the primacy of the TFV. However, Counsel notices (Appendix: para. 10) another interesting linguistic problem. The Advocate General had concluded that:

'The principle requires the balance sheet to be drawn up so as to give not only a true (even in the relative sense in which that adjective is traditionally and necessarily used as regards balance sheets) but also a fair (essentially with regard to the good faith of the persons drawing up the balance sheet) representation ...'

Counsel notes that the Advocate General's understanding of 'fair' is not what 'might be understood by an English lawyer'. Indeed, the requirement is not that the preparers must act in good faith but the more demanding requirement that the presentation must not be misleading. This is further evidence of the apparent[29] misunderstanding, noted above, by continental lawyers of a phrase invented by British accountants. One must admit, though, that an exact and settled meaning of the TFV does not exist among British accountants.

In sum, Counsel confirms the need for directors and auditors to check that statements GTFV/PF, independently from compliance with rules. Counsel also confirms the continuation of the override but notes that it is very limited. Counsel also points out some doubtful aspects of ECJ opinions and judgments.

However, in my view, Counsel is not persuasive on other issues: that TFV is the same as PF, and that 'exceptional cases' (FRS 18) are as restrictive as 'extremely rare circumstances' (IAS 1). On the latter subject, it would have been useful if the Opinion had discussed the difference between departures from law and departures from standards.

Along the way, I have noted examples of loose terminology in the Opinion (e.g. 'permits' departure instead of 'requires' it; and see the points in footnotes 10 and 14; and there are others).[30] Normally one might let these pass. However, the key point about the Opinion is its interpretation of words, so precision with words is vital, at least in an English law context. Given that the Opinion has been published by the FRC and will be a continuous source of official guidance, these lapses are of importance.

The earlier Opinions of Hoffman and Arden are iconic because they are convincing. They are also elegantly written. For example:

'The SSAP is intended to crystallise professional opinion and reduce penumbral areas in which divergent practices exist and can each have claim to being "true and fair"' (1983, para. 10);

'... the provisions of the Schedule are static

---

[29] See footnote 20.
[30] For example, readers of the Opinion should note that references in paras. 16 and 17 to paras. 6E and 6 should be to 8E and 8.

whereas the concept of a true and fair view is dynamic' (1983, para. 13);

'Thus what is required to show a true and fair view is subject to continuous rebirth' (1993, para. 14).

If others concur about the examples of unconvincing conclusions and the terminological lapses in the latest Opinion, it might not achieve the iconic status of its predecessors. It should be mentioned, though, that even the 'iconic' Opinions do not address the central issue of what directors and auditors should do to test that financial statements GTFV or PF.

US developments

Changes in the content of IFRS have, at least since 2002,[31] been dominated by convergence with US accounting. Consequently, US developments in the area of PF are likely to be relevant to further revision of IFRS.

In the above section on 'True, fair, presentation, and view', the US approach to PF was introduced, including the conclusion that PF in US practice has been regarded as weaker than GTFV in UK practice. Furthermore, unlike the position in the UK under either UK standards or IFRS, there has been in practice no 'override' in US GAAP. This feature is explored by Alexander and Archer (2000) and by Evans (2003: 320).

Until 2008, there was no specific mention of an override in US official literature directed at companies, although guidance to *auditors*[32] instructs them not to give an opinion that financial statements conform with GAAP if there is a departure from GAAP other than in 'unusual circumstances' that would make the statements misleading. This does not seem to be a particularly high hurdle for departures, but in practice an override has not been used, because it is addressed to auditors not to company management and it is presumed that the SEC would not accept departures (Van Hulle, 1997: 718; Evans, 2003: 320; FASB, 2008: para. A.11).

The FASB has now issued SFAS 162 as guidance to companies on 'The hierarchy of generally accepted accounting principles' (FASB, 2008). This does not mention PF (except in Appendices that are not part of the standard). Furthermore, the FASB explains (para. A.12) that it has deliberately excluded the possibility of an override. This

clarifies the position and renders all speculation on the applicability of the override in the US of historical interest only.

It also makes the positions of the IASB and the FASB more starkly opposed, since the IASB recently confirmed[33] the importance of the override. However, past and present American members of the IASB have questioned[34] the propriety of the override in the light of its use by *Société Générale*. It seems likely that, when[35] IFRS becomes accepted or required by the SEC for reporting by US corporations, the PF override in IAS 1 will specifically be made inoperative by arranging for the regulatory regime not to accept it (IAS 1, para. 19). This has already been done, for example, in Australia.[36]

Sir David Tweedie championed the insertion of the override in IAS 1, against the arguments of other Anglo-Saxons.[37] He is due to retire as chairman of the IASB in 2011. It seems plausible that he will be replaced by a national from another country with a long tradition of standard-setting and opposition to the override, e.g. Australia, Canada or the US. This suggests that the days of the override are numbered.

Conclusions and implications

This paper examines eight developments of 2005–2008 that affect the GTFV or PF requirement in the context of IFRS reporting by UK companies. These have not been analysed in previous literature.

IFRS reporters must now both GTFV and PF, and auditors must, in effect, give an opinion on both. All the regulatory authorities conclude that GTFV is the same as PF. However, this is not supported in the academic literature, and the arguments for the conclusion are still flimsy despite recent developments. An investigation prompted by Counsel's reference to translations of GTFV and PF in IASB documents reveals international attempts to ensure acceptance of the convenient conclusion that PF equals GTFV.

There is much literature on the TFV override in law, and some literature on the PF override in IAS 1. This paper concludes that there are several import-

---

[31] This process was officially inaugurated by the 'Norwalk Agreement' between the IASB and the FASB in 2002.
[32] Rule 203 of the AICPA's *Code of Professional Conduct*.

[33] For example, in the *Basis for Conclusions* (paras. BC 23–30) in IAS 1 of 2007.
[34] Tony Cope and John Smith; see Norris (2008).
[35] In August 2008, the SEC announced a proposal to require IFRS by 2014, and for some companies to allow it earlier than that.
[36] Paragraphs 17 to 20 of the pre-2007 version of IAS 1 are not included in AASB 101 because they are inconsistent with the Corporations Act.
[37] Camfferman and Zeff (2007: 391) record opposition from Australia and the US, and even from the other half of the UK delegation (i.e. the present author).

ant differences between the overrides in law, IAS 1 and FRS 18. Strictly, the override in IAS 1 should not be described as a PF override at all. This contrasts with the updated Counsel's Opinion, which does not discuss the differences between law and standards, and concludes that IAS 1 and FRS 18 have the same override. Several apparent misunderstandings of the TFV by the ECJ are examined. The implications are extensive. Legal opinion, especially that of the ECJ, would suggest that the PF override, although rare, might be justified rather more often that it has occurred in practice so far.

Two examples (perhaps the only two examples) of use of the PF override in IFRS were examined, with the conclusions that the UK case involved proper accounting but did not need the override, and the French case involved improper accounting and should not have used the override. The implication is that, on balance, the IAS 1 override does more harm than good, and should be removed.

Next the updated Counsel's Opinion was examined. One can agree with Counsel that TFV remains supreme. However, as noted earlier, Counsel is less than wholly convincing that GTFV equals PF or that the circumstances for the override are the same in various regulations. Other aspects of the Opinion were also questioned. The implications are that the Opinion might not become iconic like its predecessors, and that the FRC might at least wish to correct some aspects of the Opinion as published on its website.

In the US, the FASB has at last made it clear that there is no PF override for companies. Indeed, there is no PF *requirement* for them. The implication is that the FASB will argue for the removal of the override in IAS 1 as part of convergence.

Although this paper has been set in the specific context of UK companies reporting under IFRS, many of the above conclusions and implications are relevant outside the UK, especially for companies and auditors elsewhere in the EU.

Research issues
This paper has analysed and synthesised a number of technical developments. It is hoped that this will be useful to researchers in the field of financial reporting by helping them to be precise about the institutional setting. Without this precision, hypothesis development might go awry, or data might be misinterpreted.

As part of the above, some predictions have been made which can be assessed in due course. For example, it has been suggested that US regulators will not allow the PF override when they impose

IFRS, and that the IASB will abandon IAS 1's override. In addition, some propositions have been put forward that can be scrutinised and assessed by other researchers. First, it is proposed that, to the extent that the PF override is used, it is more often misused than used correctly. Second, IAS 1's 'extremely rare' circumstances should be seen as more restrictive than the 'exceptional' or 'special' circumstances found in other requirements. Third, Counsel's Opinion of 2008 is less convincing than those of 1983 or 1993.

Other hypotheses have been raised above, directly or implicitly, that can be the subject of empirical research. Initially, I present the following in the context of UK listed companies:

H1: Before 2005, the TFV override was used more often to depart from law than to depart from standards.

H2: The TFV override of law is used less under IFRS than it was under UK GAAP.

H3: The PF override is used less than the GTFV override of standards was.

H4: UK auditors tend to see TFV as a portmanteau term more now than they did before 2005.

H5: UK auditors (compared to French and German auditors) perceive TFV as nearer to 'not misleading' than to 'in accordance with the facts'.

H6: The degree to which investors perceive GTFV to be a stronger criterion than PF has decreased.

H7: Companies listed on US exchanges have a greater tendency than others to disclose compliance with IFRS and to seek audit opinions on this (in addition to reference to EU-IFRS).

There is already evidence, referred to above, that H1 to H3 would probably be confirmed by formal testing.

Most of the hypotheses could also be tested as they stand for some other jurisdictions, e.g. New Zealand. With some amendment, some of them could be applied in other EU countries. Scholars from Roman law countries might wish to investigate whether similar developments and debates to those above are occurring in their countries, and if not, why not?

References
Alexander, D. (1993). 'A European true and fair view?'. *European Accounting Review*, 2(1).
Alexander, D. (1996). 'Truer and fairer. Uninvited comments on invited comments'. *European Accounting Review*, 5(3).
Alexander, D. (1999). 'A benchmark for the adequacy of

published financial statements'. *Accounting and Business Research*, 29(3): 239–253.

Alexander, D. and Archer, S. (2000). 'On the myth of "Anglo-Saxon" financial accounting'. *International Journal of Accounting*, 35(4): 539–557.

APB (2004). *The Auditor's Report on Financial Statements*. ISA 700. London: Auditing Practices Board.

ARC (2005). *Draft Summary Report* of the meeting of the Accounting Regulatory Committee on 30.11.2005; available at http://ec.europa.eu/internal_market/accounting/docs/arc.

Arden, M. (1993). *The True and Fair Requirement Opinion*, published as an appendix to 'Foreword to Accounting Standards'. London: Accounting Standards Board.

Camfferman, K. and Zeff, S. (2007). *Financial Reporting and Global Capital Markets*. Oxford University Press.

CESR (2007). *CESR's Review of the Implementation and Enforcement of IFRS in the EU*, Committee of European Securities Regulators, 07–352.

Chastney, J.G. (1975). *True and Fair View – History, Meaning and the Impact of the Fourth Directive*. London: Institute of Chartered Accountants in England and Wales.

Company Reporting (1997). 'Issue of the month', No. 82, April.

Cowan, T.K. (1965). 'Are truth and fairness generally acceptable?'. *Accounting Review*, October: 788–794.

Deegan, C., Kent, P. and Lin, C.J. (1994). 'The true and fair view: a study of Australian auditors' application of the concept'. *Australian Accounting Review*, 4(1): 2–12.

Evans, L. (2003). 'The true and fair view and the "fair presentation" override of IAS 1'. *Accounting and Business Research*, 33(4): 311–325.

Evans, L. (2004). 'Language translation and the problem of international communication'. *Accounting, Auditing & Accountability Journal*, 17(2): 210–248.

Evans, L. (2008). 'Observations on the changing language of accounting'. Unpublished paper, University of Stirling.

FASB (2008). *The Hierarchy of Generally Accepted Accounting Principles*, Statement No. 162. Norwalk, CT: Financial Accounting Standards Board.

Fearnley, S. (2009). 'Vive la différence'[*sic*], *Accountancy*, January, p. 16.

FEE (2005). *Reference to the Financial Reporting Framework in the EU in Accounting Policies and in the Audit Report and Applicability of Endorsed IFRS*, Fédération des Experts Comptables Européens.

FRC (2005). *The Implications of New Accounting and Auditing Standards for the 'True and Fair View' and Auditors' Responsibilities*. London: Financial Reporting Council.

Freshfields (2005). *The 'True and Fair Requirement' and International Accounting Standards*, letter to the Financial Reporting Review Panel by Freshfields Bruckhaus Deringer, published by the Financial Reporting Council.

Hoffman, L. and Arden, M. (1983). *Legal Opinion on True and Fair*, published in, among other places, *Accountancy*, November, 1983: 154–156.

IASB (2008). *An Exposure Draft of an Improved Conceptual Framework for Financial Reporting*. London: International Accounting Standards Board.

ICAEW (2007). *EU Implementation of IFRS and the Fair Value Directive*. Institute of Chartered Accountants in England and Wales.

ICAEW (2008). *Guidance on the Determination of Realised Profits and Losses in the Context of Distributions under the Companies Act 1985*, Tech 01/08. Institute of Chartered Accountants in England and Wales.

Kirk, N. (2006). 'Perceptions of the true and fair view concept: an empirical investigation'. *Abacus*, 42(2): 205–235.

McEnroe, J.E. and Martens, S.C. (1998). 'Individual investors' perceptions regarding the meaning of US and UK audit report terminology: "present fairly in conformity with GAAP" and "give a true and fair view"'. *Journal of Business Finance & Accounting*, 25, (3–4): 289–307.

Moore, M. (2008). *The True and Fair Requirement Revisited*. London: Financial Reporting Council.

Nobes, C.W. (1993). 'The true and fair view requirement: impact on and of the fourth directive'. *Accounting and Business Research*, 24(93): 35–48.

Nobes, C.W. (2000). 'Is true and fair of over-riding importance?: a comment on Alexander's benchmark'. *Accounting and Business Research*, 30(4): 307–312.

Nobes, C.W. and Parker, R.H. (1991). 'True and fair: a survey of UK financial directors'. *Journal of Business Finance and Accounting*, 18(3).

Nobes, C.W. and Zeff, S.A. (2008). 'Auditors' affirmation of compliance with IFRS around the world: an exploratory study'. *Accounting Perspectives*, 7(4).

Norris, F. (2008). 'Société Générale invokes special accounting rule to absorb Kerviel losses'. *International Herald Tribune*, 6 March.

Ordelheide, D. (1993). 'True and fair view: a European and a German perspective'. *European Accounting Review*, 2(1): 81–90.

Ordelheide, D. and Pfaff, D. (1994). *European Financial Reporting: Germany*. London: Routledge.

Parker, R.H. and Nobes, C.W. (1991). 'True and fair: UK auditors' view'. *Accounting and Business Research*, 21 (84): 349–361.

Parker, R.H. and Nobes, C.W. (1994). *An International View of True and Fair Accounting*. London: Routledge.

Parker, R.H., Wolnizer, P.W. and Nobes, C.W. (1996). *Readings in True and Fair*. New York, NY: Garland.

Rutherford, B.A. (1985). 'The true and fair view doctrine: a search for explication'. *Journal of Business Finance & Accounting*, 12(4): 484–494.

Van Hulle, K. (1993). 'Truth and untruth about true and fair'. *European Accounting Review*, 2(1): 99–104.

Van Hulle, K. (1997). 'The true and fair view override in the European Accounting Directives'. *European Accounting Review*, 6(4):711–720.

Walton, P. (1991). *The True and Fair View: A Shifting Concept*. ACCA Occasional Paper No. 7. London: Chartered Association of Certified Accountants.

Zeff, S.A. (1990). 'The English-language equivalent of *Geeft een Getrouw Beeld*'. *De Accountant*, October; reprinted in Parker and Nobes (1994): 131–133.

Zeff, S.A. (1992). 'Arthur Andersen & Co. and the two-part opinion in the auditor's report: 1946–1962'. *Contemporary Accounting Research*, 8(2): 443–467.

Zeff, S.A. (2007). 'The primacy of "present fairly" in the auditor's report'. *Accounting Perspectives*, 6(1): 1–20.

Zeff, S.A., van der Wal, F. and Camfferman, K. (1992). *Company Financial Reporting*. Amsterdam: North-Holland Publishing Company.